REORIENTALISM

MODERNIST LATITUDES

MODERNIST LATITUDES

Jessica Berman and Paul Saint-Amour, Editors

Modernist Latitudes aims to capture the energy and ferment of modernist studies by continuing to open up the range of forms, locations, temporalities, and theoretical approaches encompassed by the field. The series celebrates the growing latitude ("scope for freedom of action or thought") that this broadening affords scholars of modernism, whether they are investigating little-known works or revisiting canonical ones. Modernist Latitudes will pay particular attention to the texts and contexts of those latitudes (Africa, Latin America, Australia, Asia, Southern Europe, and even the rural United States) that have long been misrecognized as ancillary to the canonical modernisms of the global North.

    Laura Winkiel, *Modernism and the Middle Passage*

    Shir Alon, *Static Forms: Writing the Present in the Modern Middle East*

    Kristin Grogan, *Stitch, Unstitch: Modernist Poetry and the World of Work*

    Aparna Bhargava Dharwadker, *Cosmo-Modernism and Theater in India: Writing and Staging Multilingual Modernisms*

    Mat Fournier, *Dysphoric Modernism: Undoing Gender in French Literature*

    Nergis Ertürk, *Writing in Red: Literature and Revolution Across Turkey and the Soviet Union*

    Cate I. Reilly, *Psychic Empire: Literary Modernism and the Clinical State*

    Adam McKible, *Creating Jim Crow America: George Horace Lorimer, the Saturday Evening Post, and the War Against Black Modernity*

    Hannah Freed-Thall, *Modernism at the Beach: Queer Ecologies and the Coastal Commons*

    Daniel Ryan Morse, *Radio Empire: The BBC's Eastern Service and the Emergence of the Global Anglophone Novel*

    Jill Richards, *The Fury Archives: Female Citizenship, Human Rights, and the International Avant-Gardes*

    Claire Seiler, *Midcentury Suspension: Literature and Feeling in the Wake of World War II*

    Elizabeth Outka, *Viral Modernism: The Influenza Pandemic and Interwar Literature*

    Ben Conisbee Baer, *Indigenous Vanguards: Education, National Liberation, and the Limits of Modernism*

    Aarthi Vadde, *Chimeras of Form: Modernist Internationalism Beyond Europe, 1914–2014*

    Eric Bulson, *Little Magazine, World Form*

For a complete list of books in this series, please see the Columbia University Press website.

REORIENTALISM

From Avant-Garde to Soviet National Form

NARIMAN SKAKOV

Columbia University Press

New York

Columbia University Press
Publishers Since 1893
New York   Chichester, West Sussex

Copyright © 2025 Columbia University Press
All rights reserved

Library of Congress Cataloging-in-Publication Data
Names: Skakov, Nariman, 1978– author
Title: Reorientalism : from avant-garde to Soviet national form / Nariman Skakov.
Description: New York : Columbia University Press, 2025. |
Series: Modernist latitudes | Includes bibliographical references and index.
Identifiers: LCCN 2025005672 | ISBN 9780231218009 hardback |
ISBN 9780231218016 trade paperback | ISBN 9780231562027 ebook
Subjects: LCSH: Arts—Soviet Union—Political aspects | Politics and literature—
Soviet Union | Motion pictures—Political aspects—Soviet Union | Art—
Political aspects—Soviet Union | Modernism (Aesthetics)—Political aspects—
Soviet Union | Avant-garde (Aesthetics)—Political aspects—Soviet Union
Classification: LCC NX180.P64 S57 2025 | DDC 709.47/0904—dc23/eng/20250423

Cover design: Barnbrook Studio, 2025.
Cover image: Eleazar Langman, *Untitled*, 1934. Productive Arts.

For Radimir, my light from the East.

CONTENTS

List of Archives ix

List of Illustrations xi

A Note on Transliteration xiii

Acknowledgments xv

Preface xvii

Introduction: Points of Reorientation   1

1. Socialist Matter: Victor Shklovsky   43

2. Socialist Vision: Aleksandr Rodchenko and Varvara Stepanova   84

3. Socialist Sound: Dziga Vertov   137

4. Socialist Time: Sergei Eisenstein   194

Epilogue: "End" Points   248

......

Notes 265

Bibliography 305

Index 319

ARCHIVES

In the references to archival materials from Kazakh, Russian, and Uzbek archives, I use the following standard Soviet abbreviation system: f. (archive, "fond"); op. (inventory, "opis'"); d. (file, "delo"); l. (page, "list"). All translations are mine unless otherwise indicated.

Auezov Archive: Mūqtar Äuezov mūrağaty, Almaty, Kazakhstan.
GARF: Gosudarstvennyi arkhiv Rossiiskoi Federatsii (the State Archive of the Russian Federation).
Gosfil'mofond: Gosudarstvennyi fond kinofil'mov Rossiiskoi Federatsii (the National Film Foundation of the Russian Federation).
Hoover: the Hoover Institution Library and Archives, Stanford, CA.
IIMK: Arkhiv Instituta istorii material'noi kul'tury RAN (the Archive of the Institute of the History of Material Culture of the Russian Academy of Sciences).
MAMM: Mul'timedia Art Muzei, Moskva (Multimedia Art Museum, Moscow).
MoMA: The Museum of Modern Art Archives, New York.
Muzei Kino: Gosudarstvennyi tsentral'nyi muzei kino (the State Central Museum of Cinema).
TsGARK: Qazaqstan Respublikasynyŋ Ortalyq memlekettik mūrağaty (the Central State Archive of the Republic of Kazakhstan).
TsGAKZRK: Qazaqstan Respublikasynyŋ Ortalyq memlekettik kino, foto jäne dybys qūjattary mūrağaty (the Central State Archive of Film, Photo and Sound Documents of the Republic of Kazakhstan).
Österreichisches Filmmuseum: Austrian Film Museum.
Productive Arts: Productive Arts, Bratenahl, Ohio.

Pushkinskii muzei: Gosudarstvennyi muzei izobraziteľ′nykh iskusstv imeni A. S. Pushkina (the Pushkin State Museum of Fine Arts, Russia).

RGALI: Rossiiskii gosudarstvennyi arkhiv literatury i iskusstva (the Russian State Archive of Literature and Art).

RGAKFD: Rossiiskii gosudarstvennyi arkhiv kinofotodokumentov (the Russian State Documentary Film and Photo Archive at Krasnogorsk).

Rodchenko-Stepanova Archive: the private archive of Aleksandr Rodchenko and Varvara Stepanova, Moscow.

VDNKh Archive: Arkhiv Vystavki dostizhenii narodnogo khoziaistva (the Exhibition of Achievements of the National Economy Archive, Moscow).

ILLUSTRATIONS

Fig. 0.1 Alfred H. Barr, *Diagram of Stylistic Evolution from 1890 Until 1935*, 1936.   xviii

Fig. 1.1 Viktor Turin, Stills from *Turksib*, 1929.   64

Fig. 1.2 Viktor Turin, Stills from *Turksib*, 1929.   71

Fig. 2.1 Aleksandr Rodchenko, Pages from *USSR in Construction [Belomor]*, no. 12, 1933.   106

Fig. 2.2 Aleksandr Rodchenko and Varvara Stepanova, Pages from *USSR in Construction [Fifteen Years of Kazakhstan]*, no. 11, 1935.   109

Fig. 2.3 Eleazar Langman, Page from *Sovetskoe foto*, no. 10, 1935.   113

Fig. 2.4 Aleksandr Rodchenko and Varvara Stepanova, Stalin Pages from *Ten Years of Soviet Uzbekistan*, 1934.   119

Fig. 2.5 Aleksandr Rodchenko and Varvara Stepanova, Pages from *Ten Years of Soviet Uzbekistan*, 1934/1935.   124

Fig. 2.6 Aleksandr Rodchenko and Varvara Stepanova, Pages from *Ten Years of Soviet Uzbekistan*, 1934.   126

Fig. 2.7 Aleksandr Rodchenko and Varvara Stepanova, Spreads from *Kazakhstan*, 1949.   133

Fig. 3.1 Dziga Vertov, Stills from *Three Songs of Lenin*, 1934/1970.   150

Fig. 3.2 Dziga Vertov, Stills from *Three Songs of Lenin*, 1938.   163

Fig. 3.3 Dziga Vertov, Stills from *The Front, To You!*, 1942.   173

Fig. 3.4 Dziga Vertov, "Construction No. 2" for *The Front, To You!*, 1942.   178

Fig. 3.5 Dziga Vertov, Stills from *The Front, To You!*, 1942.   181

Fig. 3.6 Dziga Vertov, Stills from *The Front, To You!*, 1942.   185

Fig. 4.1 Sergei Eisenstein, Stills from ¡*Que viva México!*, 1931–32.   209

Fig. 4.2 Sergei Eisenstein, "Kozy-Korpesh and Baian-Sulu [1, 2]," 1942.   225

Fig. 4.3 Sergei Eisenstein, "Kozy-Korpesh and Baian-Sulu [4, 5]," 1942.   227

Fig. 4.4 Sergei Eisenstein, "Kozy-Korpesh and Baian-Sulu [3, 6]," 1942.   229

Fig. 4.5 Sergei Eisenstein, "Totem," 1941.   233

Fig. 4.6 Sergei Eisenstein, "In Memory of Mountain Goat Hunters," 1941.   236

Fig. 7.7 Sergei Eisenstein, "The Bird Hunt," 1941.   239

Fig. 5.1 Konstantin Topuridze, "Friendship of the Peoples" sketch, 1952.   261

A NOTE ON TRANSLITERATION

In transliterating Russian quotes and citations, I adhere to the US Library of Congress transliteration system. I have transliterated proper nouns in keeping with this system except in cases where the name has been standardized in English (for example, Shklovsky rather than Shklovskii).

ACKNOWLEDGMENTS

I started my work on this manuscript in 2013, before the annexation of Crimea by Russia, and completed the first draft right before the full-scale invasion of Ukraine in 2022. These events greatly enhanced my understanding of Russian "exceptionalism" and nationalism and their role in the formation of the Soviet avant-garde and Slavic Studies in general. They also inevitably shaped my acknowledgments section, which displays many voids.

I would like to thank my mentor Julian Graffy, and my dear colleague Elizabeth Astrid Papazian for their unparalleled attention to the manuscript. The amount of intellectual generosity provided by these two readers left me forever grateful.

The "Modernist Latitudes" series editors Jessica Berman, Paul Saint-Amour, and Philip Leventhal, together with the anonymous reviewers of the manuscript, kept pushing my argument further, and I am grateful for this intellectual challenge that enhanced the book.

Many individuals provided useful feedback at different stages of my work on the manuscript and I would like to acknowledge their intellectual contribution: Konstantin Bogdanov, Eliot Borenstein, Philip Ross Bullock, Samuel Coggeshall, Alexandra Dennett, Aleksandr Deriabin, Rossen Djagalov, Victoria Donovan, Reidar Due, Adrienne Edgar, Jacob Emery, Leah Feldman, Tatiana Filimonova, Alison Frank Johnson, David Joselit, Marisa Galvez, Barry Gifford, Maria Gough, Catriona Kelly, Matthew Kendall, Martin Kemp, Klara Kemp-Welch, Naum Kleiman, Ilya Kliger, Luis Felipe Labaki, Aleksandr Lavrentiev, Steven Lee, Pavle Levi, John MacKay, Alexander Morrison, Eric Naiman, Joan Neuberger, Michael Nicholson, Kyohei Norimatsu, Karla Oeler,

George Pattison, Kevin M.F. Platt, Harsha Ram, Katherine Reischl, Ellen Rutten, Nancy Ruttenburg, Masha Salazkina, Irina Sandomirskaja, Yuri Slezkine, Galin Tihanov, Vera Tolz, Emma Widdis, Laura Wittman, and Andrei Zorin.

Finally, I would like to thank my former students for helping me to polish my academic writing: Olive Coles, Dustin Condren, Natasha Kadlec, Bohdan Koshevoi, Daria Storoshchuk, and Alice Underwood.

PREFACE

In 1936 at the Museum of Modern Art in New York, Alfred H. Barr Jr. introduced the groundbreaking exhibition *Cubism and Abstract Art*. In a decisively influential creative moment, Barr—the exhibition's curator and founding director of MoMA since 1929 at the age of only twenty-seven—would upend existing conceptions of the museum as a repository of "dead" objects, asserting the *modern* as a primary subject matter. The exhibition boldly situated modernism as a phenomenon occurring across the arts—displaying fashion and consumer products next to easel painting, photography, sculpture, typography, and architectural models. The distinctly transgeneric nature of modernism accentuated by Barr's curation reflected the all-encompassing drive of modernity: one that touched and permeated all spheres of human life.

In accompaniment to the exhibition, Barr produced the catalogue *Cubism and Abstract Art*, which almost instantly became an art-historical document of fundamental importance. In addition to the remarkable lucidity of its effort of systematization, its author displayed a distinct historical awareness of the given moment (1936)—a time in which the avant-garde experiment was brutally suppressed in centers of its very conception: Germany and the Soviet Union. In a gesture to these two sites of importance for the invention of abstraction, Barr presupposes that the catalogue "essay and exhibition might well be dedicated to those painters of squares and circles (and the architects influenced by them) who have suffered at the hands of philistines with political power."[1]

On the dust jacket of the catalogue was featured the now-iconic *Diagram of Stylistic Evolution from 1890 Until 1935* (fig. 0.1). The epochal diagram reconstructs forty-five years of art history as a continuous flow of reciprocal influence and captures the vast complexity of various avant-garde currents with

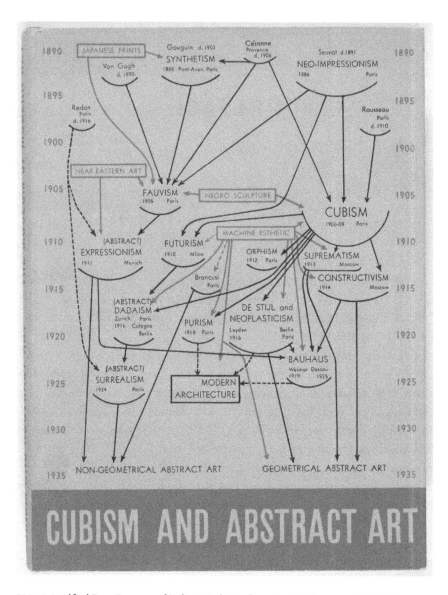

FIG. 0.1 Alfred Barr, *Diagram of Stylistic Evolution from 1890 Until 1935*, 1936. MoMA.

compelling clarity and precision. It indicated a radical and uncompromising departure from the conventional European art historiography of the time, which was reliant on the concept of "national schools." Movements are instead connected through formal and stylistic correspondence, and they are linked with cities, not countries, in a nuanced reflection of the international complexities of modern art.[2] The well-represented Soviet experimental art plays an integral part in this transnational narrative of modern art, forming a crucial backbone of Barr's conceptual model.

Barr's diagram identifies four major influences on modern art. Marked in bright orange, they hover in boxes above the movements they inspired: "Japanese Prints," "Near-Eastern Art," "Negro Sculpture," and "Machine Esthetic." The latter is cast as the only truly modern stimulus that affects ten movements while each of the remaining three relates to just two. These stimuli, disconnected from one another and safely boxed, seem to appear as if from nowhere, acquiring significance solely through incorporation within an elaborated history of Western modernism. The effect of traditional non-European aesthetic forms, nevertheless, is paramount for inventing abstraction in the Western world, for the ethnically marked stimuli played a significant role in the early stages of the stylistic evolution (1890–1905). Such a pedigree for modern art is clearly permeated with ethnic alterity, however geographically scattered and temporally nonspecific it may appear to be in the diagram.

Upon closer inspection, readers might notice an unfilled space of ten years in the diagram between 1925, marked as a limit for surrealism, Bauhaus, and modern architecture,[3] and 1935—a starting point of non-geometrical abstract art and geometrical abstract art. This void appears as a crucial space of transition—a gap, however, that Barr fails to address in the catalogue. It was precisely during this gap in 1927–28 that Barr, together with a fellow art historian, Jere Abbott, made his first trip to the USSR (by way of England and Germany). In Moscow and Leningrad, they encountered Sergei Eisenstein, Moisei Ginzburg, El Lissitzky, Vladimir Mayakovsky, Vsevolod Meyerhold, Aleksandr Rodchenko, Varvara Stepanova, David Shterenberg, Sergei Tretiakov—key Soviet experimenters in their heyday. Retrospectively, the timing of the trip was opportune: with the Great Break of 1929 and the ensuing "revolution from above" the country would set out on a totalitarian path, and Barr's new avant-garde acquaintances would need to identify new ways to continue their aesthetic quests. Some of them would fall victim to Stalinism.

Barr kept a diary during his first visit to the Soviet Union—a land he instantly characterized as "the most important place in the world for us to be." The diary chronicle is scattered with perceptive observations, most notably on the unfolding socialist modernity's overcoming of "backwardness," and the experimental art that accompanied this process. Ginzburg's famous Gosstrakh house, "one of four 'modern' buildings in Moscow . . . built in the Corbusier-Gropius style," where Barr visited Tretiakov, for example, was described as an incongruous clash between modern and obsolete: "only the superficials are modern, for the plumbing, heating, etc. are technically very crude and cheap, a comedy of the strong modern inclination without any technical tradition to satisfy it."[4]

While observing the Moscow architecture in general, Barr describes the city as "utterly lacking in any consistent style," noting that "Viennese ideas of 1905 seemed to have been imported indiscriminately." Proceeding to categorize the interior of a large food store opposite their Tverskaya Street hotel as "the frightfullest art nouveau I've ever seen,"[5] Barr perceived an unrestrained urge toward stylization and a decorative orientation to architecture (typical to art nouveau movements) as vastly at odds with technological modernity and functionality, and he did not even recognize art nouveau as a distinct movement in his diagram of stylistic evolution of modern art.

In line with Barr's intuition, the Vienna Secession, which broke away from Vienna's official academy in 1897, was indeed a pivotal aesthetic reference point for the development of modernism in the Russian Empire. Modernism, as well as modernity, was imported to Russia from the West. The society and eponymous journal *World of Art* (*Mir Iskusstva*, 1899–1904), and *stil' modern* (modern style) that it endorsed, were in many ways a belated and less radical Russian variant of the European Secession movements that set parameters for pre-revolutionary Russian culture and instigated the Russian Silver Age—a cradle of the early modernist experiment. The term *modernism* was first employed on the pages of *World of Art* in a review of the inaugural 1898 Vienna Secession exhibition. Surprisingly, the author of the review disparagingly refers to the design of Joseph Olbrich's Secession building as a " 'modernism' of ornamentation pushed to the extreme," blaming the Viennese artists for such "mannered and template 'modernism.' "[6] The journal's employment of the term *modernism* was typically in inverted commas and exclusively in relation to European art.

One of the first applications of the term *modernism* directly to Russian art is found in the 1903 article "Among Decadents" (Sredi dekadentov) by Mikhail Men'shikov, a conservative journalist and one of the earliest victims of the Bolsheviks. In this review of the fourth *World of Art* exhibition that took place in March 1902 in Petersburg, Men'shikov conceives of modernism in darkly negative terms of erosion, decay, and degeneration: "Modernism is not a renaissance [*vozrozhdenie*], as decadents cry, nor it is a sickness, it is simply a degeneration [*vyrozhdenie*]."[7] The target of the attack was Mikhail Vrubel's "The Demon Downcast," a painting that exemplified all the aesthetic evils of the modern age, according to Men'shikov. On an enormous canvas, Vrubel depicts a retelling of Mikhail Lermontov's poem "The Demon"—an Orientalist story of the love between an innocent young beauty, Tamara, and the seductive Spirit of Evil, set in the foothills of the Caucasus. The horizontal plane of the painting situates a seminaked dark-skinned "demon," splayed out across a lushly decorated cloak in the dusk-lit shadows of the surrounding mountains. His piercing gaze, directed at the viewer, is intense and unsettling. While working on the painting in 1901, Vrubel was visited by the Vienna Secession artists, who were so taken by the intensity of the work's modern archaism that they sought to exhibit the painting at the Twelfth Exhibition of the Secessionists (November 1901).[8] Vrubel, however, was not able to finish the work on time and continued to modify it even while it was being publicly exhibited in Petersburg in 1902.

For Men'shikov, however, the modern archaism of Vrubel was deeply alienating and unsettling. The critic identifies the generic "East" as an exclusive source of the modern evil that the canvas so powerfully promulgates. By assuming a transparently chauvinistic position, Men'shikov racially marks the early appearance of the term *modernism* as applied to Russian art:

> It is said that decadence came to us from the Far East, that impressionism was shipped from Japan, and that the contempt for linear perspective is borrowed from China. This is all very likely, especially if one recalls Chinese painters' passion for devils, dragons, and other repugnant stuff. But the smuggled Mongolian diabolism blossomed here by itself, in an idiosyncratic manner that is so distinctive of Europeans. The Chinese demon is only laughable in its ugliness. To reveal not a body, distorted to the point of non-distinction, but the very soul, fallen and frenzied—only Europeans could have done this.[9]

In this dizzyingly racist outburst, Men'shikov conflates various Eastern cultures into a single locus of the "hideous modernist horror." China, Japan, and Mongolia are amalgamated into the uniform and frightful Oriental Other, whose alterity vis-à-vis Europe is its only discernible point of distinction. Men'shikov also clearly identifies Russia with Europe yet fails to acknowledge that the invoked impressionism and the modernist experiment with reverse perspective constituted aesthetic borrowings brought to Russia from the West. Like Barr, Men'shikov acknowledges the impact of traditional non-European aesthetic forms on the genesis of modernism. Unlike Barr, however, he fails to recognize a productive aspect of cross-cultural interchange.

Early twentieth-century modernist culture in the Russian Empire was framed by both national and nationalist discourses. Russia always displayed a special "affinity" (whether positive or negative) for Asia, combined with its awkward and often unreciprocated relationship with the West. Self-Orientalization, Orientophilia, and Orientophobia were countered and supplemented with enthusiastically Westernizing and fervently Slavophile perspectives. A vast country,

Russia stretched itself between two geographical poles of the Occident and the Orient, and this existential indeterminacy, "a veritable geo-schizophrenia" in Mark Bassin's formulation,[10] produced discourses of Russian cultural exceptionalism. The belief that Russia was neither East nor West but enjoyed a unique, all-inclusive, and all-transcending status of "Eastern European Aryans"[11] was a claim to exceptionalism—a paradoxical shortcut from particularism to universalism, as it enabled a certain rhetorical leap from the particular to the general without effecting any real transformation. Thus, the claim to exceptionalism remained a mere rhetorical trope, sustained by racial prejudice.

Russian exceptionalism, with accompanying chauvinistic insinuations, was nonetheless deeply embedded within the political discourse of the time. In 1903, the same year as Men'shikov's incendiary application of the term *modernism* to Russian art, Lenin (in line with Marx and Engels's view of Russia as a "semi-Asiatic" country[12]) used the derogatory term *aziatchina* (Asiatic backwardness) to describe a feudal condition in Russia: "The entire working class and the entire country are suffering from this absence of rights; it is on this that all the Asiatic backwardness [*aziatchina*] in Russian life rests."[13] Such rhetoric places a commitment to a Western vision of modernity with liberal freedoms at radical odds with "Asiatic despotism," illuminating an apprehensive affinity with Asia that would only intensify during Stalin's rule. That the modernizing urge of the Russian imperial and socialist discourses conceives itself through the unreflexively racist paradigm is a distinctive aspect of Russian political and cultural orientalism, which, in Leah Feldman's apt formulation designates "not Russia's unique historical, political, and geographic alterity but rather its reverberation of European imperial culture and its appeal to the very fractured identity it hopes to sublimate."[14]

Reorientalism traces this racially colored discursive entanglement in the 1930s, when both modernism and Leninism underwent a Stalinist remolding. The radically shifted Soviet political horizon offered a corrective to both modernist exoticism and a politics of alterity via the universal socialist project. Thus, the "Cultural Revolution" following the Great Break of 1929 and the advent of "national form" as expressive of socialist internationalism function as a point of departure for the book. The complex tension between state imposition and individual (artistic) freedom lies at the core of the revisionist outlook it offers. Following the Enlightenment-inspired conviction that there is a natural association between the independent status of art and the free individual, Barr was convinced that abstract art was an expression of the liberal freedoms so starkly undermined by the politically engaged art of repressed totalitarian societies. *Reorientalism*, however, challenges the concept of irresolvable friction between political oppression and liberal aesthetic expression, highlighting a swirl of contradictory tendencies and ideas, such as emancipatory vs. domineering rhetoric and or functional vs. decorative aesthetics, that prompted an emergence of enclaves for creative imagination. Essentially, it reclaims a space for aesthetic evolution during the rise of Stalinism through geographic decentering and a temporal extension of the concept of modernism.

The nexus of the avant-garde experiment, ethnic alterity, and liberal freedoms (or their absence) lies at the heart of *Reorientalism*, which examines aesthetic practices concurrent with the conceptual framing of Barr's diagram. Despite emerging repressive policies and practices across the 1930s and early 1940s, the book will explore the continued persistence of modernism in the Soviet Union: channeled by its representatives—key early avant-garde experimenters with visual form, language, and sound—decisively eastward, in the direction of the Soviet Orient. In doing so, these artists and critics entered a new set of relations with the state and the discursive configurations it imposed, readily and enthusiastically adapting their knowledge and aesthetic convictions to the aims of the "great socialist experiment." Thus, they accomplished a leap from the avant-garde to the Soviet national form.

REORIENTALISM

INTRODUCTION

POINTS OF REORIENTATION

"There is an old proverb that all roads lead to Rome. This is the proverb of colonizers, who dragged everything to Rome. This proverb is false. Great cultures were created beyond Rome, great roads crossed our country and existed for us, not for Rome," wrote Viktor Shklovsky in 1947,[1]—a moment inflected by the very beginnings of the anti-cosmopolitan campaign in the Soviet Union. His essay discusses Aleksandr Veselovsky (1838–1906), one of the pioneers of comparative literary studies. Shklovsky's essay took a bold and dangerous stance: It defended a cross-cultural and cross-historical comparative approach at a time when the fear of an external and ideologically hostile enemy dictated Soviet politics. Veselovsky's idea of the unity and regularity of the development process of universal aesthetic production clashed with the new Soviet (anti-cosmopolitan) vision of inter-ethnic relations, marked by claims to the exceptionalism of the first socialist state and the vanguard status of the Russian nation. At first glance, the quote seems anticolonial, but the word "us" is worth examining critically. The "road" Shklovsky refers to is none other than the famed Silk Road, a set of trading routes spanning Central Asia that connected continental Europe and China with "us": the inhabitants of the Soviet Union, the country that was at the peak of its territorial extension following recent victory in World War II.

In the 1982 edition of *Theory of Prose*, Shklovsky reflects on the notion of artistic *borrowing* (Veselovsky's principal historical category) and invokes Rome again: "Rome existed. It existed for a long time, pouring the divergent into the singular. Picking all things resilient, committing injustices, which seemed to be premeditated.... Alongside the fissure, China existed. They were well separated, but accidentally and apprehensively."[2] Here, Rome is presented as just one extremity of the "inadvertent and forbidding" imperial division; it is coherent in its presumed uniformity, negating heterogeneity through oppression and further assimilation. China, in contrast, is presented as both marginal and imperial. Two pages on, Shklovsky—after discussing the "strange" effects of the genre of the Chinese novella—argues that "China has to be discovered in the same way Columbus discovered not only America but also culture, and winds, and the laws of delusion."[3] Consumed by his own cultural delusion and imperial stance, Shklovsky invokes the vast space that lies between two imperial points—the space that incorporates both "us" and "them":

> Thus, two cultures, two sets of tenets—Chinese and Roman (or rather, Greek)—lived disjointedly.
>
> Then, not instantaneously but gradually, as they became attuned to their own voices, Central Asian devices and sets of skills began to emerge between them.
>
> That was a corridor between the two cultures, which is not ascertained. It becomes self-sustaining.
>
> People of different cultures get acquainted with each other as if they're from different planets; they get acquainted through the self-sustaining, [or] in-the-process-of-becoming-self-sustaining, corridor.
>
> A third culture, perhaps equal to the two, emerges; let's call it Central Asian.[4]

Invoking the formalist lexicon, Shklovsky argues for the importance of the passageway—the route that connects the two points of radical difference. As this initially "unmarked" space gradually gains its own cultural voice and agency, the passageway becomes an identifiable locus. Shklovsky's convoluted syntax and the caustic tone of the ending, however, undermine the declared emancipatory rhetoric, as he presumptuously and only *tentatively* designates this culture as "Central Asian": an "equal" to the two great empires. The "let's call it something" rhetorical turn presupposes that there was no proper or stable appellation allotted to the vast expanse, situated between two domineering and diverse imperial structures. The very ability to designate or characterize a space or entity, however, presupposes a proprietary relationship. It is thus perhaps not surprising that by 1982, Shklovsky felt he could claim cultural ownership of the Soviet Central Asian borderlands.

Shklovsky, master of defamiliarization, was in fact very familiar with Central Asia: He had taken his first trip to Kazakhstan in 1929 and later made visits to both Uzbekistan and Tajikistan as a metropolitan emissary representing the Soviet Writers' Union. Shklovsky's early exposure to the Soviet Orient coincided with a period of great transformation for the Soviet Union, heralded by the emergence of Stalin's Cultural Revolution and the evolution of the formalist project. The period between 1929, "the year of the great breakthrough," and the beginning of the Great Patriotic War in 1941 witnessed a wholesale transformation of culture and politics in the Soviet Union. On this stage the centrifugal aspirations of modernism would be subdued, channeled instead into the centripetal flow of Stalinist culture. At the same time, an equally important focus was the preoccupation with the ethnically marked peripheries of the Soviet Union—a site where Bolshevik policymakers tested and refined key ideological tools essential for the formation of the "new Soviet man."

The Soviet state's sweeping ideological demands placed enormous pressure on the main representatives of the 1920s avant-garde: Shklovsky as well as his collaborators and colleagues Aleksandr Rodchenko, Varvara Stepanova, Dziga Vertov, and Sergei Eisenstein. As a result, the formal audacity of the modernist experiment was somewhat stifled. Yet in the East the avant-garde's work found constructive application, representing a crucial aesthetic evolution as Soviet society underwent a drastic ideological transformation. The protagonists of this book employed a variety of strategies to cope with overwhelming political demands, from Shklovsky's convoluted rhetorical equivocation and Rodchenko and Stepanova's ostensible total submission to Vertov and Eisenstein's ingenious attempts to engage with a set of restrictive aesthetic precepts by way of interiorization. These varying modes of professional behavior testify to the difficulty of drawing strict lines between conformity and nonconformity. Taken together, these stratagems of resistance, compliance, and imaginative construal demonstrate that Soviet modernism never settled into a fixed aesthetic terrain. Instead, it evolved through the 1930s and the early 1940s by means of a representational dislocation. Central Asia, as a liminal space marked by nonsynchrony and difference, evolved into the primary *topos* where the transformative dynamism of modernism could be used.[5]

Central Asia was also a product of modernity, a kind of modernist object created by geopolitical will, a space both constructed and distorted. It also aspired to become modern, which, in William Phillips's words, means being "suspended between tradition and revolt, nationalism and internationalism, the aesthetic and the civic, and between belonging and alienation."[6] At the time, however, it was at the extreme margins of modernity—"a distant cultural and territorial periphery and accordingly not easily comprehensible."[7] This marginality proved essential for the consequent radical transfiguration of the late Soviet modernist project. Imbued with foreignness, Soviet Central Asia was a space of compensation, a place, a locus, a site, where creative energies of modernism were able to get a second wind, albeit in altered form.

The newly demarcated but still peripheral territory of Soviet Central Asia proved to be a fertile ground for the inherently dialectical process of reconstituting subjectivity in line with the emerging totalitarian state. In these circumstances, the tendency of modernism to dissolve categories of self and other and to displace subjectivities, which was, in Steven Lee's words, a feature of the preceding "inclusive and decolonizing" avant-garde culture,[8] had to be restrained and its energy channeled into a more acceptable and serviceable domain. As such, the new Soviet man or woman had to be created and rhetorically sustained as an unwavering entity, rooted in a stable and bounded discursive soil.

Given these demands, it was in Central Asia that the boundary-traversing energy of modernism clashed with and was neutralized by the boundary-establishing Soviet ideology of the Stalinist mold.[9] As a consequence, "alien" cultural material was vigorously assimilated into the fabric of the new Soviet subjectivity, though not without disjunctive fissures. Thus, the long life of Soviet modernism is bound up in the politics of alterity, a process of constructing Soviet subjectivity through the ethnic other, and the consequent institutionalization of national forms. Ethnic heterogeneity was a formal possibility and indeed a necessity inherent in the process of cultural production in the first socialist society.

Reorientalism investigates the uneven continuities between early avant-garde formal experimentation and the Stalinist culture of the mid- and late 1930s and the early 1940s. The modernist cult of difficult *form* is at the center of this radical ideological and cultural shift. The general narrative of the book explores the development of the avant-garde vision of aesthetic form, which was instrumental for the later concept of socialist art as heterogeneous in form but unified in terms of content. The insistence on clarity and accessibility, fueled by the emergence of socialist realism, made aesthetic intricacy unacceptable and dramatically reshaped permissible practices of perception and expression. However, the "strangeness" of the Orient allowed the modernist valorization of defamiliarized forms to develop in new ways. National heterogeneity was directly linked with the reinvigoration of formal experimentation during the period of the development of socialist realism. Stalin's famous definition of proletarian culture as "national in form, socialist in content" provided a context in which formal strangeness could reemerge in a sanctioned way.[10] Through the domain of the "national," the potency of modernist writing and visual production found its fulfillment in the 1930s.

This book makes visible the new life of the Russian modernist tradition during the period that ostensibly repressed and decimated it. Perhaps unexpectedly, Stalin's national form, conceived as an empty vessel to be filled with socialist content, was essentially the only discursive domain that allowed and even invited aesthetic engagement with variety and heterogeneity in the dogmatic totalitarian state. It is not a coincidence that the concept of national form reached its discursive apotheosis after the statewide attacks on formalism of the mid-1930s, when the representational radicalism of avant-garde form, with its analytical decomposition of the procedure of signification, was subdued. The new socialist *content*, with its clarity and "profundity," became the foundation of the Stalinist edifice, and *form* became a secondary and almost subservient entity—a decorative encasing, an ornamented vessel holding the distilled socialist essence. Thus, formal innovation was possible only in the national context and only if singular socialist content predominated. As such, the *national form* was the last sanctuary of modernist *strangeness*.

The resulting discursive nexus animated the state-sanctioned artistic representations that lie at the core of this book. The textual and visual material I examine is the product of interpretative imagination rooted in a very specific historical experience. It dwells simultaneously in the inseparable aesthetic and political realms. I follow Raymond Williams in his conviction that formal analysis must be "firmly grounded in formational analysis" because there is a "profound connection between forms and formations."[11] My close reading of the texts and visual artifacts is thus encompassed by a cluster of divergent and often contradictory discourses—aesthetic, social, and political. In *Reorientalism*'s opening chapter, I delineate this complex discursive nexus through four steps: (1) I situate the artists, writers, and critics who defined the early Soviet experimental years in a broader discussion of the historical avant-garde and modernism. (2) I review the innate and intricate link of modernism (and the avant-garde) with orientalist and colonial discourses. (3) I investigate an understudied connection between anti-imperial socialist discourses and orientalism. And (4) I conclude with a discussion of one of the key precepts of high Stalinist culture—*national form*—and establish its discursive debt to earlier formal avant-garde experiment.

I employ the neologism "reorientalism" to describe a critical lens that, while directly evoking the notions of orient and orientalism, also preserves a sense of the derivational prefix "re-," which indicates a change of direction or backward motion. The double meaning of the noun "reorientation"—which may signify both a *new route* and a *rediscovered old path*—is crucial to the book's central argument. Continuity and metamorphosis were the two refrains that accompanied this process of reorientation. Indeed, while envoys of Soviet modernism were redirected by the state apparatus and the dictum of socialist realism, they still managed to discern a set of new aesthetic principles and push their convictions to new limits. *Reorientalism* thus recognizes the aesthetic agency of the acting subjects in the oppressive ideological environment while also acknowledging their predisposition to oriental exoticism.

This book includes several artistic projects generally considered to be fringe examples, as well as those regarded as canonical works. It sets out not only to challenge the existing canonization and theorization of this period but also to establish that the projects discussed were major pieces of work for the artists in question. The individual fates, idiosyncratic theoretical investigations, and aesthetic production of their authors should be interwoven into larger patterns of the sociopolitical experience. This is not a story about heroes and villains but a story about individuals—earnest, disingenuous, confused, determined—most of whom narrowly escaped the deathly grip of the Stalinist ideological apparatus. They were certainly swayed by powerful external political forces, but they also cultivated an equally powerful urge to evolve and refine their aesthetic convictions from *within*, not from without. Thus, I identify the protagonists of my book as artists who gave themselves the self-imposed task of evolving to transform their aesthetic precepts. Accordingly, the original modernist urge to upend deeply ingrained perceptions evolved into a fascination with an ethnic Other.

AVANT-GARDE AND MODERNISM

"Avant-garde" and, to a lesser extent, "modernism" are not historical self-appellations—they are terms employed retrospectively to situate a selection of artists and their works within a certain geographic expanse and period. The Russian term *avangard* was used almost exclusively in relation to Marxist-Leninist political theory, referring to the political vanguard that guides the proletarian masses.[12] Representatives of the Russian imperial—and later, the Soviet historical—avant-garde never applied the term "avant-garde" to describe their own artistic and trans-artistic production. Constructivism, cubo-futurism, productivism, and factography were simply known as *leftist art* (*levoe iskusstvo*). Similarly, now-canonical modernist writers and artists conceived their fin de siècle work in opposition to the nineteenth-century realist tradition and instead identified themselves with individual artistic factions such as symbolism, imaginism, or acmeism. The umbrella term "modernism" was employed only sporadically, and often dismissively; it merely conveyed a shared contemporaneity.[13]

The issue of contemporaneity presents a challenge of periodization: can modernism, as a cultural term derived from the Latin *modo* (the current, the now) be securely anchored within a defined historical period? For Astradur Eysteinsson, modernism is an oppositional cultural phenomenon, as it "signals a dialectical opposition to what is not functionally 'modern,' namely 'tradition'"; he further posits that "the self-conscious break with tradition," as embodied in Ezra Pound's famous "make it new" maxim, must be "seen as a hallmark of modernism."[14] T. J. Clark's nuanced interpretation complicates the new-old dichotomy by underscoring modernism's temporal complexity and its disconcerting concatenation of the "not yet" and the "too late," and offers a particular method of mapping out modernism in art—one that is temporally scattered as "a distinctive patterning of mental and technical possibilities."[15]

Despite taxonomical confusion and contested definitions, the terms avant-garde and modernism are operative designations, and are instrumental for historians of art and literature. In the Anglo-American tradition, they were used interchangeably by such critics as Clement Greenberg and Harold Rosenberg.[16] Theodor Adorno and Renato Poggioli, however, rejected this conflation, instead viewing the avant-garde and modernism as contemporaneous but different critical responses to the process of the commodification of art. The elitist culture of modernism, which argued for the autonomy of the arts as a strategy of resistance against bourgeois moral and capitalist economic pressures, also tended to dissociate itself from any overt political agenda.[17] The avant-garde, by contrast, correlated art and life in the most radical manner and rendered autonomy unwarranted: as Poggioli claims, "the avant-garde image originally remained subordinate . . . to the ideals of a radicalism which was not cultural but political."[18] The historical avant-garde launched an attack on the bourgeois principles of the expressive artist and organic work of art that culminated in an aestheticist withdrawal from the world. Its representatives embraced radical political agendas of the left and the right and readily affiliated themselves with emerging state institutions.

In his influential study *Theory of the Avant-Garde*, Peter Bürger further expands Adorno's argument, asserting that the avant-garde's questioning and displacement of the institutions of art comprised its focal features. Bourgeois art's aesthetic disinterest and autonomy from "mundane" affairs, that is, reality as such, were challenged by the recalcitrant avant-garde's radical (*radix*—to the root) call for the possible realization of a utopia in which art and life were integrated. Consequently, art galleries, museums, and publishing houses—along with the notions of good taste and connoisseurship, which were justified by theories of autonomous art for art's sake—underwent a profound reevaluation. Conditions of artistic production and reception were drastically transformed. Herein lies a key distinction between modernism and the avant-garde for Bürger—representatives of the former (e.g., Joyce and Picasso) disrupted old categories and genres to invent new ones, while proponents of the latter (e.g., constructivists, surrealists, and dadaists) launched an assault on the institution of "art" as such.[19]

For some critics, however, both the avant-garde and modernism comprised an anti-culture. One of the most influential critics of the radical avant-garde and the elitist culture of modernism was Georg Lukács, Adorno's fierce opponent. Writing from Stalinist Moscow, the Hungarian émigré presented an alternative to the avant-garde's art-life correlation in the 1938 essay "Realism in the Balance." Lukács's classical humanism perceives modernism, with its fixation on fragment rather than synthesis, to be an aesthetic failure. Unlike realist texts, modernist artifacts "remain frozen in their own immediacy; they fail to pierce the surface to discover the underlying essence, i.e., the real factors that relate their experiences to the hidden social forces that produce them."[20] Lukács posits that literature is capable of affecting society at large and condemns the self-indulgent individualism of novels in the Joycean mold, which he sees as merely underscoring the individual's alienation from the capitalist world. He rejects the modernist novel's "narrative subjectivity" (stream of consciousness, interior monologue, etc.), which is enabled by the abstract potentiality of its protagonists. The modernist fixation on the individual self and the denial of the possibility of objective representation results in the "disintegration of the outer world," a complete loss of social reality.[21]

Clement Greenberg, writing at the same time as Lukács and from the same moment of history that this book addresses, perceives the avant-garde and modernism in less antagonistic terms. In 1939, he wrote that "the true and most important function of the avant-garde was not to 'experiment,' but to find a path along which it would be possible to keep culture *moving* in the midst of ideological confusion and violence [through the autonomy of form]."[22] Consequently, when the avant-garde loses its radical edge and becomes institutionalized, it settles in into the modernist framework. For Greenberg, modernism did not deliver an ultimate "break with the past" but was an "evolution" of tradition—it proceeded not by "theoretical demonstrations" of new techniques, but by "convert[ing] theoretical possibilities into empirical ones."[23] Greenberg's evolutionary vision, articulated from the same point in time, provides a productive framework for the projects discussed in this book.

The cases of five experimental artists prompt a reconsideration of the temporal and geographic boundaries of the Soviet avant-garde and modernism as they collided against the dictum of socialist realism in the 1930s. *Reorientalism* questions the conventional timeline of modernism in imperial Russia and the Soviet Union, countering the widely accepted view, as expressed by scholars such as Robert Russell, that modernism emerged around the 1890s and faded with the rise of socialist realism in the 1930s.[24] In fact, late Soviet modernism led a modified, albeit fragile, coexistence with socialist realism into the late 1930s and up until the beginning of the 1940s. The preceding avant-garde formal interrogation was essential for prolonging its life.

Charles Jencks was one of the first cultural theorists to identify late modernism as a distinct period in architecture that marked the transition from modernism to postmodernism. For Jencks, late modernists took "the theories and style of their [modernist] precursors to an extreme and in so doing produced an elaborated or mannered modernism. By contrast, post-modernists have modified the previous style, while building upon it, but in addition also rejected the theories almost completely."[25] In his influential study of postmodernism, Fredric Jameson recognizes the need for an intermediary concept to characterize the cultural products of the "transition" between modernism and postmodernism, and he does so, significantly enough, by evoking socialist realism: "we should probably . . . make some place . . . for what Charles Jencks has come to call 'late modernism'—the last survivals of a properly modernist view of art and the world after the great political and economic break of the Depression, where, under Stalinism or the Popular Front, Hitler or the New Deal, some new conception of social realism achieves the status of momentary cultural dominance by way of collective anxiety and world war."[26] Jameson identifies the need rather hesitantly, and does not proceed further.

The term "late modernism" became an operative category in English studies a few years later, and is now used to describe the literature and arts created up to and during World War II. Tyrus Miller, for instance, challenges an established view of works written in the 1930s by modernist authors as mere "cultural curiosities" of a second order. Instead, these texts, in his view, "mark the lines of flight artists took where an obstacle, the oft-mentioned 'impasse' of modernism, interrupted progress on established paths."[27] This unforeseen break in continuity, prompted by new historical pressures, created a temporal lag. The resulting untimeliness allowed the late modernists to "retain the power to transport their readers and critics 'out of bounds' to an 'elsewhere' of writing from which the period can be surveyed, from which its legitimacy as a whole might be called into question."[28] The efficacy of high modernist form was questioned and drastically reconsidered. Miller convincingly suggests that late modernist works are characterized by a "struggle against what they perceived as the apotheosis of form"—they reopen "the modernist enclosure of form onto the work's social and political environs, facilitating its more direct, polemical engagement with topical and popular discourses."[29]

The notion of late modernism shares some affinities with what Selim Khan-Magomedov, a prominent Russian art historian, defines as *post-constructivism*—an intermediary period that followed radical proto-constructivist experiments of the 1920s. As early as 1988, Khan-Magomedov writes that

> "post-constructivism is a movement away from the unitary stream in different directions, or rather in the form of a fan. All these pursuits bore the birthmark of constructivism until a new powerful vector (an aspiration toward classical forms) was established in the second half of the 1930s. Thus, post-constructivism is not a mere return to neo-classicism but an artistic aspiration toward it (and not always a conscious one) through the experience of constructivism."[30]

Khan-Magomedov later acknowledged that *post-avant-garde* (*postavangard*) would have been a more appropriate term, although it could not have been applied to Soviet scholarship of the period because the notion of the historical avant-garde was not recognized as such, being referred to instead simply as *leftist art*.[31] Even so, Khan-Magomedov applies his terminological apparatus only to the field of architecture and not to other artistic practices, paying no attention to the politics of alterity that permeated all post-avant-garde artistic practices.

The literary scholar Leonid Livak explicitly argues for the late modernist case and makes a convincing argument that Russian modernism found its footing along the Berlin-Prague-Paris axis in the 1930s, a geopolitical shift that resulted in the "parallel existence of mutually isolated Soviet and émigré subsystems."[32] However, his contention that "modernist culture was extinguished [in Stalin's USSR] by the early 1930s" and that the late modernist sensibility "dissociated cultural activity from political causes" and "found its full expression only in Russia Abroad" reenacts the conventional binary opposition of avant-garde/modernism vs. socialist realism, and requires readjustment.[33]

In the period between the 1900s and 1940s, there were varying combinations of modernist, avant-garde, and late modernist impulses in the Soviet Union. The cultural process at that time was marked by its unevenness and heterogeneity. Prevailing cultural trends coexisted with vanishing forms and practices, as well as with other nascent developments. Thus, chronological points such as the February 1905 Revolution, the 1917 October Revolution, and the Great Break of 1929 do not function as strict breakpoints—they are mere chronological points of orientation that assist in establishing a continuity of aesthetic production during a period of tremendous social upheaval. But, as *Reorientalism* posits, the tripartite genealogical structure of modernism, avant-garde, and late modernism is essential for understanding the long Russian-Soviet twentieth century, and this structure resonates with the three seismic political events.

The book's four case studies of late modernism will rely on the following understanding of the process of modernist evolution. In the Russian Empire, modernism emerged as a full and capable force around the time of the February 1905 Revolution in which the Bolsheviks played a relatively minor role. These early modernists, often from the aristocratic milieu, found themselves caught in the ensuing socio-political turmoil intensified by a process of modernization that had yet to fully mature. As a response, they explored themes of decadence and disorientation and propagated the complexity of subjectivity—emphasizing the opacity and fallibility of language and image in line with European fin de siècle aestheticism. Andrei Bely's *Petersburg* (1916, 1922), a dizzying narrative of the 1905 events, is an emblematic text of this period. The rejection of realism and naturalism led to the eradication of objective representation with the consequent valorization of individual expression and an aspiration to render the ineffable in artistic forms. This version of modernism was marked by tropes of backwardness, archaism, and underdevelopment and took on, in Marshall Berman's words, "a fantastic character, because it is forced to nourish itself not on social reality but on fantasies, mirages, dreams."[34] This modernist framework dissipated in the late 1920s when the New Economic Policy was terminated, although many of its representatives continued their work abroad, as Leonid Livak suggests.

The mostly proletarian and middle-class avant-garde, on the other hand, was invigorated by the Bolshevik coup d'état of 1917 that took place after the Russian state had already collapsed and the Tzar had abdicated. The old bourgeois social structure was dismantled and replaced by the social utopianism of the revolutionary government. Soviet avant-garde artists, as a socialist vanguard, countered the early modernist cult of individual genius with trans-subjective collectivity. While relying on the modernist dismantling of conventional forms, they went beyond the realm of individual expression. This radically new trend, exemplified by Rodchenko's design for the interior of a workers' club displayed in Paris in 1925, aspired to have a transformative social impact, hence its transgeneric nature and affiliations with a consumingly "reality-defining" political agenda. Many artists, such as Kazimir Malevich, Rodchenko, David Shterenberg, and Vladimir (Volodymyr) Tatlin, held influential positions in the administrative apparatus of the People's Commissariat of Enlightenment and within various pedagogical and research institutes in Moscow and Leningrad. Most of these institutions would be eliminated in the disorienting aftermath of the Great Break of 1929 and Stalin's "revolution from above," whose impact on society, according to Sheila Fitzpatrick, was greater than that of the 1917 revolutions and the Civil War.[35] In 1932, a hierarchical structure of artistic unions was created in close conformity with the Stalinist political apparatus. The advent of this period of political rule, an emergence of "Stalinist civilization,"[36] presented an opportunity for the emergence of late modernism of the interwar years—one characterized by imaginative engagement with vernacular material provided by "national forms."

The paradigm of late modernism reconnects Soviet art to artistic trends in the rest of the world and provides important continuity between the Stalinist era and the later resurgence of interest in modernist styles in the mid-1950s. The "Cultural Revolution" that followed the Great Break had proven a turning point for the avant-garde artists; although their "tendentiousness" or "partisanship" was never complete, their practices were *inflected* by ideology. Nevertheless, because of its proximity to political power, the Soviet avant-garde was able to prolong its life into the 1930s and even further as late modernism. Most interestingly, while the transformative aspect of the avant-garde was made redundant and violently censored by the Stalinist state, its expertise in formal innovativeness and stylistic potency was appropriated. Thus, the late modernism of the 1930s seriously and arduously explored possibilities of engagement with popular, vernacular, political, and other social discourses, sanctioned by the state. For these purposes, it needed to loosen its fixation on aesthetic form and undergo what Devin Fore terms a process of "rehumanization of art."[37] This "human turn" restored the human subject as a central category of aesthetic inquiry.

It is, however, essential to distinguish late modernist practices from those of socialist realism with its alleged humanism. *Reorientalism* also contributes to the ongoing debate over the relationship between avant-garde and socialist realism. This debate is dominated by two oft-cited narratives: one of difference and one of semblance. The former, exemplified by Vladimir Paperny's *Culture Two*, sets off the egalitarian, experimental, and horizontal avant-garde of Culture One (circa 1917–1931) against the repressive, monumentalist, and vertical "neoclassicism" of Culture Two (1932–1953).[38] In contrast, Boris Groys denies such a rigid dichotomy in *The Total Art of Stalinism*, emphasizing socialist realism's organic continuity with the avant-garde project, and, more radically, insisting that the official aesthetic framework of the post-1934 Soviet Union comprises the avant-garde's culmination and its completion: "Stalinist culture both radicalizes and formally overcomes the avant-garde; it is, so to speak, a laying bare of the avant-garde device and not merely a negation of it."[39] While Paperny sees Cultures One and Two as linked through dialectical negation, Groys conceptualizes the link between the two in affirmative terms of elaboration, reinforcement, and development of the ethos of the avant-garde in late Stalinism.

Groys's critical intervention largely follows the pattern promulgated by the postmodernist criticism of modernism, yet ironically, it strives for the very totalitarian completeness that it attempts to challenge. This position regards the historical avant-garde as a fundamentally homogenous and static entity, freed from the "constraints" of history and aesthetic evolution. Without any sustained formal analysis of the works in question and without establishing points of divergence, it prescribes a normative and all-encompassing vision. Groys's *Gesamtkunstwerk* in effect deprives acting subjects of agency. Furthermore, he tends to underestimate the national heterogeneity of Stalinist culture that engendered a complex friction between notions of difference (otherness) and similarity (uniformity). Groys neutralizes it in the following manner:

> Socialist realism defined itself as "national in form, socialist in content." The central issue involved in "Sovietness" therefore had nothing to do with national form (which could be anything), but rather concerned the unified socialist, ideological work done with this form. Sovietness stood in opposition to modernism not as regional or exotic art is opposed to universal art; instead, here one claim to universality opposed another claim to it.[40]

National form, in fact, was an extremely functional category, however essence-free it was. The 1930s saw the significance of national form for the (re)development of the avant-garde. Leading experimental artists such as Vertov and Eisenstein made determined attempts to define national form and employ it in their artistic practice. The process was one of domesticating the exotic and endowing it with the potential to conform to a universal principle of modernity. The Soviet version of the "global South," with archaism and underdevelopment as its key markers, profoundly shaped a conversion from radical linguistic and visual experimentation to a subdued modernist sensibility. The resulting texts and visual artifacts perfectly exemplified the imperialist condescension inherent in the era's civilizing projects, yet they also became a space for the expression of "otherness" and for the "unfamiliar" that was central to modernism.

Thus, despite what Groys suggests, the avant-garde did not morph into socialist realism. The avant-garde evolved into late modernism, since the contestation of representational conventions was still its primary concern. The politicized aesthetics of socialist realism, on the other hand, did not contest representational boundaries; it constructed and reinforced them. Hence, the suggested continuity between the ethos of the avant-garde and the socialist realist epistemology is profoundly problematic. The "elitist obfuscation" of modernism, its concern with technique, its critique of the conventions of representation, and its claims to originality and innovation were not palatable to the emerging Stalinist culture, which was fixated on organicity, accessibility, and wholeness.

Language evolved from a means of renouncing stable meaning into a tool of assertive affirmation.

Reorientalism thus offers an alternative vision of the divide between the 1920s and the 1930s, reinterpreting that debate through a decentralized notion of modernist aesthetics. It challenges the strict binarism of Paperny and contests the totality of Groys's model of *Gesamtkunstwerk*. Socialist realism is not a completion of the avant-garde project. The official Soviet artistic method appropriated some of the avant-garde experiment's key features that were already undergoing substantial transformation. The *Gesamtkunstwerk* of the avant-garde was not total in the end; it was susceptible to internal evolution. Thus, I treat the artifacts of my book as belonging to the late modernist framework that allowed this evolution to unfold. The eastward turn of Soviet avant-garde artists was constitutive of late modernism.

The fundamental operative principle of *Reorientalism* is *heterogeneity*; it reclaims the *particular* as expressed in various national formations, distinctive aesthetic practices, and individual professional destinies. It argues that instead of accepting Paperny's approach to culture as two separate banks, or Groys's view of culture as a continuous flow, it is more productive to conceptualize it as a dam built to divert the avant-garde's river of creative impulse. This dam transformed the natural river into a man-made canal and dramatically altered the course of its flow toward the eastern periphery of the country, where it nourished the allegedly aesthetically "arid" lands and contributed to the flourishing of a new Soviet subjectivity. Moreover, within this newly reengineered waterway, each avant-garde artist had his or her own swimming lane—and often not a straight path but a curved one. In their designated space, they cultivated distinct artistic techniques: idiosyncratic strategies for applying the experimental achievements of their own celebrated pasts to engage with the political and aesthetic reality of the present.

MODERNISM AND ORIENTALISM

In a now-standard formulation of postcolonial theory, a "universal" metropolitan center is perceived as exploiting its cultural and epistemological privileges in relation to a "particularized" periphery. Edward Said's influential classification of the oriental Other as a subject of difference in the Western imagination marks the structure of this uneven relationship. Such unevenness, however, is also present in Said's selective treatment of global imperial configurations in which Russia is glaringly absent. Said acknowledges that his study "does not do justice to . . . the important contributions to Orientalism of Germany, Italy, Russia, Spain, and Portugal," but then a few pages later he conflates Russia with the East: "No one will have failed to note how 'East' has always signified danger and threat during this period, even as it has meant the traditional Orient as well as Russia."[41] More intriguingly, his postcolonial effort to expose the underlying imperialist power structures in Western artistic representations of the Orient, in fact, shares an important genealogy with the early Soviet criticism of imperial dispositions of Western oriental studies, as shown by Vera Tolz.[42] The definition of "Oriental Studies" in the second edition of the *Great Soviet Encyclopedia* (1951),[43] which comprised a summary of Sergei Ol'denburg's critique of European oriental studies, as articulated in the late 1920s and the early 1930s,[44] both anticipated and directly influenced Said's theoretical contribution through the work of the Egyptian Marxist sociologist Anouar Abdel-Malek.[45]

Said and Marxist historiography both underscore imperialism's ability to bring world communities closer together, yielding proximity that results in the "cultural integrity of empire."[46] The British and French imperial experiences in particular were marked by a unique coherence and cultural centrality. Their "unparalleled" traditions of novel-writing—for narrative plays a formative and legitimizing role in the imperial framework—serve as testimony to this integrity.[47] However, there are distinct fissures in this uneven relationship. The political project of imperial hegemony produced a paradoxical homogeneity, albeit of a heterogeneous kind: the imperial conquest, facing the difference of the Other and finding itself in the process of perpetual breakdown and regeneration, became inherently infused with contradiction and ambiguity. The experience of modernity cuts across geographic and ethnic boundaries, displacing class, national, and religious identities. As Homi Bhabha puts it, "it is in the emergence of the interstices—the overlap and displacement of domains of difference—that the intersubjective and collective experiences of *nationness*, community interest, or cultural value are negotiated."[48]

At the same time, modernity yielded a new form of unity beneath the conceptual umbrella of the nation-state. The nineteenth century gave way to the widespread creation of independent nation-states, as old monarchical structures were dismembered by the flames of romantic nationalism. Such nationalism emerged out of Western models of national identity, which were reinforced by the gradual disintegration of the institution of empire. This process would reach its pinnacle during the very advent of modernism, erupting in an explosion of political crises when the Habsburg, Ottoman, Russian, and Wilhelmine Empires collapsed after World War I. As alternative conceptions of self and territorial sovereignty were pieced together from imperial ruins, processes of claiming a national status became inextricably connected with membership in global modernity. The resulting amalgamation of former imperial centers and newly emerged nation-states produced a paradoxical hybrid, which Ernst Bloch identified as *simultaneous non-contemporaneities*.[49] Thus, Edward Said calls us to reread the cultural archive "not univocally but contrapuntally, with a simultaneous awareness both of the metropolitan history that is narrated and of those other histories against which (and together with which) the dominating discourse acts."[50]

In the twentieth century, modernism challenged literary models that relied on imperial coherence—a move both forceful and contradictory in its implications. Recently, scholars such as Jessica Berman and Rebecca Walkowitz reconsider modernism's relationship to empire in terms of a "transnational turn,"[51] a backdrop against which will emerge demands for a more cosmopolitan version of community, alert to issues of "commonality, shared voice, and exchange of experience, especially in relation to dominant discourses of gender and nationality."[52] Susan Stanford Friedman compellingly calls for *planetary modernisms*, which "encompass multitudes on a global grid of relational networks" and embrace "contradictions, tensions, oppositions, asymmetries" pertinent to both local and global modernities.[53]

And yet, modernism is also implicated in the very conditions it critiques. Andreas Huyssen describes "colonialism and conquest as the very condition of possibility for modernity and for aesthetic modernism."[54] Elleke Boehmer and Steven Matthews argue that colonialism's centrifugal forces stimulated cross-border dialogues and encouraged "the process of giving the 'other' voice—as well as of investigating who the 'other' was in the first place."[55] They further contend that empire, alongside war and modernity, made modernism possible: colonial rule produced cultural effects that consequently dismantled its very foundations by means of "the dissociation of subjectivity, the dislocation of western sensibility, the valorization of the fragment, the reification of the alien, and the fascinated glance at the stranger."[56] Imperial infrastructure—railways, maritime navigation, and various communication channels—provided physical access to distant cultures.

Modernity rendered the Other physically reachable and accessible. But whether the Other was ever fully and unconditionally seen is up for debate, given that the radical otherness of the colonial mode of existence, as an unmediated experience, was virtually unavailable to metropolis dwellers. Modernist representation is born out of a sociopolitical situation in which the colonial Other is invisible. Raymond Williams goes a step further to suggest that modernist works exploit the cultural privileges provided by the empire to enact a "metropolitan perception."[57]

Similarly, Fredric Jameson contends that the aesthetics of modernism serve to disguise the forbidding realities of imperialism, given that modernism fails to provide a substantive criticism of the institution of empire and its exploitative mechanisms, nor does it attempt to undermine its discursive fundamentals.[58] The imperial capital is merely substituted with a commodified and rarefied cultural artifact. Jameson further argues that *spatial* aspects of the Western imperial project had a profound effect on modernist aesthetics:

> "A significant structural segment of the economic system as a whole is now located elsewhere, beyond the metropolis, outside of the daily life and existential experience of the home country, in colonies over the water whose own life experience and life world—very different from that of the imperial power—remain unknown and unimaginable for the subjects of the imperial power, whatever social class they may belong to. Such spatial disjunction has as its immediate consequence the inability to grasp the way the system functions as a whole."[59]

Because of this structural condition, wherein the Other is distanced and made imperceptible to most inhabitants of metropoles, modernism's formal experiment becomes a means to expose the absence of subaltern agency. A modernist text thus comprises an intricate veil concealing the indecency of capitalism.

However, more charitable accounts of modernist cross-culturalism underline imperial expansion's ability to bring the unfamiliar Other into proximity. Terry Eagleton, for instance, views modernism as the product of imperial dislocation and renders it as the implicit precursor to postcolonial literature.[60] Jahan Ramazani develops this argument further, highlighting "the overlap, circulation, and friction between postcolonialism and modernism" by examining "various ways of vivifying circuits of poetic connection and dialogue across political and geographic borders and even hemispheres."[61]

As Barr's diagram from the preface shows, modernism's preoccupation with formal innovation was indeed nourished by exposure to alien cultures that inspired new artistic forms. These "outlandish" influences played to the modernist obsession with defamiliarization—a strategy of enhancing perceptions of the familiar. Thus, for instance, Ezra Pound's engagement with traditional Chinese and Japanese literary forms, or Pablo Picasso's and Gertrude Stein's use of African masks, resulted in productive tensions between modern and archaic elements. Michael North identifies these practices as a case of "dialect *of* modernism" that sees linguistic mimicry and racial masquerade as essentially modernist strategies.[62] The genuinely and "primordially" unfamiliar indeed found its place in the everyday artistic life of the European avant-gardes. Through the return to the past and pronounced awareness of the present, the modernist aesthetic form underwent a process of historicization. On the other hand, these "alien" forms, emanating from outside the Western hemisphere, functioned as archaic remnants or anachronisms and comprised an exotic supplement that was appropriated and reshaped by the experimental master, whose original locale was frequently a metropolitan center. This master metamorphosed the archaic into the vanguard and made alien forms transcend their "primeval" origins.

The case of Russia in the context of these debates is compelling. The prerevolutionary avant-garde's obsession with the East is well documented. Such figures as Mikhail Larionov, Natalia Goncharova, Velimir Khlebnikov, and David Burliuk were consumed by the Russian Empire's own Eastern "primitive" culture. Indeed, in her 1914 draft letter addressed to Marinetti, Goncharova boldly identifies Russia with Asia,[63] while Benedikt Livshits, a prominent futurist, referred to Russia as "the inherent part of the East" during the dispute "Our Answer to Marinetti" held in Petersburg in the same year.[64] Jane Sharp categorizes this affectionate gaze eastward and inward as *orientophilism* (vostokofil'stvo) that "represents the avant-garde's turn to the East as a condition of its radicality."[65] This is elaborated in Harsha Ram's argument that the early avant-garde's analytical decomposition of the linguistic sign or the material principles of art was related to a "geopoetics" of Eurasia premised on a reconfiguration of time and space, with Khlebnikov as a leading exponent.[66] This comprised an act of spatial deterritorialization that affirmed the unbounded authority of the artist, who delivered new ways of seeing.

The 1920s and 1930s, however, presented a modified version of the Soviet state's orientation toward the Orient. Emma Widdis deems the Eastern preoccupation "both threat and opportunity."[67] In the late postrevolutionary context, she claims, the "primitiveness" of the Soviet Orient was considered something to be overcome by way of modernization and, more importantly, was seen as "a model of pre-capitalist life that was a source of considerable fascination and allure for those seeking a specifically communist reformulation of mind-body experience."[68] I would like to expand this argument, however: while the prerevolutionary avant-garde strove to renew categories of perception by incorporating "archaic" forms, the 1930s practice of late modernism normalized their difference, at least on a thematic level. The "primitivist" component was thus radically renegotiated and turned into a trope of modernization with the beginning of the first five-year plan: the fetishized archaic past evolved into the bright communist future and a new socialist subjectivity was created. As a result, tensions between the alien and the familiar, universal drives and ethnic particularism, center and periphery, aesthetics and politics were elevated to a new level. The cross-cultural transposition of Marxist values resulted in a unique articulation of the discursive challenges presented by orientalism and the question of subaltern agency.

Both epochs—the revolutionary era and the era of high Stalinism—witnessed formal experimentation motivated or mediated by an eastward turn. However, the structure of these encounters was different: the early avant-garde celebrated unevenness of development, while the late modernists sought to abolish it in the service of progress. Furthermore, the late modernists' projects were utilized to reterritorialize space in sync with the political project of delimitation (in contrast to a "cerebral" concept of Eurasia). This orientation toward real political space endorsed the authority of the state, to which the artist was now subordinated. The avant-garde aesthetic trajectory was conditioned by the political realia of the first socialist society, while ethnic difference was the primary vehicle for the displacement of formal experimentation away from the sweepingly epistemological concerns of the 1920s.

The fate of modernist experimentation in the Union of Soviet Socialist Republics (USSR)—a country that set itself on a quest against the institution of empire and claimed to celebrate national equality—presents a unique case. The Bolsheviks' challenge to universalized imperial structures problematized modernism's complicity with empire. The resulting ideology did not produce a simple homogeneity of aesthetic practices. Instead, it complicated the politics of modernist form, whose conviction of historical constructedness gave way to the notion of organic temporal wholeness, and in so doing relinquished the notion of non-universality in favor of the internationalist appeal of the socialist project, which gradually acquired a status of universal authority. The turn to it constitutes a kind of intricate self-portrait of Soviet political modernity. Unlike Western culture that, according to Said, "gained in strength and identity by setting itself off against the Orient as a sort of surrogate and even underground self,"[69] the Soviet attentive gaze toward its own Eastern territories was not a case of mere projective narcissism; it was a bold reaffirmation of the universality of the socialist project.

At the same time, the emancipatory and idealist nature of the Soviet turn to the East gave it an essential ambivalence. The anti-imperial October Revolution was supposed to be a liberation and emancipation of oppressed nations, but despite its embedded critique of imperialism, Soviet policy in the East also represented a strong display of innately orientalist clichés. The Bolsheviks continued to replicate some of the colonialist stereotypes that they tried to disavow under the guise of universal socialist values. Consequently, Soviet modernity produced hybrid and regenerative syntheses of discourses and policies: they were both progressive and reactionary.

The reoriented Soviet avant-garde correlated with the geopolitical space of the Stalinist state. Various avant-garde and modernist concerns—such as the role of the capitalist market and cultural institutions, or the function of mass culture and the vernacular—were vigorously addressed by Soviet ideologues after the abolition of the New Economic Policy in 1928. Consequently, Soviet late modernism acquired markedly different resonances under the banner of anti-imperialism and internationalism.[70] Its impulse of transformative radicalism was subdued and reoriented. The anxieties and discontents of imperial conquest pertinent to the modernist text were replaced by the self-confident enthusiasm of socialist modernity during the late modernist period.

ORIENTALISM AND SOCIALISM

"In Russia the center is on the periphery," Vasilii Kliuchevsky famously wrote in the 1890s.[71] The lack of a clear geographic border between the supposed metropolitan areas and peripheral zones, including colonies, characterized the Russian Empire for this prominent Russian historian of the late imperial period. Kliuchevsky's aphoristic endorsement of the centrality of the marginal reverberated some thirty years later, in a drastically different political context, in Iurii Tynianov's vision of a literary process: "It is not only the *borders* of literature—its 'periphery,' its liminal regions—that are fluid, but this [fluidity] affects its very 'center.'"[72] Mikhail Bakhtin, a contemporary of Tynianov, argues that the very notion of culture implies a boundary and any cultural act takes place at a borderline separating I and the Other, or everyday life and art. As he succinctly states, the "aesthetic act always operates on the boundaries (form is a boundary)."[73] What these statements imply is that a closed, immobile, and stable center does not exist in either a topographical or ontological sense. A process of constant interchange and mutual displacement defines the geographic space and temporal framework of the cultural process, and it also defines the very structure of being.

Russian political realities, however, imposed a more pragmatic and less malleable understanding of the border concept. After the October Revolution in 1917, the new government inherited a vast territory with ill-defined and contested borders from the collapsed Russian Empire. Many borderlands were ethnically heterogeneous, with fluctuating and disputed political and national affiliations. Conceptually, however, the territory was *boundless*, and thus in alignment with the dictum of the "borderless" international proletarian revolution, which aspired to nothing less than a total transformation of the global political structure.

As Stalin boldly put it in 1924, the Russian communists could not "confine their work within the narrow national bounds of the Russian revolution" because they had "to transfer the struggle to the international arena . . . in order to facilitate the task of overthrowing capitalism for the proletarians of all countries."[74]

The very first step toward the bordered Soviet state was the Treaty of Brest-Litovsk—a separate peace treaty signed on March 3, 1918, between the new Soviet government and the Central Powers. The treaty, a deeply unpopular decision that had split the Party, conditioned Russia's withdrawal from World War I upon a relinquishing of its western borderlands (Ukraine, Poland, Belarus, and the Baltic provinces), and enforced further territorial cessions in the Caucasus in favor of the Ottoman Empire. The treaty was annulled eight months later by the Armistice of November 11, 1918, according to which Germany surrendered to the Western Allied powers. During the Russian Civil War (1917–1922), the Bolsheviks tried to restore power over the lost territories after Germany's defeat; eventually, they established control over most domains of the former Russian Empire.

The Red Army, however, was defeated in the Russo-Polish War (1919–1920). Poland was of crucial importance to the Bolsheviks, who planned to reach Germany via the "Polish Corridor" and help socialist revolutionaries in Bavaria, thus instigating a truly international socialist revolution. The Treaty of Riga, signed in Latvia on March 18, 1921, concluded the Russo-Polish War and established Russia's western border. After the defeat in Poland, the Bolsheviks were forced to develop an alternative to the revolution without borders. The concept of the "socialist border" was subsequently conceived, leading to the founding of the USSR, as a conventional nation-state with fixed geopolitical boundaries, in 1922.[75] Yet Russia, as the largest constituent state, served as a handy synecdoche for the entire collective throughout its existence. The Marxist ideal of proletarian internationalism and the eventual "withering away of the state" were subsequently adjusted, and the revisions led to Stalin's 1925 doctrine of "socialism in one country," which later began to conflate revolutionary internationalism with Soviet patriotism.[76]

Between 1924 and 1936, when the Soviet Union gained control over formerly imperial territories in Central Asia, the boundary-enforcing culture of Stalinism further solidified its state borders. These territories included the future constituent Soviet republics of Kazakhstan, Kyrgyzstan, Tajikistan, Turkmenistan, and Uzbekistan, which emerged in place of the former imperial General Governorate of Turkestan, as well as two protectorates—Bukhara and Khiva. Ethnic communities acquired national identities through social engineering. The new borders of the new Central Asian republics were altered along ethnic identities—a process that was accompanied by the suppression of independence movements categorized as "right deviations" by Stalin. This signaled a shift toward a stronger centralized Soviet identity and greater Russification; the autonomy previously given to national cultures was increasingly curtailed. By the late 1930s, Russian national identity within the ethnic structure of the Soviet state had become the centerpiece of the country's ideological identity and the Russian nation assumed the role of the vanguard of the socialist movement.

The political reality of the formation of the Soviet *state*, as a halted revolutionary movement, was preceded by Lenin's theoretical work on the institution of empire. Russia, despite being the least-developed capitalist country in Europe, was the place where the socialist revolution ensued. Its intermediary status—an underdeveloped country among the developed—was key for Lenin's conceptualization of the empire-colonies interaction.[77] In *Imperialism, the Highest Stage of Capitalism* (1917), Lenin argues that the fact that Russia was a colony in relation to Europe made it the weakest link in the capitalist chain: it was fertile ground for the revolution to take place.[78] Thus, Russia—as an "underdeveloped empire" with a largely uneducated and "backward" population, and in which archaic and modern modes of production coexisted—could use its economic, cultural, and political in-betweenness to its advantage.[79] It is crucial that the trope of backwardness was an integral part of Soviet Marxist historiography. This was never seen as a stumbling block on the way toward complete enlightenment and economic advancement. On the contrary, backwardness was seen as a condition under which revolutionary potential could flourish. The suppressed "retrograde" constituents, not the urban proletariat of the industrialized societies of Western Europe, were destined to deliver world revolution.[80]

Dismantling the institution of empire lay at the heart of the Russian articulation of Marxism. Lenin provided a forceful economic and political argument for empire as the ultimate stage of capitalist development, to be superseded by communism. By generating profits from imperial colonial enterprises, financial capital creates a systemic power imbalance: it divides the world between monopolist corporations and the great Western powers, a key feature of which is the corruption of native elites who, in turn, suppress local worker revolts. This imbalance of power was supposed to provide an impetus for world revolution since the millions of suppressed colonial subjects possessed enormous potential to launch a revolt against the global capitalist system.

Furthermore, according to Lenin's theory, the colonized Orient's structural dependence on imperialism was a beacon of revolutionary hope. Thus, Lenin's contribution to Marxist theory incorporates the East into a global whole. It was no longer a docile territory—a mere archaeological or cultural curiosity—but an integral, albeit suppressed and exploited, part of the capitalist circulatory system. Lenin's Soviet nationality policy directly derived from this conviction:

establishing the right of nations to self-determination was not only a means to mobilize the working class against national oppression under capitalism; it was also the most radical way to dismantle imperialism—the highest stage of capitalism—altogether and forever. The early Bolshevik state was the sole political entity at the time that not only rhetorically denounced colonialism but also invested heavily in challenging it both on their territory and beyond.

Lenin's conceptualization of the role of the dedicated professional vanguard (*avangard*) of the party was another theoretical addition to Marxism: Unlike capitalists, who undermine radicalism by granting incremental improvements to the working class, the vanguard, fueled by its clear understanding of political reality, accelerates historical progression. However, Lenin's concept also establishes a structurally colonial relationship between the vanguard of the party and the world proletariat by maintaining that neither the proletariat nor the peasantry could gain socialist consciousness without external assistance.[81] Thus, in classic orientalist fashion, Lenin calls for intervention by the elites—an action justified by the presumed lack of agency in the "object" of transformation. The subaltern, in the Spivakian sense, had to be represented and spoken for.

This "turn eastward and inward," to use Immanuel Wallerstein's formulation,[82] was a key event of the 1930s that amplified these two Leninist conceptual additions to Marxism. Central Asia served as a topos where the past would meet the present, and the clash between the two would produce a bright socialist future. It was imagined as an ideal premodern *Gemeinschaft*, ready to join the universal socialist collective once its "backward" inhabitants were reshaped through social engineering. Thus, the Soviet project evolved into a peculiar blend of the classic Weberian idea of modernity with its drives toward industrialization, bureaucratization, and secularization on the one hand; and utopian and inherently collective communist ideals on the other. The Soviet Union was a space of contradiction and ambiguity, and the Soviet Orient lies at the heart of this conceptual muddle, for it was an ultimate *contact zone* marked by perils of "miscomprehension, incomprehension, [and] absolute heterogeneity of meaning," as in Mary Louise Pratt's conceptual model.[83]

The Soviet culture of the 1930s tended to respect cultural differences, albeit in the context of a "backward" periphery's structural dependence on an advanced center. In classic orientalist manner, the "retrograde" region was deemed incapable of transcending its borders on its own and of making sense of its political self—there was a need for a "middleman," a revolutionary agent. As early as 1923, Stalin had argued that some republics, due to their cultural and economic underdevelopment, "are incapable of making full use of the rights and opportunities afforded them by national equality of rights; they are incapable of rising to a higher level of development and thus catching up with the nationalities which have forged ahead unless they receive real and prolonged assistance from *outside*."[84] Therefore, Soviet ideologues exploited a key aspect of orientalism: its inherent mediating role between "unenlightened" ethnic populations and the values of "universal" civilization. Inadvertently, Stalin's vision of the national question undermines its own claim of addressing the specificity of vernacular forms.

Soviet Central Asia was profoundly heterogeneous, and this inherent heterogeneity posed a political risk. As Marlène Laruelle argues, while "the Soviet period both continued and discontinued the late tsarist regime's nationalities policy and its definition of ethnicity . . ., techniques of population control in the name of scientific knowledge took on unprecedented scope with the officialization of Marxist-Leninist science."[85] The Bolshevik modernity project faced a vast Eastern territory where ethnicity and statehood simply did not coincide—it was inhabited by multiethnic, multilingual, and generally dispersed and disorganized local populations. This remarkable ethnic complexity was discursively and politically addressed through the project of national delimitation—the demarcation of national territories in Central Asia between 1924 and 1936. The delineation thus constituted both a division and a unification: a push toward the universal idea of communism via demarcation and territorial nationhood. Terry Martin, among others, highlights the fact that Soviet ideologues never explained how the promoting minorities' particularistic identities at a sub-state level would contribute to the unity of the newly founded country.[86] The Soviet nation-building initiatives resulted, in Yuri Slezkine's words, in "a spectacularly successful attempt at a state-sponsored conflation of language, 'culture,' territory and quota-fed bureaucracy."[87] However, the policies that enthusiastically affirmed diversity were implemented against a background of ideological and institutional "sameness," so that the universal appeal of communism could never be forgotten. Cloé Drieu's concept of *heritagization*, constituted by the capacity for national resilience through the adaptation of nationalist sentiments under totalitarian subjugation, reveals the contradictory logic of the Soviet construction of nations and cultures during the interwar period.[88]

The project of national delimitation effectively ended the long and animated scholarly debate on how to understand the territory of Central Asia. There were two dominant approaches to this concept in post-revolutionary Russia: a *regional* one that saw the expanse as a larger whole, with close historical ties between sedentary and nomadic civilizations; and a *national* one, which perceived the territory as consisting of distinct national pieces. The regional approach, embodied in the overarching concept of Turkestan, was professed by the prominent orientalist Vasily Bartold, while the national vision received strong support from Soviet ideologues. Consequently, the idea of a unified Turkestan was rejected due to fears that a Muslim constituent might threaten the unity of the USSR. Instead, the project of national demarcation established individual "nations," each with its own respective history. This marked the culmination of the Stalinist endorsement of national forms. No transnational identification, such as Turkestan or Transcaucasia, was to compete with the wholeness and integrity of the USSR.[89] This political integrity shaped Georges Bataille's 1949 vision of the Stalinist state as a case of *imperial socialism*. The Soviet Union was "a framework in which any nation can be inserted," and, for Bataille, "it could later incorporate a Chilean Republic in the same way as a Ukrainian Republic [was] already incorporated."[90] The very name of the country could accommodate any preexisting national formation.

The 1930s saw the "resolution" of another issue related to nationality: the Marxist historiographical concept of Asiatic Mode of Production (AMP). Marx refers to AMP only once, describing it as one of the four stages of social development: "In broad outline, the Asiatic, ancient, feudal and modern bourgeois modes of production may be designated as epochs marking progress in the economic development of society."[91] AMP is thus the only mode of production that Marx identifies as geographically circumscribed. The concept presented itself as an almost insolvable conundrum for Soviet ideologues and Stalin himself, for the nondevelopmental character of the Orient contradicted the universal logic of the development of forces of production. The presumed particularistic nature of Asiatic society undermined a universal pattern of development common to all societies. The teleology of inevitable progression toward socialism was thus suspended.

Karl Wittfogel, a disenchanted German communist, later expanded Marx's concept of AMP to advance a theory of a perpetual Asiatic society that functions as the prototype and progenitor of despotic society, reborn in the Soviet Union under Stalin.[92] Wittfogel's notorious 1957 study *Oriental Despotism: A Comparative Study of Total Power* establishes two points: "the peculiarity of a non-Western semi-managerial system of despotic power and the interpretation of Communist totalitarianism as a total managerial, and much more despotic, variant of that system."[93] He finds a resemblance between "hydraulic-bureaucratic official-states" of the past and the Soviet political system with its state planning, social engineering, preference for monumental architecture, and absence of a strong institution of private property. Essentially, Wittfogel argues that the USSR was a contemporary version of oriental despotic rule based on AMP.

Indeed, the turn to the East coincided with the beginning of the first five-year plan, the crux of Soviet modernity, with its mass-scale infrastructural and industrial projects, among which the construction of thousand-mile canals occupied a special role. The Soviet hydraulic empire, according to Wittfogel's account, relied on centralized bureaucratic despotism to implement large-scale irrigation works ("people's," or forced labor, construction projects). This comprised a process of construction through subordination, in which the state apparatus essentially assumes the role of the exploiting class. Wittfogel even directly invokes and rebukes Stalin's "national in form, socialist in content" formula: "Stalin claims that in a modern industrial apparatus state the culture of a national minority is national in form and socialist in content. Experience shows that the 'socialist' . . . substance quickly wipes out all but the most insignificant national elements. A similar mechanism is at work in the agrarian apparatus state. Paraphrasing Stalin's formula and replacing myth by reality, we may truthfully say that hydraulic despotism is benevolent in form and oppressive in content."[94]

In his attack on Stalinism, Wittfogel's account, locked in rigid binarism, enacts essentializing and Eurocentric features of Marxism. However, it presents a valuable contemporaneous account of debates on how the universal appeal of communism had to negotiate national particularities. Indeed, for Gayatri Chakravorty Spivak, AMP "marks a venerable moment in theorizing the other" for it endeavors to answer the question: why is there difference?[95] It is "imaginary fleshing out of a difference in terms that are consonant with the development of capitalism and the resistance *appropriate* to it as 'the same.'"[96]

1934 is the year in which the discursive life of AMP in the Soviet Union officially ended.[97] The exceptionalist AMP was replaced by the rigid historical model of *piatichlenka* (five-stage development), a uniform pattern of historical development divided into five different stages: (1) primitive communism, (2) slave society, (3) feudalism, (4) capitalism, and (5) socialism. In June of 1933, the prominent Soviet orientalist Vasily Struve delivered a paper entitled "The Problem of the Genesis, Development, and Disintegration of the Slave Societies of the Ancient Orient" at the State Academy of the History of Material Culture.[98] In it, he argued that AMP was not a stage of slave society, merely an Asiatic variant. This was followed by the earliest attempt to formulate the basic premises of *piatichlenka* based on Marx's and Lenin's works. Stalin officially endorsed *piatichlenka* in his 1938 work *Dialectical and Historical Materialism*,[99] and famously excised Marx's reference in *Critique of Political Economy*, as Wittfogel puts it, in "modo Tatarico—with a meat cleaver."[100] The unilinearity of *piatichlenka* became a doctrinal truth.

Stalin vehemently rejected the notion that geographic environment could be "the chief force determining the physiognomy of society, the character of the social system of men, the transition from one system to another."[101] With the role of geographic factors thus denigrated or outright denied, Stalinist discourse openly promoted the empowerment of human subjects through their ability to transform the face of the environment. A similar solution was offered in the cultural sphere. AMP posited the existence of a fixed and unchanging national form, while the stadial development model emphasized the universality of historical progress. In the end, the exceptionalist AMP model was absorbed into the discourse of universal socialist culture, which incorporated distinct yet transient national forms. This shift allowed the Soviet Orient to progress from being the object of imperial domination to an active historical socialist subject.

SOCIALISM AND FORM

In "The Nation Form: History and Ideology," Etienne Balibar explores how historical identities of modern social formations, affected by political forms, evolved into national forms. He argues that *"every social community reproduced by the functioning of institutions is imaginary*, that is, it is based on the projection of individual existence into the weft of a collective narrative, on the recognition of a common *name* and on traditions lived as the trace of an immemorial past (even when they have been created and inculcated in the recent past)."[102] Thus, as Rogers Brubaker argues, the nation is an instutionalized form—both a practical category and a contingent event.[103] The Eastern republics of the Soviet Union were undergoing a process of formation in the 1930s in line with what Balibar and Brubaker describe: nation-ness was a curated event. The central state apparatus provided these republics with a firmly institutionalized set of novel forms—new borders, new languages, new alphabets, new literary canons, and new identities— and thus created "nation forms."[104] The end product of this formational orientalism, however, was the development of the supranational proletarian state. While being nationally "different," the republics aspired to ideological sameness.

The USSR was initially conceived as a transitory political entity rather than a permanent state. It was a purgatory situated on the path from the hell of capitalism to the paradise of stateless proletarian unity. However, this prefiguration of a future proletarian non-state gradually developed into a chronic condition: the Soviet Union persisted, while the stateless universal unity was postponed. Despite their varying national forms, the state projects discussed in *Reorientalism*— Kazakh, Tajik, Turkmen, and Uzbek—were microcosms of that desired but suspended homogeneity. Such uniformity, aspiring to proletarian universality, was fundamental to Soviet subjectivity and the Stalinist state, which concerned itself with the project of overarching centralization and homogenization. The Soviet system of institutionalized multinationality was its main driving force.

The notion of national form lies at the heart of what can be labeled "Stalinist Orientalism."[105] Stalin's formula of "national in form, socialist in content" has received considerable scholarly attention.[106] However, existing scholarship on the topic operates on a reductive and loose vision of the notion of *form*, limited to the problem of translation and vaguely defined customs of everyday life (or, as Stalin put it in 1925, "forms corresponding to the languages and manner of life of [various] nationalities").[107] It must therefore be reconsidered within a broader concept of *aesthetic form*, one that facilitated the convergence of formal and exotic elements, and in which exoticism served both as a justification and a catalyst for formal innovation. Indeed, Stalin's formulation is a radical and rather unique coarticulation of artistic and political forms. In this sense, *Reorientalism* shares Caroline Levine's broader theoretical understanding of the category of form as an ordering procedure that delivers shapes and configurations of socio-political and aesthetic experiences.[108] For example, Vertov's conceptualization of folklore within his umbrella concept of *radio-eye*, and Eisenstein's reassessment of ornament as a gateway to a general system of representation, both strongly resonate with the coarticulation of artistic and political forms.

With the demise of formalism, national form—legitimized by socialist content—assumed discursive dominance in the 1930s. But if Stalin's national form were to be filled with socialist content, it had to be *empty* to begin with. The process of neutralization, containment, and emptying of form took place as early as 1913, in Stalin's refutation of Otto Bauer's 1907 vision of the national question from a Marxist vantage point. Bauer, a prominent Social Democrat who served as Austria's minister of foreign affairs, perceived the nation as a product of the transformation of isolated communities into modern industrial societies, with literacy-based high culture playing an instrumental role.[109] He thus challenged the established Marxist view that capitalism annihilated all national cultures by treating them as a singular borderless world market. In his interpretation, Bauer posited that in modern societies, "increased contact with foreign cultures in fact resulted in promoting a differentiation of human personalities, not their mutual assimilation."[110]

For Bauer, "community of character" was a central category that defined and essentialized the category of nation.[111] National character, in turn, was framed by a common "human destiny"—a historical vector connecting the past (cultural values from earlier generations) with the future. The function of socialism was thus to acknowledge the existing alterity of national characters and destinies while trying to standardize all aspects of material life. Therefore, he wrote, "socialist society will see an increasing differentiation of nations, a sharper definition of their specificities and a sharper separation of their character."[112] It appears that the creation of the Soviet Union was a paradoxical and perhaps unwitting realization of this vision. As Benedict Anderson put it, the Bolshevik state fulfilled Bauer's dream by "transcending the problem of nationalism by formal recognition of the terrains and cultures of its major nationalities while subordinating them fully to a universal project."[113]

However, Stalin vehemently contested Bauer's definition of the nation as a "community of character." As he wrote in *Marxism and the National Question* (1913), "Bauer's point of view, which identifies a nation with its national character, divorces the nation from its soil and converts it into an invisible, self-contained force. The result is not a living and active nation, but something mystical, intangible and supernatural."[114] Stalin was confounded by the fact that nations are identified with the "immaterial" concept of national character: "It might appear that 'national character' is not one of the characteristics but the *sole* essential characteristic of a nation, and that all the other characteristics are, properly speaking, only *conditions* for the development of a nation, rather than its characteristics."[115] This challenged the absolute importance of a presumed national consciousness dissociated from material conditions. Furthermore, Stalin historicized national character by framing it as variable, "not a thing that is fixed once and for all, but [that] is modified by changes in the conditions of life."[116] His own "classic" definition of nation is built upon this: "*A nation is a historically constituted, stable community of people, formed on the basis of a common language, territory, economic life, and psychological make-up manifested in a common culture.*"[117] By historicizing national character and culture, and by making them directly dependent on material conditions of life that are also mutable, Stalin *animates* the category of nation. A nation's changeability is framed by the ultimate endpoint of history—universal supranational socialism.

This rhetorical move laid the discursive groundwork for Stalin's later formula, "national in form, socialist in content," pronounced in the 1925 speech "The Political Tasks of the University of the Peoples of the East." According to this definition, which was cited ad nauseam in the Soviet press throughout the 1930s, the *national* is devoid of any self-contained essence and becomes a mere casing, a mode of expression, for *socialist content*—the ultimate essence:

> We are building proletarian culture. That is absolutely true. But it is also true that proletarian culture, which is socialist in content, assumes different forms and modes of expression among the different peoples who are drawn into the building of socialism, depending upon differences in language, manner of life, and so forth. Proletarian in content, national in form—such is the universal culture towards which socialism is proceeding. Proletarian culture does not abolish national culture, it gives it content. On the other hand, national culture does not abolish proletarian culture, it gives it form.[118]

Stalin initially used the adjective "proletarian" when referring to content, but by 1930, this had shifted to the canonical phrase "socialist in content," and proletarian (emphasizing class struggle) devolved into a more abstract category of socialist state. This reflected a broader transition from class conflict to state-building, where class was subjugated to nation. However, the distinction between form and substance remained, and it lies at the heart of Stalin's vision of the national question. While the former is variable and can assume different shapes, the latter is permanent and remains exclusively socialist. Thus, the formula "national in form, socialist in content" establishes a valorized dichotomy in which form is subordinate to content. Furthermore, content is restrained by the qualifier "socialist," as seen in socialist realism, the defining method of Soviet art. The new socialist content, marked by clarity and profundity, was to become the foundation of the Stalinist edifice, evolving into an overarching, unifying category. Form, in turn, was not treated as a self-sufficient entity with autonomous discursive terrain. It was instead strictly confined to a delimited national framework, while the "national" aspect was subordinated to the socialist nature of the content.

Per Stalin's logic, once oppressed nations are given freedom of national self-expression, proletarian enlightenment is inevitable: national solidarity would not be able to resist proletarian class consciousness (content). Thus, the conviction that nation is a mere essence-free form lies at the heart of Stalinist orientalism. In a truly dialectical manner, ultimate proletarian unity was to be achieved through diversity: the development of existing national forms. As Stalin put it in 1930:

> The national cultures must be allowed to develop and unfold, to reveal all their potentialities, in order to create the conditions for merging them into one common culture with one common language in the period of the victory of socialism all over the world. The flowering of cultures that are national in form and socialist in content under the dictatorship of the proletariat in one country *for the purpose* of merging them into one common socialist (both in form and content) culture, with one common language, when the proletariat is victorious all over the world and when socialism becomes the way of life—it is just this that constitutes the dialectics of the Leninist presentation of the question of national culture.[119]

Stalin articulated the concept of national difference as a rhetorical tool for enforcing uniformity and infused his vision of multiculturalism with latent discourses of cultural domination and superiority; the asymmetrical and even hierarchical division of national cultures within the Soviet Union was testimony to that. Cultures marked by "difference" had to integrate themselves into the fabric of "the same." Similarly, Irina Sandomirskaia describes early Soviet identity politics as rooted in a "not-as-yet-sameness" that had to be overcome with proper guidance from above.[120] In this context, national forms would have to be abandoned altogether once undergoing socialist remodification; only in this way would a normative standard, a "transparent" socialist culture without deviations, be achieved.

Stalin consistently uses the metaphor of the *flowering* of cultures (*rastsvet*)[121] in relation to national forms, as if cultural blossoms after blooming and withering were destined to deliver the ultimate fruit of socialist universalism—a unified world culture that would be socialist in form and content. Strikingly, Stalin's metaphorical rendering of the emergence of national forms as *blossoming* is rooted in the prerevolutionary avant-garde milieu and specifically in Iakov Tugendkhol'd's writings. Tugendkhol'd (1882–1928) was a prominent art critic specializing in the Western and Russian avant-gardes before the October Revolution and later became an influential proponent of the art of Soviet national minorities.[122] In a 1913 discussion of Goncharova, he coined the term *vostokofil'stvo* (orientophilia) to distinguish her art from orientalism and Slavophilism.[123] After the 1917 October Revolution, he oversaw *Pravda*'s art section and was a key ideologue of the successful Soviet pavilion at the 1925 International Exhibition of Modern Decorative and Industrial Arts, held in Paris. The exhibition featured designs by prominent avant-gardists Konstantin Mel'nikov, David Shterenberg, and Rodchenko. More importantly, he chaired sections for the arts of Soviet nationalities at the State Academy of Artistic Sciences (GAKhN) and the People's Commissariat of Enlightenment. He was a principal intermediary between the Western-oriented avant-garde tradition and early Soviet attempts to conceptualize the art of national minorities.

As early as 1915, Tugendkhol'd attempted to conceptualize the art of different nationalities as *flowers* at different stages of blooming: "And world art is like one single bouquet of wonderful flowers. Some are still at the early stage of blooming, others are at the stage of mature beauty or even are found gently dying; in some, there is the modesty of the North, in others the exoticism of the East or the splendor of the South. In this variety lies the source of eternal novelty."[124] These are not simply suggestive parallels between Stalin and Tugendkhol'd; for both, cultural ethnonational heterogeneity would result in the social congruence of cross-pollination. The same metaphoric rendering of blossoming was later extrapolated to Soviet nationalities' artistic practices. Tugendkhol'd, this time as a Soviet cultural functionary, posited that every cultural form, regardless of its level of development, was invaluable for its uniqueness: "in this variegated bouquet of Soviet art one nevertheless has above all to get to know each separate flower, in all of its individual distinction."[125]

Heterogeneity, however, must be cultivated, and Tugendkhol'd highlighted the dangers of deviation that Stalin did not warn of until 1932—equally harmful trends associated with Russian chauvinism, local nationalism, and radical internationalism. Tugendkhol'd resolved the conundrum between the universal and the particular by suggesting a critical appropriation of "progressive elements" from every cultural form through the unifying prism of class consciousness.[126] The latter assumes a role of content, the meaningful essence of a socialist agenda that could productively coexist with the formal ethnic variety.[127] The unity of the singular theme is counterpoised by the variety of its formal-national renderings.

The figure of Paul Gauguin and his experience in French Polynesia, as an iconic nexus between Western modernism and the "primitive" other,[128] was an important point of reference for Tugendkhol'd. He argued that Soviet artists did not need to travel far to have an aesthetically "rejuvenating" experience through exposure to alien cultures, for Russia had its own living (*zhivaia*) counterparts to Polynesia, Africa, and Mexico inside its own territory.[129] The "primitive" folk arts, which survived due to lack of industrialization, were an inexhaustible reservoir for artistic inspiration. They performed a productive function, much like how Russia's economic underdevelopment was an enabling condition for the socialist revolutionary movement. Years before Gorky highlighted the significance of folklore for Soviet arts, Tugendkhol'd claimed that through its longing for "synthetic beauty," modern art overcomes bourgeois individualism and returns to "primordial collective roots" through engagement with folklore.[130]

However, Tugendkhol'd also claimed that the inherent heterogeneity of the Soviet arts differed from art made in the colonial context—be it England and India, or Austria and Galicia.[131] Instead, socialist diversity is marked by a "common, natural [*zakonomernoe*—conforming to some set of laws], and expedient" factor—"the *Eastern* foundation of the arts in the USSR."[132] This Eastern factor is rooted in the decorative-utilitarian essence of artistic practices found in the region—every artifact, whether a Central Asian carpet, Tatar boots, or a Caucasian saddle bag, has a practical function and does not belong to the domain of contemplation.

Tugendkhol'd's stance on the utilitarian aspect of national arts, and their embedded connection with the practice of labor, resonated with the principles of constructivism. However, like its avant-garde counterpart, his stance did not survive into the 1930s, when several attempts to define national form and turn it into an operative category took place. These early definitions reiterated Lenin's stance on the tension between the national and international aspects of the proletarian movement, although they did not yet undergo Stalinist molding.

For Lenin, national features were by no means ephemeral; they were tangible elements that played a constructive role in a socialist state. In his 1913 article "Critical Remarks on the National Question," Lenin writes:

> The *elements* of democratic and socialist culture are present, if only in rudimentary form, in *every* national culture, since in *every* nation there are toiling and exploited masses, whose conditions of life inevitably give rise to the ideology of democracy and socialism. But *every* nation also possesses a bourgeois culture (and most nations a reactionary and clerical culture as well) in the form, not merely of "elements", but of the *dominant* culture. Therefore, the general "national culture" is the culture of the landlords, the clergy and the bourgeoisie.... In advancing the slogan of "the international culture of democracy and of the world working-class movement", we take *from each* national culture *only* its democratic and socialist elements; we take them *only* and *absolutely* in opposition to the bourgeois culture and the bourgeois nationalism of *each* nation.[133]

Subsequently, Lenin provides his famous concept of *two nations*: "There are two nations in every modern nation—we say to all nationalist-socialists. There are two national cultures in every national culture."[134] The national culture of the oppressed, whether proletariat, peasantry, or simply poor, should take precedence over the national culture of their oppressors. Lenin rhetorically reinforces the possibility of a national proletarian culture—national in form and *nationally marked* socialist in content.

At the same time, Lenin emphasizes that every progressive proletarian national culture possesses the centrifugal quality of the internationalist drive. For him, all national distinctions comprise an ephemeral phenomenon, while horizontal class distinctions cut across national formations. In 1913, Lenin offered his radical solution to the "national question": "Only the clericals and the bourgeoisie can speak of national culture in general. The working people can speak only of the international culture of the world working-class movement. That is the only culture that means full, real, sincere equality of nations, the absence of national oppression and the implementation of democracy."[135] Indeed, as Marx put it, "the working men have no country."[136]

Lenin's vision of every progressive proletarian national culture as international is what consequently neutralized all national markers in relation to socialist content during the Stalinist period. The rhetorical shift from the concept of *two nations* (democratic proletarian and reactionary bourgeois) in every national formation to a *single* national form among the Soviet constituents dramatically changed the political structure of the USSR and its ensuing politics of internationalism, which was infused with a celebration of national differences. This tension reached its peak in the early 1930s. In the space of two or three years, all distinctly national aspects, however democratic they were (with the notable exception of Russian culture), underwent a process of erasure and subjugation to singular socialist content.

A classical Leninist articulation of national form is exemplified in the writings of Sergo Amaglobeli, a Georgian playwright and art critic who was the director of the State New Theater, housed in the House of Government across from the Kremlin. Amaglobeli delivered a series of lectures on national art at the Correspondence University of the Arts. His attempt to define national form faithfully applied Lenin's vision of *two nations*: "we . . . must take the socialist and democratic elements of the given national culture to build a proletarian national culture, but we must not take feudal and bourgeois 'styles,' mechanically applying them to proletarian content."[137] Amaglobeli also warns of ethnographic exoticism, a remnant of the colonial past, for it reproduces the colonial division between a powerful and universal metropolitan culture and a passive exotic periphery, which is exploited in a representational sense. He boldly identifies "Great Russian chauvinism" as assuming the role of the colonial oppressor in the Soviet Union:

> If the working masses have already come out of the enclosures of their ethnographic, narrowly national life but the art pulls them back, cultivates exoticism, savors ethnography, and creates national romanticism—then this ethnography is reactionary; it becomes a tool in the hands of nationalistic elements [to achieve] their reactionary goals.
>
> A protective attitude toward this kind of movement is a concrete manifestation of Great Russian chauvinism, for which "national art" is identified with exoticism, and it also reverberates with local nationalism, which confines cultural life within narrowly national bounds.[138]

For theorists who held a more conservative position and were not in favor of radical emancipation and egalitarianism, the Leninist conceptualization of national form acquired different undertones. In 1932, Lazar Rempel', a Soviet art historian who specialized in Central Asian and Transcaucasian art at the Communist Academy, provided his vision of national form as essence-free, thus emulating Stalin's take on the national question.[139] In a radical manner, Rempel identifies national form as lacking any conceptual essence—"taken on its own, national form does not exist."[140] For him, national form "means only a *particular* 'approach' toward the resolution of the unified international tasks of the proletarian class struggle."[141] He also emphasizes that the "unity of culture" that characterizes any given nation "and the 'psychological mindset' that is manifested in it or a 'national character' do not comprise anything once and forever given but change together with the conditions of life."[142] Thus, national form becomes a transient category.

The pinnacle of all classification efforts is arguably the normative definition of national literature written for the *Literary Encyclopedia* by Isaak Nusinov, a Soviet literary critic and specialist in Yiddish literature who was also an opponent at Mikhail Bakhtin's unsuccessful defense of his doctoral thesis on Rabelais. Nusinov employs the structure of the Leninist argument, opposing the view that there is a primordial and singular national form for each national literature: "Bourgeois national form, then, is a means for national isolation, narrowness, and the cultivation of national animosity, because it is defined by content that is fixated on [capitalist] property. Proletarian national form, in contrast, is a means of overcoming national disagreement because it is imbued with internationalist content, with socialist principles [*ideinost'*]."[143]

The ethnic particularism of form, its embeddedness in capitalist property, had to be neutralized by the ideational universality of content that dramatically reconsidered the notion of private property. A variety of national forms, however, did not stand for cultural polycentrism. Nusinov explicitly argues that true internationalism emanates from cultural centers of "advanced" nationalities: "Russian, Ukrainian, or Jewish proletarian writers, whose art comprises an ideological factor of socialist construction, are doing international socialist work for the entire proletariat. Their art, internationalist and socialist in its orientation, is national in form to the extent that it reveals the distinctiveness of the struggle for socialism in the conditions of a given people."[144] Nusinov reinforces the unevenness of the relationship, where representatives of "advanced" nationalities assumed a position of a universal, or rather internationalist, authority over their "minor" and "backward" counterparts. "Russian, Ukrainian, or Jewish proletarian writers," for him, were capable of transcending national divisions—they were the ultimate curators of a display of Soviet national heterogeneity.

This curatorial work was accelerated by the First Soviet Writers' Congress, held in 1934, in which "minor" national literatures and their oral and written traditions were celebrated. The concept of *national* had to be defined, essentialized, and placed on the preexisting cultural map to be used as a solid building block for the universal proletarian cultural edifice—but only as a rhetorical trope. After the resolution abolishing all artistic organizations and forming the Writers' Union in 1932, a committee was established to oversee the organization of the

First Soviet Writers' Congress. It took more than two years and three plenary sessions of the organizing committee because of the time-consuming process of consolidating national literatures. At the same time, the status of the national was purely nominal. Despite the substantial amount of time allocated to reports on national literatures, and the fact that delegates from the republics were celebrated at the Congress, all major decisions and theoretical discussions of socialist realism were made by the Moscow branch. Only Abolqasem Lahouti, representing Tajikistan, and Ivan Kulik, representing Ukraine, both as national minorities, were part of the All-Union Organizing Committee.

The committee viewed Russian literary interests as the ultimate needs of Soviet literature, while national literatures comprised a supplement, albeit an important one. The strangeness of the periphery reaffirmed the normality of the center. Consequently, one of the central resolutions of the All-Union Organizing Committee was to send envoys to every national republic to supervise, direct, and mediate the process of integrating local writers into structured, functional bureaucratic entities and to prepare them for participation in the Congress. The list of writers included several notable modernist names: Shklovsky was sent to Tajikistan, Andrei Platonov to Turkmenistan, Boris Pil'niak to Azerbaijan, Boris Pasternak and Iurii Tynianov to Georgia, and Andrei Bely and Osip Brik to the Russian Soviet Federative Socialist Republic (RSFSR) nationalities, while Iurii Olesha, Ilya Il'f, and Evgenii Petrov traveled to Tatarstan.

The minutes of the first plenum of the All-Union Organizing Committee reveal widespread complaints about the orientalist attitudes of Russian writers toward their national counterparts. Several members of national delegations objected to the inherently exotic representational strategies employed by Russian writers depicting the Soviet East.[145] Some of the national minority writers, however, had clearly interiorized their "backwardness" and did not contest the uneven relationship with their metropolitan colleagues. As Said Baduev, a Chechen representative, put it, "we [writers from the mountain peoples] did not have any culture before Sovietization, there was only sheer darkness."[146]

But these critical and self-effacing voices were eventually swamped by torrents of praise and celebration during the 1934 Congress itself. The first two days were filled with reports on Ukrainian, Belarusian, Tatar, Georgian, Armenian, Azerbaijani, Uzbek, Turkmen, and Tajik literatures, and praise predominated. The culmination of the Congress was a poetic performance by Suleiman Stal'sky—a prominent Lezgin epic poet from Dagestan. Sitting at the presidium, Maxim Gorky proclaimed him the Homer of the twentieth century. With Gorky's declaration that the oral tradition was to be a cornerstone of socialist realism, the presence of that tradition, which emanated primarily from the Eastern territories of the USSR, became consistently conflated with general ideological epic narrative characterizing the country's progression toward the communist future. However, it is notable that Gorky employed exclusionary rhetoric—the first-person plural "we"—to distinguish himself and other Russian writers from those representing national republics.

In fact, all pronouncements about national form made at the 1934 Congress, despite being overtly celebratory, were ultimately either ritualistic or purely redundant. They lacked analytical precision and were shaped by the teleological orientation of the Stalinist mode of socialism. These pronouncements were clearly in line with a classical definition of socialist realism, although the political governed the aesthetic, and the national "formal" aspect played a purely nominal role. Form, then, assumed a subservient position in relation to all-encompassing socialist content, since socialist realism, in the words of Evgeny Dobrenko, was the sole guarantor of the reality of socialism.[147] Formal diversity manifested itself in "exterior" and multifarious cultural attributes that derived from indigenous folklore and customs. Form, in a rudimentary way, was perceived to be an outward (that is, essence-free) manifestation of a given cultural heritage. This "framing" of form, relegated to a subservient entity, was emblematic of the endorsed socialist realist practices.

The apotheosis of the national form was reached with festive celebrations of internal Soviet diversity, where a predominant role was played by the Eastern republics. Though the Stalinist ideological system witnessed the decline of the political diversity project of *korenizatsiia*,[148] it discursively celebrated the country's heterogeneous constituents. Starting in 1936, Moscow and other key cities throughout the country hosted so-called decades (ten-day festivals) of non-Russian arts and literatures. At these events, artists and both professional and amateur collectives showcased their artistic achievements in the spheres of dance, vocal performance, visual arts, and literature. Each event highlighted a particular culture: Ukrainian (1936), Kazakh (1936), Georgian (1937), Uzbek (1937), Azeri (1938), Kyrgyz (1939), and Armenian (1939).[149] These spectacles were a symbolic exhibition of the rhetorical trope of "friendship of the peoples." But the alleged celebration of difference was in fact infused with blatant orientalist exoticization.

By the late 1930s, Stalin's insistence on the possibility of a union of socialist nations (unity)—and, at the same time, his vision of the primordial character of ethnicity (divergence)—had succeeded in imposing a set of contradictory practices.[150] This contradiction was perceptively rendered by Osip Mandelstam in *Journey to Armenia* (Puteshestvie v Armeniiu, 1932). In a censored passage, Mandelstam writes: "Love of the other [*chuzheliubie*] is not among our virtues. The peoples of the USSR cohabitate like schoolchildren. They know each other only as desk-mates and from the lunch break, while the chalk is being crumbled."[151] Mandelstam suggests that *inter*-national interaction within the Soviet Union is of a shallow or accidental character with no continual meaningful engagement among various socialist nations, only intermittent and superficial encounters. These occasional encounters operate under an implied disciplinary mechanism that oversees and structures the nation's so-called schoolyard. And Stalinist management of difference was the mechanism in question.

The concept of the "friendship of the peoples"—a new principle of unity for the multiethnic Soviet state—lay at the heart of Stalinist management of difference. Articulated for the first time in 1935, the "friendship of the peoples" was, in Terry Martin's words, the only "officially sanctioned metaphor of an imagined multinational community."[152] As such, it shifted the concepts of nation and nationality from constructivist to essentialist. Its stress on domestic unity allowed the party, as David Brandenberger argues, "to preserve its promotion of national difference while at the same time discouraging discussions of cultural autonomy or separatism."[153] The metaphor, which relied heavily on a primordial conception of nationality, gradually became a core aspect of the Stalinist variant of nationalism. Consequently, the primacy of class consciousness over national consciousness faded. Furthermore, cosmopolitanism, a product of Western modernity and a driving force of capitalism, was seen as antithetical to this Stalinist vision of interethnic relations. Capitalism's globalist aspirations, expressed through cosmopolitan values, were regarded as a threat to the "flowering" of socialist nations. As one Soviet official put it, "Comrade Stalin showed us what the Soviet ideology of 'friendship of the peoples' consists of and explained what a vast chasm separates proletarian internationalism and bourgeois cosmopolitanism . . ."[154] Similarly, the internationalist drive of the historical avant-garde was conceived as a negation of the professed primordial conception of nation.

The endorsement of the "friendship of the peoples" metaphor took place at a Kremlin gathering of Tajik and Turkmen kolkhoz shock workers on December 4, 1935. Progressive national elements from the two heavily agrarian republics were gathered to witness the birth of a new paradigm of interethnic relations in the Soviet Union. In a notable rhetorical move, Stalin elevated social relations (friendship) over material commodity (cotton):

> But, comrades, there is one thing more precious than cotton—it is the friendship between the people of our country. The present conference, your speeches, your actions, go to show that the friendship between the people of our great country is growing stronger. . . . The present conference is vivid proof of the fact that the

former mistrust between the peoples of the USSR has long ago been laid to rest, that mistrust has been replaced by complete and mutual trust, that the friendship between the peoples of the USSR is growing and gaining in strength.[155]

The birth of the formula is permeated with floral symbolism. Distinguished cotton farmers are praised for their cultivation efforts. However, the value of the natural commodity (cotton) is overshadowed by an abstract conception of interethnic relations (friendship), one not cultivated organically but rather articulated from above. Friendship is rendered more valuable than crops. Stalin uses this discourse about produce to "naturalize" the nation. Furthermore, by suggesting that "the former distrust" has been overcome, Stalin equalizes all forms of nationalism and effectively prohibits any mention of great-power chauvinism. Friendship becomes the only sociopolitical construct able to "correctly" represent the multiethnic dimension of Soviet culture. In this way, Stalin creates a seemingly horizontal plane that cleared the ground for the return of the Russian imperial discourse in a modified form.[156]

This speech started the process of normalizing the exceptional status of Russian culture within the political structure of the USSR, which was soon followed by its discursive ascent: Russian cultural form started to enjoy a privileged rank. The ascent of Russian form was consequently presented not as an artificially imposed hierarchy, but a natural one—Russians being the advanced "vanguard" nation, great precisely for their role in helping other Soviet cultures in their ascents. On February 1, 1936, a Pravda editorial, succinctly titled "RSFSR," emphatically delineated new discursive grounds that solidified Russian priority within the multi-ethnic Soviet state:

> All the peoples [of the USSR], participants in the great socialist construction, can take pride in the results of their work. All of them from the smallest to the largest are equally Soviet patriots. But the first among equals is the Russian people, the Russian workers, the Russian toilers, whose role in the entire Great Proletarian Revolution, from the first victory to today's brilliant period of its development, has been extraordinarily great.[157]

The Russian national form was assigned a primary role, but its endorsement did not imply the straightforward formation of a Russian-dominated Soviet nation. The "friendship of the peoples" provided a smokescreen that created a nebulous discursive space, one that presumed an unequal status and that elevated Russian culture, however speculatively. The centrality of Russian culture was justified by the leading role of the Russian proletariat in the October Revolution and the immense "brotherly help" Russians provided non-Russians in the latter's class struggle with their oppressors. The appreciation of this help "from without" was solidified even further after World War II.

Reorientalism challenges traditional historiographies of the Soviet avant-garde, and late modernism more generally, by uncovering the complex discursive nexus between avant-garde, modernism, orientalism, socialism, and form. A sociopolitical analysis of aesthetic (national) form in the 1930s is impossible without taking into consideration the eastward reorientation of the main representatives of the early Soviet experimental tradition. *Reorientalism* reframes modernist time by considering a networked range of artistic practices from a period that, according to the established narrative, repressed the avant-garde and delivered the triumph of socialist realism. These practices originated in the experimental 1910s and 1920s, and underwent dislocation and dispersal in the 1930s and 1940s.

The crossing of metropolitan boundaries was accompanied by a revision of the avant-garde's radicalism and by the channeling of its creative impulse into a more conventional, yet still pronouncedly modernist, representational domain. These "transgressions" into the Soviet Orient—the forefront of the Soviet particularized modernity or the Soviet "South"—were accomplished through the concept of national form, promoted by the state and framed by the agenda of political vanguardism. Thus, the long life of Soviet modernism is bound up in the politics of alterity. Ethnonational heterogeneity was a formal possibility and indeed a necessity inherent in the process of cultural production in the first socialist society. The historical construction of ethnicities in the late 1920s and 1930s coincided with a campaign against formalism and the subsequent advent of national forms. Fascination with the other, non-European, primitive was a source of formal innovation in the Soviet 1930s and early 1940s as part of politics of anti-imperialism and decolonization.

Reorientalism also posits that, in principle, only former representatives of the left avant-garde, such as Vertov and Eisenstein, made genuine attempts to discern and produce sophisticated theoretical treatments of the concept of national form, while others, such as Shklovsky, Stepanova, and Rodchenko, imaginatively engaged with the concept in their texts and visual artifacts.[158] Thus, the national form functioned as a point of *interconnection*, and, at the same time, a *distinction* between late modernism and socialist realism.

With a few exceptions, the textual and visual material of this book constitute largely neglected material. Despite its marginality, this material possesses the potential to elucidate the political and aesthetic mechanisms of the Soviet state in its attempt to create a supra-national proletarian communion—one that would, nevertheless, respect and preserve national peculiarities. The study of these artifacts can also help us to understand the socialist project as an efficient tool for developing and reinforcing national identities.[159] Furthermore, while the avant-garde form and avant-garde socialist content of the 1920s produced an effect of aesthetic *difference*, the national form and socialist content of socialist realism fabricated aesthetic (and political) *semblance*. However, the late modernist engagement with national form, as discussed in the following four chapters, generated a *semblance* that was pronouncedly infused with *difference*, this being a critical reverberation of the experimental 1920s. Thus, each chapter of the book makes a necessary detour into the avant-garde 1920s to reveal a continuity of aesthetic praxis, however modified, that had profound political implications.

Each of the five artists on whom I focus was accused of overindulgence in formal experimentation, and the chapters carefully examine their subsequent repentances, which comprise meaningful statements that consequently shaped late modernist aesthetics. The critiques of the artists centered around the category of *form*—they were condemned for very specific formalist devices: defamiliarization (*ostranenie*), foreshortening (*rakurs*), texture (*faktura*), kino-eye (*kino-glaz*), and montage of attractions (*montazh attraktsionov*). All of them, as per Stalinist rituals of repentance, acknowledged their mistakes and promised to become productive contributors to socialist culture. These were not mere empty declarations and acts of self-subjugation. The direct outcome of their repentance was a set of projects exploring various ethnic identities, meant to serve the larger cause of socialist construction and the formation of a new Soviet subjectivity. Thus, I treat the Stalinist genre of repentance as an evocative rhetorical tool that allows a scholar of the period to discern discursive precepts that were to be pivotal for the prolonged life of late Soviet modernism.

I intervene in the way we talk about the Soviet artists and the idea that these artists are almost algorithmic in their predictability, even if we claim that the algorithm itself changes. After all, algorithms are unambiguous specifications for performing calculation and data processing and are widely used today for automated reasoning. But, as we know, artificial intelligence is incapable of doubting—current AI models do not include "self-doubt" in any reasonably describable form. The heroes of my book, in contrast, did doubt a lot: their hesitations and, at times, confusions, discharged a productive energy. Thus, I am interested in models we have been using to describe their creative evolution, but I am also sensitive to the ways those models fail. Finding that space between theoretical assertions and practical contradictions is crucial for our understanding of the 1930s.

Through focused analyses of the key figures of the Soviet avant-garde, this book also employs a set of four categories—*matter, vision, sound,* and *time*—through which to understand the longer history of Soviet modernism. While vision and voice (sound) are human categories of perception and communication, matter and time constitute the base from which physical existence is derived. Thus, through Shklovsky's reconceptualization of the notion of *thing* (*veshch'*); Rodchenko and Stepanova's theoretical and practical contributions to the process of setting up the Soviet *optics* of perception; Vertov's experiments with the emancipatory potential of *sound*; and Eisenstein's theoretical reassessment of the notion of *regress* in art I can examine the intricacies of the material environment of Soviet modernity and the acting subjects who inhabited it.

Late modernist exposure to the Soviet Orient was a defining feature of artistic and sociopolitical concerns during the 1930s. The resulting projects forged often surprising pathways and created their own spaces in relation to the power structure of the metropolitan center and the officially endorsed discourse that emanated from this center. As a result, ideological conformism was entangled with the problem of artistic form, viewed as a mode of structural rearrangement. In other words, the sheer adulation of totalitarian power was intermingled with strategies of resistance to the epistemic violence of the Stalinist state. The tensions, contradictions, and asymmetries that defined the cultural space of the country in the 1930s were amplified in the works of the late modernists, who genuinely attempted to follow the delineated pathway of the state-sanctioned socialist realist genre. The detours that these writers and artists made to inscribe themselves into official Soviet culture carry tremendous aesthetic and ideological value, which this book aims to reveal and reinforce.

CHAPTER 1

SOCIALIST MATTER

Viktor Shklovsky

In the landscape of Soviet culture, Viktor Shklovsky occupies a strange place. Born in 1893, he actively fought as a Socialist Revolutionary militant against the Bolsheviks yet managed not simply to survive the Stalinist purges but to thrive as a key Soviet cultural figure. He passed away at the age of ninety-one, a mere three months before Mikhail Gorbachev was elected general secretary of the Union of Soviet Socialist Republics (USSR). One of the key theoreticians of avant-garde form in the 1910s and 1920s, he ostensibly was the first formalist to yield to ideological pressure, years before the full-fledged assault on formalism in the mid-1930s.

Shklovsky's tumultuous biography and contentious scholarly legacy raise many questions. Was he an evasive master of accommodation who easily yielded to political pressure, a playful subverter who managed to smuggle his early radical theoretical convictions into seemingly conventional texts, or an ever-evolving thinker fueled by the energy of transformation? Was his persona somehow capable of synthesizing these three distinct identities?

Conscious evasiveness, forced accommodation, and self-directed evolution all seem to have shaped his career as a scholar. In *Sentimental Journey* (Sentimental'noe puteshestvie, 1923) he confesses his pliability: "I have the capacity to flow, to change, even to become ice or steam. I can fit into any kind of shoes. I went along with the others."[1] But Shklovsky's practice of accommodation was never about complete surrender. His theoretical acumen allowed him to contrive aesthetically sound and ideologically acceptable rhetorical moves. Thus, the accommodation–resistance binary should be supplemented by the act of (subversive) interiorization, wherein individuals appropriate for their own purposes the discursive structures and social practices of the opponent.[2] The ever-increasing political pressure indeed demanded courage and some degree of internal conviction from Shklovsky, who found himself in a peculiar position between the rock of socialist realism and the hard place of defamiliarization.

Retrospectively, however, the hard place of the formal method does not seem to be unconditionally solid. The movement displays inherent mobility and discursive flexibility with its belief in culture as a process entailing the continual formation and modification of aesthetic horizons. This conviction was never betrayed. The tumultuous evolution of the key term *ostranenie* (defamiliarization, making strange), from the moment of its inception in 1916 to Shklovsky's retrospective musings in the early 1970s, is a testimony to that.

The canonical essay "Art as Device" (Iskusstvo kak priem, 1917/1919) refers to Aristotle's concept of *xenikon* (alienation) and maintains that "poetic language ought to have the character of something foreign, something outlandish."[3] The essay conceptualizes Russian literature's fixation on dialects as a manifestation of strangeness while also positing that Russian literary language, originally alien to Russian speakers, played a normalizing function as it leveled many vernacular varieties.[4] The notion of ethnic alterity as a constructive element of Shklovsky's poetics thus was present in his very first attempts to formulate its key principles.

In 1970, fifty-four years after its introduction, the term *ostranenie* reappeared, albeit transiently, in *Bowstring: On the Dissimilarity of the Similar* (Tetiva: O neskhodstve skhodnogo). Shklovsky's late work of theoretical autofiction is marked by the critic's signature paratactic fusion of scientific and self-reflective personal discourses. In *Bowstring*, these discourses envelop *ostranenie* and allow it to acquire a broader set of connotations:

> I am convinced now that the very fact of perception of art depends upon a comparative juxtaposition of a work of art with the world.
>
> The artist, the poet orients himself in the world with the help of art and introduces into what we call the surrounding world his own artistic perception.
>
> There used to be an old term—*ostranenie*. It is often printed with one "n," even though the phrase originates from the world *strannyi* [strange]. The term came into usage in 1916 spelled in that particular way.
>
> Often the term is mispronounced or mixed with the word *otstranenie* [estrangement], which means pushing the world aside.
>
> *Ostranenie* is the sensation of surprise felt toward the world, a perception of the world with a strained sensitivity. The term can be established only by including the notion of "the world" in its meaning. This term simultaneously assumes the existence of so-called content and supposes that content is the constricted, close examination of the world.[5]

Shklovsky begins with the almost commonplace statement that the essence of art lies in a combination of the fictional and real realms. But this stance serves to reevaluate his long-standing formalist fixation on the binary opposition between the everyday and the artistic, in which the latter overcomes or defamiliarizes the former so that its perceptibility can be renewed. He proceeds to claim that the artist *orients* herself in the world by artistic means and that her perception, once enhanced by the act of defamiliarization, becomes an integral part of reality: when the object is taken out of its mundane environment, the artist's perception of it is renewed and it is returned to reality as a qualitatively different entity. The world and the artistic impression thereof are presented as contingent: antagonism is replaced by mutual dependence. However, this is accomplished by pushing the notion of perception into the material realm: perception is the prolonged examination of the world materialized in the form of content.

This was a rather fundamental rethinking of the first, futurist-inspired vision of *ostranenie* as a procedure that undermines the ontological validity of the everyday. The poetic word disrupts the chain of signification as its referential meaning is expanded; it unsettles the linearity of the word's relationship with the object it signifies. Literary language disrupts patterns of perception imposed by the mundane use of language, social-ideological conventions, and preceding literary traditions. The following statement exemplifies the "primal" definition: "we futurists . . . have emancipated art from daily life, which plays in creative work only the role of fleshing out forms and may, perhaps even be driven out altogether."[6] Hailing the election of his futurist comrades as members of the People's Commissariat of Enlightenment, Shklovsky declared the militant banishment of the everyday. But later, as the excess and autonomy of signification became problematic for unitary Soviet discourse and the energy of the riotous and experimental 1920s dissipated, Shklovsky does not depict unyielding irreconciliation but rather a peaceful interaction between the artificiality of art and the familiarity of reality.

In fact, the foundation of Shklovsky's radical reassessment of the term had been laid much earlier, in the late 1920s, while he was completing a key methodological cycle and was forced to *reorient* the course of his theoretical thought.[7] After his travels within the new borders of the Soviet Union, the device of *ostranenie* took a new direction. In this new direction for *ostranenie*, perception was subjugated by the materiality of the world and the utility of its objects. The ontological status of raw material and the everyday in general were renegotiated. The change resulted in a series of somewhat hesitant but persistent gestures toward the notion of *content*, which gradually fused with the concept of *material*. The formalist method then underwent a drastic transformation: *material*, something that is transmuted by the futurist artist, evolves into material-as-content, a *meaningful* and formally integral component of the late modernist work of art. Form, previously an agent of change, consequently becomes a stable vehicle for meaning.

Yet it was through discursive engagement with the Soviet Orient that the "strange" impetus of *ostranenie* finds its partial and subliminal discharge. Shklovsky's journeys to Kazakhstan, Uzbekistan, Tajikistan, and Georgia, as well as his imaginings of Marco Polo's adventures in China, allowed him to experiment with the notion of ethnic alterity within the premises of the Stalinist definition of proletarian culture as "national in form, socialist in content."[8] Formalism, which emerges from a fascination with the strange and alien, finds a proper socialist outlet for the late modernist energy of *ostranenie*.

Shklovsky's systematic involvement with the fringes of the country started in 1928 when he was commissioned to write several screenplays for the Georgian film studio. Among them was an adaptation of Tolstoy's novel *The Cossacks*, which fuses two popular Russian nineteenth-century Oriental motifs: the Caucasus and the Cossack way of life. Establishing the screenplay required a scouting trip to remote Georgian mountains, and this resulted in Shklovsky's 1930 book *Mountainous Georgia: Pshavi. Khevsureti. Khevi* (Gornaia Gruziia: Pshaviia. Khevsuretiia. Mukheviia). It arguably comprises the most colonial narrative the critic ever produced—it both domesticates the Orient and amplifies its otherness. The text is full of the usual "uncivilized Orient" clichés: from local women washing their hair with cow urine, since there is no soap, to men cutting each other's faces in a knife fight.[9] It also delivers an uncompromising message of modernization that is specifically oriented around technological advancement and infrastructure development: cream separators and churns should suffice to move the distant region out of its backward state by introducing "culture."[10] The dynamics of transformation are prized by Shklovsky, for whom "things are more interesting where they are changing."[11]

Transformative dynamism permeates the body of work that Shklovsky produced in the 1930s, in connection with the creation of a Soviet multiethnic socialist literature. The works are full of theoretical observations that consistently attempt to reconcile differences between the autonomous form of the avant-garde and the national form of Stalinist culture. Neither in the early- and mid-1920s, the period of "high" formalism, nor in the 1940s, when the main aesthetic and theoretical premises of Soviet culture were already solidified, could Shklovsky make his tactical and theoretical moves of ostensible surrender and intentional accommodation. The 1930s, a period in which the basic principles of Soviet culture were under intensive revision, on the other hand, allowed him to rethink his uncompromising early convictions and to articulate new theoretical avenues.

The pages that follow examine how Shklovsky applied the possibility of reorientation. The first section addresses his quasi-conciliatory "Monument to a Scholarly Error" (Pamiatnik nauchnoi oshibke). This 1930 article can be considered a *starting point* of late modernism in the Soviet Union, for it initiated a major impetus toward reformulating the main premises of *ostranenie*, which was transmuted into a hybrid entity that incorporated correlated notions of variety and heterogeneity and posited the work of art as delivering a literally meaningful message. These were crucial theoretical developments for the late modernist aesthetic practice. The second section registers Shklovsky's shift away from "Baroque" formal intricacies toward simplicity and clarity—in essence, a step toward the singular content of Stalinist culture. The urge to transform is also an important motif of the "Formalist Things" section, which explores how Shklovsky attempted to pass off the materiality of things as socialist content; as such, *ostranenie*, enhanced by professional, hands-on knowledge, became a real agent of change in the world, not a mere shift in perception. These first three sections, while not directly engaging with Oriental material, examine the ontological reverberations of the familiar-strange dichotomy. They provide the essential theoretical groundwork for understanding the late stage of modernism by establishing two of its key aspects: a pursuit of clarity over strangeness and a focus on utility over materiality. These two aspects were key to the defamiliarizing reformulation of *ostranenie* in the 1930s, as the following four chapters will demonstrate.

The appearance of "Monument to a Scholarly Error" was quickly followed by several "minor" texts that reflected this methodological rupture: *Potboiler Work* (Podenshchina, 1930), *Turksib* (1930), *Marco Polo, Explorer* (Marko Polo, razvedchik, 1931) and *A Hunt for Optimism* (Poiski optimizma, 1931). These short books, at first glance, may seem like minor, isolated works within the author's creative biography as well as in the broader context of Soviet cultural history generally. Because of this perceived lack of significance, they have attracted little scholarly attention. Nevertheless, they express and expose Shklovsky's forced and, to some extent, self-inflicted transformation. The four books project ethnic alterity onto the process of socialist modernization. They register the evolution of *ostranenie*: from bewilderment by the strange, to exploration of the unfamiliar, and then to the familiarity of the useful and practical. *Potboiler Work* and *A Hunt for Optimism* are accomplished in a *variété* style, unified solely by the narrating voice of the "maestro." Important theoretical observations occasionally emerge in these largely biographical sets of texts, infused with stylized letters addressed to the critic's contemporaries. Cryptic and mostly sporadic reflections reveal Shklovsky's radical reassessment of the function of form and content in the work of art and art's ultimate relationship with reality.

The two concluding sections of this chapter explore how *ostranenie* found its application in the exotic lands of the Soviet Union and China. *Turksib*, which celebrates the most important industrial project of the first five-year plan (the Turkestan-Siberia railway), and *Marco Polo, Explorer*, which reimagines the oriental travels of the famed Venetian explorer and makes them relevant to the Soviet reader, both function as discursive sites where the notion of otherness is negotiated. These two books for children were written during a time when the Soviet Union was undergoing a process of radical spatial transformation: industrialization had reconfigured the landscape and the process of national delimitation had created a new geography. The Soviet Orient, which lies at the discursive core of these books, emerged as a meaningful topos, and its advent required the renegotiation of the relationship between form and content.

THE ERROR

Between 1928 and late 1929, after the dissolution of *New LEF* (Novyi LEF), Shklovsky actively sought to revive the OPOIAZ (Society for the Study of Poetic Language) as an officially recognized organization with access to state funding and publishing contracts. The initiative reformulated the movement's key positions under the guise of theoretical theses and was welcomed by the primary members of the circle—Iurii Tynianov, Boris Eikhenbaum, and Roman Jakobson. The latter famously wrote to Shklovsky: "A departure from formalism does not mean a crisis in formalism, but rather crises for the formalists."[12] Shklovsky ardently agreed with Jakobson's characterization of the situation: "What you wrote about the crisis of the formalists is very true. I also partly yielded to the crisis, which is explained not by the feebleness of my frame but by the enormity of the load."[13] The tremendous political pressure seemed to suppress Shklovsky's urge to reformulate and revive the formalist movement, for it came to a standstill in the early 1930s when he suddenly attempted to distance himself from the movement altogether—or rather, to move along the thoroughfare of the Soviet socialist project.

Shklovsky's infamous "Monument to a Scholarly Error" appeared on the front page of the January 27, 1930, issue of *The Literary Gazette* (Literaturnaia gazeta). In this article, Shklovsky pronounces the importance of the Marxist method for literary studies for the first time and establishes a direct connection between the literary and economic-material planes, clarifying that his earlier attempt to separate the two was merely "a working hypothesis that was useful for the initial accumulation and systematization of facts."[14] Now, with that preliminary stage completed, the critic aspired to find a new path—and this, to the average reader of the main literary periodical, had to be a Marxist one.

But nothing is straightforward about Shklovsky's line of reasoning. He highlights the impossibility of arguing for the "non-tendentiousness" (*nenapravlennost'*) of socialist art and acknowledges, though somewhat hesitantly, that there is a current trend to study epochs in which the teleological-journalistic mode of literary production predominates. The hesitation becomes more prominent when Shklovsky retreats in the very next sentence: "At the same time, it turns out that art's non-tendentiousness—its [semantic] mitigation—also pursued very real and intentional aims."[15] A circle, whether vicious or not, is formed. But what is, and what has been, the direction of his scientific pursuit, according to the article?

As has been suggested elsewhere, transgression was one of Shklovsky's favorite discursive strategies.[16] It works together with a rather idiosyncratic understanding of the notion of *error* and its functional capabilities. Long before the appearance of the eponymous article in the 1930 issue of *The Literary Gazette*, Shklovsky muses about the notion of error in a stylized letter to Lev Iakubinsky in *The Third Factory* (Tret'ia fabrika, 1926). After completing his stints at the "first factory" (family and school) and the "second factory" (his involvement with OPOIAZ), Shklovsky finds himself moonlighting at the third factory (the Third Factory of Goskino). He writes:

> I have made a lot of mistakes, Lev Petrovich, and I am still making them hand over fist. But then, flowers are unreliable, as opposed to botany.
>
> I spent the second factory thinking—or, to put this in terms of an object being processed—undergoing the thought of freedom.
>
> What concerns me now are the limits of freedom, the deformations of the material.
>
> I want to change. I fear negative unfreedom. The denial of what others are doing links you to them.[17]

Shklovsky points out that being erroneous about a particular instance never undermines general scientific principles as such. Being mistaken is a productive principle for sustaining the general truth value of science, for this leaves space for doubt and intellectual freedom at large. Thus, scientific inquiry for Shklovsky is a constant quest for an opportunity to err. Epistemic freedom is restrained both by uncompromising affirmation and pure negation. Three years after publishing the "letter," Shklovsky, in *Theory of Prose*, attempts to conceptualize a "story based on error" (*novella oshibki*), a text whose narrative is structurally driven by a mistake: "In the story based on error the confusion of two given concepts is motivated by an external resemblance in circumstance that involves an ambiguous interpretation."[18] Semblance, as a source of confusion, evolves into a potent generator of new meaning that emerges from the semantic tension of the error.

"Monument to a Scholarly Error" channels the energy of error and initiates a major impetus toward reformulating the main premises of *ostranenie*. While retaining the original connotations of strangeness, *ostranenie*, is transmuted into a hybrid entity that incorporates correlated notions of variety and heterogeneity. This is how he redefines the key notion of literary form: "Very little was left of the first, rather naïve, definition that a literary work equals the sum of its devices. The parts of a literary work are not summed up but correlated. Literary form itself in its ostensible monosemy [odnoznachnosti—literally, *one-meaningness*] turns out to be *uni-formed* [odnoformennoi], but not monosemic [odnoznachnoi]."[19]

Denying the preeminence of literary form is an evolutionary move toward late modernism, which restrained the ostentatious avant-garde exultation of the category of form and directly engaged social discourses. The work of art is no longer a coherent sum of the devices present in it that enhance the perception of the familiar. The *supremacy* of form is replaced by formal *integrity* (uniformity), a more content-friendly concept. The push toward polysemy, heterogeneity, and hence semantics, is a new aspect of the formalist way of thinking that the article introduces. This becomes Shklovsky's theoretical lifesaver. Now, the place previously held by "complication of the form" is taken by formal integrity and heterogeneous content.

Shklovsky amplifies the tension between strangeness-familiarity and heterogeneity-homogeneity by admitting that he used to ignore diachronous and synchronous aspects of literary evolution and treated the work of art as a self-contained phenomenon:

> The error was not in the division of the system but in the anchoring of the division. My error was that I took distant or disparate examples of literature *from different epochs and nationalities* and proved their aesthetic *unambiguousness* [odnoznachimost'], i.e., I tried to study literary works as an isolated system, without investigating their correlation with the whole system of literature and the economic base that shapes culture.[20]

The earlier erroneous conviction argued for the uncomplicated rendering of space (geography of national literatures) and time (literatures of different historical epochs) as manifestations of aspatial and atemporal aesthetic form. Although the formalist method glorified strangeness for its own sake, this technique ultimately proved reductive; it failed to convey alterity and the heterogeneity of divergent social phenomena that are both temporally and spatially scattered. However strange it may sound, the process of defamiliarization failed to recognize difference as such, according to the essay.

Shklovsky resolves what seems to be a discursive dead-end by emphasizing the notion of evolution, which animates artistic form and adds a crucial temporal—that is, historical—dimension. As he puts it, "literature must study the uninterruptedness of the changing system of modes of social impact."[21] Thus, the pressure of time works together with social factors as agents of change to "emancipate" form from the restraining effects of a singular work of art or individual consciousness. Here, Shklovsky responds to substantial shifts that were taking place within the formalist school in the mid-1920s. Developments such as Tynianov's introduction of the category of evolution and his attempt to explore the nature of the boundary between literature and life, or Eikhenbaum's interest in the literary everyday (*byt*), were already signaling a shift from the notion of autonomous and technical form.[22] These directions were supposed to comprise the reformulated theses of the reorganized OPOIAZ of the late 1920s. Shklovsky seems to acknowledge them as a possible way forward.

Nevertheless, a sense of methodological disorientation and lack of any stable theoretical ground permeated the essay—it was an exercise in proactive defense and conciliatory retreat. As Shklovsky phrased it in the early 1980s in a private conversation with his secretary Aleksandr Galushkin, "'Monument to a Scholarly Error' settled accounts with formalism, while itself remaining a formalist text."[23] This was noted even at the time of publication of the "manifesto." The editorial board of *The Literary Gazette* very soon published an attack written by Mark Gel'fand, one of the editors of *The Literary Encyclopedia*. Gel'fand argued that not only did the "renewed" formal method still fail to view literature as a weapon in the class struggle and as a tool for molding the social psyche, but that Shklovsky's article was also a "mere maneuver of retreating formalism."[24] In 1949, during the anti-cosmopolitan campaign, Shklovsky fully affirmed the truth of this critique by acknowledging that the formal method was not a mere scholarly mistake, it was political, too:

> It was a scholarly error because it was based on an incorrect assumption about the self-sufficiency of literature. It was a political error because it made an inaccurate assessment of literary phenomena, asserted that art was emotionlessness and essentially non-teleological, and thus deprived the proletarian revolution of [using] art as a weapon. The main error was political. The scholarly error emerged from it.[25]

FROM BAROQUE INTRICACY TO SOCIALIST CLARITY

The unconditional acknowledgment of the political instrumentalization of the arts was preceded by theoretical "detours" and a new vocabulary to describe the passing times of "radical" formalism. The reappropriated term *baroque*, which entered the Soviet literary scene's discursive field in the late 1920s and early 1930s, was one of the lexical additions. Shklovsky first used the term in 1929 in his review of Sergei Eisenstein's *October*, which he called "a film in the style of the 'Soviet baroque'" because it disintegrated objects by metaphorizing them.[26] To Shklovsky, the baroque, with its tendency to overload the metaphoric plane, seemed compatible with the left-wing avant-garde sentiments he once shared and even propagated.

There are specific features of the historical tradition of baroque—etymologically deriving from the Portuguese *barroco*, meaning an unevenly shaped pearl—that played a crucial role as descriptors of avant-garde aesthetics. For Gilles Deleuze, baroque comprises an operative function, endlessly producing folds that have a potential to differ and grow despite consistent operation.[27] The open-endedness of the baroque structure is crucial: it undermines boundaries by omitting the division between inside and outside. The resulting unboundedness is achieved by means of folds that bring inside and outside together in close proximity. Because of this interweaving, the detail either stands for the whole or is completely devoured by it.

This state of constant movement, or rather agitated oscillation, is another important element of baroque's aesthetic structure. According to Heinrich Wölfflin's nineteenth-century account, which was likely known to Shklovsky,[28] baroque conveys a feeling of discontent with the present and is oriented toward a postponed future fulfillment; it anticipates something yet to come.[29] The agitation of baroque aesthetics, shared by the avant-garde with its negation of stasis, became superfluous to the immediacy and monumentality of the emerging Stalinist era. Its irregularity and elaborate form were not desired qualities in the context of Soviet discourse prioritizing clarity, uncomplicated forms, and straightforward discursive lines. It is no coincidence that Lazar Kaganovich, one of Stalin's main associates, issued a "recommendation" on how to define the baroque epoch in 1935. The definition had "to reveal the style's decadence [upadochnost'], narcissism [samovliublennost'] and parochialism."[30] Socialist classicism's zest for life, collective spirit, and universality would function as a healthy alternative.

The excess of detail—baroque's signature element—was essential to Shklovsky's critique of his formalist past and of his fellow experimenters, including

Eisenstein, Vladimir Maiakovsky, and Vsevolod Meyerhold, whom he refers to as "people of the baroque" who are "preoccupied with intensive detail."[31] As a result of this fixation on detail, the wholeness of form is undermined: "A larger form is not necessary: as with the phenomenon of the baroque, every separate fragment unfolds on its own."[32] The curved and entwined baroque structure strives for a state of organic wholeness but never fully achieves it, remaining instead a formless and dynamic mass. With its valorization of detail and hence particularity, baroque proved to be an unsuitable concept for the emerging Stalinist culture. Comprehensibility and clarity of content were needed. Consequently, the nation, as an instance of particularity, and its cultural articulation through national form, had to be "clarified" (essentialized) and integrated into a comprehensible whole.

The intricacies of baroque aesthetics thus served as a negative example of the socialist realist principle of clarity. In the March 31, 1930, issue of *The Literary Gazette*, just below Shklovsky's response to Gel'fand, there is an article by Boris Ol'khovyi, then the newspaper's editor. Titled "On Simplicity and Intelligibility," (O prostote i poniatnosti), the article argues against artistic works that favor formal experiments over content, declaring that formal innovation should not be elevated above accessibility.[33] This was a crucial signal of the radical discursive shift to come. On behalf of the new mass Soviet reader, formerly an illiterate peasant, the state demanded simplification. As Maxim Gorky had expressed in his influential article "On Language" in *Pravda* mere days earlier, words devoid of sense have no place in a socialist society, for every word is either on the side of truth or falsehood.[34] Gorky called for a purification of language, establishing nineteenth-century literary language as the gold standard. He reaffirmed the linguistic heterogeneity of the country but also argued that although Soviet literature is "heteroglot [raznoiazychnaia] in terms of languages, it has to be ideologically unified."[35] National difference must be intelligible, that is, its alterity needs to be rendered in the "familiar" terms of socialist ideology.

Shklovsky responded to new sociopolitical pressures in a 1932 essay for *The Literary Gazette*, written in the form of stylized appeals addressed to fellow modernists: "One must take a simple thing, or in fact any thing, as if it were a simple thing. The time of the baroque has passed. It is a time of a continuous [nepreryvnoe] art."[36] For the first time, the notion of simplicity enters Shklovsky's theoretical vocabulary; in announcing the end of the baroque with its montage of fragments and details, he simultaneously ushers in the continuous and semantically translucent aesthetic framework of the Soviet state. A year later he presents a more complex argument, asking rhetorically what exactly the notion of simplicity is and who is its designated beneficiary. Unexpectedly, he reintroduces the notion of form:

> We have to speak not about simplicity as such but about a concrete simplicity and a concrete metaphoric plane, taking into consideration a functional orientation of the stylistic device.
>
> It is a matter not only of simplicity, but also of form. If form comprises the principle of the object's design, and not only its appearance, then the form is simple.[37]

Shklovsky argues that simplicity must be conceptualized in formal terms. Simplicity is not an end in itself; it is rather a functional *orientation* of a stylistic device within an aesthetic framework. Simplicity then is an artifice; it is an illusion of transparency. In the unpublished article "On Simplicity" (O prostote), which opens the unrealized book *On Soviet Prose* (O sovetskoi proze, 1932–34), Shklovsky is even more uncompromising: "There is no simplicity as such. There are instances when the elements of a work of art reach equilibrium. Intelligibility does not equal simplicity. If something is not clear, one can ponder it.... Craftsmanship is not about concealing difficulties; it is a means to overcome them."[38] The notion of formal intricacy (*zatrudnennaia forma*) is revived, but now the function of art is not to impose difficulty of perception but to overcome the inherent complexity of the material. The essential aspect of the formalist agenda remains in place, though there is a shift away from the author (making it difficult for the reader) toward the author and reader (overcoming interpretive difficulty).

The tone of Shklovsky's criticism softens substantially during and after Stalin's Great Terror. Initially, he was highly skeptical of Gorky's push for clear and simple literary language and speech, particularly in his article "Gorky as a Reviewer."[39] However, over time, he became a strong proponent of *kul'tura rechi* (literally "culture of speech," meaning cultivated speech). In 1948 he wrote "On Cultivated Speech" (O kul'ture rechi) in which the notions of clarity and simplicity are central.[40] As he says on the first page, "cultivated speech above all is grounded in the fact that its practitioner treats the word very seriously and learns how to delete, to cross out—not for the sake of writing something complicated, but in order to write something simple—precisely what the writer needs."[41] Shklovsky perceives Lenin's speech as an exemplary use of language that animates words: even adverbs and conjunctions have a dynamic feel to them. Notably, from Lenin's article "On the National Pride of the Great Russians," a condemnation of imperial Russia's oppression of smaller nations, Shklovsky quotes the following passage: "We are full of national pride because the Great-Russian nation, *too*, has created a revolutionary class, because it, *too*, has proved capable of providing mankind with great models of the struggle for freedom and socialism."[42]

Shklovsky emphasizes that the adverb "too" is italicized twice in the original text, and no single word can be substituted by any other one. Precision and simplicity are on full display. What is crucial here is the strong opposition to any artifice of language: Lenin "struggled against the impurity of language and pointed out any bureaucratese, any artificiality of the word."[43] Similarly, Stalin's speech, according to Shklovsky, is an etalon of clarity—"these speeches can be studied in the same way as crystals are studied, for all their facets are examined."[44] These comments make clear Lenin's understanding of cognitive activity as an adequate *reflection* of reality that forms the basis of any materialistic epistemology; Stalin's *crystals*, on the other hand, do not reflect but *refract*. Nevertheless, putting the particulars of Marxist optics aside, Shklovsky's shift away from artificiality and baroque intricacies toward simplicity and clarity displays how his preoccupation with form transformed into a preference for content (versus material) displaying discursive intelligibility; it is also a shift from art to rhetoric.

As of the mid-1930s, the aesthetic form became a pejorative term. Clear socialist content evolved into an omnipotent discursive spell performed on all theoretical debates. The fierce condemnation of Shostakovich's opera *Lady Macbeth of the Mtsensk District*, which launched the frontal attack on formalism in all artistic spheres in 1936, was driven by the accusation of a lack of clarity. As the infamous *Pravda* editorial puts it, "from the first minute, the listener is shocked by deliberate dissonance, by a confused stream of sound. Snatches of melody, the beginnings of a musical phrase, are drowned, emerge again, and disappear in a grinding and squealing roar."[45] Instead of this "muddle," the article calls for "simple and popular musical language accessible to all," and establishes "simplicity, realism, clarity of image, and the unaffected spoken word"[46] as a golden standard of Soviet culture.

Formalism, according to Gorky's 1936 programmatic article "On Formalism," published a few months before the writer's death, seems to function as a smoke screen to conceal (spiritual) emptiness.[47] The founding father of socialist realism pushes aesthetics into the realm of ethics: "Formalism is employed because of the fear of the simple, clear, and sometimes coarse word by those who are afraid of answerability for such a word."[48] Remarkably, the article concludes with a call for a new internationalism in arts: "Our literature, in its own, limited way, has already become international. It is time for us to understand that this is its path, its purpose."[49] The concluding remarks gesture to the internationalism of content manifested in Stalin's formula—"national in form, socialist in content." The ultimate end of formalism thus coincides with the reinforcement of Soviet literature's internationalism by linking it to epic traditions that frame proletarian content.

Lukács adds more theoretical nuances to Gorky's ideological attack. Inspired by Hegel's argument that the material and formal aspects of a work of art are derivative in relation to its philosophical contents, Lukács laconically declares that "content determines form."[50] He advances the concept of *Weltanschauung* (worldview), whose structure delineates the semantic field of any given work of art. Lukács maintains that "it is the view of the world, the ideology or *Weltanschauung* underlying a writer's work, that counts."[51] In a truly Aristotelean way, he argues that the literary text, as a privileged form of consciousness, provides a reflection of the world and reveals the dynamic tendencies of historical development. Mimetic correspondence defies defamiliarizing transposition. This is precisely why Lukács fiercely challenged the autonomy of the aesthetic function earlier professed by the formalists. By extension, his concept of modernism is driven by the same belief in aesthetic autonomy and self-contained formal experimentation, and thus "means not the enrichment, but the negation of art."[52]

However, the vigorous Marxist-Lukácsian challenge to the formal method refused to deal in an unbiased way with key elements of its opponent's theoretical positions. The formalists never undermined the category of content as such; everything which is already included in a work of art is formal. Yet as early as 1923, Shklovsky maintained that the formal method's "most remarkable feature is that it doesn't deny the idea-content of art but treats so-called content as one of the manifestations of form."[53] He vehemently attacks the understanding of form as an external husk merely enclosing the kernel of content.

In the classic rendering of formalism, the conventional static dichotomy of form and content is replaced by a transformative relationship between device and material. Literature, as a result, is not a reflection of reality but a specific mode of signification—it does not represent but distorts everyday material. However, this conversion resulted in the fact that content became, in Hansen-Löve's words, "a passive object upon which the principle of form exerts its influence."[54] This passivity was alien to the fiercely enthusiastic project of socialist construction. Hence, the critics of formalism fixated on the theory's reduction of content to the level of pre-aesthetic material. Following the fierce debates of the mid-1930s, Shklovsky's renowned hierarchical formula—the "content ... of a literary work is equal to the sum of its stylistic devices"—was replaced by the equivalence of form and content, wherein the notion of pre-aesthetic material was neutralized.[55] The "form made difficult" (*zatrudnennaia forma*) was replaced by the cohesion and clarity of the form-content relationship. Consequently, perception was replaced by comprehension and observation was supplanted by cognition.[56]

FORMALIST THINGS

In 1936, after the attacks on Formalism become more vigorous and widespread, Shklovsky wrote another "conciliatory" piece bearing the same title as Gorky's programmatic article of the same year, "On Formalism" (O formalizme).[57] The text, rarely discussed in scholarly literature, contains a key passage in which the critic conceptualizes thingness and its role in the Formalist project. Honoré de Balzac's prose serves as a point of departure for Shklovsky's attempt to justify his theoretical past:

> Balzac represented his world in an entirely real manner. He objectifies the world. He represents a man through an accumulation of objects, like a miser who collects things.
>
> The whole of art was the art of details. That was a completely distinct world, with a distinct sense of things that had newly emerged. The successors of this world—which was already dead by the time of their inheritance—were the formalists. The conditions that created the profound perception of a real picture of the world had passed. We stood in front of the old world. Many of us had an impression that this world could be made anew.[58]

The process of literary reification taking place on the narrative level in Balzac's novella *Gobseck* is elevated to the level of poetics. Afraid to sell too cheaply, the miser refuses to sell anything—food decomposes, and things perish in his apartment. Reification leads to disintegration. Similarly, the formalists yielded to the temptation of aesthetic hoarding, according to Shklovsky, for they relied too much on detail—that old baroque habit of the avant-garde. The result was a handicapped poetics that failed to appreciate the organic complexity of the world. As he puts it, "we used to think that the world was almost imperceptible, that [only] things could be perceived."[59]

In the same article, Shklovsky compares his theoretical dead end of 1930 with a train stuck in a snow drift. The mass of accumulated details turns into an unsurpassable obstacle. He professes that working on the Marco Polo book and the history of the White Sea–Baltic Canal led to a gradual change in perspective.[60] Whether the alleged acknowledgment of transformation was forced or not, it seems that historicization was key for Shklovsky's theoretical survival. Socialist realism prescribed that literature ought to reflect the revolutionary development of reality: the past, present, and future had to be presented through the Marxist prism of historical development. Accordingly, Shklovsky's works of the 1930s and 1940s had—almost without exception—an important historical dimension, which replaced general theoretical observations. As he puts it: "I used to think that objects did not change, that only immobile things could be assembled. I thought about the history of literature and the history of art ahistorically."[61] Indeed, in *The Prison-House of Language*, Fredric Jameson reproaches early formalism for its inability to leave the maze of language and for its aimless wandering through infinite passages of verbal matter.[62] This linguistic suspension results in a failure to establish a meaningful relation with the flow of history. In the Stalinist state, historical narratives emerged as predominant discursive means in ideological matters, and this trend profoundly affected Shklovsky. Time, introduced with the general historical flow, animated things; the formal method had to undergo a process of historicization.

Shklovsky's self-proclaimed transformation occurred over several stages before reaching the state of "blessed socialist historicism." The defamiliarized thing was replaced by the artifact, whose materiality was pronounced so that its material structure could be better understood. The artifact was then replaced by the "utilitarian" socialist thing, which had a clear role in the process of historical development. The varied and extensive textual corpus of the 1930s reveals these discursive shifts. In *Potboiler Work*, for instance, drawing from his experience as a military mechanic, he claimed an understanding that "aluminum is shaggy, nickel is slippery, and cast iron feels somehow greasy to the touch."[63] Tactile and "strange" encounters with different metals signal a move toward concrete material perceptibility—not a mere abstract mental perception. The physical encounter with matter replaces detached cerebral experience. Consequently, in the late 1920s and throughout the 1930s, a process of sensory renewal through tangible qualities of real objects and substances becomes a new avenue for the development of Shklovsky's concept of *ostranenie*. Matter's inherent qualities, and the idiosyncratic perception of these qualities by an individual who is consuming or interacting with them, are paramount.

In the mid- to late 1920s, Shklovsky worked with *LEF* (Left Front of the Arts, Levyi front iskusstv) and was exposed to the factography movement, which, as Elizabeth Papazian has convincingly shown, was a key transitional movement of the historical avant-garde of the late 1920s *en route* to socialist realism.[64] Factography helped Shklovsky develop his new direction for *ostranenie*. In this hypostasis, the device moves away from the aestheticizing *naïve* point of view (that of a stranger, a child, or an animal), where perception plays a crucial role. He instead develops a notion of professional, hands-on knowledge of the subject that allows the writer to engage with the material world and then provide its artistic rendering. The writer is no longer a perceiving outsider and contemplator; she is an active participant in production processes. Shklovsky's brochure

Technique of the Writing Craft (Tekhnika pisatel'skogo remesla, 1927) and his entries for the volume *The Literature of Fact* (*Literatura fakta*, 1929), which proclaimed that the writer should be a "literary screw of socialist construction," testify to this shift.[65]

In this understanding, an essence of the aesthetic procedure lies in writers' ability to know material things and processes associated with their "real" first profession, "for the professional—a person with a profession—describes things in terms of a professional relation."[66] Arguably, the manual as a genre (Shklovsky wrote another manual on how to write screenplays) emerged from the initial understanding of *ostranenie* as a procedure drawing attention to the madeness (*sdelannost'*) of a work of art. The deep knowledge of a professional craft results in a real and physical proximity to objects. The ability to depict things from this unmediated position—in essence, from a position of *familiarity* with the world—becomes fundamental.

In 1930 Shklovsky contributed the essay "The Way I Write" (Kak ia pishu) for a volume of collected essays by a group of prominent writers of the era, led by Gorky.[67] This was intended to be the definitive manual for aspiring writers. In this context, Shklovsky remarks:

> When I write, I proceed from facts. I try not to change facts. I try to connect facts that stand far apart. This might be coming from Lomonosov's idea of bringing together "rather-far-removed ideas" [dalekovatykh idei] or else from Anatole France who mentioned hurling epithets against each other.
> As for me, I try to hurl not epithets but things, facts.[68]

The collision of facts provides the needed energy—the energy of *ostranenie*, for the produced kinetic force resonates with the disruptive defamiliarizing function of Shklovsky's canonical device. The process of drawing together distant entities, things and ideas that should not be in a state of propinquity creates a dynamic interplay between different formal conventions and semantic structures. A few paragraphs below the quoted passage, Shklovsky suddenly switches to his "factographic" mode of writing by recalling his recent Turksib trip:

> I traveled through Turksib. It was dusty and hot there, and lizards were squeaking. Tall grass stood upright—sometimes it was feather grass, sometimes wormwood; sometimes it was rigid, sometimes thorny; it was desert grass and tamarisk that looked like not-yet-bloomed lilac.
> The freshwater Balkhash is over there, a freshwater lake with salty gulfs. In the fall, salty rivers flow in. The people over there ride bulls and horses like we

ride trams. Kazakh greyhounds gallop through the feather grass as if not using their legs but just curving their thin backs, as if they are cut out from cardboard.

Goats walk in the sand. Cars get stuck in salt marshes for weeks. Camels pull carts. Eagles fly hundreds of miles to sit on a telegraph pole because there is nothing to sit on in the desert.

That's where they're building Turksib. It is very necessary and very hard.

It is so hot there that the Kyrgyz people walk around wearing boots over thin felt boots, fur trousers, and fur hats. And they are called Kazakhs, not Kyrgyz.[69]

Shklovsky's signature syntax is terse and compact. Short paragraphs, infused with sudden discursive changes, work by means of association and contrast. The travelogue account is full of collisions and incongruities: fresh water of the Balkhash Lake, yet salty rivers; heat, and warm clothes used to fight it; flattened but speedy "cardboard" greyhounds; center and periphery, jumbled with a variety of settings; nature versus modernity. Saken Seifullin, one of the founders of modern Kazakh literature, criticized Shklovsky's conflation of the Kazakh and Kyrgyz identities into a generic Other in his speech during the First Soviet Writers' Congress.[70] According to Russian imperial nomenclature, the Kazakhs were referred to as Kazakh-Kyrgyz and the Kyrgyz as Kara-Kyrgyz. Seifullin argued that there was no place for fiction, exoticization, or confusion in documentary sketches depicting the reality of Soviet life. Nevertheless, the orientalist gaze of *ostranenie* in Shklovsky's passage rises to meet the factographic mode of writing, with Stalinist modernity in the background. The result is a strange blend of discourses. The Turksib digression concludes with musings on the hardship of socialist construction and the hardship of writing—a typical defacilitating (*zatrudnenie*) move:

> The construction of the road is strenuous. There is little water. Bread must be delivered.
> Bread must be obtained. Bread must be stored somewhere. There are many workers and each of them needs a roof over his head.
> But they went on building anyway.
> Good books turn up when a man must master a subject at any cost, and when he is courageous.
> This is also called inspiration.[71]

The hardship of physical labor here coincides with the anguish of artistic craft. Physical burden replaces cognitive intricacy. It also evolves into a source of artistic inspiration and Soviet enthusiasm for transformation. In a later report titled "How One Writes and How One Ought to Write about Technical Equipment" (Kak pishut i kak pisat' o tekhnike, 1947), given at the Writers' Union, Shklovsky again reminiscences about his trip to Kazakhstan, where he observed various industrial processes. The theme of hardship reemerges: "One can remember fantastic moments in the construction of Turksib when rails were split in one go. A man of my build split the rails with one blow. This is where the difficulty begins. Art is a thirst for concreteness, yet here they write without taking their gloves off, without palpable sensation."[72]

The enormous strength of the worker laying railway tracks is compared to aesthetic *zatrudnenie*; the laborious practice sets an example of how to interact with the material world tangibly to produce aesthetic-sensuous effects. This instrumental application of modernist accomplishments is discernable in the way the device of *ostranenie* is transformed, with the Turksib experience functioning as a catalyst of the change.

SOVIET MODERNITY AND ITS ROAMING SUBJECTS

The construction of the 1,400-kilometer Turkestan-Siberian (Turksib) railway, connecting Central Asia with Siberia and the larger Soviet railway network, was one of the most economically vital and symbolically significant construction projects during the first Five-Year Plan. It took more than four years (from December 1926 to January 1931), and upon its completion, it was called "the First-Born of the Five-Year Plan," though its construction began before the planned economy was even introduced. It was both a civilizing mission in the "wild" East and a celebration of the economic and ideological unity of the Soviet nations. The reality, of course, was different and was more reminiscent of blatantly racist colonial rule. As Matthew Payne observes, the Kazakhs at the construction site "were despised, discriminated against, and beaten not just because they spoke a different language or belonged to another culture. For both managers and European workers, Kazakhs were the embodiment of Asiatic primitiveness, savages who ill fit with their conceptions of industrialism."[73]

Shklovsky likely witnessed firsthand this racial discrimination and attempts to exclude local Kazakhs from the ranks of proletarians: xenophobic echoes are found in his orientalizing descriptions of the Kazakh workers, which will be discussed below. Indeed, writing about Turksib served as a way for him to inscribe his theoretical perspective into the emerging Soviet modernity. In this context, his extensive visit to the railway construction site proved memorable and would reverberate throughout many of his later texts. One text in particular holds the key to his Turksib experience: the eponymous 1930 book where Shklovsky assumes the role of a mediating narrator. Although written for children, the book has a serious purpose—instilling the psyche of the Soviet child, the possessor of the socialist future, with a deep understanding of the material grandeur of the epoch. Thus, the book presents the child reader with a travelogue describing the "firstborn" of Stalinist modernity through the all-encompassing gaze of the formalist undergoing a theoretical conversion. However, just as the gaze of the formalist is a constructed perspective, so too is that of the child reader. Contemporary critics of children's literature have observed that the child is often blatantly "colonized" by adults; for Karin Lesnik-Oberstein, the very concept of "childhood" is artificially framed and maintained by "adults" who perceive children as empty spaces and project onto them their perceptions of themselves.[74] Thus, Shklovsky's *Turksib*, intended to glorify the Soviet anticolonial and industrial projects, is in fact a double colonial gesture aimed at the abstract Soviet child and real Kazakh workers.

Shklovsky's preoccupation with the genre of children's literature developed during his work on *Turksib*. Yet again he managed to smuggle in his formalist convictions, this time into the "uncorrupted" world of children's literature. He dedicates a whole section to the topic in *Potboiler Work*, starting with a statement that a child's development is not an even process; it is full of ruptures and leaps and is inherently revolutionary rather than evolutionary.[75] Children, in the early stages of development, do not need "prudence and instructiveness."[76] Thus, Shklovsky maintains that the traditional nursery rhyme is perfectly "constructed" for a child, for it gives "orientation to the word's self-articulation;"[77] the very articulation of the word and its rhythm create a "sufficient" experience for a child. Furthermore, the very content of a children's book should not be primarily didactic; its "semantic load" (*nagruzka*) should be evenly distributed and "should be comprised of a sense of the work of art's form and of a light, extremely simple and playful humor."[78] Even when he discusses books for teenagers, Shklovsky insists on formal aspects and the key role of the texture of the word. Good examples include books that provide a "sense [*oshchushchenie*] of the word," "a word that is discerned because it is correctly constructed, made difficult to a degree [*v meru zatrudnennoe*] and therefore sensed [*chuvstvennoe*]," and those that "have a loose, simple, and intelligible plot, which usually finds its resolution comically."[79] These are exemplary formalist pronouncements, offered under the pretext of formulating the aesthetic conventions of books for children.

The same can be said of the device of *ostranenie*, which, with its fixation on strangeness, finds some of its entropic dispersion through the exotic lens of *Turksib* and *Marco Polo, Explorer*. These books allow for a narrative voice animated by some variation of the classic defamiliarization technique, albeit through a somewhat simplified point of view that is accessible to a child. Both display a set of unresolved discursive tensions: perception versus cognition, strangeness versus familiarity, modern versus archaic, and delimited versus boundless space. Samuil Marshak, the patriarch of Soviet literature for children, argued that exemplary books for children take issue with seemingly objective geographic and ethnographic depictions, thereby revealing "the changing nature of phenomena" and cultivating a transformative approach to nature.[80] This is what *Turksib* attempts to accomplish.

Shklovsky's *Turksib* was written in conjunction with Viktor Turin's earlier documentary *Turksib* (1929), whose screenplay Shklovsky co-wrote with Turin, Aleksandr Macheret, and Iakov Aron. Significantly, both the book and the film were produced while the railway network was still under construction: the artifacts commemorating this achievement of socialist labor were being forged at the same time as the railway network itself. Artistic and physical labor merged to create a significant element of Soviet infrastructure and its representation.

While the book and the documentary film share a basic theme—the modernization of archaic space—there are still significant differences. The documentary creates a vision of the Soviet Union as a heterogeneous but unified space. Its attempt to fashion the country into an imagined and indivisible community is accomplished with the trope of "taming wild elements." Turin posits the wind as a principal enemy in the deserts and steppes of Central Asia. Throughout the film, the director employs a motif of wandering as a manifestation of physical and cultural instability, declaring "the war on the primitive," as the film's intertitles read, and literally undermining the traditional way of life (for instance, in one scene engineers use dynamite to clear the landscape for the construction of the railway). At the same time, peoples of Central Asia are consistently depicted as archaic-natural elements of the steppe: they are always surrounded by animals and appear against sweeping landscapes. However, their "natural" way of life is soon to be eroded. The conflict reaches its apogee in the depiction of a stylized race between Kazakhs on camel- and horseback and a brand-new locomotive—a visual realization of a 1930 statement by the leading official of the Commissariat of Nationalities Semyon Dimanshtein: "The advanced peoples are tearing along in the fast locomotive of history.... Whereas the backward people must 'race like the wind' ... to catch up."[81] In the end, however, the nomads of *Turksib* do not catch up with the locomotive of history; the film fails to depict the transformation of nomads into the proletariat and thus lacks a key motif of class struggle. It was pulled from circulation in 1936, probably for this reason.[82]

FIG. 1.1 Viktor Turin, Stills from *Turksib*, 1929.

While Turin's documentary celebrates the dynamic geography of Soviet modernity on an epic scale, Shklovsky's book focuses more on the subject itself, offering a narrower perspective that is more suited for a child. Thus, in Shklovsky's *Turksib*, the strangeness of the distant place is contrasted with the familiarity of socialist production. The opening section is simply entitled "Ordinary Things/Common Goods" (*obyknovennye veshchi*). It begins with a description of various food items (tea, bread, butter), commodities (curtains), and raw materials (cotton and timber). The author seems to be employing the reifying logic of economic discourse. But, in contrast to the commodity fetishism associated with bourgeois society, socialist matter resists fetishization. Its essence is practical—it occupies physical space, rather than the value-space of the capitalist commodity. Shklovsky's very first page appears to radicalize Marx's famous critical definition of the commodity as "abounding in metaphysical subtleties and theological niceties."[83] Soviet matter is devoid of any metaphysical aspects—it is familiar and concrete.

A similar discursive change can be discerned in Shklovsky's other texts of the time. In the section titled "How Things Are Changing" in *Potboiler Work*, for instance, he maintains that "there is no longer meaning in having ownership of the thing. The thing, as a fetish, becomes senseless because of its easy replicability."[84] He also notes that technical progress renders things obsolete too quickly for the human psyche to catch up.[85] As a result, the critic offers a new socialist ontology of things: goods and technical equipment all work for the collective good, and their orientation toward the future as agents of change is a guarantor of their present value. The thing is animated not by an act of defamiliarization (the realm of perception) but by the resourceful will of the worker (the realm of active transformation). This was a radical reorientation of early formalism: it left the realm of pure aesthetics and entered life through the fact of *modernization* (industrialization and cultural construction). Political pressure made the method evolve: theory became a subject of the formalists' theory of evolution.

This evolution is especially visible in *Turksib*. The book's narrative strategy and conceptual approach replace the tendency of tropes to "move around" or circumvent objects—that is, the author's tendency not to call objects by their proper and direct names. Instead, the text strives to merge with the thing (*veshch'*) itself. The matter-of-fact enumeration of various food items, commodities, and natural resources not only exposes the ideological and economic underpinnings of socialist matter, but also reveals a rather novel aesthetic foundation for that representation. By providing the provenance of the thing,

Shklovsky resolves the problem of its strangeness. This approach echoes Gorky's musings found in his late notes about literature and games for children. The most prominent Soviet writer imagines a *papier-mâché* globe cut in half, with the uncovered earthly entrails exposing the planet's structure to reveal layers of natural materials: "coal, iron ore, salts, oil, peat, etc."[86] Through this imagined demonstration, natural resources are exposed and made immediately comprehensible to the child.

Turksib, with its constant references to raw materials, welcomes the discourse of utility. It is not the renewed perception of the material that is preeminent, but the social usefulness of the processed material. The produced thing is close at hand, in proximity to the Soviet child who was the intended reader of this work. This vision reached its culmination two years later in the already quoted passage from a 1932 issue of *The Literary Gazette*: "The world is simpler these days.... One must take a simple thing, or in fact any thing, as if it were a simple thing."[87] The famous categorical statements that "*art is a means of experiencing the process of creativity*" and "*the artifact itself is quite unimportant*" are replaced by the notion of utility.[88] In a Turksib *ocherk*, a documentary sketch, preceding the 1930 book for children, Shklovsky writes:

> We built Turksib but never depicted it, that railway connecting two countries. When I traveled there, I was told: "don't swim in Balkhash, its waters are salty," but they turned out to be fresh. We thought that we would go through the desert, yet it turned out there was copper, molybdenum, tungsten. It was the discovery of the country. There are people there who study, produce concrete, walk around in trousers made of uncured sheep skins, and manufacture steel frames.[89]

Shklovsky unconsciously excludes the Kazakh Soviet Socialist Republic from the Soviet "family" by referring to them as "two countries." But what is crucial in this passage is that anticipated strangeness evolves into discovery and then literally becomes a productive entity. This was a key point of the reorientation of Shklovsky's understanding of the function of *ostranenie*: from bewilderment by the familiar made strange, to exploration of the unfamiliar, and then to the familiarity of utilization—a quintessential late modernist procedure.

The author-narrator of *Turksib* rather erratically navigates the Orient, while objects and people oscillate around the narrative points he establishes. The point of departure is not revealed, but is presumably the center of the country—Moscow. Shklovsky's text does not demonstrate a conscious displacement of the metropolitan center but rather an involuntary transposition of the center achieved by taking on its point of view. From here, differences and similarities are established, and ideological implications are enforced:

> In Central Asia, like here, they also eat bread. And the sky over there is blue. From the blue, cloudless sky, there isn't any rain. The grain also must be watered. The grain takes water from the cotton. The cotton lacks water, and the whole country lacks cotton. There is a strictly limited amount of water. You can build the *aryks* better, and they're being rebuilt right now, but still, there isn't enough water.[90]

Shklovsky begins with a similarity (bread is eaten both "here" and in Central Asia) but then goes on to highlight differences. No rain falls from the blue sky of the steppes, and this creates a chain of nationwide shortages: growing wheat, from which bread is made and which is also eaten "there," diverts limited water resources away from cotton fields; as a result, cotton is scarce. The local irrigation system (*aryks*) cannot cope with the demand. Turksib is supposed to resolve the issue by connecting Siberia and Central Asia; the former will supply wheat and timber and receive cotton in return.[91] The railway network, with its flow of carriages, takes the irrigation system's place as a major economic artery in the vast and fertile body of the country.

However, the railway network as a trope also contributes to the process of colonial normalization of the Orient. Indeed, *Turksib*, with its preoccupation with the materiality of production, aesthetically challenges and, at the same time, reenacts some of the key premises of colonial importation. Revivification of the Central Asian economy is possible only through its annexation to the country's whole. The notion of planned economy was supposed to unseat the imperial economic system's reliance on distant colonies. As mentioned earlier, for Fredric Jameson, the imperial economic system is inherently segregated since its significant structural segments are located beyond the metropolis.[92] This spatial disjunction creates a certain semantic crisis: the impossibility of comprehending the country and its economic system as a whole.

Transcending borders and uniting people and markets, the railway is the ultimate feature of modernity. It began as a spatial practice of late nineteenth-century capitalism but evolved into a socialist entity. Marx, discussing a physical system of moving goods, claims that the generative phenomenon of capital, with its interminable impulse to sell products in distant markets, is the driving force behind railway development: "Capital by its nature drives beyond every spatial barrier. Thus, the creation of the physical conditions of exchange—of the means of communication and transport—the annihilation of space by time—becomes an extraordinary necessity for it."[93] But as Wolfgang Schivelbusch argues, the alteration of spatial relationships by the speed of the railway train did not just annihilate space; instead, it "was both diminished and expanded."[94] The railway network stretched space by incorporating new areas.

The expansionist and unifying aspects of the railway phenomenon were crucial to the Turksib project. Imperialism's geographical conquest was supposed to be replaced by socialist unity, and the wholeness of the planned economy in this sense was crucial. At the same time, this "new" idea of regional industrial specialization replicated the Russian Empire's vision of economic division of labor in different regions, according to which the Turkestan cotton industry supplied textile manufacturing in Russian cities. As Shklovsky puts it at the very end of *Turksib*:

> The road will connect Siberia, Kazakhstan, Turkestan, and the overall planned economy. Cotton will be sown not only in Turkestan, but also in Transcaucasia, in the Taman Peninsula, located between the Black and the Azov seas, and in Ukraine.
>
> Turksib is only one part of the general plan; it is only a method to merge separate parts of the country's economy into one system, into one plane.[95]

The concluding passage of the book vehemently defends a vision of economic unity for the Soviet Union: natural resources and manufactured goods would flow freely through the country's circulatory system, thus ensuring the efficient use of economic "nutrients." In the *Potboiler Work* chapter "Roads to Kazakhstan," Shklovsky ironically notes: "With regard to roads, there weren't any."[96] He ridicules the pre-Turksib road network for covering only the country's periphery and also points out that one had to make a transfer in Moscow to travel from eastern Kazakhstan to its western part.[97] Both Turksib and *Turksib*, the rail line and the book, follow the trope of transforming the Soviet land to its logical extreme.

Shklovsky fully exploits the symbolic potential of the railway network to captivate the imagination of Soviet children, transporting them to the exotic Socialist borderlands, which take on the function of the irrational. However, he presents a dichotomy in which the archaic is gradually being normalized. This process is captured by a photograph of the outmoded locomotive and Shklovsky's textual inscription for it: "This is the first steam train in the Kazakh steppe. The train's smokestack, as you see, is not like the one we have, but an old one."[98] Even this innovation is not that new—it is still permeated with archaism. Nevertheless, the text affirms without reservation that the outdated locomotive is still better than a young, strong horse.

The exotic land being depicted, at the time still an autonomous republic within the Russian Federation, is far from being economically self-sufficient. Shklovsky paints a rather bleak picture—the natural economy does not provide necessities, and the space desperately awaits modernization:

> The Kazakh lives in the desert. He weaves ropes from wool. He eats meat rarely—only when there is meat. He wears skins. He covers his yurt with felt. He fries grain on a bonfire. He pounds grain in a mortar.
> The Kazakh lives in a desert, in a yurt.
> He buys very few things, sells very few things. This kind of economy is called natural.
> In the vast, rich steppe, the Kazakh lives poorly.
> If the ground is crusted in ice [dzhut], or if the ice covers the grass when there is a frost after a thaw, herds cannot get grass from under the snow and they die, and the steppe becomes poor and dead for many years. The Kazakh lives in isolation, helplessly.[99]

Shklovsky's prose, written in terse sentences and opening with an image of emptiness (the desert), creates a sense of sparseness and bleakness. Every aspect of traditional nomadic life revolves around a natural element (wool, felt, leather, meat, wheat). This is how Shklovsky introduced the Soviet child to the natural mode of production and basic economics. Nomads' complete dependence on unpredictable natural forces makes their premodern lifestyle—images and descriptions of which abound in the book—unproductive. This dismal "natural" state is placed in sharp juxtaposition with a photograph of naïvely cheerful Kazakh workers and the explanatory inscription "Kazakh-workers. The worker on the left wears a Kazakh hat called a *malakhai*. Many wear workers' glasses, or so-called cans [konservy], for protecting their eyes from the dust."[100] The combination of overtly didactic image and text reduces Kazakh nomads to ethnographic material and neutralizes their alterity, rendering it non-formidable, even facetious. The text suggests that overall, the "Kazakh" lives his life in an isolated and dismal way and is barely able to cope with natural forces. Fortunately, however, the train of modernity is on its way to "rescue" him.

Of course, the fusion of foreign archaic elements and universalizing features of modernity seen in *Turksib* is not Shklovsky's own invention. Indeed, cultural works combining the promise of modern technology with the archaism of folkloric tradition were quite commonplace at the time. Similarly, at the turn of the twentieth century, while discussing the impact of railways on human consciousness, H. G. Wells—who visited the USSR on several occasions and even met with Shklovsky—acknowledged both the limits of technological development and its connection to irrational pre-modernity: "Before every engine, as it were, trots the ghost of a superseded horse, [which] refuses most resolutely to trot faster than fifty miles an hour, and shies and threatens catastrophe at every point and curve."[101] Trains embodied the technological rationalism of modernity, but also directly appealed to premodern irrational (natural) instincts. The resulting incongruous effects find theoretical reflection in several passages of *Turksib*. In one of them, Shklovsky writes: "Cars will overtake bulls and camels. The feather-grass steppe will see a hay-mowing machine."[102] Here he highlights the classic tension between archaic, natural forces and the mechanical forces of modernity that supplant them. In another passage, Shklovsky shows his imagined Soviet child reader a photograph of a camel and reminisces: "I saw this camel myself and told Turin, the director who shot *Turksib*, about him. He liked the camel, and now I see him in all the journals. The camel is sniffing the rail. He doesn't seem to like the smell of the rail. It smells like competition."[103]

The cover of Shklovsky's *Turksib* refers to the same conflict-succession—the top depicts a caravan of camels going slightly downhill, while a locomotive steams across the bottom portion. It is also remarkable that Shklovsky's surname is incorporated as the steam coming out of the locomotive engine—this literal sign of authority provides a certain connection (which is already being disconnected) between the archaic caravan and the train of modernity.[104] The train emerges from the caravan, but the two exist on dramatically different planes: The sepia photograph of the caravan, together with the plain desert background, underlines its archaic nature, while the retouched photograph of the train is a collage insert in which the real object (the train) is withdrawn from its natural environment and inserted into the vacuum of what might be termed a real-mythic socialist realist space. While the caravan belongs to the conditionally real realm, the train incontrovertibly emerges from the symbolic domain that is more real than reality itself.

Later, in his 1964 memoirs, Shklovsky perfected this conflation of the road and the thing, of structure and material. Speaking about his time in Persia, he confesses: "In this country, my heart was worn down in the same way a harsh road is worn down by the shaggy feet of camels. . . . I felt like a camel and the road at the same time."[105] One can argue that in *Turksib* Shklovsky himself must undergo a major transformation—no longer called upon to travel the dusty roads of Persia on shaggy camel feet, he was compelled to become the steel tracks and wheels of the Soviet project of modernization. Stalin, the "man of steel" himself (also referred to by Lazar Kaganovich as "the great engine-driver of history's locomotive"), was the key enforcer of this transformation.[106]

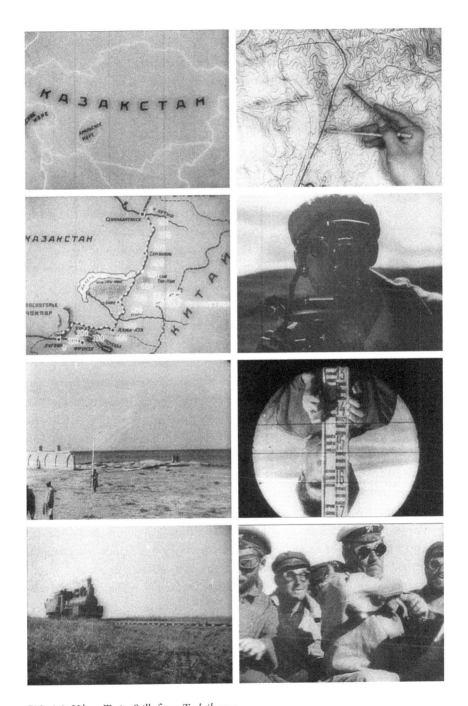

FIG. 1.2 Viktor Turin, Stills from *Turksib*, 1929.

However, there was a much larger group of affected subjects—local inhabitants—who were being called upon to accomplish a much more significant transformative leap. The construction of Turksib, tangible sign of the Soviet state's commitment to ethnic modernity, had the ambition of forging the Kazakh proletariat. Introducing modern infrastructure was supposed to help transform Kazakhs by assimilating them into a pan-Soviet, albeit Russified, workers' identity. The Stalinist distinction between sameness and difference was reconciled by the "not yet the same" formula. This temporal orientation, an emphasis on the process of becoming and transformation, suspended discrepancies of all kinds.

The Soviet Orient—Central Asia, the Caucasus, and the fringe Northern territories—presented a case of dynamic spatial interaction between center and periphery, and a temporal coexistence of past and present. Soviet ideologues attempted to reconcile these tensions and converge them into an integral system of Soviet modernity. They characterized imperial colonialism as envisioning the oriental territories outside of history, in an irrelevant state of perpetual stagnation. The Soviet project of modernization was going to resolve this historical and political "injustice," emancipating nations from the chains of backwardness and imperialist exploitation. The process of rapid industrial development guaranteed a leap in history—from feudalism straight to socialism.

Ernst Bloch, in a text written in 1932, identifies the uneven temporal development of various capitalist nations as *nonsynchronism* (*Ungleichzeitigkeit*). The essay commences with a bold statement that "not all people exist in the same Now."[107] If heterogeneous stages of social and economic development can coexist in one space under capitalism, this developmental unevenness must be eliminated from a socialist society. However, it was still discursively framed as a certain advantage: the state of underdevelopment provided unmediated access to the primordial values of a classless society.

Primitive communism, slave society, feudalism, capitalism, and socialism comprise five stages of social development, according to a Soviet interpretation of orthodox Marxism (the five-stage system, *piatichlenka*). Marx and Engels argue that hunter-gatherer societies, traditionally based on egalitarian social relations and common ownership, present a case of primitive communism. These societies had neither hierarchical social class structures nor capital accumulation; inequalities of wealth and power were minimal.[108] Soviet modernity conceived the socialist future of its "underdeveloped" territories as a form of reconstructed past: the primordial classless paradise of primitive Communism. As Yuri Slezkine puts it, the "dichotomy of native (nature) versus Russian (culture) was overcome by the discovery that natives had a high (communistic) culture of their own."[109] As societies of primitive Communism, the former subjects of imperial colonialism were expected to make an easier transition to socialism.

However, the start of the first Five-Year Plan marked a major shift in how "primitive" societies were perceived. The master narrative of the ideology of modernization posited that "backward" nomads, those who had been "left behind" in the historical progression, now had to catch up.[110] Collectivization and sedentarization must proceed hand in hand; Kazakh Communist Party officials had resolved in December 1929 that collectivization was impossible without mass sedentarization. As Filip Goloshchekin, first secretary of the Kazakh Communist Party (who possessed little knowledge about the nomadic way of life and was openly xenophobic toward Kazakhs) put it, "settlement is collectivization."[111] This was a clear display of what Francine Hirsch identifies as "state-sponsored evolutionism."[112] It was also the beginning of the nomadic economy's end, leading to the devastating famine of 1932–33.

THE LAST OUTPOST OF STRANGENESS

Settling the nomads of Soviet Central Asia was one of the key "sociocultural" initiatives of the Stalinist 1930s. Halting the movement of nomadic tribes was not just another restrictive biopolitical procedure; the transformative passage from a "homeless" nomad into a "cultured" sedentary was equated to the transformation of a peasant into a proletarian. It had major ideological consequences: as one of the articles in *Our Achievements* (Nashi dostizheniia) put it in 1931, "The cultured and semi-settled part of the East strides toward communism, bypassing the banker; the nomads are forcing their way to socialism straight from their primitive tribal communes."[113] The possibility of reaching socialism and avoiding the "painful" stage of capitalism for archaic feudal societies was a discursive "coping" mechanism through which nomadic "backwardness" was conceived in the Stalinist state. Although Vladimir Paperny argues that the ordinary person of Culture Two is rendered immobile in geographical space, with the prerogative to "move around" instead given to heroes-conquerors of space (pilots, explorers, etc.),[114] nomads present a peculiar case. Completely devoid of heroism, they use mobility as a natural mode of existence. However, their physical mobility is appropriated for sociopolitical purposes and thus transformed into an ability to accomplish the ideological leap from archaic feudalism to glorious socialism. But they had to halt their movement in physical space. Nomadism was literally a transitory state.

The theme of wandering on the fringes of the socialist land is addressed yet again in *Marco Polo, Explorer*, another of Shklovsky's books for children. Published only a year after *Turksib*, *Marco Polo* also foregrounds the theme of spatial exploration and explores both symbolic and real places. Indeed, both books penetrate each other's discursive territories: traces of *Turksib* are easily discernable in this narrative about the famed Venetian traveler who was profoundly influenced by the cultures of the medieval East. Shklovsky commences his description of Marco Polo's itinerary with a topos not that alien to the Soviet child—Soviet Central Asia—as he mentions the region's past glory: "And it is not always the most famous nations that created the greatest things. Agriculture, for instance, spread from many centers—one of them, the currently godforsaken fields of Central Asia."[115] He reasserts the importance of the current Soviet periphery by stressing its past glory in land cultivation. However, it is still a space of transition for the Marco Polo narrative. As Shklovsky writes: "For a year, the brothers traveled from Bukhara to the Great Khan's capital. Presumably, they crossed the Tian Shan mountains through Ghulja after getting across Syr Darya and passing by Samarkand. Thus, they made the beginning of the road, in contemporary terms, alongside the present Turksib."[116]

The Venetian traveler commences his journey along the not-yet-existing Turksib route (the actual Silk Way), causing divergent spaces and times to intersect on the pages of the book. But it seems that the region's "exoticism" performs a structuring function. In fact, this is a driving theme of the narrative: Marco Polo, per Shklovsky's daring interpretation, was a master of defamiliarization whose appreciation of strangeness allowed him to describe phenomena that were unknown and had no adequate lexicographic referent in Europe at the time. Among other descriptions, he depicts banisters as several regularly placed poles, decorated with seated lions. As Shklovsky concludes, "here Marco Polo describes handrails on a bridge as something unheard of. He not only has to describe them but also explain their purpose."[117] Here, openness to strangeness serves as a step toward comprehending how the unfamiliar thing functions. The same operation takes place when Marco Polo encounters a breadfruit tree. He carefully describes a wondrous plant and then prudently explains how to use it as sago to make bread. Astonishment leads to instrumental appreciation. Shklovsky, as Anja Tippner observes, emphasizes not redundancy and unreality, which usually accompany orientalist travelogues, but abundance and progress: "He turns Polo's travels into an exercise in curiosity and objectivity thus heavily re-writing and editing the original text that does not lack in orientalism as well as in prejudice."[118]

The tension between the familiar and the strange is also present in the way Shklovsky describes currency circulation in thirteenth-century China. Chinese paper money, the use of which was compulsory under Kublai Khan, functions as a refrain throughout the text. Paper money has the quality of a trope—it stands in for something else (a certain amount of gold or silver). Shklovsky develops the money-as-trope idea in the following manner: "The Great Khan made gold out of paper money. He printed the money, as Marco Polo says, on mulberry tree bark. The bark's fiber was ground up and turned into a firm dark paper. This paper was cut into oblong pieces, and then an exact value was printed on them."[119]

Mulberry tree fiber stands in for a precious metal. Here, something that is familiar and utilitarian in the extreme is presented from an unusual perspective—as physical matter. Marco Polo was indeed the person who introduced banknotes to Europe. However, the famous Venetian traveler's narratives were perceived as pure fiction by his contemporaries, and only approximately fifty years after his death were its geographical observations recognized as truth.

The 1931 short book for children *Marco Polo, Explorer* undergoes a substantial expansion to become the 350-page biography *Marco Polo* (1936) as part of the canonical series "Lives of Remarkable People," which Gorky revived in 1933.[120] The book is permeated by a set of tensions between reality and fiction, truth and error, East and West. As Shklovsky writes, the fifteenth century saw a transformation of the Marco Polo accounts, known by then as *A Novel about the Great Khan*, into a documentary text that was destined to influence several explorers, Christopher Columbus among them. In it, the figure of the traveler was progressive: he pushed the boundaries of the known and moved mankind ahead. The biography concludes with the following sentences: "Thus the truthful book of Marco Polo labeled the traveler a liar, while the mistake of this book led another traveler to the discovery of America, which he took for Asia."[121] Disbelief turned the author into a liar while the mistake "inspired" by the text led to a remarkable discovery. Shklovsky underlines the productive nature of error and miscalculation as if gesturing toward his "Monument to a Scholarly Error."

Remarkably, Shklovsky's 1936 book also commences not with Venice or China but with nomads dwelling in the Caspian region. It starts with the trope of circular movement by nomads and their cattle on the bare steppes:

> There are nomads on the steppes. Some of them leave for the mountains in the summer, and in winter they descend into valleys where cattle eat dried grass or extract it from the snow. Some of them wander through their steppes, making a complete circle from year to year.
>
> There are wells dug along the circle route. The circles' locations are defined by tradition.
>
> The people don't herd the cattle; the cattle go, and the people follow them.
>
> In the Lokai Valley in Tajikistan, shepherds still tie themselves to rams, so they do not sleep past the time when the ram wakes up and starts grazing.[122]

The preoccupation with mobility derives from a belief that it brings renewal and evolution along with it. As Anne Dwyer puts it, Shklovsky's emphasis on "the shifting, but lasting, marks of the caravan routes" comprises a mode of nomadic resistance: "while empires come and go, the writing and the wandering they sponsored—such as Marco Polo's account—can, at times, against all odds, outlast them."[123] By endorsing nomadism as a theme, Shklovsky justifies it as a formal element—a device. In fact, the circular movement described in *Marco Polo* is itself a reemerging trope. It also appears in *Turksib* in the following rendition:

> Beyond the semi-desert lies the desert. People live in the desert as well. Some kind of grass grows in it, and nomads wander. Don't presume that nomads wander at random. They move in rings. In a huge circle that they complete every year.
>
> Herds, when they eat up all the grass, move on and the people follow the herds. They proceed in a perpetual, closed ring.
>
> The herds move. They eat the grass; they loosen the soil under their hooves. The wind blows, lifts the dust, whirls it around, and carries it to fields. The desert advances.
>
> I used to know one village in the Lower Volga region. There was a meeting. They talked about the necessity to plant willow trees to stop the sand.[124]

What is striking about this passage on eternal nomadic circles is the fact that Shklovsky himself enters a circle of intertextual reference. Firstly, the sentence "the desert advances" already appears in *Third Factory* when Shklovsky describes his encounter with Andrei Platonov as a land reclamation engineer: "Comrade Platonov is very busy. The desert is advancing."[125] The passage resonates with another text: a script based on Platonov's 1926 short story "The Teacher of the Sands" (*Peschanaia uchitel'nitsa*), on which Shklovsky was working with the writer in the late 1920s and which was consequently turned into a film by Nikolai Tikhonov in 1931.[126] The short story indeed takes place in the Lower Volga region and describes tension between nomadic and sedentary groups. After three years of land reclamation efforts, which included the planting of willow trees, the protagonist faces a threat from the nomadic people who are expected to arrive: "Every fifteen years they traversed this nomadic circle in the desert."[127] It is notable that Shklovsky attempted to amplify the antagonism between the settled people and the nomads (he even suggested staging a military confrontation between the two), while Platonov's text presents a much more ambiguous mode of interaction between the two groups.

While nomadism functions as a prominent theme and trope in Shklovsky's 1930s texts as he attempted to reforge his poetics in terms acceptable to the

Stalinist state, it also permeated his earlier texts. Perhaps Shklovsky's most renowned quotation connected to the nomadic way of life was written before the onset of external political pressure. In *Zoo*, he writes: "As a cow devours grass, so literary themes are devoured; devices fray and crumble. A writer cannot be a plowman: he is a nomad, constantly moving with his herd and wife to greener pastures."[128] The writer must lead a nomadic mode of existence, constantly renewing devices and themes. The cultivation of land and the resulting spatial stasis prove to be an unsustainable practice in a purely cultural sense.

Retrospectively, Shklovsky finds traces of cultural nomadism as a progressive force in ancient times. As he notes in his 1931 rendering of the Marco Polo story, the whole medieval world was encompassed by the hectic movement of ethnic groupings: "Then the Greeks were replaced by the Genoese. People in Crimea were also replaced. This type of change took place many times. After all, our world and our way of life are not original. Culture began many times, and different places were interconnected at different times."[129] Culture is presented as an inherently dynamic process, undergoing constant change and oscillating between the poles of heterogeneity and homogeneity: different ethnic formations were interconnected with different peoples at different stages of history. Shklovsky depicts a world devoid of everlasting cultural paradigms.

The dynamism of culture was not Shklovsky's exclusive theoretical invention. In 1924, Iurii Tynianov wrote the seminal essay "Literary Fact" (Literaturnyi fakt), dedicating it to Shklovsky. In the already quoted passage, the influential OPOIAZ member argues that the cultural process can be understood as a relationship between a center and periphery that are constantly swapping places:

> It is not only the *borders* of literature—its "periphery," its liminal regions—that are fluid, but also its very "center." It is not a matter of some primeval, successive stream moving and evolving in the center of literature while new phenomena flow in only at the edges—no, these new phenomena themselves take place in the very center, and the center itself moves away to the periphery.[130]

Tynianov makes a claim—radical for the time—that there is no such concept as an immobile permanent center. The grand narratives of culture rise and fall, and the only constant is the process of interchange. Remarkably, Shklovsky's fellow critic conceptualized this idea in (proto-)postcolonial terms. That fact was not accidental; three years later, Tynianov commenced his 1927 article "On Literary Evolution" with a criticism of the history of literature as a discipline that is comparable to a colonial state, for it imposes its terminological apparatus and general theoretical assumptions on "neighboring" cultural disciplines.[131]

As a result, the latter rely on jargon and scientific postulations alien to their "native" discursive soil. In his article, Tynianov emancipates the field of literary evolution from oppressive literary history, as it was known in the early twentieth century. His theory of evolution defined aesthetic influence as "the transference of the key compositional device from the art of a different artist or a foreign literary tradition."[132] Hence the foreign element plays a crucial role in the literary process and ethnic alterity, by extension, was able to become a driving force.

"On Literary Evolution" marks a major discursive shift for the formal method as well as Shklovsky's subsequent turn toward historicism. Tynianov advocates for the study of literature as an independent and self-regulating system of internal and external relations, animated by historical progression. This was a response to various critics of formalism, who, like Pavel Medvedev, maintained that formalism disregards "the living interactions of concrete social and historical life" or, more fundamentally, delivers a "radical negation of the past ... combined with complete absence of inner content."[133] With the understanding that the temporal flow of history animates formal aspects of any given work of art, it emerges that the seemingly rigid aesthetic system is full of dynamism, manifested in such modes of resistance as parody or appropriation. As Steven Lovell suggests, "it is via history that Tynianov heads away from 'pure' formalism."[134] This statement can be applied to Shklovsky as well. A prime example of this shift is Shklovsky's polemics with Lukács in the late 1930s. In an internal review of Lukács's typescript *The Historical Novel* (Istoricheskii roman) for a state publishing company, Shklovsky criticizes the proposed theory of the novel for underestimating the importance of historical components.[135] Specifically, he argues that the given atemporal view, a view outside history, does not establish a clear connection between the novel and the epic—a connection much needed for understanding the role of folklore in the literary process current at the time (the Soviet late 1930s). This was a crucial historical turn for his late modernist theoretical vision. Shklovsky's conceptualization of folklore, discussion of the impact of modernity on the artistic process, and engagement with the Soviet oriental periphery and the Russocentric populism of the mid- to late 1930s were all taking place through the historic prism.

The newly acquired historicism and the fascination with the oral tradition of the Soviet East emerge in the report Shklovsky wrote after his 1934 trip to Tajikistan, yet another transitional space of the Soviet periphery. The emissary of the Writers' Union fearlessly starts his assessment of the state of the literature of Tajikistan by revealing flaws in the material base of the republic. He notes economic devastation stemming from such detrimental reforms as the rapid expansion of cotton production: as a result of an economic "optimization" campaign during which almost all wheat fields were resown with cotton, the majority of the local population was fed from grassland.[136] This was a rather courageous and risky criticism of the Soviet collectivization project and, at the same time, a reassertion of the Marxist mode of understanding the cultural process. Shklovsky then establishes the need to work with local materials through the example of metal roofs. Metal is scarce in the Central Asian republic, so the insistence on laying metal roofs is irrational. He is convinced that "one has to take the local material and national culture into account"[137] in order for construction projects to be effective.

Driven by the call for economic rationality, he then addresses the ideological-cultural superstructure. Herein lies the importance of folklore for Shklovsky. He emphasizes that the folkloric tradition is still alive in Tajikistan and that it should serve as a foundation for Soviet Tajik literature, for its poets know traditional poetics very well. The idea would become dogma at the First Soviet Writers' Congress a few months after the report. This "local" cultural material, according to Shklovsky, could comprehend the new Soviet thematics and reinforce it with the knowledge of the native everyday life. The smooth fusion of the archaic and the modern was essential.

But the most notable aspect of Shklovsky's report is his unexpected attack on the classically colonial obsession with the "exotic" aspects of the republic's cultural life. He perceived the majority of Soviet-Russian writers sent to produce socialist narratives about the region as colonial agents; they simply projected their epistemic and aesthetic principles onto the supposedly empty slate of foreignness: "People view the country as a barren place while perceiving only its culture as variegated; they do not use the old experience of production and do not understand those contradictions that are found in the old, and in the collision between old and new."[138] It is interesting how Shklovsky conflates the two seemingly incompatible qualifiers: bare and variegated. Tajikistan is a place of cultural emptiness, yet it is filled with "useless" motley items. This approach, Shklovsky continues, cannot yield results. One must consider the preceding traditions, both economic and aesthetic, and their collision with the socialist present.

Despite the political reality of the time, which included the forced resettlement of the local population and the burgeoning Basmachi resistance movement, Shklovsky concludes on a constructive note. When commenting on how Tajikistan was made a separate constituent republic of the Soviet Union in 1929, he sees the positive results of the Soviet nation-building project which was bringing drastic changes to the region: "a new nation is already being created, a national feeling is emerging. Tajikistan was not a nation in the past. People already see themselves as subjects, not objects, while writers often examine them like a landscape."[139] The regaining of subjectivity was already taking place, but the foreign gaze of the colonial mediator still prevailed. That gaze took in a natural inland scenery, devoid of agents of action (whether people or things)—a passive object of contemplation. But Shklovsky, as a key cultural functionary, showed his uninhibited faith in the constructive and edifying nature of culture. This constituted a major discursive shift.

The shift corresponded to the dramatic reformulation of the proletarian culture that was taking place in the 1930s. One of the key components of the socialist realist paradigm was orientation toward the people (*narodnost'*). Folklore, as a lore of the *populi*, provided a point of access to the people: it was supposed to make their voice heard. However, what that voice enunciated had to be within the clearly defined boundaries of homogenous socialist content, which would replace the primitive, patriarchal, feudal content of the past. Thus, folkloric, epic elements functioned as an container—a manifestation of national form—for socialist content. In a cultural sense, they also made the region valid in the socialist present.

Folkloric elements were always present in—even central to—the formalist discourse. As Jessica Merrill has shown, folklore and nineteenth-century theories of folklore played a key constructive role for Shklovsky's *Theory of Prose*.[140] Folklore was a buffer zone where art and life intersected. Moreover, formalism had left a considerable methodological imprint on the study of folklore in the Soviet Union. Such key Soviet theorists of folklore as Vladimir Propp and Viktor Zhirmunsky were profoundly influenced by the formal method. But folklore reemerged with a new intensity and a much more important function in the late 1920s and the early 1930s. Shklovsky's *Matvei Komarov, Resident of the City of Moscow* (Matvei Komarov, zhitel' goroda Moskvy, 1929) and *Chulkov and Levshin* (Chulkov i Levshin, 1930) explore the works of eighteenth-century Russian writers whose texts were informed by fairy tales, folk songs, and *lubok* literature. This comprised a qualitatively different engagement with folkloric material.

This historical turn was yet another crucial point of reorientation. The pressure to conform to the general discursive line of patriotism with national-epic overtones did not fully overwhelm Shklovsky, who still managed to inscribe formalist logic even in supposedly anti-formalist texts. In the 1939 *Diary*, for instance, renewal of the perception of the world remains a rallying cry: "The fight against formalism is a fight for the perceptible [*oshchutimyi*] world, for a method as method and not for a method as the content of art.... We need to get rid of formalism, a phrase that is routine and false in the current circumstances, and get used to the language of heroism. We need to remember the national pride of the Great Russians, and not be afraid to display good fortune."[141] Ilya Kalinin's argument—that the "language of heroism," together with the role of the individual in the flow of history, can be understood as the final stage in the development of the device of *ostranenie*—should be modified:[142] the importance of the historical component led to Shklovsky's renewed interest in folklore and the cultural "fringes" of the country, where the defamiliarizing energy of *ostranenie* could have been utilized with renewed vigor. Yielding to historical pressure to transform, Shklovsky discovered this last outpost of strangeness.

In 1939, acknowledging the wealth of ethnic traditions in the Soviet Union, Shklovsky writes: "Folklore in our country has not perished. It is here, it is right next to us. The relationship between folklore and new literature has not yet been resolved, but the strength of our literature is in folklore."[143] The anonymity of the ancient oral texts that developed into authorial folkloric stardom during the Soviet 1930s appeals to Shklovsky. He signals the development of a new theory of authorship that is not limited to the artistic sphere and incorporates every practice of labor. He argues that almost all labor processes cease to be anonymous in a country where labor is a central category: "our time and our labor have become authors. In our country, the labor of a concrete worker, the labor of a bricklayer, the labor of a combine operator are all signed [like a work of art]."[144] The tension between the individual and the collective—individual heroic effort and mass enthusiasm—is resolved by the all-encompassing recognition of authorship. Professionalism, comprehensive knowledge of one's vocation, fuses with the enthusiasm of socialist construction to serve as a guarantee of prominence. This results in the emergence of a new type of authorship: Tikhon Semushkin (a teacher from Chukotka), Aleksandr Beliakov (a jet pilot), and Ernst Krenkel' (an Arctic explorer), all professionals whose deep knowledge of their respective crafts allowed them to produce mesmerizing texts ("book-documents about a life that didn't pass by"),[145] represent a new type of Soviet artist. Shklovsky concludes that "we have art everywhere."[146] Art finally enters life; it has stopped defamiliarizing it.

During the late 1910s and the early 1920s, the significance of raw materials and the objects made from them was largely irrelevant: the obliteration of the old world and the things that constituted it dominated political discourse. In the avant-garde context, the materiality of the everyday constituted an inert force of capitalism that resisted the transformative force of the revolution. Kazimir Malevich famously stated in one of his manifestos: "Objects [things] have vanished like smoke; to attain the new artistic culture, art advances toward creation as an end in itself and toward domination over the forms of nature."[147] For the Shklovsky of this period, form, in relation to everyday material, was endowed with an ability to intensify the *sensation of things*. For the Shklovsky of the late 1920s, on the other hand, a deep professional knowledge of the technical aspect of the thing, whether a film script or an armored car, became a guarantee for effective formal experiments.[148] But for the late modernist Shklovsky of the 1930s, form as such did not *defamiliarize* the thing, but rather made it look and feel *simple* and *useful*. The emphasis on renewed perception was replaced by the acknowledgment of materiality and its utilitarian potential. Formalism leaves the cerebral seminar room of the avant-garde, as it were, and exits out onto the Central Asian roads. It becomes "real," physical, and seeks to be productive.

This transformation constitutes a substantial discursive shift, for it makes the notion of content finally relevant to the formal method. Content entered Soviet cultural life together with an "orientation" toward "human values." Shklovsky, in his very short penitential speech at the First Soviet Writers' Congress in 1934, highlighted his own shift as a former member of avant-garde movements:

> We, in particular the former LEFers, removed everything practicable [*poleznoe*], thinking that this was an aesthetic move; we, being constructivists, created a construction that turned out to be unconstructive. We underappreciated humanity and the universal appeal of the revolution. Now we can solve the question of humanity and new humanism. Humanism enters the structure of the epoch.[149]

Stalin's infamous declaration of 1935, "Life has become better! Life has become happier!" is further testimony to the transformed Soviet *byt* (the everyday), how its everyday objects manifested the fullness of life. It was a celebration of the new content of the socialist state because Stalinist civilization began as a leap toward the mass production of things that defined the wealth and well-being of the nation. For the formalists, the *everyday*, with its mundane tediousness, was a point of departure. For Stalinist culture, the *everyday* equals everyday heroism— it is profoundly self-sufficient and needs to be celebrated, not defamiliarized.

The reoriented Shklovsky mused about producing a thematic album with Stalin's maxim as its title; there is a two-page description of the project in his archive. The first half was supposed to provide dismal pre-revolutionary statistics and quotes from the great Russian authors (Pushkin, Gogol, Tolstoy) who had exposed czarist Russia as "a poor, sick, dreary, malnourished country."[150] The second half intended to glorify achievements of Soviet everyday life, from the emergence of bed sheets to the disappearance of wooden spoons. As Shklovsky puts it, "this is how fork, plate, boots appear in our lives and the window gets bigger."[151] The construction of this sentence mirrors the critic's famous line depicting the effect of automatization: "And so, held accountable for nothing, life fades into nothingness. Automatization eats away at things, at clothes, at furniture, at our wives, and at our fear of war."[152] Now life, instead of disappearing, becomes better and happier. Things do not dematerialize because of automatized perception—they emerge because (nominally) they are produced by the new society for its consumption. These new and practical items drastically redefined the Soviet way of life and also created a sense of astonishment that functioned as a surrogate *ostranenie*: "We present the everyday life of a child and surround him with things as if they've newly emerged."[153] Shklovsky concludes his proposal by highlighting the positive change the Revolution brought to the daily lives of national minorities: the emergence of the proletariat and professionals in Kazakhstan.[154] The unsung hymn of the new Soviet life glorified both material everyday objects and the diversity of the country—the two aspects that provided *ostranenie* with a new discursive territory for expansion.

CHAPTER 2

SOCIALIST VISION

Aleksandr Rodchenko and Varvara Stepanova

The year 1914 was a defining period in the personal life and professional career of Aleksandr Rodchenko (1891–1956). Two pivotal events took place in Kazan, a key oriental outpost of the Russian Empire, where he studied easel painting at a local art school. He attended a reading of futurist poetry by David Burliuk, Vasilii Kamensky, and Vladimir Maiakovsky, after which he immediately became an adherent of the most radical aesthetic movement in Russia. In the same year, at a student party, the new convert to futurism met his future spouse Varvara Stepanova (1894–1958), a collaboration that would last until his death.

Rodchenko and Stepanova, the celebrated couple of the avant-garde, had great influence on theoretical debates of the time and shaped the trajectory of Russian and Soviet art in the twentieth century. Among the so-called "Amazons" of the avant-garde, Stepanova was an original and influential theorist of art. Her theoretical investigations into the domain of material composition, photomontage, and constructivism in general are indispensable. Rodchenko, in turn, is one of the most notable theorists of the image. His excursuses into the sphere of non-objectivity and his *LEF* articles on photography have become required reading for students of the visual arts. His 1936 "repentance," by contrast, comprises a rather bizarre but informative set of reflections on the fate of the visual arts in the first socialist society.

In addition to their corpus of theoretical writings, the couple's often playful and affectionate letters to each other functioned as another site for aesthetic deliberation. In 1925, for instance, Rodchenko traveled to Paris to participate in the International Exhibition of Modern Decorative and Industrial Arts where he exhibited the now-canonical design for the Workers' Club. This trip prompted a torrent of impressions, as is evident from his multiple letters to Stepanova. In one of them, written on May 4, 1925, Rodchenko reflects on Russia's uneasy relationship with the West: "The light from the East is not only the liberation of workers; the light from the East is in the new relation to the person, to woman, to things. Our things in our hands must also be equals, also be comrades, and not these black and mournful slaves, as they are here. The art of the East should be nationalized and rationed."[1] Rodchenko, while using emancipatory rhetoric, establishes a new set of affective relationships with the world of things by glorifying what Christina Kiaer identifies as "the comradely object of socialist modernity."[2] He also sees socialist art as the art of the East, as if assuming a Eurocentric geographical position. Its advent is a radical revision of the world order of things. The egalitarian "Eastern" socialist culture of which Rodchenko was a representative in Paris, an Eastern ray of light, would subsequently be replaced with the totalizing dark force of Stalinism. But in 1925 the radiance was still there.

Seven years prior to Rodchenko's private exchange, Joseph Stalin's article "Light from the East" was published as an editorial in several newspapers. The text describes the growing proletarian resistance to the "national bourgeoisie" in the Baltic states and opens with the following sentence: "Slowly but surely, the tide of the liberation movement is rolling from East to West, into the occupied regions."[3] Stalin proceeds to claim Soviet Russia's role as a leader, "the standard-bearer of world revolution" of "these stupendous developments . . . for the benefit of world socialism."[4] Russia, with its centuries of conquest and subjugation by and of oriental lands, assumes an emancipatory role in relation to the Western-oriented Baltic states. Stalin emphatically concludes his article with the following words: "Light is coming from the East! The West, with its imperialist cannibals, has become a breeding ground of darkness and slavery. The task is to destroy this breeding ground, to the joy and comfort of the working people of all countries."[5] The revolution is identified as an annihilator of the old order of things, which to him, as well as to Rodchenko, is a source of darkness and slavery.

The Latin phrase "Ex Oriente lux" refers, in its original sense, to the sun rising in the East. The East is a point of origination and a point of orientation since the sun's path functions as a natural indicator of temporal progression. However, this stance would undergo a substantial modification in the mid-1930s. Russia as an oriental outpost would be transformed, or rather it would be reoriented towards its own Orient: the republics of Central Asia. It would assume the role of the enlightening Westernizing force while building socialism in one country.

Unlike the other protagonists of this book, Rodchenko and Stepanova never traveled to Central Asia—they visualized the region from the comfort and convenience of the metropolitan center as "virtual tourists."[6] Neither did they systematically theorize their engagement with Soviet oriental material but left only sporadic remarks. However, their body of work dedicated to the oriental periphery, which emerged after the torrent of attacks on Formalism and thus comprised a hands-on attempt at reorientation, is considerable and prominent. Among these works is a 1935 issue of the journal *USSR in Construction*, dedicated to the fifteenth anniversary of the creation of the Soviet Republic of Kazakhstan, and two large photobooks: *Ten Years of Soviet Uzbekistan* (1934) and *Kazakhstan* (1949). The significance of Rodchenko and Stepanova's theoretical legacy is difficult to overestimate, and the three works, despite their own attempts to inscribe them into mainstream Soviet culture in order to comply with an imposed set of representational instructions, indicate deep reflection and imagination. These works constitute a testing ground for the avant-garde's will and compulsion to evolve, however erratic and incongruous its tactical moves might appear.[7]

Rodchenko and Stepanova's professional trajectories were not in sync with each other. Stepanova was much more theoretically active during the early period and covered foundational questions of material form, while Rodchenko thrived as a theorist of the photographic image in the late 1920s. However, it is evident that the two were in constant conversation, as were their aesthetic conceptions and perspectives. In terms of practical activities, there is no material evidence of who did what, and hence I will treat their work on the three photobooks in question as indivisibly collaborative. Their respective theoretical contributions will be treated individually.

The chapter begins with an overview of the principles of early constructivism, including the critical distinction between *depiction* (*izobrazitel'nost'*) and *painterliness* (*zhivopisnost'*). The next section explores Rodchenko's infamous repentance and his earlier involvement with the October Group, as well as the debates they initiated. The question of national form and alterity was a focal point for the group's theoretical concerns. The "Reconstruction of the Country" provides an overview of Rodchenko and Stepanova's highly modernist book-design experiments, commissioned for *USSR in Construction*. The subsequent section, "Construction of the Nation," shifts focus to a seemingly more conservative photobook, *Ten Years of Soviet Uzbekistan*. Finally, I use the 1949 album *Kazakhstan* to examine a drastic aesthetic shift in the couple's working method.

PRINCIPLES OF CONSTRUCTIVISM

The early Greek philosophical concept of form, as a non-physical essence of all things, is strongly linked with several words that relate to vision. In *The Republic*, Plato employs aspects of sight and appearance to explain the Forms and the Good; the Greek words εἶδος (eidos) and ἰδέα (idea) derive from the Indo-European root *weid*—"see." Traditionally, *vision* has not just been identified with the mere faculty of being able to see but has also been an inherently conceptual tool. Stalinist culture shared this expanded understanding of the word. Ushakov's dictionary, while defining the noun *zrenie* (vision), immediately offers an instance of its figurative use: "adhering to a Marxist point of view."[8] Indeed, a Marxist point of view, though loosely defined, shaped sociopolitical and aesthetic discussions of the 1930s and was instrumental in the process of setting up the Soviet optics of perception.

Photography represented the ultimate visual domain of Stalinism. The political apparatus valued its monumental stillness over the dynamism of the cinematic image while its indexicality and immediacy were considered more instrumental than labor-intensive easel painting. Prolifically used in party-controlled media and propaganda, photography established visual standards that enforced a "correct" Marxist point of view. *Pravda* and *Izvestiia*, the two leading Soviet newspapers, switched to a visually saturated format in 1933, thus utilizing the instant persuasiveness of the photographic material to its full extent. Numerous propaganda posters and brochures cultivated a correct ideological outlook and instructed the Soviet people on how to see and perceive the world. In this sense, Rodchenko's and Stepanova's theoretical legacy and practical achievements in the visual sphere are indispensable for any analysis of how Soviet visual standards were conceived and modified in the 1920s and 1930s.

The couple also played an instrumental role in the formation of the Working Group of Constructivists, which came into existence in March 1921 and immediately evolved into one of the central hubs of the avant-garde movement. Constructivism was both a product and a constituent of modernity. Christina Lodder influentially defines the movement as an artistic practice with "an approach to working with materials, within a certain conception of their potential as active participants in the process of social and political transformation."[9] The constructivists attempted to achieve their goal by disrupting sets of binary pairs such as art vs. reality and reflection vs. production. Rodchenko's spatial structures, which were made from real materials with a pronounced industrial emphasis, were produced by the "artist-constructor" and the "artist-engineer." The factory, as a collective enterprise, an antithesis to bourgeois individualism, was the movement's ultimate locus not just for material production but also as a source of creative force in the world. Art and life no longer comprised an antagonistic pair: mass production and industry merged them into one entity. As Rodchenko puts it, "the art of the future will not be cozy decorations for domestic apartments. It will be as necessary as forty-eight-story skyscrapers, grandiose bridges, as the wireless telegraph, aeronautics, submarines, and so on."[10] Indeed, in March 1921, the constructivists announced that they intended to abandon easel painting altogether and would concentrate their efforts on the production of utilitarian objects. The concept of construction was an antidote to the toxic decadence of painting. Technology functioned as a means of active creation and replaced representation in the narrow sense.

Constructivism's productivist shift toward the industrial process and away from the making of works of art defined early Soviet aesthetic coordinates. Escaping subjectivity was one of the key aspirations in this anti-representational quest. In place of the subjective aesthetic experience, adherents of the movement offered objectivity of structures and forms. The constructivist object was an empirically derived, impersonalized, utilitarian product that lacked any aesthetic aspects. Rodchenko and Stepanova's early preoccupation with the material formation of the object repudiated any form of superfluous aesthetic decoration. However, as Lodder convincingly argues, though the constructivist-designed object was allegedly devoid of style, as a superfluous artistic rendering, it still employed its own formal language that can amount to a style: "the constructivist system of organizing form became expressed in skeletal angular structures, in rectangularity, simplicity, economy of line and material and a geometric solution to surface arrangements."[11]

Constructivism is known for its pronounced engagement with physical materials: glass, concrete, cast iron, and wire lent themselves to simplicity of man-made forms and referenced the technologized worlds of modern engineering. However, *vision* constituted an important immaterial operative category. During a discussion in April 1922, Rodchenko boldly argued that the difference between the engineer and the artist "lies in just this fact that *we know how to see.*"[12] Only artistic vision, combined with the engineer's technical knowledge, can produce a constructivist artifact. Non-representational in essence, this artifact must participate in a process of renewal of human perception through a radical transformation of the material. Thus, the constructivists radically dissolved the discursive and material boundaries between representation, perception, and consumption with vision and technical knowledge playing a key part. This resonates with Shklovsky's suggestion that the constructivist "artist" aspires toward "the creation of a new world of sensations, the transference or dissemination of the materials of the construction of artistic things to the construction of the 'things of daily life'."[13]

Materiality, perception, and vision were all amalgamated in one of the key fundamental notions of constructivism—*faktura* (*texture* or *facture*). One of a troika of elements that were initially theorized by Aleksei Gan (with *tektonika* and *construction* being the other two), it stands for "the processing of the material as a whole."[14] *Faktura* is a testimony to a conviction that the form of a produced object is largely determined by the material from which it is made. Furthermore, "the purposeful use of the material means its selection and processing, and the nature of its processing for a specific purpose is *faktura*."[15] Thus, *faktura* is not a state but a process of handling material. The transformative aspect is its key feature.

In Stepanova's rendering, *faktura* was instrumental in the evolution of the arts, conceived as a departure from *depiction* (*izobrazitel'nost'*) through *painterliness* (*zhivopisnost'*) and toward *functionalism*. The fundamental difference between *depiction* and *painterliness* is principal. Stepanova, in her appeal to Gan, identifies artists who are more concerned with emotion and literariness (e.g., Leonardo, Vermeer, the Russian Wanderers) as adherents of *depiction*, while those who are preoccupied with materiality and plasticity (e.g., Rembrandt, Cézanne) are seen as practitioners of *painterliness*. The presented tension lies between a fictional representation that erases the presence of the material on one hand, and on the other, an attempt to imprint reality, to mold an impression of it by material means—the Russian word for painting (*zhivopis'*) literally means "writing live." The latter strategy played a formative role for the constructivists. As Stepanova puts it, "the painter who gradually adopts an increasingly formalist position moves first of all from the manner of painting to elaborate the plane, and then goes on to working up the state of the material."[16] This subjugates the category of meaning through an effort of material form.

This stance aligns with some aspects of Rodchenko's perspective on the history of art. According to notes made by Stepanova on March 5, 1919, one of Rodchenko's first reflections on art was strongly infused with the discourse of *defamiliarization*: he argued that art as such emerged only when a brush stroke that reflected an illusion of naturalness from a distance appeared instead of a smoothly painted face.[17] Thus, the defamiliarized impression of reality (the coarseness of the brush stroke), and not a perfectly imitated imprint of it, forms the core of artistic practice: "this exaggeration of the object, its underscoring, even its irregularity in comparison with its natural state [*natura*] is art, it is creative work."[18] A conscious departure from aesthetic illusion is imperative for both Stepanova and Rodchenko.

A process of overcoming *depiction* marked Stepanova's early printing experiments. In the late 1910s, she produced handmade books that were displayed as separate sheets pasted on boards. Stepanova treated each sheet's surface as a space for the collision of textual and visual elements by establishing synesthetic connections between the acoustic sound of the verse (*phoneme*) and its visual representation (*grapheme*). The book, as a medium, operated as a neutral field on which the tension between the two was enacted—it allowed the reader to overcome the monotony of printed letters through painterly graphics (*zhivopisnaia grafika*).[19] Very often (e.g., in *Gaust chaba*) the artist incorporates printed texts cut from newspapers and sets it against handwritten—or rather, hand-drawn—trans-sense verse (the newspaper text is usually "misplaced" on a vertical plane; viewers can read it only by turning their heads or the work itself). Text functions in multiple ways: as semantically stable and ready-made (e.g., mundane newspaper reportage), and as meaning-transcending *texture*. As the futurist book came to displace the established hierarchy in book design, the visual component ceased to be a supplement to the text. The two evolved into a composite image (*obraz*) that was simultaneously literary and visual. As Alexander Lavrentiev argues, these cut-and-paste experiments prepared the formal ground for subsequent photomontage and book-design practices.[20]

Once the artist makes the material of the canvas or paper salient for the viewer, *faktura* accomplishes a further qualitative leap, as is evident from constructivism's evolution. Everyday utilitarian function supersedes artistic practice, revealing the inherent qualities of the material: "When art moved from a contemplative domain to an active one the productive process, that is the concept of facture, changed with it. I consider facture to be a production process."[21] *Faktura* ceases to operate at the level of representation altogether and evolves into a concept that reveals the very technological process used to produce it. It acquires functional attributes and starts serving the industrial and ideological agenda of the proletariat.[22] As a purposeful necessity (*tselesoobraznaia neobkhodimost'*), *faktura*, together with construction, prompts a radical rethinking of the function and nature of art: "The contemplative and representational activity of art is shifting to an active conscious action, by that very process destroying the concept of the spiritual nature of the artist's creative process, which has existed till now."[23] Construction and *faktura* comprised an attack on the spiritual and ideational aspects of the work of art and entered the domain of design and production.

The constructivists described their design endeavors as "artistic construction" (*khudozhestvennoe konstruirovanie*) that reflected a need for artistic and technical skills. Their skill set found practical application in typographical and printing projects in the 1920s.[24] The functional-technical and rational technological expediency of graphic design allowed the constructivists to search for novel forms. In their experiments, they utilized a newspaper layout and radically attacked the symmetry of the book page. The physical qualities of typographic material were made perceptible. As a result, excessive decoration was replaced by simple shapes, sans-serif typefaces supplanted ornate lettering, and photomontage took over the illustration.

A call for functionalism found its partial fulfillment in photomontage, as an ideologically and socially meaningful practice with an aspiration toward the redefinition of the representational systems of the new socialist society. The constructivists believed that photography neutralized the need for *depiction*, for no other art could contest its ability to produce the likeness of the real. Besides, its innate and direct connection with reality, through the precise fixation of fact, made it utilizable. The photographic image, a documentary fact, is integrated into the fabric of photomontage as a constitutive element. Meticulously interspersed and amalgamated photographic images effectively provided both documentation and presentation of a process of social transformation and constituted, in Benjamin Buchloh's words, "an artistic procedure that supposedly carries transformative potential *qua* procedure."[25] The real achievements, whether ideological or industrial, were endowed with clear political meaning, and photomontage fulfilled its utilitarian function by molding the psyche of the proletariat.

In this context, Stepanova's 1928 article "Photomontage" is arguably a watershed that divides the classic Constructivist vision from the emerging late modernist reformulation of the movement's basic principles that would take place in the 1930s.[26] Practices of photomontage served as a catalyst, a certain shared discursive territory that integrated the productivist agenda with the ideological indoctrination of emerging Stalinist culture. Constructivist compositional nonobjective and spatial experiments, which transformed passive, contemplative modes of seeing, provided the formal vocabulary for photomontage with its active instrumental orientation.

Stepanova begins her article by arguing that printed media such as newspapers and posters record phenomena, whereas a drawing can only fail to capture their real documentary nature. The construction of a photomontage requires an indexical photographic image and its transformation by means of montage and assemblage (*montirovanie i komponovanie*).[27] The productivist turn forced artists to employ "documentary precision" and thus they had to engage with the photographic apparatus. Rodchenko seems to be in full agreement with Stepanova when he argues that photomontage essentially assembles photographic facts and not fictional representations (drawn images): "Precision and documentality make such a strong impression that is not achievable for painting and graphic [works]. A poster with photographs has a much stronger impact than a poster with a drawing on the same theme."[28]

However, there was a substantial difference in how the photograph was utilized in photomontages throughout the period. According to Stepanova, photocollages of the early 1920s were characterized by "the combination of a large number of photos into a single general composition by cutting out separate photo-images" resulting in "planar mounting on the white field of the paper."[29] The later, politically oriented photomontage, however, was exemplified by individual snapshots that were "no longer cut up and now had all the characteristics of an original document."[30] The photographic image, as a nexus of the artistic and the real, becomes self-sufficient: it "is no longer raw material for montage or for some kind of illustrated composition, but has now become an independent and complete work [in itself]."[31] *Completeness* can be understood as a totality aspiring towards a full confluence with reality—representation converges with the represented.

Lodder persuasively suggests that the indexicality and visual accuracy of a photograph was "a compromise with that powerful move towards realism and the attempt to create a popular Soviet art."[32] The photographic image gradually evolves into a powerful artistic medium capable of contesting easel painting. The real object, as the subject matter of a photograph, was mechanically reproduced and made available for ideological consumption. The belief in a totalistic artistic vision, which replaces aesthetic representation in the narrow sense with a real-life transformative agenda, was enacted and utilized for the purposes of socialist construction. Photographic indexicality starts pointing to a vision of a rapidly changing socialist society.

In the early 1920s, Rodchenko relied on a personal photographic archive and stock photos while working on his photomontages. Freely cutting and pasting images and combining them with graphic elements, he "authorized" his final creations using his signature. The signature inscribed his authorial presence, though the documentary nature of the components stood for his presence as a mounter-assembler, not an author. In 1924, he exhausted his archive and felt a compositional need to engage in single-frame still photography and produce his own oblique-angle photographs. In a way, photomontage experiments influenced and even enabled Rodchenko's photographic practice, allowing the artist to complete a full representational circle: from the easel painting image, to construction, and then back to the image, this time a photographic one. For Buchloh, the move signaled a transformation of *faktura*—it was replaced "by a new concern for the *factographic* capacity of the photograph, supposedly rendering aspects of reality visible without interference or mediation."[33]

Rodchenko quickly mastered the camera and developed his signature set of devices that he also substantiated theoretically. For him, modernity, with its unprecedented speeds and heights, impacts the way humans perceive the world. Spatial fluidity and distortion of conventional proportions and forms are necessary to keep up with it. As he writes in one of his most important articles, "The Paths of Contemporary Photography," in 1928:

We don't see what we're looking at.

We don't see marvelous perspectives—foreshortening [*rakursov*] and the positioning of objects.

We, who have been taught to see the customary and inculcated, must reveal the world of the visible. We must revolutionize our visual thinking.

We must remove the veil that is called "navel level" from our eyes.

"Photograph from all viewpoints, except the 'navel,' until all viewpoints are recognized."

"And the most interesting viewpoints of today are the 'top-down' and 'bottom-up' perspectives, and their diagonal counterparts."[34]

Rodchenko's shooting instructions announce a vision of a new Soviet man—a subject of modernity. These are not merely aesthetic preconditions, for they comprise a new vision, an epistemological principle deriving from an industrial experience. *Foreshortening* (Rodchenko uses the word *rakurs* which stands for an unconventional camera angle, a diagonal viewpoint)[35] radically challenges the recognizability of the photographed object. Sharp optical foreshortening brings an object's structure into an amplified visibility. By manipulating space and proportions it accomplishes an axonometric exploration of the world. Rodchenko experimented with horizontal planes, and some of his most radical photographs defy gravity—there are no clear-cut spatial relations that can be easily identified (for instance, his 1935 photographs of divers). Depth flattens. Space collapses.

Retrospectively, in 1958, Sergei Morozov provided a summary of Rodchenko and his followers' key principles. The critic disapprovingly identified several tenets of the "internal montage" of the shot (*vnutrikadrovvyi montazh*): *upakovka*—"filling the frame," literally "packing-in" of the material; *razgon po uglam*—"pushing the composition to the corners of the frame" or "working the corners of the frame" when all four corners are compositionally active; *kosina*, "obliqueness" or "slantiness"—the vertical or horizontal compositional lines of the frame meet "at oblique angles"; the application of optics "in reverse"—using wide-angle or telephoto lenses to shoot subjects that would usually be photographed using lenses with different focal lengths.[36]

For the inventors of this set of defamiliarizing devices, however, it accomplishes an important cognitive function. The unusually tilted viewpoints of Rodchenko's photographic images give "a full impression of the object."[37] The radical distortion of proportions and scales of the represented people and objects is a clear *ostranenie* procedure that leads to a new way of looking at the world—it produces a new vision of reality that, in turn, enriches human vision.

Foreshortening's defamiliarizing function is, of course, endorsed by Shklovsky, who argues that "everyone shoots from his point of view and this point of view replaces an artistic orientation [*khudozhestvennuiu ustanovsku*]."[38] But an *artistic orientation* cannot be a steady constant, according to the principles of formalism. Thus, foreshortening is engaged in a process of perpetual defamiliarization—and this stance strongly resonates with Rodchenko:

> They say: "We're sick of Rodchenko's pictures—everything's photographed from the top down or the bottom up."
>
> But they've been taking pictures from "the middle to the middle"—for about a hundred years; not only should I, but the majority should take pictures from the bottom up and the top down.
>
> But I will photograph from "side to side."[39]

Thus, when the "top-down" and "bottom-up" viewpoints become a convention, the photographer chooses to shoot "from side to side." Herein lies his deep disagreement with the critic Boris Kushner, who provided a comradely critique of Rodchenko's prescriptive insistence on the primacy of radical foreshortening.[40] The misunderstanding arises from the fact that point of view, for Rodchenko, is always a variable entity. Its unconventionality is facilitated by an evolutionary aesthetic drive.

This variability defines Rodchenko's vision of photographic art in opposition to painting. For him, the claim of the leading journal *Soviet Photo* (Sovetskoe foto) that the "photo-picture" is "something closed and eternal" is profoundly erroneous.[41] Instead, he asserts the validity of the photographic image by referencing its triumph over established painterly representations: "Take the history of art or the history of painting of all countries and you'll see that all paintings, with negligible exceptions, are painted either 'from the navel' or at eye level."[42] Conventional photographic shots from "center to center," from the navel level, thus, comprise an anachronism that was cultivated by centuries of painting. Overcoming the plane of *depiction* resonates in photography. Foreshortening defamiliarizes the perspectival convention and refuses to follow the reactionary inertia of artistic representation. It turns photography into an autonomous and progressive artistic practice.

How to represent a human subject in photography naturally becomes one of the most immediate concerns with the increasingly cultlike aspirations of the Stalinist state. In 1928, *New LEF* published several articles attempting to prescribe certain practical and conceptual ways. In one, Osip Brik argued forcefully against staged shots, which present political leaders as isolated "heroic" individuals and thus reference imitate painterly portraits.[43] He suggested they should instead be presented in their habitual environment, and in natural (not always perfect) postures, engaged in routine activities. The connection with a broader social stratum was crucial: "The task of the contemporary photographer is not to catch a people's commissar when he is alone and is found in a photographic position, but quite the contrary, it is to catch him when he is connected with his environment to the greatest extent and acts in reality, not photographically."[44]

In the very next issue, Rodchenko published an article on the difference between painterly and photographic portraits, "Against the Synthetic Portrait for the Snapshot." The article opens with the observation that an easel painting depicts a human subject as the sum of observations made through the prism of the artist's subjective vision—it presents an "ultimate" truth about the sitter. Modernity, with its fast pace and discoveries that constantly challenge established truths, lives in an ever-evolving moment. Thus, Rodchenko argues, the "instantaneous" (*momental'nyi*) photographic shot is the most efficient way to represent a human subject in the twentieth century: "Record [*fiksiruite*] man not by a single 'synthetic' portrait, but by a mass of instantaneous snapshots taken at different times and in different conditions."[45] Basically, an instantaneous shot is a certain visual take on a human subject.

In 1928, Lenin remained the central human figure prompting debates on photographic representation. Sets of conceptual binary pairs—document versus fiction, instantaneity versus history, the particular versus the general—delineated these debates. As Rodchenko argues:

> I maintain that there is no summation of Lenin, and there cannot be one and the same summation of Lenin for everyone ... But there is a summation of him. This is a representation based on photographs, books, and notes.
>
> It should be stated firmly that with the appearance of photographic documents, there can be no question of a single, immutable portrait. Moreover, a man is not just one sum total; he is many sum totals, and sometimes they are quite opposed.[46]

This comprised a consistent attempt to challenge any attempts at generalizations. Only a documentary archive, as part of a broader social reality, can present the figure of Lenin in its entirety. As far as photography is concerned, Lenin is many Lenins. Pluralism is essential.

RECONSTRUCTION OF THE SELF

Rodchenko was engaged in theoretical debates about photography at the time when he joined the October Group (officially, the All-Russian Association of Workers of New Types of Artistic Labor "October") that was founded in 1928. His membership, at first in the interior design and then in the photographic section, proved to be fateful for his career. Initially, however, the group did seem to be a comradely union of professionals with considerable artistic and ideological influence. It united a significant number of prominent avant-garde architects, artists, filmmakers, and critics such as Aleksandr Deineka, Sergei Eisenstein, Aleksei Gan, Moisei Ginzburg, Gustav Klutsis (Gustavs Klucis), Esfir' Shub, and Aleksandr and Viktor Vesnin. The very first sentence of its manifesto, published in *Pravda* in 1928, states that spatial arts, including architecture, painting, sculpture, photography, and cinema, should submit "to the task of serving the concrete needs of the proletariat as a hegemon, leading the peasantry and backward nationalities."[47] The statement highlighted the group's practical and enlightening mission of eliminating social and national "backwardness." It also reconfirmed the avant-garde's demand to endow art with an important social function, thus undermining the life-art divide.

The October Group's theoretical stances were instrumental to Rodchenko's "fall" and the discursive backlash he received in the early 1930s. A barrage of pointed attacks following the group's photography exhibition in 1931 forced him to move to the outer reaches of Soviet artistic life until 1935. But before this event, which was a harbinger of the emerging cultural shift, October played a pivotal role in shaping discourse within the domain of visual arts in the Soviet Union—it was the most prominent post-*LEF* coalition of supporters of the avant-garde. The group was well-funded, and it supervised the work of Izogiz (the State Fine Arts Press)—the chief state publishing house for the visual arts. Its activities and theoretical elaborations comprised a singular attempt to function as a discursive viaduct connecting the already fading experimental tradition with emerging but not yet clearly articulated late modernist trends.

The February 1931 brochure, titled *Struggle for Proletarian Class Positions on the Front of Spatial Arts* (Bor'ba za klassovye proletarskie pozitsii na fronte prostranstvennykh iskusstv), was designed by Solomon Telingater, a VKhUTEMAS-educated graphic designer, who applied a somewhat restrained constructivist-inspired typography. The stylistic choice was conscious and reflected the movement's aspiration to depart from the abstract aesthetic radicalism of early Soviet aesthetics and to serve the proletariat's ideological and artistic needs in a more conventional manner.

In its published vision of the formation of proletarian culture, the October Group identified three possible ways of dealing with preceding styles: *imitation*, *contraposition* (*protivopostavlenie*), and *transformation*.[48] Imitation is immediately discarded as a superfluous practice, but contraposition and transformation are heralded as two possible ways to form a progressive proletarian culture. Contraposition, as an expression of class antagonism, is conceived as a productive negative force fueled by a daring artistic experiment that challenges established bourgeois positions. Its role, essentially synonymous with that of the avant-garde, is pronounced as an indispensable emancipatory force. Transformation, however, is also identified as another way forward: a critical appropriation of selected artistic styles should result in the creation of an advanced proletarian culture that is conscious of preceding formal achievements.

The avant-garde initially opposed the vision of socialist culture as edification or as a proletarian inheritance of bourgeois culture, but this radical position had to be reconsidered. The authors of the manifesto stress that the creation of a new artistic style should be an inherently "organic process."[49] This position shares a striking similarity with the later definition of socialist realism as a critical appropriation and reworking of the world's cultural heritage. However, socialist realism, which gradually evolved into the practice of stylistic *imitation* of realist nineteenth-century art (albeit with socialist content), is at clear odds with the October Group's vision.

In another October publication, the association proclaims its intention to serve the concrete needs of the Soviet proletariat—"a total hegemon, leading the peasantry and backward nationalities" by organizing its psyche and everyday life (*byt*).[50] The group was one of the first to introduce the term "proletarian realism."[51] This realism was dynamic: "showing life in movement, in action, systematically revealing perspectives of life in a planned way, a realism that makes things, rationally transforms the old everyday life, acts with all artistic means in the thickness of struggle and construction."[52] This represented the avant-garde's voluntary transformation since the proclamation rejected the "abstract industrialism" and "naked technicism" of the past—elements used in productivist and constructivist experiments—as revolutionary practices.

The October Group also prominently included the Nationalities Unit, which sought to weave a national dimension into the fabric of proletarian culture. In its declaration, the Unit acknowledged the uneven development of different nationalities and proclaimed that backward nationalities ought to skip the capitalist stage in their effort toward building socialism.[53] It also argued that the uneven development of national forms did not affect in any way the "ideological content of the Soviet arts."[54] National heritage and its formal achievements should be critically reassessed and appropriated for socialist construction and the creation of a new "proletarian style."⁵⁵ This comprised one of the earliest conceptualizations of the interdependence of socialist content and national form.

In 1931, Lazar Rempel' wrote an important article "On National Art" in *Brigade of Artists*, the October Group's journal. This comprised October's official stance on national form as such and the article was conspicuously featured on the very first page of the issue. Rempel' tackles the content-form conundrum in terms that are exceedingly close to those that would be articulated five years later as an official Soviet position:

> The proletarian content of national art is not simply defined by a topic [*siuzhetom*], but by a relation to reality that is expressed by the artist, as a representative of class ideology. This relation is expressed in art through the unity of content and form, where "content is not formless and form is rich in content [*soderzhatel'na*]," with content playing the leading role.
>
> The content of proletarian national art is the construction of socialism.⁵⁶

The question of "national form" and its symbiotic unity with content acquired more orientalist undertones during a conference held in April of 1931 at the Leningrad branch of the Communist Academy. The conference featured many prominent October members, including János Mácza (Ivan Matsa), a Soviet art critic of Hungarian descent specializing in the Soviet avant-garde, who led a discussion about the aesthetic coordinates of visual arts and their ideological implications. In his opening address, Mácza approaches the problem of realism in the Soviet poster through the prism of national consciousness. He argues that the path of realism is not a straightforward one for people from the national republics of Central Asia and the Caucasus who "for centuries have been accustomed to the perception of a schematic form of representation, to stylized-ornamental [*ploskostno-uzornoi*] interpretation of plot and which themselves produce images of human figures, objects, etc., that are driven by schematism."⁵⁷ Mácza points to the example of the "schematism" of Persian miniatures to which a proletarian Azeri might be accustomed. The alleged inability to grasp the visual accuracy of a photographic image is also shared by a backward Russian peasant, a *lubok* connoisseur. Photography's combination of indexicality and iconicity fails in the "backward" oriental domain.

As a solution, Mácza insists on a "special type of poster": "It is essential to find such forms that are capable of tearing [workers and peasants] away from the religious world-view of 'their own' Persian miniatures, to bring them nearer to the level of perception, which has been developed at higher levels of economic, technical and cultural development."⁵⁸ In effect, he argues for a hybrid form that would combine "adapted" distinctive features of national aesthetics and the photographic image's indexicality, both affected by "content, deriving from a dialectical-materialist interpretation of [socialist] reality."[59] This again was a discursive attempt to conceptualize the form-content symbiosis where content would play a leading role. However, this hybrid form ought to gradually dispense with the national component because of its close interrelationship with an oppressive religious worldview. Thus, the photographic camera functions as an agent of progressive change that enables proletarian realism.

This stance had clear implications for the operative principles of photomontage, an artistic practice that was already emerging as the most important medium to fulfill the teleological and aesthetic concerns of the state. National form's radical distinctiveness had to be subdued and pushed into the domain of realism with the help of the photographic apparatus. The axonometric planes in the avant-garde's photomontage produced multiple perspectival viewpoints, as did the "national form" of the Persian miniature, and these planes also had to be either restrained or eliminated. Fragmented photomontage was rejected in favor of the smooth amalgamation of *real* images. Seamless and invisible visual assembly delivered a coherent narrative, in contrast to the constructivist "noise" of juxtaposition. The informational excess of the early photomontages disappeared and was replaced with rather austere composition defined by a few dominant elements: the singular leader-*vozhd'* counterposed with the masses.

However, the October photographers faced a fierce and powerful opponent. ROPF (the Russian Association of Proletarian Photographers), which counted leading photojournalists Semyon Fridliand, Arkadii Shaikhet, Max Al'pert, and Yakov Khalip among its members, published their own declaration that challenged some of the aesthetic premises of the October group.[60] They defied the "pure" and "abstract" aesthetic qualities of the photographic image propagated by *LEF* and still discernible in the October declaration. Rodchenko was the main target of the proclamation indicting the October photographers and their ability to shoot "only from below or from above and only with a lopsided horizon."[61] Leonid Mezhericher, an editor of *Soviet Photo*, blamed the October Group, and specifically the "stubborn leftist" Rodchenko, for valorizing composition at the expense of political meaning; for Mezhericher, such meaning resided in *siuzhetnost'*, or the ability to convey a clear narrative line.[62] *Siuzhetnost'* guarantees that form will be subservient to content. Thus, the photojournalists argued against any formal prescriptions, and the quality of the photographic image was largely defined by its political usefulness in delivering a meaningful message.

Fridliand, for instance, promoted both the "synthetic" photographic image and the serial *photo-ocherk*, given that their main function was to analyze reality by drawing out its key elements and highlighting their interaction.[63] Synthetic unity, which had earlier been challenged by Rodchenko in his discussion of photographs of Lenin, performs a significant function for ROPF—it animates the documentary and formal aspects of the photographic shot by fusing them to a superficially introduced narrative line. This narrative line, *siuzhetnost'*, would later devolve into mere fabrication, but at the time, it was a purely teleological element.

A few months later, ROPF seized the opportunity to aggressively articulate its position. The photo section of the October Group organized an exhibition in May of 1931 where Rodchenko exhibited his "Pioneer Girl," "Pioneer-Trumpeter," and a series of photographs from Vakhtan Timber Mill near Nizhny Novgorod. The "Pioneer-Trumpeter" photograph was the main target of criticism: *Proletarian Photo* pronounced it as being shot "either from the point of view of [Rodchenko's] own navel or from the point of view of a worm crawling near his feet."[64] An unsigned editorial from *Pioneer Truth* (*Pionerskaia Pravda*), the chief news outlet of the Pioneer Movement, made a public appeal to "finally stop showing pioneers from the point of view of a drum or a horn."[65] Foreshortening had become identified with an *incorrect* point of view.

The problem with Rodchenko's pioneer series lies in the fact that the employed close-up with radical foreshortening severs the depicted subjects from their surroundings. These are not conventional frontal view full-body images that reveal the physical build and social significance of the young builders of socialism, who were seen as real human subjects and ideological incarnations at the same time. Instead, the series offers a multivalent vision of a rather abstract social type that refuses to be immediately intelligible and fails to deliver a distinct narrative line.

The escalation of such attacks reached a high point when Rodchenko's close associates were required to denounce the master. Ilya Sosfenov, Rodchenko's former associate and a member of the October Group, gives a more nuanced yet more callous assessment of the "Pioneer-Trumpeter" image:

> The object is framed in such a way that the physiological function of breathing, adapted to a job on a certain wind instrument, turns out to be its theme.... Rodchenko has exterminated objects themselves. His trumpet is not a trumpet but a part of some kind of machine, his pioneer is not a pioneer but a working detachable device of this "synthetic machine." Stylistic rendering of the object is reduced to attaining a construction wherein objects lose their essence and turn into the abstract schemes of an ideal mechanism.[66]

Foreshortening defies organicity by reducing a human figure to a spatial structure. The excessive physiology of the pioneer overshadows his ideological function. What the unusual angle accomplishes is a "debasement" of the real body; it turns it into an inanimate material assemblage. The valiant and ideologically charismatic figure of the pioneer had to be transmitted as a boldly real and socially active human being without any "aesthetic" noise of abstraction. Rodchenko failed to accomplish this task.

The October Group was consequently forced to publish a public denouncement of its own method, now defined as "a leftist principle of abstract documentarism that is alien and antagonistic toward the dialectic-materialist nature of the proletarian ideology."[67] On January 25, 1932, Rodchenko was expelled from the October Group for his "systematic reluctance to take part in the practical reconstruction of the group."[68] His *rakurs* became history.[69]

A few months after his expulsion, Rodchenko was employed by Izogiz as a photo correspondent and later sent to the construction site of the White Sea–Baltic Canal. According to the contract, he had to produce a minimum of forty negatives a month.[70] In 1935, with his glorious experimental days behind him, Rodchenko participated in the Masters of Soviet Photography exhibition, which restored his professional reputation. He also rejoined the editorial board of *Soviet Photo* and contributed articles praising his former ROPF opponents. The period between 1932 and 1935 is exactly when Rodchenko, together with Stepanova, produced the first issues of *USSR in Construction* and the photobook *Ten Years of Soviet Uzbekistan*—key artifacts of this chapter. However, it also culminated in Rodchenko's notorious 1936 apologia "Reconstruction of an Artist."

In this seemingly self-critical document, which begins with a strictly chronological narrative written in the third person, Rodchenko turns his "mistakes" into virtues:

- 1916–1921: he is a non-objective artist, and his experiments revolve around compositional issues.
- 1921: abandons painting and goes into production.
- 1921–1922: starts working on photomontages.
- 1923–1924: enters the realm of photography where he pursues compositional issues and returns to abstraction.
- 1925–1926: *LEF* years which redefined photographic language. Foreshortening reigns supreme and the experimentation "was not a mistake, it was necessary, and it played a positive role in photography, refreshed it, raised it to a new level."
- 1926–1928: years of photojournalism and attempts to depart from "the easel approach, aesthetics, and abstraction."

1929–1930s: three trips to the White Sea–Baltic Canal, which reforged him; the canal becomes his "salvation, it was a ticket to life."

1934–1935: years of "silence" and work on *USSR in Construction* issues and various photo albums with Stepanova.[71]

After recounting these steps of his professional path, Rodchenko suddenly turns his judicious gaze outward: "Now, as for others."[72] He critiques the work of every major Soviet photographer at the time: Shaikhet is blamed for staging facts, for the absence of life in his work, and for a poor grasp of technique; "sentimental" Fridliand falls "into photographic melancholy, mediocrity"; Al'pert's work is "a little boring, a little too photographic"; Boris Ignatovich, "a former friend, student, and colleague," is terminally leftist and mannerist; Abram Shterenberg, though a first-class studio portraitist, does not dare to do photo reportage; Mikhail Prekhner "does not have his own creative identity"—and the inventory goes on.[73] The supposedly contrite text turns into a denunciation of other artists. Rodchenko concludes it with a standard oath proclaiming his loyalty to socialist realism in highly templated terms:

And lastly. Henceforward I want to decisively reject placing formal solutions to a theme in the first place and ideological ones in the second place; at the same time, I want to search inquisitively for new riches in the language of photography, in order, with its help, to create works that will stand on a high political and artistic level, works in which photographic language will fully serve socialist realism.[74]

RECONSTRUCTION OF THE COUNTRY

Rodchenko uses the same reflexive mode of the verb "to reconstruct" when he talks about his own artistic self and the White Sea–Baltic Canal worker-prisoners: "Man came and conquered, conquered and reconstructed himself."[75] The process of constructing the canal—the forceful transformation of nature—coincides with the reconstruction of human subjects, including the artist himself. The self-confessed makeover took place at the construction site of the Belomor Canal, the first Stalinist project to rely purely on prisoners' labor. Correctional labor turns a former criminal into a "productive" member of society while the artist rediscovers his aesthetic path. The waterway, of course, was a dubious way out. This makes Rodchenko's exclamatory rhetoric even more suspect: "I was bewildered, amazed. I was caught up in this enthusiasm. It was all familiar to me, everything fell into place. I forgot about all my creative disappointments. I took photographs simply, not thinking about formalism."[76] The legacy of avant-garde experiments perishes together with the thousands of prisoners who did not survive the hard labor, malnutrition, and extreme weather conditions.

Rodchenko's highly problematic role as a chief producer of visual propaganda for the Belomor project inscribed his artistic identity into the fabric of Stalinist culture. The Soviet secret police (Unified State Political Directorate, or OGPU) was his employer and collaborator: it oversaw Rodchenko's work, built an on-site photo laboratory for him, and retained sole ownership of all the negatives. OGPU decided which images could go public and regulated the photographer's work (for instance, certain lock structures could not be photographed due to security concerns). Rodchenko produced thousands of images of the Belomor construction site, but only a few made it into official publications. Most of the published photographs appeared in the 1933 special issue on Belomor in the photo journal *USSR in Construction*, for which Rodchenko worked as a layout artist.[77]

Rodchenko's entry into the sphere of book design was an organic continuation of his engagement with "printed matter." Constructivism's forceful drive for experimentation lost its edge towards the late 1920s when it evolved into a dominant force in the sphere of book design.[78] This was a moment when the adherents of the avant-garde started incorporating traditional graphic design patterns and synthetic neoclassical forms in the late modernist manner.

Rodchenko's Belomor issue certainly bears qualities of an artifact in transition between two stylistic paradigms. It opens with landscape shots of untamed Karelian nature and portraits of the worker-prisoners, who are ready to undergo a process of radical change. The visual narrative elaborates the process of construction with images of the laborers themselves and of their "mentors"—the officers of the Main Directorate of Correctional Labor Camps (GULAG). The whole issue is framed by two collages of Stalin: the head of the leader superimposed on a boundless aquatic surface (an abstract image of water) at the beginning, and the leader with his associates inspecting the completed canal (the concrete waterway) at the end. Rodchenko chooses a photomontage technique for both images, even though the latter was meant to establish a documentary truth (that is, that the canal was constructed and that Stalin was there to witness its opening). There are many visual "anomalies." The leader and his deputies in blue tones do not converge with the green-toned canal in terms of perspective. Furthermore, Rodchenko leaves white edges on the figures' contours to emphasize that they do not belong to the space of the canal (see fig.2.1). And almost all photographs of the canal in this issue employ radical foreshortening. The canal, the ultimate product of construction that "cured" Rodchenko of the disease of formalism, is both a monument to and a burial stone of formalism.[79]

Indeed, the influence of the factographic movement is obvious: the presence of numerous maps, statistical data sheets, newspaper clippings, and other documents signifies the reality of Belomor. Rodchenko's camera registers the process of radical transformation of nature, which goes hand in hand with the no less radical "reeducation" of former criminals through the practice of labor. In the end, nature is tamed, and the convicts are turned into productive members of society—two factual achievements are accomplished.

The importance of documentary fact for Rodchenko is evident in the way he dealt with the figure of Stepan Dudnik, a former Odesa thief who developed certain artistic talents while working at the construction site and began to produce agitational material there. Rodchenko's camera took multiple shots of the man at work, and these were meant to play a prominent role in the Belomor issue of *USSR in Construction*. However, Rodchenko refused to "reconstruct" Dudnik's former life, and the material, in the end, did not appear in the final version.[80]

The refusal to stage a photograph had deep theoretical roots. The first issue of *USSR in Construction* for 1932 featured the *photo-series* (or photo essay) "Giant and Builder" (Gigant i stroitel') by Maks Al'pert and Aleksandr Smolian, which prompted a radical change in the journal's design.[81] Officially hailed as groundbreaking, it tracked the conversion of Viktor Kalmykov, an illiterate peasant, into a highly skilled Magnitostroi shock-worker, a member of the Party and a recipient of the Order of the Red Banner. To depict Kalmykov's transformation, the photographers had to stage his arrival and first days at the construction site. Al'pert theoretically substantiates his stance against a "conservative" conviction that "you can deliver only that which you can see, and under no circumstances can you go further than this."[82] He argues that only his method of "the reconstruction of the fact" (*vosstanovlenie fakta*) can display all the achievements of Soviet society. Staging becomes a key component of the socialist mode of representation.

Some critics challenged the staged nature of the issue by pointing out that since Kalmykov is wearing the same bandage on his finger at what are supposedly different points in time, the temporal progression of the photo-series—and, more importantly, its claim to truth—is disrupted. In response, Mezhericher likened the bandaged finger to a physical photographic flaw, such as a scratch, which could easily be touched up to avoid any distractions that might hinder the reader's comprehension of the artist's creative intention.[83] He concludes that the reconstruction of a fact does not contradict the documentary essence of the photographic image: proletarian propaganda is rooted in reality, and the reconstructed fact simply adds to it.[84]

"Giant and Builder" was Al'pert's second photo-series project. A year earlier he, together with Arkadii Shaikhet, famously documented one day in the life of the Filippovs—an "ordinary" Soviet family. The daily routine of this Soviet poster family was meticulously documented, beginning with their morning breakfast, continuing through their respective work and school obligations, and ending with an evening of relaxation at Gorky Park. The photo-series was shot at the request of the "Society of Friends of the USSR" in Austria and appeared in *Arbeiter Illustrierte Zeitung* (Workers' Illustrated Newspaper), better known by its acronym *A-I-Z* in 1931. The material, delivered in a very innovative form, proved to be a major success for Soviet propaganda abroad.

The photo-series allowed the viewer to witness a historical continuity in the photographic image's stillness. It created a set of dynamic interrelations between disparate images and a concocted narrative. As one of the proponents of the photo-series puts it, "*in a series something should take place, there should be a narrative line.*"[85] The photo-series read essentially as a storyboard for a great Soviet film about the economic and social transformation of the country. The viewer was witness to a valiant change and had a pronounced sense of historical perspective. The dynamism of the photo-series reflected the dynamism of the USSR's development.[86] According to Shaikhet and Al'pert, a photo-series "must bring to light the social essence of objects and events as a whole, in all of their dialectical variety."[87]

Tretiakov, who was behind the idea to document the Filippovs' life, wrote the article "From the Photo-Series to the Prolonged Photo-Observation," published in the December 1931 issue of *Proletarian Photo* that literally framed the photo-series: its first page preceded the photographs while the second page followed them. In his article, Tretiakov argues that the photo-series and photomontage "allow us to feel the thickness of reality, its authentic weight."[88] They do so by incorporating several instantaneous-incidental shots—which, in isolation, merely reveal the arbitrariness or randomness of an event—into a generalized and cohesive picture of a greater phenomenon. As a result, the Filippovs' photo-series presents a Soviet subject "not as an isolated person, but as a particle of our active social fabric."[89] At the same time, Tretiakov points to several factual distortions, including unrealistically empty Moscow trams, a discrepancy between declared and shown receipts, and the glamorous representation of young tennis players. Facticity should reign supreme.

Rodchenko certainly shared his avant-garde comrade's convictions. His refusal to "reconstruct" Dudnik's former life signified a principled allegiance to the documentary fact. Transformation of reality by artificial means (staging)

FIG. 2.1 Aleksandr Rodchenko, Pages from *USSR in Construction [Belomor]*, no. 12, 1933. Productive Arts.

should yield to factual transformation of reality. In this sense, Rodchenko's Belomor issue of *USSR in Construction* attempted to provide a truly documentary equivalent for the narrative dynamism of the photo-series, by then an officially celebrated mode of visual representation in the Soviet Union. It registers the process of the transformation of space (the natural landscape) through time—the progression of the canal's construction and the prisoners' "reconstruction."

The inherent link between the canal and people it "reconstructs" is at play in what is arguably Rodchenko's most famous photograph of Belomor—"Work with a Band on the Canal" (Rabota s orkestrom na kanale). The photograph did not appear in the *USSR in Construction* issue. It was instead displayed at the Masters of Soviet Photography exhibition of 1935, and it would rescue him from oblivion. Rodchenko registers a moment when workers are fixing the lagging of one of the canal's locks, while a brass band is rehearsing one level above, on a concrete platform. The shot is taken from another, third level, and hence reveals a multilevel composition that compellingly engages horizontal and vertical lines. This seemingly was "the beauty of genuinely heroic creative labor"[90] to which Rodchenko referred in "Reconstructing the Artist." Nevertheless, Mezhericher criticized the image for not revealing the "happiness" of labor but instead imposing a sense of abasement, prompted by the camera's point of view. To this Rodchenko responded: "It's shot this way on purpose to show that the orchestra on the production site are also workers and that there is nothing solemn about it, it's an ordinary work situation."[91] Thus the conflation of labor and art becomes the norm in a country undergoing a drastic transformation. But Rodchenko also insinuates that his own questionable contribution to glorification should be seen as ordinary: the forced penal labor of these prisoners, the forced art of the prisoner-musicians, and the "forced" art of Rodchenko all stand for a new norm. This was not staging; it was reality itself.

In the same year as the Masters of Soviet Photography exhibition, Rodchenko collaborated with Stepanova on another issue of *USSR in Construction* that would represent their entry into the sphere of the Soviet Orient. Since the early 1930s the Soviet oriental periphery had a regular place in illustrated Soviet press outlets, such as *Ogonek* and *Pravda*. The periphery's visual representation through "a form of consumable *othering*"[92] served the purpose of confirming the success of the Soviet modernization effort. Rodchenko and Stepanova's *USSR in Construction* issue was dedicated to the fifteenth anniversary of Kazakhstan, an autonomous republic and part of the Russian Soviet Federative Socialist Republic at the time, and it largely reflected the journal's tendency to even out regional and cultural differences.[93] Its visual structure is dominated by the imposed contrast between cliché and fact. The first third of *Fifteen Years of Kazakhstan* displays the agricultural riches for which the republic was known: sheep, goats, cows, camels, horses, fish, grain, cotton, and fruit. The remaining pages establish a new truth: the space is now known for its industrial progress that, in turn, emancipates its inhabitants. Most photographs and photomontages apply avant-garde foreshortening and are compositionally innovative. This symbiosis of triumphant modernity and ethnic particularism overcoming backwardness is implemented, in Timothy Nunan's formulation, by the force of "chauvinistic ethnophilia" that defined the journal's general editorial strategy.[94]

The issue enacts a fetishistic obsession with raw materials as a manifestation of the newly industrialized Soviet "order of things."[95] Indeed, one of the key texts in the journal is titled "Socialist Metabolism" and it metaphorically elevates the republic to the status of an organism with a life-sustaining chain conversion of "food to energy" to run cellular processes:

> Uninterruptedly and unrecognizably changing, transforming, assuming the most various and unexpected forms, the industrial blood of Kazakhstan pulsates in its veins, obedient to the pumping of its mighty and wise heart—the Kremlin. It spreads throughout the whole union, nourishing factories and construction sites.

> Enriched by the complex process of the socialist metabolism, it returns to Kazakhstan its riches—by way of planes, tractors, excavators, cars, turbines....
>
> The riches of the bowels turn into the riches of the surface—into meat, wool, leather, fish, they grow into ears of wheat and cotton bolls.[96]

The metropolitan heartbeat of the Kremlin sustains the body of the peripheral republic: what is extracted from below is transported away but then returns to nourish life on the surface. Thus, a cohesive and succinct storyline, reminiscent of the one in Shklovsky's *Turksib*, is created: Kazakhstan was known for its natural and primitively gathered agricultural produce but has emerged as an industrial nation, developing at a quick pace and taking part in the larger metabolic process of the whole country. A clear plot starts defining the work of Rodchenko and Stepanova. The plotless fragment of formalist experimentation cedes its place to the organic continuity of an overarching narrative line.

As in the Belomor issue, the geometrical basis of composition, an echo of constructivism, is evident in *Fifteen Years of Kazakhstan*. The most striking instance in this regard is a sophisticated centerfold dedicated to the mineral riches of the republic. Comprised of two foldable inserts with circular cutouts, it presents close-ups of earthen and alpine surfaces (fig. 2.2). Miners working underneath are seen in these cut-outs. Once the inserts are turned, they reveal geodesic slits—the bowels of the Kazakh earth. Thus, the circular cut-outs perform the function of a peephole—they disclose the invisible. Indeed, the text in the insert refers to the hidden riches as "unmined, uncreated, and unfertilized by labor."[97] The device finds its echo on the penultimate page where Stalin is represented in a circular shape, superimposed on dozens of Soviet newspapers in the Kazakh language. However, his circular opening does not open—the Soviet leader is visible and invisible at the same time. His immobile presence is sufficient.

Rodchenko and Stepanova's layout forcefully delivers a representational model that conveys the promise of the historical inevitability of the abundant socialist paradise. Notions of production, economic efficiency, and rapid development permeate every page of the journal. A fetishistic obsession with social and industrial construction is more than evident—and this was in line with the key ideological stance of the time. Yet it also radically contradicted the reality of the situation; Kazakhstan was just emerging from the 1932–1933 famine that resulted from the collectivization campaign. As Dobrenko argues, "the sphere of representation was the domain of expanding production itself" and the Soviet notion of "abundance" was a purely rhetorical construct and "can be regarded as a by-product of this process."[98]

FIG. 2.2 Aleksandr Rodchenko and Varvara Stepanova, Pages from *USSR in Construction* [*Fifteen Years of Kazakhstan*], no. 11, 1935. Productive Arts.

The photographic image was a driving force of *USSR in Construction*. Its veracity provided visual evidence of the country's radical transformation. Galina Orlova convincingly argues that the Soviet preoccupation with the photographic image derives from a conviction that "the experience of unprecedented accomplishments is difficult to think of, to imagine or to describe—it can only be seen."[99] This was a realized utopia that could be witnessed immediately. As a result, the decision to employ a certain formal device was dictated by the transfigured reality itself, and the photographer's role was reduced to the identification of a suitable lens, angles, and lighting that would allow this reality to manifest itself.

The editorial article of the very first issue of *USSR in Construction* (1930), written by Gorky himself, states that the language of numbers, diagrams, and schemes causes suspicion abroad: "To deprive our enemies inside and outside of the Soviet Union of the ability to distort and to denigrate the testimony of words and figures, we decided to turn to light-writing [*svetopisi*], to the sun's work—to photography. The sun can't be accused of distortions, the sun illuminates that which exists, as it exists."[100] The sun illuminates the truth, and the photograph becomes an ideal illustration. Indeed, the word *illustration* derives from the Latin verb *illustrare*, which means to illuminate and to explain. It is a visual entity with a similarly dazzling cognitive function. Furthermore, the photographic camera offers images "uncontaminated" by interpretation—it supposedly provides a judgment-free representation, pure visual evidence.

However, the textual elements in *Fifteen Years of Kazakhstan*, unlike in the Belomor issue, play a prominent role. Text and image are closely integrated. Approximately one-third of its pages feature a substantial amount of text. And every image but one has a corresponding caption. This signified compliance with the emerging obsession with narrativization in the Soviet ideological apparatus's logocentric tendencies. Lenin famously left only one (succinct) comment about photography, which was still oriented toward text: in his 1922 instructions for the People's Commissariat of Enlightenment, he ordered them "to show not only cinema but also photographs suitable for propaganda [purposes] with corresponding titles [*nadpisiami*]."[101] The image fails to have an impact if it is not supplemented by a textual explanation or a factual description. Its visual immanence is not self-contained.

Fifteen Years of Kazakhstan is very Leninist in this sense. It also more or less conforms with a general set of instructions on captions. The 1932 brochure *Caption for the Photo-Shot* (Tekstovka k foto-snimku) claims that the resistance to the inclusion of captions below photographs is a leftist deviation.[102] A caption should make an image more informative (*soderzhatel'nyi*) by providing concrete information and factual data. If it is a shot of a shock worker, a caption should provide his or her surname, the name of the production plant where he or she works, and describe his or her achievement. It cites Rodchenko's "Pioneer" as a photograph for which no caption can be introduced since it radically distorts reality and does not correspond to any tangible fact.[103]

While Rodchenko and Stepanova provide names for most of the workers and farmers depicted (and, of course, for all political leaders), the most famous Kazakh worker at the time—Tusup Kuzembaev—made his way into the issue without any textual recognition. The image of this prominent shock worker of the Karaganda coal mine region can be found in one of the industrial "circles."[104]

The Kuzembaev photograph was shot by Eleazar Langman who, together with his student David Shul'kin, authored all the images in *Fifteen Years of Kazakhstan*. Langman did not begin photographing actively until 1929 when he met Rodchenko and Ignatovich, already October members. Their influence on him is hard to deny: he also joined the October group and participated in the fateful exhibition of 1931. Yet Langman's foreshortening is arguably even more extreme than that cultivated by his teachers. Radical experimentation with the forward plane was one of his signature devices. The object-free foreground, which could take up to 90 percent of the shot (e.g. in "Daesh' '1040'" published in the same issue of *Soviet Photo* as Rodchenko's pioneers), dominates in Langman's typical framing.[105] By foregrounding real actors in the frame, the bare space creates a socially meaningful message. This comprised a novel take on Rodchenko's signature foreshortening that prominently features in *Fifteen Years of Kazakhstan*.

In the early 1930s, Langman traveled to Central Asia to develop a large portfolio of photographs for several forthcoming editions, including *Fifteen Years of Kazakhstan*, an issue produced by Rodchenko and Stepanova for *USSR in Construction*, and *Ten Years of Soviet Uzbekistan*. The Kazakh trip was somewhat different, as it was sponsored by the Kazakh government. Its main purpose was to collect materials for the publication *Fifteen Years of the Kazakh ASSR*, which was being designed by Nikolai Troshin, the art director of *USSR in Construction*.[106] Langman was the head of a brigade that consisted of photographers, technicians, a graphic designer, and an editor who all traveled to the republic for a period of four and a half months to collect material and give it a conceptual framework in situ.

The photograph of Kuzembaev, together with Langman's discussion of his method, was published in the same issue of *Soviet Photo* as Rodchenko's "repentance."[107] The two artists even exchanged critical jabs. For Rodchenko, Langman "has enormous experience, taste, wit, ... [and] lyricism," but the former teacher is concerned that his student "might run off 'for a minute,' either 'to the right' or 'to the left.'"[108] Such erratic formal "rushing about" irritates Rodchenko—and it results in Langman's failure to present the "real" people of Kazakhstan and

Uzbekistan. Rodchenko concludes that "it won't be easy for him to work, having rejected 'obliqueness,' but Langman has all the necessary requirements for creating talented works."[109] Langman, in his turn, challenges Rodchenko's rhetoric of reconstruction. He conceptualizes his development in therapeutic terms by referring to disease and the distress of pain:

> I've understood a great deal, I was really "ailing" in terms of my art. I'd say that the word "reconstructed" doesn't define all those sensations that are had by someone who really is leaving old convictions behind if he does it earnestly. To be reconstructed is very difficult, it's painful. Here reflections don't always help. Here one must feel and go in depth. More importantly, one must know how to grow.[110]

Langman claims that the work on the Kazakh material prompted his reorientation and evolution as an artist—it was his "university." He almost completely abandoned the close-up for "there is nothing to be 'cut'—everything beyond the shot was grand and necessary," and "no wide-angle lens could capture this magnificent material."[111] The long shot reigns supreme. Furthermore, there was an attempt to rethink the oblique angle:

> I set an interesting task before myself and my pupil D. Shul'kin. "We're on our way to shoot Kazakhstan, I told him, let's set one condition—not to take oblique angle shots." Maybe this was a somewhat primitive way to pose the question, since one shouldn't limit oneself. However, it seemed to me that it's more difficult to produce a straight shot than an oblique one, since in those instances when you can't understand the essence of the object, you can mechanically warp [*perekosit'*] it, so that everything falls into place, and it becomes engaging. The mechanical application, as a result, delivers an insipid thing, but, again, I highlight the fact that obliqueness [*kosina*] justifiably applied, obliqueness that underscores the content, is needed.[112]

Foreshortening undergoes a process of late modernist evolution—it needs to discard its tendency to present objects mechanically. Langman hints at an organic mode of representation that relies on classical perspectival conventions. Nevertheless, foreshortening can be employed as one of the devices of socialist realism:

> After all, realism is not a path along which you can walk in some given direction. Nothing of the sort! It is an immense radius on which you can arrive at one point by countless paths, and obliqueness too can be one of these paths that leads to realism, but this should be justified in a socio-realist sense.[113]

FIG. 2.3 Eleazar Langman, "Kuzimbayev," *Sovetskoe foto*, no. 10, 1935. Harvard Library.

Foreshortening starts to underscore content and to make it more pronounced. Indeed, the editors of *Soviet Photo*, who published one of Langman's most famous photographs, praised the formal solution: "There is an exceptional foreground in Langman's Kazakh shots. The carpet in shock worker Kuzinbaev's [sic] yurt is quite rightly justified by folklore."[114] The attributes of national ornamentation justify the avant-garde foreshortening. It merges with a formalist device, and this results in the advent of a "national form." The combination of two formal aspects delivers truly socialist content—a Kazakh Stakhanovite enjoying a tea break.

The May-June issue of *Soviet Photo* in 1936, which included Rodchenko's repentance, Langman's reflection, and the Kuzembaev photograph, was a landmark of Stalinist discursive intervention into the sphere of photography. Adorned with a portrait of Gorky on the cover, it opened with the article "Towards Realism and Narodnost'" by Sergei Morozov, a leading young critic at the time and the author of the first history of Soviet photography. The programmatic article tried to establish the basic premises of realism, attacked formalist experimentation, and reinforced the concept of *narodnost'* (popular spirit). *Narodnost'* ensures that Soviet art is accessible to the people and expressive of the people. This is achieved by means of a clear narrative component. *Narodnost'* should manifest as something profoundly evocative—it should display the concrete achievements of the people, but this should not be attained through a mere dry reportage.[115] The documentary shot, reportage, should be replaced by a meaningful image (*obraz*) that delivers another quality of *narodnost'*—the expression of the deepest sentiments and ideas of the people. The final aspect of *narodnost'* reveals itself in the employment of various national motifs, such as ornament or other folkloric elements in the photographic shot. This now comprised the full advent of national form.

In the same article, Morozov praises Langman's attempts to reconstruct his artistic method—the mastered formal devices are now in the service of the socialist content and make it "sound more expressive."[116] The critic justifies foreshortening in terms identical to the assessment by the editors of *Soviet Photo* and equates national form with ornament: "this is what provides an excellent foreground in the Kazakh shots: the carpet in Stakhanovite Kuzinbaev's [sic] tent ... Langman quite rightfully justifies this carpet through folklore."[117] Form, manifesting itself in the dominant foreground space that still operates within the premises of internal montage, is acceptable as long as it prompts certain connotations. It evolves into an element subservient to content—it becomes meaningful.

CONSTRUCTION OF THE NATION

In 1933, a year after they joined the newly formed Moscow Artists' Union as book designers, Rodchenko and Stepanova were commissioned to produce a luxurious volume to commemorate the tenth anniversary of the formation of the Uzbek Soviet Socialist Republic. The scope of this project, which was completed in 1934, is truly impressive: more than 250 pages in length, it allowed the artists to blend their earlier experiments with typography and photomontage with some recent achievements of the Soviet book design industry. They utilized all kinds of printmaking techniques, including innovative use of embossing, full-color and duotone printing, and incorporated costly color acetate transparencies, high-gloss coated paper, and lithographic paper. *Ten Years of Soviet Uzbekistan* was a compendium of the most advanced techniques of visual representation.[118]

The transformative agenda of nation-building lies at the narrative core of the work. A clear storyline, a certain temporal progression from one point or state to another, more advanced one, shapes *Ten Years of Soviet Uzbekistan*.[119] At the time, the Central Asian republic was seen as an exemplary space: its "inherent" emptiness was filled in through construction—a new home for the emerging Uzbek proletariat, built during the first five-year plan. By the mid-1930s, after ten years of intense construction, this home had to be suffused with symbolically meaningful content. The *foto-al'bom* (photobook) created and endorsed this meaning. The word "album" derives from the Latin *albus*, meaning white, and it highlights the whiteness of the sheet. *Ten Years of Soviet Uzbekistan* is an interplay between the empty whiteness and the meaningful socialist content inscribed on its surface.

The result is an impressive graphic design achievement. Real and virtual intersections are created through various kinds of visual materials. Paintings and drawings by Uzbek artists,[120] as well as arts and crafts by anonymous artisans, were reproduced in color. These reproductions, which are significantly smaller than most of the photographs in the folio, point to oriental opulence in terms of their color palette—*Pravda*, in its review of the work, referred to it as "an orgy of colors that intoxicates" the viewer.[121] But these reproductions, numbering a half dozen at most, were overwhelmingly overshadowed by the photographic material. Elaborate large-scale photo collages, uncut photographs, and portraits of the political elite accompanied by textual inserts, dominate the layout. In the resulting work, epic visual compositions overcome the spatial limits of the page: a great number of the collages are presented on folded inserts and inlays, which can be opened in every direction. Altogether, they create the intricate rhythm of the work, a typographic oriental carpet, and present Uzbekistan simultaneously as an exotic fairy-tale land and an advanced socialist topos, an enacted utopia.

Vladimir Favorsky, who chaired the VKhUTEMAS graphic design department, identifies two tendencies in the sphere of book design in the early twentieth century: design as a traditional applied craft that treated the book in a decorative mode, and the constructivist trend that aimed to enhance the book's functionality.[122] For the latter, script was one of the expressive elements and the photograph replaced conventional book illustration. However, as Favorsky notes, "if you take a left, you will arrive at the right,"[123] and strict leftist engineerism unwittingly ended up in the decorative plane itself—its functional principles became a style. This passage from sharp left to right is evident in *Ten Years of Soviet Uzbekistan*. The photobook reveals a peculiar blend of late modernism and socialist realism: the revised formal language of the avant-garde is still manifest, yet the clarity and straightforwardness of content, infused with decorative motifs in line with the official artistic method of Stalinist culture, are also clearly discernible.

The most avant-garde aspect of the work is certainly its slipcase. There are two versions of the slipcase, and both resonate with the early constructivist experiments in volumetric construction. The first one has a semicircle shape segment that opens vertically. It is a haptically active case made of deep red velvet-like fabric that delivers a pronounced sense of materiality. The other one, used for the limited edition, is a case made of two overlapping modules that open in the manner of a turnstile. An experiment in nonrelational progression, it turns into a Roman "X" when open, standing for ten years of Uzbekistan. It was morphologically constructivist in its design—the functional construction of the object met Rodchenko's modularity. As Aglaya Glebova observes, the credits refer to Rodchenko and Stepanova as "authors of the artistic construction [*khudozhestvennogo postroeniia*] and design of the album"—a veiled homage to constructivism.[124]

Yet another constructivist aspect of the work is the design of its title and chapter title pages. According to Favorsky, the title page is the entrance to a book. However, unlike the cover, it is an internal, invisible door that allows one to have a glimpse of the "entrails" of the book.[125] The title page's design is marked by the dominance of typographic elements, themselves derived from the abstract geometry of nonrepresentational art over graphic elements. The page is treated as a modular grid in the classic constructivist mode. A strict geometric structure is augmented by a restricted color palette (black, white, and red as primary colors). Rodchenko and Stepanova employ a sans serif font, one of the signature devices of constructivism, and experiment with the script's size, type, and color.[126]

The lapidary title page, however, is preceded by two of the book's key photomontages. The images of Lenin and Stalin, who appear to endorse the development of the Central Asian republic, comprise a peculiar blend of styles. Lenin, who is represented as a monument, seems to be unnaturally tilted as if about to fall. However, the vertical line of his back is strictly parallel to the right side of the collage and thus, compositionally, the "tilted" monument performs its function—it reveals dynamism within stasis. The monumentality of the monument is grounded and animated at the same time. The Lenin in *rakurs* points toward the "sky," an empty space in pink gradient producing a smooth color transition. The sky is festooned with the slogan "Proletarians of the world, unite!" written in Uzbek. The Turkic language underscores the international appeal of the slogan—it is a point of ultimate aspiration. Furthermore, the pedestal is surrounded by two red banners and a cotton shrub that has not yet produced flowers or bolls. This is a promise of proletarian and national blossoming. Indeed, a few pages later, when Rodchenko and Stepanova present large studio portraits of four regional leaders—Bauman, Ikramov, Khodzhaev, and Akhunbaev—the two sets of photographs are divided by a much larger cotton shrub, which has almost grown into a tree. When Rodchenko and Stepanova produced the folio, Uzbekistan was entering the mature stage of what Julia Obertreis calls the "cotton fever"[127] and was consequently reduced to a cotton-producing region. Cotton monoculture manifests itself in the very first photograph utilized in the work—a close-up of cotton flowers that, once pollinated, will drop off and be replaced with cotton bolls. The inscription below laconically states: "Uzbekistan is a country of cotton."

Stalin, in turn, makes his entrance in a photographic close-up pasted on a white background, typical of avant-garde collages. The "Lenin-today," represented using a photographic document, anchors the whole composition. His slightly tilted figure is placed in the bottom left corner and thus mirrors the right-leaning composition of the Lenin collage. Stalin inspects a parade procession and waves his right hand at the viewer. His broad shoulders conceal banners with political slogans that, in turn, disguise miniature figures representing the Uzbek proletariat. In terms of perspective, the parallel lines of banners and people recede into the top left corner where the vanishing point of the composition is located. This also creates a sense of dynamics, but of a different kind. The photograph of Stalin, his gaze directed at the bottom right corner, still predominates; it grounds the composition while Lenin's monument, with its orientation towards the sky, points to something aspirational. The airy ideal of Lenin encounters Stalin's weighty reality.

The traditional genre of photomontage is supplemented by a rather innovative representation of Lenin and Stalin in the "Uzbekistan Today" section, where the leaders are rendered in silhouette. Silhouette, or profile portraiture, was the most popular way to recreate an image of a human subject before the invention of photography. Its embeddedness in reality—the sitter's profile is mechanically captured by a tracing device—delivers a transparent physiognomy. Silhouette renders the face as a *line* and its interior is featureless. For Rodchenko, the *line* was a key element of any construction, serving as its skeleton or carcass, and he dedicated a whole brochure to the subject. "The perfected significance of the line" is manifested in its kinetic qualities: "The line is the path of passing through, movement, collision, edge, attachment, joining, sectioning."[128]

Line as a constructive and kinetic element is enacted in Lenin's silhouette, which is pronouncedly spectral but nevertheless complete. The line's dynamic curves make the deceased leader materialize with a seemingly minimal effort. The image is drawn in gold on an acetate transparency with Lenin's chin slightly lifted. But he is not an outline devoid of "semantic feeling," for his image covers a black page filled with a red script. The text is his 1919 letter (in fact, it is addressed to Ukrainian workers!) that calls for the peaceful coexistence of all nations and the emancipation of those who were formerly repressed. Once the page is turned, Lenin's profile, now in red, finds itself on an almost-empty yellow page with his spectral nature enhanced. The page contains a much shorter quote from a 1920 report on national and colonial questions that establishes a different set of power relations: it claims that a more advanced proletariat can help its backward comrades and accelerate their development. Lenin's spectral presence vacillates; it is enfolded in two rather discordant discourses—the emancipatory and the domineering.

The transparency of the profile plays a more complex role in the instance of the pages dedicated to Stalin (fig. 2.4). The living leader's profile is a hollow-cut type of silhouette—it is cut from a piece of paper, so that the middle drops away, and is covered with a clear acetate transparency. Unlike Lenin's drawn, wraithlike outline, Stalin comprises a void, a capacious and physically marked space. The materiality of his profile is very pronounced because he is not superimposed on a transparent surface as is the founder of the Soviet state—the form creates a tangible imprint and makes space for itself. The hollow cut, authorized by Stalin's signature, covers the text in red on a silver background that remains disjointed and fails to deliver meaning until the page is flipped. The text turns out to be a quote derived from Stalin's famous 1925 speech "The Political Tasks of the University of the Peoples of the East," that enforced the notion of national form, and this text occupies the next three consecutive pages. But the profile has a double meaning that is changed once the page is flipped—the silhouette is now filled in with an ornamental carpet design. Thus, the hollow-cut silhouette is an interface between a national tradition and a text that discursively validates

SOCIALIST VISION 119

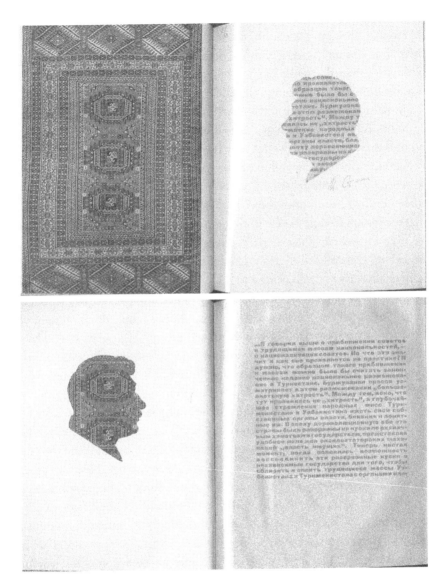

FIG. 2.4 Aleksandr Rodchenko and Varvara Stepanova, Stalin Pages from *Ten Years of Soviet Uzbekistan*, 1934. Productive Arts.

it. Carpet and text enact a confluence of, or tension between, national form and socialist content. Incongruously, however, the selected Uzbek national form is in fact Turkmen. The depicted carpet in dark red color with a hint of brown, a typical Turkmen carpet color scheme, features a *göl* (flower or rose)—a distinctive octagonal medallion-like design element that appears on most Turkmen carpets. The *göl* has a twofold rotational symmetry that produces a strict geometric pattern. Uzbek carpets, on the other hand, are more stylistically varied—they tend to lack a pronounced rhythm and often feature floral elements. Rodchenko and Stepanova inadvertently highlight the generic essence of the Soviet Orient. National form is replaceable and variable.

The tension between real and symbolic, material and ethereal that is in play in the Stalin and Lenin photomontages and silhouettes is also enacted in the front and back endpapers of the work. They feature the two most celebrated natural products for which the republic is known: cotton and astrakhan fur (*karakul'*).[129] However, there is a substantial difference in the way the two natural products are represented: the hand-drawn cotton buds and flowers are flatly superimposed on a red background, while the fur manifests as a photographic close-up to emphasize, even to celebrate, the material's texture.[130] The symbolic order of the drawn cotton buds is positioned against the real of the close-up of the astrakhan fur. The sterile artificiality of the drawing is in sharp contrast with the close-up of animal fur that discloses otherwise inapprehensible materiality—it reveals the hidden formations of matter. Here, natural resources do not simply dwell on the level of the real; their ideological-symbolic (drawn) potential is equally vital. This is an unexpected move by the two constructivists, who consistently celebrated the photographic image's veracity, vehemently guarding it from the fictionality of the drawing.

The symbolic-real tension continues to be in play in the chapter dedicated to the "ordinary" inhabitants of the republic. The "Country and Its People" section differs from its counterparts in that it applies uniform color filters and the photographs it contains are presented in varying tones of orange, blue, and green. The sense of monotony in the progression of the work is eliminated through variations of hue that create a chromatic rhythm and deliver an illusion of color photography. With a primary focus on land and body, its images of prominent shock workers, farmers, simple village dwellers, athletes, and scientists are all rendered in color. Thus, the color filter becomes an emanation of the national form. As a marker of difference, it makes diversity literally visible. But filters also perform a homogenizing function—they turn people into types, who stand in for something.

The filters can also be read as echoes of Rodchenko's famous monochrome series (*Pure Red Color*, *Pure Blue Color*, and *Pure Yellow Color*), exhibited in 1921. Radical non-objectivity for Rodchenko "cultivated color as such, engaged in its full expression, its treatment, its condition, giving [it] depth, intensity, density, weight, and the like."[131] Rodchenko rejected expressive abstraction and distilled the art of painting into the primary colors from which all others can be made.

This was a radical formalist experiment that could be said to go even further than Malevich's suprematist studies. As Rodchenko put it in 1931: "I reduced painting to its logical conclusion and exhibited three canvases: red, blue and yellow. I affirmed: it's all over. Basic colors. Every plane is a plane and there is to be no representation."[132] However, in *Ten Years of Soviet Uzbekistan*, colored monochromes, as the end of the chain of representation, evolve into photographic filters, which in turn reveal reality per se. The radical negation becomes a vehement assertion. The sharp left again brings Rodchenko and Stepanova to the right.

Filters are abandoned altogether in the pages that immediately follow, which are dedicated to the reconstruction of agriculture, industrialization, and culture-building. Stylistic uniformity reigns supreme in these sections. They are strictly factographic in nature and the documentary impression delivered by black and white photography is fully appropriate. Their focus is emphatically less on human subjects and more on the process of production, produced matter, and the industrial equipment used to make it. Strict compositional order and hierarchy, which are enforced by uncut photographs, predominate and become a fundamental visual idiom for these sections.

It may not be coincidental that Rodchenko and Stepanova use the same photograph of an empty desert with sparse vegetation initially as a background for a collage, and then as an uncut photograph. The image appears as a background for a centerfold collage with a shepherd surrounded by lambs at the end of the "Country and Its People" chapter (pages 130 and 131). Pastoral in its mood, it presents a joyous man shielding his eyes from the sun and looking into the distance with other people and animals moving far away behind him. The desert photograph serves as a background for the scene. The same image, now uncut and without any superimposed elements, features on the very first page of the chapter that immediately follows: "Socialist Reconstruction of Uzbekistan's Agriculture" (page 140). Reconstruction requires one to build and to produce artifacts. Hence the section commences with empty land, which is gradually filled up with objects and equipment, represented in similarly uncut shots, thereby gaining a socialist meaning of an industrial kind. The uncut photograph serves here as documentary evidence for emptiness, which will be subsequently surmounted.

The cut-uncut tension present in *Ten Years of Soviet Uzbekistan* is one of the key points of reorientation for the artists. The experience of photomontage allows Rodchenko and Stepanova to move naturally into the niche of photobooks—that is, their artistic production started to include such processes as the mediation and curation of already produced artifacts, rather than strictly adhering to the construction of new things and images. It is noteworthy that the photographs incorporated in *Ten Years of Soviet Uzbekistan* are not individually attributed and do not comprise a coherent aesthetic whole. This was the final stage of constructivism, wherein an understanding of form underwent a baptism of content. The latter, in the guise of already existing images produced by other artists, demanded a "broader" understanding of formal interrogation that invited conceptual curatorial thinking.

Rodchenko and Stepanova suppress their signature photomontage technique, the agglomeration of photographic fragments to produce a composite image. The dynamic intersection of vertical and diagonal lines, an integral feature of the constructivist visual artifact, also disappears. Instead, they now use photomontage to create the semblance of an uncut photograph that reveals human subjects in their natural habitat.[133] This tendency effortlessly fuses with the side-by-side placement of uncut photographs predominant in the interior layout of the Uzbek folio. The wholeness of uncut photographs stands for its self-sufficiency as a mode of representation. As a result, clusters of photographs constitute spaces of seamless association.

Ten Years of Soviet Uzbekistan indicates that its photographs were made by Langman, who had also contributed images for *Fifteen Years of Kazakhstan*, Abram Shterenberg, and some anonymous photojournalists of Soiuzfoto and Izogiz. Shterenberg, like Langman, was a member of the October group. However, his membership, for some critics, was considered accidental for his style was extremely eclectic and his preference for studio portraits sharply contrasted the formalist experiments of his October comrades.[134] However, he had previously managed a photographic studio in pre-revolutionary Tashkent and certainly knew the region well, so his pairing with Langman as a chief producer of photographic material was pragmatically justified. Maks Penson, another prominent local, is probably the most famous contemporaneous photographer to be concealed behind the "Soiuzfoto" designation. At least two photographs by Penson that were used in the work had been previously published in *Soviet Photo*.[135] For years he visually framed the republic and was considered its official local "eye" (he famously never visited Moscow, the metropolitan center, during his entire career).

Significantly, *Ten Years of Soviet Uzbekistan* provides a space for a redefinition of foreshortening, evident in the photographs by Langman and Penson. The Soviet Orient, as a reservoir of unfamiliar and novel experiences, did not seem to require any foreshortening. What it truly needed was a form of representation that would make it familiar and thus accomplish a cognitive closure. This is evident in numerous collages and photographs showing shock workers and political leaders: they are all represented from a waist-level perspective, the use of which Rodchenko had vehemently resisted only a few years before. However, foreshortening still infiltrates the style of representation in various photographs shot by Rodchenko's October associates: those of ordinary people, civil buildings, factories, and even mosques. The two aesthetic frameworks jointly and dialectically negotiate icons of the new Soviet subjectivity.

The process of negotiation is evident in two instances when, in 1935, Rodchenko and Stepanova replace two images from the 1934 edition with photographs that are thematically identical but stylistically dissimilar. Unlike certain swapped photographs of political leaders, who had perished during the nine-month period separating the publication of the two versions of *Ten Years of Soviet Uzbekistan*, this was a purely aesthetic choice without any political underpinnings. On page 111 of the 1934 edition, the artists place Langman's photograph of four athletes, only one of whom seems to be Uzbek, standing in a row, their arms lowered but their chests straining (fig. 2.5). With two-thirds of their bodies in the frame, the athletes are shot with a substantially tilted bottom-up angle and the foreshortening makes their solemn figures dynamic (the bare arms of the athletes produce pronounced diagonal lines that accentuate the composition). The photograph is a classic Rodchenko-type shot—it makes for a defamiliarized take on a mundane situation and creates dynamism out of static figures and objects.

The 1935 edition, however, contains a very different photograph on the same page, though it is also made by Langman.[136] Similarly, it depicts athletes, but this time there are about one hundred of them and they are marching in a formation that emerges from the bottom left corner and then splits in the upper part of the frame into two rows, thus forming a sickle-like shape. The shot is taken from a top-down perspective and is also inherently dynamic—the core formation anchors the composition against the two rows that split in different directions, thus bracketing the edge and creating spatial tension. The depicted body in this photograph is not that of an individual worker-athlete but a collective body in the shape of an ideological attribute. What takes place is a process of ideological incorporation.[137] As Ekaterina Degot' describes Rodchenko's photographs of parades in the 1930s, instead of reality presented from an unusual human point of view, it is reality itself that has already incorporated a vision full of dynamism and this must simply be revealed and presented: "the tension of the poses significantly exceeds the tension of the photographer's vision: reality itself has gained a *rakurs*."[138]

By replacing the bottom-up angle and defamiliarized human subjects with the top-down perspective of a collective body, Rodchenko and Stepanova accomplish their reorientation in line with already-dominant aesthetic principles. The aerial shot, with its inevitable foreshortening, evolved into one of the signature

FIG. 2.5 Aleksandr Rodchenko and Varvara Stepanova, Substituted photographs from *Ten Years of Soviet Uzbekistan*, 1934/1935. Productive Arts.

Stalinist viewpoints: celebrating the scale of the country's physical transformation. A transformed landscape or a complex formation must be witnessed from a distance so its splendor can be appreciated. P. Krasnov, in the Rodchenko installment of the prominent "Profiles of the Masters" series, justifies the aerial *rakurs* in the following terms:

His famous "top-down" viewpoint, which previously gave purely formal effects, is now admired by everyone and comprises a bottomless source for visual representations. Take, for instance, our people's celebrations, mass spectacles in the open air, carnivals, and parades. Who would shoot these huge streams of human joy and exultation in an old-fashioned way, from the navel viewpoint, and wouldn't prefer an aerial shot from a roof or even a plane? The camera lens, situated at this level, provides an opportunity to dynamically capture an immensely bigger angle of vision in one frame.[139]

Similarly, in the 1939 brochure *Photo-Illustration in the Newspaper*, Morozov argues that this "top-down" viewpoint should be used primarily in the depiction of objects in open space (e.g., parades), while the "bottom-up" viewpoint should be avoided altogether since it disrupts human perception of an object's proportions.[140] Soviet reality finally receives a prescriptive set of representational directives that defy perspectival deformations but celebrate the scale of social and material transformations.

The second substitution, which takes place on page 200 of the later edition, deals more with the subject matter. A photograph by an unidentified artist is replaced by Max Penson's image—a photographer who was repeatedly praised for abandoning exoticism and for showing the real Uzbek proletariat "who are reconstructing their country."[141] The 1934 photograph is a full-page vertical shot of a weaver in a traditional Uzbek garment standing right in front of an industrial loom. The man's facial expression is tense; his hands rest on the cloth. The shot is done from a slight bottom-up viewpoint that creates dynamic tension by animating the vertical and horizontal lines of the loom. However, the dynamism is immediately "muted" by the solemn figure centered in the bottom. The shot depicts a representative of a national minority mastering industrial equipment.

Nevertheless, the emancipatory photograph is replaced with Penson's image in the 1935 edition. The new image, a version of which was displayed at the Masters of Soviet Photography exhibition and appeared in the May 1935 issue of *Soviet Photo* under the title "Work on Wood," depicts two Uzbek wood carvers at work. With various tools and a wooden block that is being decorated in the foreground, the light in the shot accentuates the craftsmen's inclined heads and hands working at a carved ornament. The latter, as an ultimate manifestation of national form, prominently holds the whole composition. The emergence of the ornament's intricate pattern under the craftsmen's hands is strikingly photogenic. Rodchenko and Stepanova's decision to use it instead of a "secular" industrial shot can be read as an endorsement of Stalin's definition of proletarian culture:

 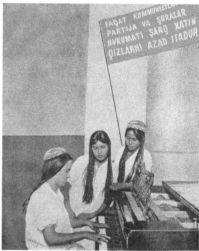

FIG. 2.6 Aleksandr Rodchenko and Varvara Stepanova, Pages from *Ten Years of Soviet Uzbekistan*, 1934. Productive Arts.

liberated ethnic artisans producing a socialist artifact while still incorporating bedrock elements of their culture.

However, not all aspects of national heritage were acceptable to the new socialist society. One of the most impressive sections of the book reveals a reverse passage: from national to secular. The centerfold, dedicated to the emancipation of Uzbek women, is adorned with Ural Tansykbayev's triptych "Liberation of the Uzbek Woman" that faces a green-colored photograph printed on acetate transparency, depicting a sitting patriarch "guarding" six fully covered women in traditional garments (fig. 2.6).[142] The work of the unveiling is enacted by the acetate transparency—once the page is turned, the women's veils are removed. What is revealed is a rather sterile black-and-white photomontage (a "documentary" fact) of three young Uzbek women in secular dress wearing traditional embroidered skullcaps. The women sit at a piano; the slogan pasted awkwardly above them claims that only the Communist Party and the Soviet government can deliver freedom to the women of the East.[143] The contours of the two photographs are nearly identical—one image conceals the other. Uzbek women, who had traditionally been associated with the natural and premodern, became the beneficiaries of the *hujum* (assault), the unveiling campaign launched on March 8, 1927, International Women's Day. They leave the space of repression, unveil themselves, and enter the secular space of the Soviet worker's club. Rather symbolically, a photograph of the unveiling activist Jahon Obidova formed part of the 1935 edition, only to be blacked out later with India ink—a Stalinist "veil"—in Rodchenko and Stepanova's private copies of *Ten Years of Soviet Uzbekistan*.[144]

The fate of Obidova's photograph comprises the most arresting act of concealing-revealing in the *Ten Years of Soviet Uzbekistan*. It has stood the test of time, but not without the scars to prove it. The oriental fairy tale bears tangible traces of the Stalinist terror. Within a year of the publication of the book's second edition, the political establishment of the USSR became subject to new levels of violent repression, and many of the individuals whose portraits proudly adorned the folio's pages were purged. The artists' two personal copies register the rupture that took place:[145] by defacing with India ink the faces and names of those who had fallen out of political favor and ceased to exist, they thus took part in what Leah Dickerman describes as "Stalin's perpetual rewriting (and reimaging) of history."[146] This editorial intervention was driven by an instinct of self-preservation, for the possession of books with photographs of "enemies of the people" was a punishable crime. However, over time, it evolved into a radical artistic gesture, defying fears of the political machine and its consumption of human flesh. The obscuring ink stains conceal the victims of Stalinism.[147] At the same time, these blacked-out spaces and resulting voids offer a striking portrayal of the horror of the moment. This was a Stalinist black space: a dark corner of extermination, competing in its representational radicalism with *Black Square*.

Richard Brilliant has argued that portraits express a profound relationship between the portrait image and the human original by enacting "the oscillation between art object and human subject."[148] The oscillation comes to a standstill in the mutilated centerfold of *Ten Years of Soviet Uzbekistan*. The portraits are defaced, and the "human originals" are repressed. The foldout renders the past as a void, as nothingness. The glory of socialist construction in Uzbekistan is infused with the work of mourning.

"DECONSTRUCTION" OF PHOTOGRAPHIC IMAGE

Surprisingly, Rodchenko's diaries offer a handful of insightful theoretical observations, but one entry made on September 1, 1940 stands out. Here, the disillusioned master reflects on the state of visual arts in Russian history through the prism of his career path:

> Russian painting was always literary: the Wanderers, World of Art, suprematism, and AKKhR.
>
> Deineka—is an illustrator and poster designer.
>
> There are no exhibitions. No artists.

But now, art is a teacher, it's all about teaching, teaching, and propaganda...
The war swallows everything...
If I had known all this earlier, I would have become an airplane builder [konstruktor].[149]

A preoccupation with narrative and fictional representation made the Russian visual arts conveniently subservient to ideological indoctrination. Rodchenko returns to Stepanova's early constructivist distinction between *depiction* (*izobrazitel′nost′*) and *painterliness* (*zhivopisnost′*) and yearns for *functionalism*, which was supposed to radicalize the plasticity of painterliness by forcing it into the material reality of the world. He wishes to be a real-world airplane builder, who could rise above the overbearing reality of literariness.

Rodchenko dreams of reversing time at the very moment that the dramatic reversal of the avant-garde's challenge to artistic representation in the narrow sense, accomplished with a return to figuration, was fully completed. Even Malevich, the apostle of non-objectivity, celebrated "a new object that the proletarian revolution had brought to the fore" before his untimely death in 1935: "Enriched by a new painting spectrum, by form and composition, the new arts must give this object shape on an artistic level, that is to say, they must elevate every thematic subject into a painting, and that painting is the plane on which a two-dimensional and frontal development of the content takes place before the spectator."[150] "Thematic subject" and even "content" enter the avant-garde's lexicon. The proletarian object has "to be raised to the level of a work of art."[151]

The 1949 *Kazakhstan* folio was Rodchenko and Stepanova's last engagement with the Soviet Orient and their penultimate collaborative project. What is at work in this rather perplexing artifact is an attempt to elevate the socialist object and subject to the level of a work of art: *Kazakhstan* is completely bereft of ordinariness. The genre of the photographic book is utilized as a mode of representation for the ethereality of socialist life in the Soviet Orient. "Life has become more joyous" to the extent that it resembles a fairy tale. Light and happiness emanate from every single shot (with the solemnity of the "Great Patriotic War" section as the only exception). The clash between the archaic past and socialist present, which produced a new kind of constructed identity in the visual propaganda of the 1930s, is no longer enacted. It is all one continuous present moment, and a very jubilant one at that.

Kazakhstan, unlike earlier works, is structured like a conventional book with accompanying—though numerous—illustrations. Not a single foldout or insert disrupts its fully intact architectonic structure. It includes a table of contents and page numbers, begins with a lengthy textual introduction without any images, and is followed by five distinct chapters. Text evolves into the chief means of representation; exceedingly informative captions frame and enable the images. The book chapters tell the story of a successful cultural and industrial integration and the self-sacrificing contribution of the Kazakh people to the national patriotic resistance during World War II. The narrative is comprehensive and clear.

Photomontage, in its classical sense, is completely absent in *Kazakhstan*. Ten years before the book was published, photomontage had already fallen out of favor as a preferred mode of representation. A reviewer of the All-Soviet Agriculture Exhibition in 1939, an event of major ideological importance, highlights the fact that the most effective exhibition displays, among which is the Kazakh Soviet Socialist Republic pavilion, are those that reduced the use of "scissors and glue" to a minimum.[152] It also establishes that "an original shot, rich in content, is almost always more intelligible, truthful and artistically full-fledged than an ordinary (even competently executed) photomontage."[153] V. Akhmet'ev and G. Volchek, who were in charge of the design for the main exhibition area, claimed that they utilized a photomontage of a "different type" in which a single photographic image is taken as a foundation for the whole composition while other elements are added on (*narashcheny*), thus extending the picture's horizon.[154] This "expansion," instead of the juxtaposition and packing-in of traditional photomontage, created a sense of airiness and delivered a panoramic impression. It endowed the work with a a much-desired epic aura, however synthetic it might be. The erasure of the modernist, constructed nature of photomontage, according to Buchloh, was replaced by "the awe-inspiring monumentality of the gigantic, single-image panorama" that "naturalizes the perspective of governance and control, of the surveillance of the rulers' omnipresent eye in the metaphor of nature as an image of a pacified social collective without history or conflict."[155]

In *Kazakhstan*, the playful and intrepid combination of photo fragments from earlier graphic designs succumbs to the meticulously choreographed placement of uncut photographs. Differently scaled figures, spatial depth, and superimposition all vanish. Diagonally based layouts are replaced with strictly rectangular compositional patterns wherein an "anchoring" central image imposes a structural equilibrium and defies any dynamism. What remains is a complete and total regularity. Such a rudimentary placing of portraits in a linear manner, "shoulder to shoulder," predominates in pages representing the political elite, war heroes, and prominent workers; other pages are organized around strict symmetrical principles. When Rodchenko attempted to define composition in 1942, he distinguished three primary types: "Ordinary: everything is on the right; unusual: everything on the left; and mystical-religious, pacifying: evenly in the center."[156]

The Kazakhstan of *Kazakhstan* occupies this very center—it is both mystical and pacifying in its evenness.

Across an overwhelming number of the incorporated photographs, all the verticals are parallel. They also stand for a static world order. Everything, even movement, is presented as steady and immobile. Unlike foreshortening, which geometrically radicalizes space, the strict verticality and horizontality of these images establish a rhythm of alleviation. Those images that still employ a moderate degree of foreshortening are compositionally subdued by the regularity of their placement on the page. A pattern of hues (orange, blue, and green tones), identical to the one employed in *Ten Years of Soviet Uzbekistan*, creates a rhythmic variety that overcomes the monotony, but it is substantially muted and is not one of the work's conspicuous features.

Staged photographs overwhelmingly infiltrate Rodchenko and Stepanova's final book on the Orient. Whether it is a farmer spraying apple trees with insecticide dust, a steel founder tending to a blast furnace, a fisherman proudly displaying his catch of fish, an affable grocery shop assistant offering her produce, a nursery schoolteacher minding her pupils, a graduate student preparing for math exams, or a young musician rehearsing in a newly built conservatory, they all pose for the camera. Their postures and gestures tend to be awkwardly unnatural but are almost always accompanied by a radiating smile.

Photography, as a truth-establishing medium, has undergone a radical transition. The indexicality and iconicity of the photograph are replaced by its symbolic potential. *Index*, which refers to the object and the photograph's real connection to it, and *icon*, which indicates a resemblance to the object, are both superseded by *symbol*, which makes the object open for interpretation. In some sense, this "evolution" is an enactment of Roland Barthes' suggestion that photography is not a replica of reality but rather its emanation.[157] When the Soviet critic Volkov-Lannit argues that, apart from likeness (*skhodstvo*), a photographic portrait should reveal "the spiritual countenance of the Soviet worker,"[158] it seems likely that he has such a symbolic emanation in mind.

The entry into the symbolic field is abetted by the practice of retouching, which is overwhelmingly present in the folio. Rodchenko had initially opposed the invasive retouching of photographic images. While working on the "History of VKP(b) in Posters," according to Volkov-Lannit, he determinedly avoided cutting and retouching the photographs he worked with and treated them as sacred documentary objects.[159] The visual accuracy of the photograph performed a postulating function in the assembly of portraits. This conviction also resonated with the avant-garde's fervent resistance to the aesthetic "glossing over" of reality. As Boris Arvatov, puts it: "Instead of obscuring [*zatushevat'*] the operating function of art, one needs to reveal it explicitly. Otherwise, there will be an illusionary drift away from reality, a harmful self-delusion, a pseudo-life that is needed by the bourgeoisie but dangerous for the class of real builders."[160] The device must be laid bare instead of being glossed over.

Nonetheless, as early as in the 1930s Rodchenko began experimenting with retouching, and the practice was not imposed on him by any means. He manipulated the surface of his own ideologically unassuming photographs with crayons and gouache (for example, "Portrait of Regina Lemberg" of 1936).[161] The purpose of this invasive procedure, which made every individual shot original, was simply to create the semblance of a color image. In the Lemberg photograph, the primary "victims" of the retouching brush are the highly ornamented background and the sitter's dress. In terms of human appearance, only the woman's lips receive a vestige of red pigment.

In the case of *Kazakhstan*, retouching reaches inconceivable heights and this time the main object of corrective manipulation is the human body: lips, teeth, eyes, eyebrows, noses, hair, chins, hands, and the general body contours of the inhabitants of the transformed republic undergo alteration. In this case, retouching aspires to produce a generalized image. It defies documentary exactitude and veracity. But, as Tom Gunning puts it, "a photograph can only tell the truth if it is also capable of telling a lie."[162] Rodchenko and Stepanova's work thus enters the domain of fictional representation by enabling the covert abilities of the photograph.

It is not a coincidence that images of Lenin and Stalin, conventionally placed at the beginning, appear in the form of classic socialist realist paintings by Petr Vasil'ev and Dmitrii Nalbandian, and not as photographs or montages. The avant-garde photographic image that contested the representational dominance of easel painting thus evaporates. The photograph becomes a photo-painting that only invokes (and undercuts) the photographic accuracy of truth. As retouching starts to dominate the surface, the function of the latter becomes reduced to simply providing an outline; it degenerates into a simulation of the documentary image.

The retouched photographic image, however strange its emergence, is not what most obviously differentiates Rodchenko and Stepanova's *Kazakhstan* from the duo's earlier photo albums. The most striking feature of the 1949 artifact is, arguably, the predominant presence of ornament. The book contains an astounding variety of Kazakh ornamentation, most of which is an adaptation of a prevalent Kazakh pattern—*koshkar muyiz* (the ram's horn). All the renderings of the ornament are appropriated from a Soviet visual compendium of Kazakh ornament published in 1939.[163] *Kazakh National Ornament*, illustrated with drawings by Evgenii Klodt—a member of the Soviet Artists' Union—tried to replicate the seminal 1856 design sourcebook *The Grammar of Ornament* by Owen Jones. All the variations of Kazakh ornament, drawn in color, are compiled into groups and presented on twenty tables with a pretension of systematicity.

The ornamental inundation of *Kazakhstan* adorns, frames, and connects the photographic images and creates rhythmic patterns between clusters of photographs (fig. 2.7). The condensed ornamental lace completely persists in the composition of each chapter title page and then erupts as a lush, graphically composed carpet on the very last page of the book, where the Kazakh people's pledge to keep on the path of socialist construction is delivered. The created pattern becomes a manifestation of national radiance, it is a variation of "an ornamental halo," which Benjamin defines as "the characteristic feature of genuine aura."[164]

The interplay between form and content is vigorously enacted through ornamentation. *Ornamentum* in Latin means decoration and adornment and denotes a clear supplemental function in relation to the formal structure of an object or space and its social meaning. According to Wilhelm Worringer, however, "strong metaphysical content is inherent"[165] in ornament, and every single line of a primeval ornament bears a considerable semantic load, for it comprises an attempt to conceptualize the chaos of the external world. For many nineteenth-century critics, the formal outline of the ornament has connotative implications, usually of a religious or mystical character. John Ruskin, for example, regarded ornament as a reflective emblem that represents the world in a divinely inspired and rigorous order.[166] Alois Riegl, on the other hand, attempted to discern a transformation of "universal laws" that govern ornamental composition.[167]

In contrast to this, Gottfried Semper, an influential German art historian and architect, theorizes ornament exclusively in relation to material structure and practical purpose. For him, all "correct" stylistic aspects of work, including ornament, manifest themselves in one attribute that comprises "a *natural and logical consequence of the raw material*."[168] Semper's correlation of ornament with the structural arrangement of an artwork, as Kristin Romberg argues,[169] resonates with the avant-garde's—and Gan's in particular—notions of *tectonics* and *faktura*, both of which correspond to the material and technical processes used in manufacturing. Similarly, for Favorsky, ornament is defined in *faktura* terms. The former VKhUTEMAS professor conceives ornament not as a static entity but as a process: it is "working on the surface. Endowing it with a quality. Character. Not at all a decoration of the surface."[170]

The form-content tension, an inherent feature of ornament, was forcefully enacted in the twentieth century. Most representatives of the avant-garde were skeptical about the value of ornament in the new age of non-objective and productivist trends.[171] For Wassily Kandinsky the danger of ornamental form is

FIG. 2.7 Aleksandr Rodchenko and Varvara Stepanova, Spreads from *Kazakhstan*, 1949. Productive Arts.

that it can be "outwardly expressive and inwardly expressionless."[172] Sergei Tretiakov, in turn, critically labeled traditionalist trends in the field of form as "a new ornament, a new embellishing device, a new addition to the assortment of aesthetic embroideries and rattles offered to the public."[173] Similarly, for László Moholy-Nagy, form ought merely to express purpose, whereas "ornamentation almost always goes beyond the functional."[174] The culmination of the modernist rejection of ornament was Adolf Loos's bold statement that the "*evolution of culture is synonymous with the removal of ornament from utilitarian objects.*"[175] Ornament was virtually erased from modernism's quest for form.

The ornamental patterns found in *Kazakhstan* completely defy the avant-garde relation to ornament: they are proliferations of organic forms, which, moreover, had undergone a process of unimaginative orientalist appropriation. The ornamental "constructions" rely on the effect of excess, but all the same, produce a hollow discharge. National form is reduced to an ornament that is missing its primordial connection to a way of life. Similarly, the real inhabitants of the republic, who are represented in the book, are turned into exhibition display models.

The reduction of the human body to an expendable element of an imposing spectacle was certainly a universal feature of modernity. "The bearer of the ornaments is the *mass* and not the people,"[176] writes Siegfried Kracauer in 1923 of the Tiller Girls, a group of militarily trained dancing young women named after their choreographer John Tiller. The "girls" would synchronically condense into complex geometric patterns of colossal dimensions during their stadium spectacles. The geometry of human limbs, "a pure assemblage of lines," creates a mass ornament—a new type of collectivity that defies the natural bonds of the community but generates an abstract unity of functionally efficient individuals; this heralds the emerging "American distraction factories."[177] The end product, for Kracauer, "is the ornament, whose closure is brought about by emptying all the substantial constructs of their contents."[178] Kracauer, using terms similar to those of constructivism, empties the ornament and turns it into a functional formal device.

A comparable procedure takes place in the last image of *Kazakhstan* (fig. 2.7). It comprises an extremely primitive variety of photomontage—a cut-out from a photograph of three young Kazakh women and four men standing behind them and holding a giant coat of arms of the republic, a massive ceremonial ornament, on their shoulders. The cutout is pasted on the white plane of the page, thus creating a solemn, if sterile, impression. The group's picture was likely taken at a parade—a Stalinist version of a Tiller Girls' performance in which eroticized bare legs are replaced by rather desexualized military and athletic bodies. Stalinist parades, an inherent part of "stage dictatorship," were always a complex interplay between homogeneity and variety.[179] The unified pledge to serve the socialist cause was supplemented by the display of the multiple layers of diversity in Soviet society. External appearance is crucial in this sense—the young people all wear a stylized national garment, punctuated by an ornament.

Compositionally, the human figures form a column that literally supports the key ideological attribute—the coat of arms. With their lowered arms, the young Kazakhs are reduced to an architectural element. The final touch to this "photomontage" is the superimposition of two identical square ornamental patterns, also taken from Klodt's compendium, atop the photographic cutout.[180] The ornament validates the composition. It reinforces the identity of the group of people wearing ornamented clothes and holds the republic's key decorative attribute. That was an inadvertent return to what had been identified critically as a form of stylized-ornamental schematism in the pronouncements of the October Group years before.

Constructivism did not simply yield to external political pressure in the 1930s. The passage from the avant-garde experimentation of the early period to neoclassical socialist realism included many backwater byways. Although stagnant, these channels still nourished and even (re)directed some official cultural tendencies of the 1930s. Rodchenko and Stepanova's engagement with the material of the Soviet Orient bears witness to this process. Their body of work reflects the political evolution of Soviet photography, which is presented as a five-stage development process by Mikhail Karasik: "photo-document—the documentary recording of events; photomontage—the modeling of life; reportage—a politically committed approach to the recording of events; the photo-epic—investing reportage with artistic and epic features; the photo-painting—a new artistry, enriched by the method of Socialist Realism."[181] While the *USSR in Construction* issues represent a blend of the first three stages and rely heavily on the constructivist theory of photographic image, *Ten Years of Soviet Uzbekistan Kazakhstan* enters the domain of photo-epic, and *Kazakhstan* fully embraces the form of photo-painting.

The formal, technical, and ideological elements of the constructivist movement all aspired to reject any display of aestheticism—they defied any artistic predilection, however radical this may have been. Purified by the experience of non-objective representation, the constructivists had to exit the canvas plane altogether. The rejection of conventional artistic form was accomplished by endorsing the distinction between *depiction* and *painterliness*, which subsequently led to *functionality*. This position permeated almost all the operative principles of constructivism: *faktura* was inherently linked with *painterliness*, while construction realized itself in *functionality*. Mass-produced items of everyday utility comprised a new "artistic" form.

In 1932, Rodchenko wrote an article for the newspaper *Soviet Art* to provide his reflection on Stalin's call to master technology. He attempts to frame the challenge in clear productivist terms: "Stalin's slogan obliges us to abandon our individual cells and studies and go out into all kinds of production anywhere where there is an artistic need."[182] The artistic need seemed to be located in the sphere of the visual representation of the state. Photography becomes a surrogate artistic form, which fulfills a representational function yet does it with documentary precision. The instantaneous photograph, while respecting the unboundedness of the human subject and its embeddedness in the material world, provides a useful snapshot of reality that can be deployed in newspapers and turned into an ideologically and socially meaningful artifact through photomontage. However, photomontage, with its ability to select phenomena and to synthesize them into a generalized vision, gradually evolves into a means of blatant manipulation of photo-epic and photo-painting—signature artistic modes of Stalinist culture. It accomplishes a return to *depiction*, while its *functionality* is reduced to the level of propaganda. By passing from the function of reconstituting an object to performing its celebration, the leftist constructivists will now find themselves on the right.

CHAPTER 3

SOCIALIST SOUND

Dziga Vertov

"Dziga," according to Mikhail Kaufman, a famed cameraman and Dziga Vertov's brother, is a sound produced by the whirring film when it rolls through the spinning wheel of an editing table, while "Vertov" means to turn (*vertet'*) the montage table's handle.[1] It is noteworthy that Dziga Vertov, also known as Denis Arkad'evich Kaufman,[2] one of the opponents of Eisenstein's theory of montage, was, to a certain extent, a figurative extension of the editing table rather than of the camera apparatus that "catches life off guard" and thus reveals factual aspects of life.

Vertov's struggle with the theatricality of fictional, acted cinema resulted in a fixation on cinematic documentary fact and the camera that makes its emergence possible. Nevertheless, the montage procedure, though redefined, remained important to his project, which was marked by "a completely different significance toward *editing*" and was regarded "as the *organization of the visible world.*"[3] Montage, for Vertov, is not the process of *manipulation* (orientation toward a certain narrative line) but *organization* of phenomena. It is not a procedure that creates an illusionary presence; rather, it comprises an organizational or structuring method that allows the real to transpire. Documentary is a reality-driven mode of representation, but despite its goal of achieving objective representation, it inevitably employs fictive elements and is subject to creative intervention. Thus, the tension between the artistic-artificial and the factual permeated Vertov's theory and practice.

In 1920, Vertov was involved in organizing the agit-train "Red East," which was supposed to enlighten the inhabitants of the Russian Orient.[4] A few years later, the expansive, borderless urge of his aesthetic and political project was conceived in bolder theoretical terms. In January of 1925, after the first meeting of the Left Front of the Arts in Moscow, Vertov wrote an appeal to the *kinoks* of the "South" in which he proclaimed: "The basis of our program is not film production for entertainment or profit... but *a film bond between the peoples of the USSR and the entire world based on the platform of the communist decoding of what actually exists.*"[5] The aspiration of his avant-garde project was fundamentally planetary. However, the ideological and bureaucratic apparatus of the Soviet state would gradually assume a mediating role and confine Vertov's borderless ambitions.

Roland Barthes' famous statement that ideology is, in effect, "the image-repertoire of a period of history, the Cinema of a society"[6] resonates on many levels with Vertov's cinematic project. If ideology is the cinema of the real, then documentary, as a process of the communist deciphering of the world, is the ultimate all-encompassing imaginary, for it operates on both the real and the fictional planes and even collapses the distinction between the two. The tension was recognized by the Soviet state—the chief commissioner of Vertov's films. However, unlike the proposed "organization of the visible world," the state preferred the world's manipulatory representation. In May 1924, at the Thirteenth Congress of the Russian Communist Party, Stalin famously pronounced: "The cinema is a most valuable means of mass agitation. The task is to take this matter in hand."[7] The stance echoes Lenin's renowned dictum, "of all the arts, for us the cinema is the most important,"[8] but it also noticeably adds an important aspect to it—Lenin's immediate successor wants to keep the medium close at hand. Stalin underscores even further the manipulatory (from the Latin *manus*, for "hand") character of the art of cinema.

Vertov's response was not simply to passively face such inconsistent ideological demands but to engage in a theory and practice that emblematized the inherent incongruity of Soviet ideology. He was in a continuous dialogue with the Soviet ideological imaginary. Though this dialogue was gradually transformed into the latter's monologue, Vertov's conceptualization of the documentary film persisted throughout its evolution. In the mid-1930s he increasingly would start referring to "Vertov" in the third person, as if putting himself on a cinematic pedestal and, at the same time, distancing his theoretical self from his actual physical body.[9] This theoretical self-presentation does not comprise a clear-cut or homogenous referential system. Nevertheless, it incorporates a set of terms and operative principles that to a certain degree remained stable, though they were subject to a (forced) reorientation over time.

The chapter opens with a section on Vertov's early experiments with sound. The director's work on *Enthusiasm: Symphony of Donbass* (Entuziazm: Simfoniia

Donbassa, 1930) was crucial for the conceptual transference from the seeing *kino-eye* to the seeing and hearing *radio-eye*. This experience largely shaped Vertov's subsequent engagement with the oral tradition of the Soviet East in *Three Songs of Lenin* (Tri pesni o Lenine, 1934). However, as Vertov's archive establishes, the emancipated "primordial" voice of the Orient was essentially framed by previously transcribed and translated material. The tension between written and oral cultural traditions, and, by extension, between modern and archaic, is further enacted in the way the filmmaker conceptualized the transference of power from Lenin to Stalin. The following section investigates the director's late and substantially underexamined engagement with the wartime material in *The Front, to You!* (Tebe, front!, 1942), in which the Eastern oral tradition, now competing with a voice-over by the omnipresent Russian narrator, plays a constructive function. Finally, I conclude with Vertov's reconceptualization of "documentary fact" in his late writings and argue that he accomplishes a shift from the demystifying kino-eye toward a process of active mythmaking, prompted by his preoccupation with folkloric material.

FROM KINO-EYE TO RADIO-EYE

The key operative principle for Vertov is *kino-eye* (*kino-glaz*, cinematic eye). Kino-eye is a compelling ideological tool, capable of revealing sociopolitical perspectives that remain invisible to the human, biological eye. Thus, a film is a factual vision of the world, unmediated by subjective retinal impressions. As Vertov puts it, "the position of our bodies while observing or our perception of a certain number of features of a visual phenomenon in a given instant are by no means obligatory limitations for the camera which, since it is more perfect, perceives more and better."[10] The camera diminishes the size of retinal blind spots and has the potential to greatly expand the horizon of human perception: it is "more perfect than the human eye, for the exploration of the chaos of visual phenomena that fills space."[11] What is more, kino-eye overcomes limitations of the temporal fixity and spatial immobility of the human eye. Cinema can intermix unrelated spaces and move forward and backward in time, creating "the possibility of seeing without limits and distances."[12]

The kino-eye's aesthetic capacity was illustrated by one physical act, accomplished by the director himself and registered by a camera around 1919: a jump of one-and-a-half stories (a ledge above a grotto), filmed from a house in Moscow. Vertov describes the feat as recorded on celluloid film:

> A man approaches the ledge above a grotto; fear and indecision appear on his face; he's thinking: "I won't jump." Then he decides: "No, it's embarrassing, they're watching." Once again he approaches the edge, once again his face shows indecision. Then one sees his determination growing, he's saying to himself, "I must," and he leaves the grotto edge. He flies through the air, flies off-balance; he's thinking that he must position himself to land on his feet. He straightens out, approaches the ground; once more his face shows indecision, fear. Finally his feet touch the ground. His immediate thought is that he fell, then that he's got to keep his balance. Next he thinks that he jumped nicely but should not let on that he has, and, like an acrobat who's performed a difficult maneuver on the trapeze, he pretends that it was awfully easy. And with that expression the man slowly "floats off."
>
> From the viewpoint of the ordinary eye, you see untruth. From the viewpoint of the cinematic eye (aided by special cinematic means—in this case, accelerated shooting) you see the truth. If it's a question of reading someone's thoughts at a distance . . . then you have that opportunity right here. It has been revealed by the kino-eye.[13]

The footage of Vertov's jump revealed a range of emotions of which the jumper himself was not aware and observers failed to detect. The camera exposed what was previously hidden, as it did in Muybridge's horse movement experiments, where a duplicated version of reality redeems it as a whole. This very discovery is also linked to Vertov's preoccupation with the camera's ability to capture the *synchronism* (or correspondence) between words uttered and the inner feelings of the speaker, something that will be amplified in later sound films.[14] However, in the context of silent cinema, this was a great epistemic discovery—the cinematic apparatus assumes the function of a revelatory device and allows everyone involved (the actor, the recording crew, and the spectators) to leave the realm of ignorance and attain the domain of consciousness.

This process of enlightenment is also connected with another key notion of Vertov's theory and practice—"life caught off guard" (*zhizn' vrasplokh*).[15] The director identifies three modes in which it can manifest: "1) hidden-camera filming where [people] are completely unaware that they're being recorded; 2) such a technique when they're artificially distracted; and 3) when people themselves are naturally distracted."[16] Life caught off guard is the guiding principle for the kino-eye: a hidden camera or its unobtrusive presence is essential because it captures people and phenomena in their natural state, as facts of life.

Vertov argues that the ordinary human eye only observes "a series of scattered perceptions"[17] and fails to appreciate the ultimate fluidity of movements and complex interrelationships between various phenomena and objects. The film records these and, once edited, arranges everything into harmonious and intelligible patterns. Vertov's hostility toward human eyesight and his attempt to replace it with the superior mechanical vision of the kino-eye is driven by a clearly articulated ideological agenda. In one of his early speeches, he unambiguously connected the invention of the movie camera and its early uses with the capitalist tendency to "entertain the masses" in order "to divert the workers' attention from their basic aim: the struggle against their masters."[18] It was an affordable substitution for a theatrical experience. Vertov challenges the reactionary factory of illusions—"the toxic sweetness of artistic drama."[19] Instead, he argues for the enlightened consciousness of the proletariat and conceives his artistic agenda in terms of a "class vision": "We need *conscious* Revolutionaries, not an unconscious mass submissive to any passing suggestion. *Long live the class consciousness of the healthy with eyes and ears to see and hear with!*"[20] Human perceptual limitations are overcome, and the true nature of social reality is revealed.

The camera is what ultimately provides a Communist film vision—it enlightens and emancipates. It is not merely a recording device registering the visible, it is also a tool that accomplishes critical analysis—it scrutinizes the material world with visual capacity inaccessible to the ordinary human eye and thereby creates a new critical perspective. Vertov's camera is a Latourian *instrument* that analyzes objects of scientific study and thus participates in a process of social construction.[21] Reverse motion, manipulated speed of projection, tilted camera angles, and split screens: all are among the necessary cinematic tools that appear as "seeming irregularities" and that are employed "to investigate and organize phenomena."[22] They lie at the heart of the truly Communist method of the "cinematic deciphering of the visible world,"[23] which provides ultimate documentary supra-objectivity.

The filmmaker valorizes mental cognition and diminishes the value of perception by the senses. The cognitive process (fact) replaces the detached reflection of traditional narrative arts (fiction). Vertov thus abolishes art for its fictionality-untruthfulness. He accomplishes a radical displacement of forms of mimetic figuration that prevailed at the time—art ceases to imitate reality. The kino-eye fills in the gap between human cognition and the perceived world as such while the proletarian class, the carrier of the correct Marxist vision, is the sole possessor of the "accurate" cognitive vision.

The kino-eye allegedly provides "unmediated" access to the real and reveals true revolutionary reality without any embellishments and distortions, though

Vertov never actually theoretically conceptualized cinema's purported ability to grasp the real as such. This unmediated access ostensibly did not involve any representational practices. However, the process of overcoming the representational barrier is abetted by the kino-eye's refusal to recognize the difference between the realms of the real and the fictional. It does not merely contemplate; it actively participates in the process of building socialism. Accordingly, in Vertov's view, Lenin, with his enlightened theoretical outlook (dialectic materialism) and practical transformative agenda (such as the project of electrification), was the first true kino-eye. Unmediated access to reality "as it is" is followed by an impulse to transform the world.

Vertov envisaged a situation in which the technical advancement of mobile cameras would create an army of *kinkors* (*kino-correspondents*) that would film every noteworthy event, and from whose footage statewide film journals would be produced. This participatory model of newsgathering would result in mass authorship—a collective artistic body: "The millionth part of each man's inventiveness in his everyday work contains an element of art, if one must use that term."[24] For Vertov, cinema made by *kinkors* produces reality and this clearly resonates with one of the foundational principles of Marxism. In the very beginning of *Theses on Feuerbach*, Marx identifies a key problem with all preceding materialist frameworks: "things, reality, sensuousness are conceived only in the form of the *object, or of contemplation*, but not as *sensuous human activity, practice*, not subjectively."[25] This condition creates an obstacle to grasping "the significance of 'revolutionary,' of 'practical-critical,' activity."[26] The kino-eye, with its active participatory and scientifically materialist outlook, thus fulfills Marx's vision.

However, Vertov's orthodox Marxist technocratic vision of the documentary genre was bound to be challenged with the emergence of Stalinist culture, given its organicity and valorization of content at the expense of form. On January 11, 1930, two weeks before the appearance of Shklovsky's "Monument to a Scholarly Error," the newspaper *Kino* published a programmatic article attacking formalist practices in cinema.[27] It denounced formalist experiments, claiming that they are cut off from "social content": the fetishistic preoccupation with fact prevented the formal experimenters from engaging with content as such. It also emphasized Vertov's role in passing these experiments off as revolutionary art. Vertov drafted a response, published only recently, where he argues that the widely hailed achievements of the Soviet film industry, such as Turin's *Turksib*, owe much to his theoretical postulates and films.[28] More importantly, he highlights the incompatibility between "reactionary form" and "revolutionary content" without realizing that the state had developed a preference for a stable meaning that replaced revolutionary content.[29]

Vertov's treatment of the cinematic shot as a documentary *fact* presented a different set of problems for the Soviet ideologues of cinema. This fact of life was to be treated not as a self-sufficient domain of objective truth, but as a building block in the overarching ideological narrative, which revealed the socialist realist tendency to outstrip reality by incorporating fictional elements. For Vertov, on the other hand, the move toward "adequate correspondence to reality" and the ultimate outstripping thereof, as demanded by socialist realism, took place largely in the domain of sound. The visually presented fact of the kino-eye was supplanted by a *speaking* subject. However, this reorientation took place within the premises and in accordance with Vertov's early conceptualization of sound, and was largely informed by his early avant-garde experiments.

The advent of sound in cinema does not merely coincide with the Soviet modernization project; it also parallels the rise of the ideological voice of Stalinism and reflects a substantial change in Soviet internationalist rhetoric—from expansionist internationalism to diversity within one country. Furthermore, as Masha Salazkina highlights, the transition to sound substantially contributed to the shift from avant-garde theory and practice to the basic premises of socialist realism.[30] "Talking cinema is as little needed as a singing book,"[31] bluntly stated Viktor Shklovsky in 1927. The following year, a group of leading Soviet filmmakers—Eisenstein, Pudovkin, and Aleksandrov—issued their famous statement on sound. The joint declaration denounced the use of sound that corresponded with movement on the screen and proclaimed that "*only a contrapuntal use* of sound in relation to the visual montage piece will afford a new potentiality of montage development and *perfection*."[32] The directors strove for an "*orchestral counterpoint* of visual and aural images."[33] There was no place for *talkies*, with their use of linear naturalistic sound. Moreover, the question of sound had clear international-national inflections. The statement's concluding paragraphs read:

> The contrapuntal method of constructing the sound film will not only not weaken international cinema but will bring its significance to unprecedented power and cultural height.
>
> Such a method for constructing the sound film will not confine it to a national market, as must happen with the photographing of plays, but will give a greater possibility than ever before for the circulation throughout the world of a filmically expressed idea.[34]

The statement posits that non-synchronization of the visual and auditory planes is crucial for cinema to maintain its international appeal since, in that case, sound would function as a purely formal element and not as a narrative-driving one. Vertov fully agreed with the internationalist impulse of the statement. The kino-eye has intrinsically borderless aspirations and Vertov consistently referred to Lenin's vision of radio as a paperless newspaper able to overcome distances. This position resonates with the essence of his documentary project, described as a process of the "establishing of a class bond that is visual (*kino-eye*) and auditory (*radio-ear*) between the proletarians of all nations and all lands, based on the platform of the communist decoding of the world."[35] The resulting hybrid—*radio-eye*—comprises "one of the shortest ways to fulfill the formula '*proletarians of all countries, unite!*' "[36]

However, his nonsynchronization of visual and auditory material was even more radical than that of the authors of the sound statement. The question of narrative, and the contrapuntal or diegetic function of sound in relation to it, was irrelevant to him. For Vertov, what mattered is the sound's origins: whether it was recorded as documentary material or artificially reproduced for fictional purposes. The documentary-factual essence of sound overshadows its diegetic function. The image's optical-aural rootedness in reality allows it to have a cognitive effect that, in turn, leads to a tangible impact on the real world.

Vertov also shares a belief in the transnational aspiration of sound with the authors of the "Statement." As he puts it in the 1930 article "March of the Radio-Eye":

> We have to see the radio-eye as the most powerful weapon in proletarian hands; as a possibility for proletarians of all nations and countries to hear, see, and understand each other in an organized manner; as an opportunity, not limited by spatial distance, for activism and propaganda by means of facts; as an opportunity to contrast the radio-documents of our socialist construction to documents of suppression and exploitation—radio-documents of the capitalist world.[37]

Although Vertov does not formally address how different languages can be intelligible to proletarians of different countries, an explanation can be found in his inherently avant-garde treatment of language as such. The word, as a rhetorical entity, is redundant for the director—he aspired toward cognition unmediated by words. In this vein, *Man with a Movie Camera* (Chelovek s kinoapparatom, 1928) comprised a radical visual investigation that attempted to subjugate language as such: as the titles announce, "this new experimentation work by Kino-Eye is directed toward the creation of an authentically international absolute language of cinema on the basis of its complete separation from the language of theatre and literature." To a certain extent, the films that followed it continued this epistemic experiment.

Vertov's non-semantically driven understanding of the function of language seems to derive directly from his early sound experiments. He started his artistic career in 1916 with experiments in the sphere of sound recording while pursuing medical studies in Saint Petersburg. Within two years, he had produced what he termed "verbal montage structures." As he writes, "I had an idea about the necessity to expand our ability to hear in an organized manner. Not to constrain this ability by the limits of ordinary music. I included the whole heard world in the notion 'I hear'."[38] What is remarkable is the fact that Vertov's "failed" (for they did not fully satisfy him) early experiments with sound subsequently led him to make films. As Douglas Kahn succinctly puts it, the kino-eye "was born of a keen but frustrated ear."[39] Vertov recollects:

> Once I was sitting in the cinema. Some picture was being screened, I don't remember exactly which—maybe something about an explosion in a mine or something else, but it was newsreel footage. So, I thought, while looking at the screen, that an apparatus exists that has the capacity to record for the eyes the waterfall that I could not record for hearing. I decided that I had to temporarily abandon all endeavors in the sphere of sound and see if I could do something in the sphere of the visual examination of phenomena.[40]

Vertov highlights here the fact that he theorized the employment of sound in cinema (audio facts) long before there were technical means to generate it.[41] In 1923, four years before the release of *The Jazz Singer*—the first sound film which is also notorious for its blackface performance—Vertov conceptualized his approach to sound in "Kino-Eyes: A Revolution." According to his credo regarding the "organization of the heard world," sound was not supposed to create a naturalistic illusion or to be used to synchronize dialogue.

A few years later, in 1929, Vertov wrote down a plan for a treatise on documentary film in which he conceived his work with sound as central to his oeuvre. He identifies four types of sound experiments under the very first rubric of the book—"Rhythmic montage of verbal-sonic material": 1) the montage of words ("Cities of Asia"); 2) the montage of noises ("sawmill"); 3) the projection of music fragments on words (Scriabin); and 4) the Laboratory of Hearing.[42]

The passage is further elaborated in Vertov's later (1935) autobiographical sketch in which he recollects presenting Oriental toponyms (cities of Asia Minor) as a rhythmic sequence for purposes of memorization while at school: "Miletus, Tegea, Smyrna, Halicarnassus, Samos, Ephesus, and Mytilene on the Isles of Lesbos,

Cyprus, and Rhodes."[43] Through their organization in rhythmic and cadenced sequences, the "outlandish" names are reclaimed as familiar. Vertov's schoolboy experience led to later experiments with recorded sound—a montage of fragments of different gramophone records (basically, a case of early sound mixing).

Yet the available repertoire of recorded music did not satisfy the future filmmaker. He began to extend the borders of the audible world by experimenting with sounds other than music. During a summer break at Lake Ilmen, while waiting for his girlfriend by a sawmill, he started to perceive industrial noises as though he were blind, and then tried to reconstruct the sounds using words and letters. He quickly realized that this was an inadequate means of representation since certain sounds could not be transcribed. Even musical notation failed to solve the problem, given the preponderance of atonal sounds.

Vertov subsequently returned to poetry. His early asyntactic attempts were imitations of the futurist tradition that vigorously created idiosyncratic lexical associations and specular phonetic patterns. He also developed an interest in the music of Aleksandr Scriabin, who had created a substantially atonal and dissonant musical system, infused with mysticism and his personal brand of synesthesia (association of colors with various harmonic tones of his atonal scale). Vertov conceived of writing poems that could be recited to Scriabin's music, thus creating a contrapuntal effect. The semantics of words were to be engulfed by auditory strategies. Vertov identified this poetic-musical practice as "the Laboratory of Hearing."

For Vertov, the practical transference from the realm of the purely optical to the optical-aural occurred when he made his first sound film—*Enthusiasm*. The director referred to the film, released in March 1930, as "March of the Radio-Eye"—a new beginning and an evolution from the mere *kino-eye* to the *radio-eye*, which comprised a visual-sonic exploration of the visible and audible world.[44] In Vertov's own words:

> *Enthusiasm* is the first train of sound to have burst through the velvet studio walls onto the open expanses of audible life. The film was shot not in the conditions of the deadly silence of a soundproofed room, but in Donbass, in the conditions of clamor and clatter, in production workshops shattered by sound. The significance of the film lies also in the fact that it exceeded the limits of musical notation (do-re-mi-fa-sol-la-ti) and brought millions of sounds to active life; it sharply expanded our sound horizon.[45]

Vertov experimented with the process of recording sound while working on the industrial sensory environments of the film. He used a recently designed portable set of equipment, built specially for him by Aleksandr Shorin's Leningrad-based workshop. The recording camera was attached to a stationary sound recording studio linked to several microphones placed in different parts of the city.[46] The cinematic apparatus literally brought distant industrial topoi together into a single audio-visual field. The industrial sound recorded remotely with portable microphones and thus detached from its source in the film was comprised of sirens, a steam whistle, wheels turning on the railroad track, and rotating engine sounds.[47] To emphasize the film's technical-experimental nature, Vertov appeared in its titles not as a "director" but as an "engineer."

The sound of labor—the cacophony of factories—was a unifying international phenomenon for the proletariat, who had no motherland. It was a sound that defied translation and narrow national identities. Indeed, palpable industrial sound was an essential component of the expansionist modernist aesthetics of the 1920s, and it was actively appropriated for ideological purposes. In the words of René Fülöp-Miller, an Austrian cultural historian writing in 1926, the "true" proletarian music "emphasized the rhythms that corresponded to the universal and impersonal elements of humanity. The new music had to embrace all the noises of the mechanical age, the rhythm of the machine, the din of the great city and the factory, the whirring of driving-belts, the clattering of motors, and the shrill notes of motor-horns."[48] There was a clear emphasis on the sounds of labor as a universalizing element and *Enthusiasm*, which erupts with a hustled motif of "The Internationale" (still the Soviet national anthem at the time) at the end, followed that trend.[49]

However, Vertov argued that there was no single noise in his film, for the notion of *noise*, for him, is framed by the conception of musical harmony, while any worker can distinguish sounds made by a particular piece of machinery in the "industrial cacophony."[50] "Noise" becomes comprehensible and familiar to those who make it. The initial plan to overlay industrial sounds with revolutionary speeches failed to be accomplished due to technical difficulties, so *Enthusiasm* remained within a purely acoustic field.

The film commences with an image of a young woman wearing headphones and looking for the "correct" radio station, which transmits the march from the soundtrack of the film itself. The self-referential nature of this episode is very pronounced. The woman in earphones makes the viewer aware of the very act of listening.[51] In Oksana Sarkisova's words, the scene "sets up the spatial coordinates, demonstrates the creation of an 'imagined community'" and does so "through the simultaneity of shared experiences based on the presupposed interest in and importance of the received information for the listeners."[52] Sergei Tretiakov, for instance, conceived of radio as a means of directing the movement of those who march and, at the same time, representing the action of movement for those who could not participate in the parade.[53] It performs both an instrumental and representational function.

However, the avant-garde's imagined proletarian community, unified by auditory means, did not resonate deeply with critics of *Enthusiasm*. Stalin criticized *Enthusiasm* for its "erroneous abstruseness [*oshibochnoe zaumnichan'e*]" and raised concerns over its arbitrary treatment of documentary material.[54] The Soviet leader, who was once shown a documentary about the Cheliuskin expedition without a soundtrack, emphasized that "cinema really presupposed music and that this helped perception enormously."[55] *Enthusiasm*'s radical soundscape contrasted strongly with melodious soundtracks written to help in the achievement of this desired cognitive clarity. Mikhail Cheremukhin, a Soviet composer and a prominent advocate of folk art, wrote that song had become a crucial component of the filmic image ever since the advent of sound film; it was a guarantor of comprehensibility.[56] Turning away from musical harmony and language as the governing medium of ideology was no longer possible.

INVENTING ORALITY

Over the subsequent years, Vertov gradually neutralized the machinist aspect of his theory and practice. The industrial noise of the highly experimental *Enthusiasm* was consequently replaced with the human voice, which introduced human organicity and allowed for the invention of alternative forms of anthropocentric experience. Two years after the completion of his first sound film, Vertov embarked on a path toward discovering the people's primordial voice through the study and recording of Central Asian folklore.[57] Shorin's sound-recording device, tested in Donbass, was relocated to the Soviet periphery where it became one of the earliest mobile sound studios used to record local musical compositions. These recordings were later featured in *Three Songs of Lenin*.[58] Vertov viewed this documentary sound film as a "symphony of thoughts," in contrast to *Enthusiasm*, which he considered a symphony of industrial sounds.[59] This was a conscious move toward conceptualization of the thinking (and singing) Soviet human subject. The documentary orientation, however, still prevailed. Vertov claimed that the film about Lenin "is written with cinematic documents":[60] documents of socialist construction, documents that preserved the image and voice of Lenin, and documents of folkloric art.

Three Songs of Lenin glorifies the exploits of Vladimir Lenin, presented through flashbacks of his life, and mourns his death by means of stylized songs performed by women of the generic Soviet East. Emancipated female singers cast off their veils, only to put them over their heads once more to mourn the leader's death. But the emancipation and the ensuing act of mourning are eventually superseded by the promise of resurrection and eternal afterlife. On June 13, 1933, while filming in Tashkent, Vertov makes the following entry in his diary:

> Lenin is when an Uzbek woman on a tractor starts spring with plowing.
> Lenin is when the melancholy songs of slavery grow gay and lively.
> Lenin is a power station on the Dnepr. Ukrainian girls awarded medals, an Uzbek farmhand as head of administration, a Turkmen woman who has thrown off the *yashmak*, an orchestra of Uzbek Pioneers (former waifs) playing in a red tearoom, the newspaper *Leninskii put'* [Leninist Way], a nursery school in a collective farm.
> Lenin is honesty, uprightness, selflessness, enthusiasm, and straightforwardness.[61]

Lenin's image undergoes a process of radical dissipation: all aspects of the new Soviet life evolve into metaphoric extensions of the figure of the first Soviet leader. The dead man finds his numerous reincarnations in forms from various domains: the corporeal (Stalin, shock workers, emancipated women of the East), the mental (honesty, uprightness, etc.), and the inanimate (dams, power stations). This omnipresence and profusion define the aesthetic strategy of *Three Songs of Lenin*.

The singularity of the figure of Lenin is balanced by a topographic diversity, for the documentary film has the texture of a complex Oriental rug. It was shot in several of the Eastern republics of the Soviet Union: Azerbaijan, Turkmenistan, and Uzbekistan—disparate spaces that interweave to form an image of a rather generic Soviet Orient that is not distinguished by any particularities and that stands for a homogenous Soviet identity.[62] Such a blatant conflation of spaces is directly linked to the kino-eye's ability to connect disparate places. It does not know borders and its spatial ambitions know no limits. Vertov discusses the question of crafted geography in connection with *Three Songs of Lenin*: "From the human eye's viewpoint, I haven't really the right to 'edit in' myself beside those who are seated in this hall, for instance. Yet in kino-eye space, I can edit myself not only sitting here beside you, but in various parts of the globe. It would be absurd to create obstacles such as walls and distance for the kino-eye.[63]

The accepted avant-garde practice of montage, an amalgamation of various topoi, resonates with the declarative opening of the film: "In different corners of

FIG. 3.1 Dziga Vertov, Stills from *Three Songs of Lenin*, 1934/1970.

the world, in Europe and America, in African countries and beyond the Arctic Circle, songs of Lenin, the friend and liberator of every exploited man, are sung. No one knows the unnamed authors of these songs, but they pass from mouth to mouth, from *yurt* to *yurt*, from settlement to settlement, from *aul* to *aul*, from village to village." Vertov delineates or rather extends Lenin's impact throughout the entire world (the rarely mentioned subtitle of the film is "about the leader of the repressed of the whole world"). The Soviet leader's emancipatory drive, like the expansion of an electric field, permeates all corners of the globe. However, it is not a process of mere spatial extension. Oksana Sarkisova points to the fact that because the mourning women in the documentary are filmed years after Lenin's actual death, the director's action of interspersing the funeral with the songs creates "a single spatial-temporal event": "The women, who 'never saw Lenin,' epitomize the changing function of vision as they incorporate his mediatized presence."[64] The documentary thus gestures toward a complex spatiotemporal interweaving with a clear mythological potential.

Kristin Thompson, in her pioneering article, argues that Vertov chooses a more conventional path when it comes to the sound design in *Three Songs of Lenin*: there is no contrapuntal tension between sound and image, and the soundtrack is comprised of reverent music and bits of on-screen diegetic voice.[65] Oksana Bulgakowa echoes these concerns and suggests that Vertov "posited the ear above the eye, above the analytic visuality of silent cinema, on his way from modernism to archaism."[66] Diegetic voice and folkloric music, as "semantically unburdened" aesthetic phenomena, smoothly guide the viewer toward ideological comprehension and replace the cerebral visuality of the early Vertov. The film's assumed formal conventionalism, which enables ideological indoctrination, was a result of elaborate theorization of the human voice and agency. An analysis of the sound design and archival materials related to it, together with the director's own theoretical reflections and intentions, point to a more nuanced evolution in line with late modernist human turn. Vertov's "drastic" reorientation was not as straightforward as has been contended.

Vertov insists that *Three Songs of Lenin* is a self-sufficient original and not an artifact of a secondary order "translated from the language of theatre and the language of literature,"[67] and that its director performs the function of a composer, and not that of a translator or pianist-transmitter. This treatment of sound as something lying beyond conventional semantics allowed him to work with the songs of the East as sonic material. What was sung about, as conveyed by intertitles that translated songs' lyrics, mattered less than the sound experience as such. Indeed, pre-1933 drafts of the film did not contain a single reference to Central Asian songs.[68]

This rather radical undermining of the connotative potential of words was a crucial component of Vertov's aesthetic strategy in the 1930s. He elaborates further in the essay titled "Without Words" (Bez slov):

> The point is that the exposition of *Three Songs* develops not through the channel of words, but through other channels, through the interaction of sound and image, through the combination of many channels; it proceeds underground, sometimes casting a dozen words onto the surface. The movement of thought, the movement of ideas, travels along many wires but in a single direction, to a single goal. Thoughts fly out from the screen, entering without verbal translations into the viewer's consciousness. The written and spoken words have their own contrapuntal route within the film. Before us is a huge symphony orchestra of thoughts; an accident to a violin or cello does not put an end to the concert. The flow of thoughts continues even if one of the interconnecting wires is broken.[69]

Even the interviews with the Dneprostroi shock worker Maria Belik and the kolkhoz activists, the most poignant speech acts of the film, transcended the realm of comprehensibility. Vertov recollects the writer H. G. Wells's impression of the film, which he watched without a translator: "those who spoke, their awkward gestures, the sparkle in their eyes, the embarrassment in their faces, and other details enabled him [Wells] to read their thoughts, and he felt not the slightest need for a translation of those words."[70] The interview with Belik, who in a very shy voice full of dialectal specificity, narrates the exploits for which she received the Order of Lenin, was one of the earliest records of synchronous sound and image in the Soviet Union. It was the ultimate manifestation of Vertov's vision of the kino-eye catching life off guard. The shy concrete worker does not seem to be aware of the camera's presence and the interview with her is an example of an accented, unkempt reality manifesting itself.

In fact, Vertov directly connects the Belik interview with his early kino-eye experiment—the celebrated jump. For Vertov, both reveal a rich scope of emotions hidden from the human eye: "Why does she have an effect? Because she's good at acting? Nothing of the kind. Because I got from her what I got from myself during the jump: the synchrony of words and thoughts."[71] The synchrony between words and thoughts, a quintessentially epistemic aspect of filmmaking for Vertov, defines the film's structure. The director emphasizes that while the method as such was consciously laid bare in his early films, it remained hidden in the 1930s projects, so the viewer sees only the result and not the process of formal construction. As he puts it in his diary in 1936, after having made the film: "My goal was the truth. Kino-eye was [its] means."[72]

However, the most unexpected manifestation of the kino-eye is found in the key component of the film, from which it takes its title—the songs of the Soviet East. Folklore, carefully gathered by Vertov and recorded by Petr Shtro, who had worked on *Enthusiasm*, plays both a structural and a poetic role. As Vertov notes in his diary, the film was inspired by his early experiments in "the laboratory of hearing," for it includes records of unmediated folkloric material that the director also refers to as "song-documents":[73] "We included several songs of the Soviet East in the film. Some songs are present on the soundtrack, some on the image track; still others are reflected in the intertitles."[74] The Eastern voice is dispersed within the formal structure of the film. This diffusion, however, results in an ornamental pattern, as the enunciating power of the word remains a prerogative of the Russian-speaking subjects.

The first song of the film, "In a Black Prison Was My Face," registers the transition from the repressive feudal past to a modernized socialist present. The unveiling of Muslim women, so that they can face the world both literally and metaphorically, functions as a key motif. As Emma Widdis puts it, "unveiled, the ethnic woman is permitted a hands-on encounter with socialism."[75] After showing various images of repression and misery, the most striking of which is a sequence that depicts a woman staggering aimlessly through the streets of Bukhara, Vertov shows images of socialist modernization: a group of pioneers marching cheerfully and in unison, in sharp contrast to the lone woman's directionless wandering. Equipment such as planes, combine harvesters, tractors, and cars; production plant machinery; modern institutions such as women's clubs, universities, and hospitals; and various tools such as microscopes and theodolites are all presented in oriental settings with formerly repressed women operating or engaging with them professionally.

The second song, "We Loved Him . . ." (My liubili ego . . .), reveals the reaction of ethnic minorities to the death of Lenin. The song's lyrics are not sung but projected in translation on the screen and accompanied by a Western-style funeral march. The scenes of mourning are intermixed with the documentary chronicle of Lenin's actual funeral procession. A moving funeral train transporting the coffin—the train of modernity—bids farewell to the great modernizer. The song establishes the leader's international appeal but also concludes with a gesture toward a specific Russianness at the end: "Founder of the Communist International. Banner of the exploited East! Head of the proletarian dictatorship in Russia. He was simple and direct in his conduct and Russians used to call him

'Il'ich.'" This is followed by one of the central sound documents of the film—Lenin's Red Army speech, accompanied by spiraling titles.

The vital aural presence of the leader is supplemented by a complex interplay of movement and stillness in a montage sequence that shows mourners counterposed with the deceased lying in a coffin. This sequence is accompanied by succinct intertitles: "Lenin, but not moving, Lenin, but silent ... The masses are moving, the masses are silent." The movement of the masses implies that the immobile Lenin continues his life in the movements and deeds of the masses. The structure of this montage sequence, however, has literary roots. As Viktor Listov has observed, there is a textual source for Vertov's visual treatment of the funeral sequence—the *Pravda* ocherk "The Final Journey" (Poslednii reis) by Mikhail Kol'tsov, *Pravda*'s leading correspondent and Vertov's longtime comrade, who had offered him his first job in cinema.[76] As Kol'tsov writes two days after Lenin's death, "Lenin, but he does not move, does not gesticulate, does not buzz with excitement, does not wave, does not hurry along at an angle with brief cheerful steps. Lenin, but he lies down, hopeless and straight, hands at his sides, shoulders in a green army jacket."[77] The text is literally animated by Vertov. The importance of the textual provenance of this episode and its entrance into the visual field is further enhanced by the fact that the director uses ellipses instead of commas, periods, exclamation marks, or question marks. The ellipsis, which usually indicates the omission of a word, points at Lenin's absence textually while the camera displays his immobile presence. Lenin's physical death is negated by the enduring life of Leninism, which is "paraded" in titles abundant with exclamation marks at the end of the film.

The funeral song concludes with the piercing and pensive gaze of the Eastern woman Melkiu, played by the Azeri party activist Aishat Gasanova.[78] Melkiu has the function of a silent guide throughout the film—she is arguably the first possessor of human subjectivity in Vertov's oeuvre, for she is not presented as a mere "fact." But it is a poignant incongruity that this truly emancipated figure remains silent throughout the film even though it takes the oral tradition as its structuring device. The voice of the collective is given to her European counterparts, the workers and peasants of the European parts of the Union of Soviet Socialist Republics (USSR). Her subordinate status is further reflected by the fact that she is connected through montage with the symbolic (metropolitan) center of Red Square, where the funeral guard is firing its rifles in a ceremonial act of mourning. The sound of the salute reaches different parts of the country, and every inhabitant of the vast territory is shown to be frozen in place.

This mournful petrification is subsequently overcome in the third song "In the Great City of Stone" (V bol'shom kamennom gorode) that brings the film's narrative back to Moscow. The melancholic song invites the viewer to find consolation and inspiration in Lenin's mummified body in the mausoleum. Conceived as a sacred relic legitimatizing Soviet power, the petrified body prompts the birth of Leninism as an ideological movement: the concluding part of the song is accompanied by a sequence showing an incessant flow of ideological mourners entering the mausoleum. An upward curvilinear movement of the funerary procession is contrasted with a downward movement of a printing house conveyor belt carrying Lenin's books in different languages. The birth of Leninism then reveals the full scope of the Soviet modernization project. The concluding sequence shows how the ideological energy of Leninism acquires its industrial socialist flesh. Dneprostroi is presented as a site of feats of labor and a source of light: the hydroelectric station is depicted as the ultimate monument to Lenin—the first bringer of light. The industrial (though muted) noise of Magnitostroi, the Moscow–Volga canal, the SS Chelyuskin, and the Moscow Metro seem to overwhelm the feeble "tune" of the last oriental song. The final titles of the film reinforce the main discursive premise that time will pass but Lenin will live on: "Centuries will pass with an iron gate, and people will forget the names of the countries in which their ancestors lived but they will never forget the name Lenin, Il'ich Lenin." The overall structure of the film thus presents a temporal continuum that extends from the first song's rootedness in the oppressive past to the last song's glorification of the socialist future, with the middle song reflecting a transitional state that registers Lenin's death and anticipates the future life of Leninism.

The combination of epic socialist content and exotic form made manifest in the three songs is a late modernist corrective to Vertov's avant-garde aesthetics. This corrective reopened the enclosure of form onto the film's social and political environs, facilitating its more direct engagement with topical discourses of the time, such as *narodnost'*. It resonated with Shklovsky's simultaneous denial of the preeminence of aesthetic form and inclusion of the content-friendly notion of heterogeneity in 1930. In a 1936 diary entry, Vertov asserts that the key feature of collected folkloric material is indeed the unity of form and content.[79]

In the 1920s, however, Vertov vehemently argued that the attempts of many Soviet filmmakers to accommodate revolutionary material in a conservative form was done in vain, since the two are simply incompatible.[80] He drastically reformulates his vision of the form-content tension while working on *Three Songs of Lenin*. In order to achieve the desired unity between form and content, Vertov argues, the director has to abstain from confusing the viewer by "showing him a trick or technique not generated by the content and uncalled for by necessity."[81] This stance was a characteristic accommodation of the aesthetic-ideological trends of the time and it resonated with the classical definition of the method of socialist realism, as defined in the leading cinema journal: "in its images, the method of socialist realism reaffirms truthful art—content that is simple in its artistic clarity and precision, form that is simple in its clarity and precision."[82] Offering an audience readily comprehensible content was crucial. In "On the Struggle against Formalism" (1936), Vertov again concentrates on *Three Songs of Lenin* as his redemptive project: "This connection with folk art will help us in our struggle for the unity of form and content.... The pivotal role, in this dialectic unity, is given to content.... We will not achieve simplicity and clarity in art with a separation of form from content."[83]

Folklore, as a document of reality, supplants the avant-garde fact. Mariano Prunes has highlighted the interconnection between the aesthetic principles of factography and Vertov's treatment of the documentary chronicle and photographic image in the first part of *Three Songs of Lenin*.[84] However, the film gradually evolves into a "mythographic" artifact, where factographic iconicity is replaced by symbolism and romantic pictorialism. As a *Pravda* reviewer noted, the first two songs are infused with delicate lyricism that overcomes the documentary fact's dryness, while the last song yields to the factographic pressure due to the overwhelming presence of industrial labor images.[85] The final product is not a documentary film per se, for it does not merely document reality. Vertov manipulates documentary material to achieve clear ideological ends by creating a hybrid (fictional-real) filmic space.[86] The departure from the documentary realm of the real towards the mythographic ideological space defines the discursive coordinates of *Three Songs of Lenin*.

The documentary's mythic potential resonated with the key premises of the emerging high Stalinist culture that prompted the discursive ascendency of folklore and epic. Epic, as a genre that could accommodate a creation myth, was instrumental in the process of Soviet nation-building. The new socialist society needed a symbolic narrative justifying and solidifying its political arrival. *Three Songs of Lenin* thus was a well-timed artifact, produced at the moment of discursive ascent of folklore and socialist realism that prompted a replacement of the category of class consciousness with "folk consciousness." *Narodnost'* claimed "eternal" values and provided a mythical connection between the oppressive past and the socialist present.

The conceptualization of folklore as relevant to and constituent of Socialist modernity is reflected in a revision of formalist studies of folklore. Viktor Zhirmunsky, for instance, originally defined oral tradition as "living antiquity" (*zhivaia starina*) prevalent among intermediary social groups (peasants and handicraft workers) in capitalist societies.[87] Slow to be influenced by the historical progress of modernity, those social groups preserve the archaisms of the past. Thus, folklore is not a contemporary phenomenon—it is a relic of cultural life rooted in the peasant and petty-bourgeois ways of life.[88] For Zhirmunsky in the early 1930s, folklore had no place in a classless socialist society and was destined for eventual demise. Fellow folklorists, such as Mark Azadovsky and Nikolai Andreev, fiercely attacked this stance in a meeting at the Leningrad Institute of Oral Culture in 1931. Subsequently, Zhirmunsky's "folklore as a relic" formula was pronounced "formalist" and was widely denounced. It was clearly established that there was a place for folklore in the first socialist society.

As noted in the introduction of this book, orality was ardently celebrated at the First Soviet Writers' Congress. Suleiman Stal'sky, an illiterate poet from Dagestan, performed a work about the Congress in Lezgian (one of the languages of Dagestan). It was followed by a Russian translation, and both met with enthusiastic applause. Gorky famously witnessed the "miracle" of the foundational spoken artistic act and presented the poet as a naïve genius whose art has an immediate impact and should thus be appreciated and understood beyond a standard critical framework: "I saw how this elder, illiterate but wise, sitting in the presidium, was whispering while he created his poems. Then this Homer of the twentieth century read them outstandingly."[89] The illiterate Stal'sky is hailed by Gorky in a rather confusing manner: the *ashug*, a traditional Lezgian poet, "read" the freshly composed poem. What is taking place is a domestication of orality, for the form can be conceived only in the terms and established conceptions of the "high" culture of reading and writing.

Gorky's praise was not a mere condescending compliment—it signaled the discursive interdependence of literature and folklore within the framework of socialist realism. As he puts it in the same address: "the beginning of the art of the word is in folklore. Collect your folklore, learn from it, process it. It provides a lot of material for yourself and for us, the poets and writers of the Union. The better we know the past, the more easily, the more deeply and joyfully we will understand the great meaning of the present that we are creating."[90] Ursula Justus emphasizes that Gorky, by treating folkloric texts as historical documents, legitimizes epos and makes it a valid component of Soviet culture.[91] With folklore becoming a primordial form of literature that reflects real historical events, epic narratives enter the realm of the real. Consequently, the difference between the mythological idealization of reality and its factual depiction is completely erased. As Katerina Clark has elaborated, socialist realism thus combined "what hitherto seemed uncombinable: verisimilitude and mythicization."[92] Folklore was instrumental for the Stalinist state given its attempts to diffuse the boundary between fiction and reality, art and life.

In 1934, Lazar Kaganovich commissioned a folklore-gathering expedition in the Moscow region. This created a template for future expeditions to the peripheral regions of the country. Active collecting was propagated, and results of fieldwork were published in leading Soviet newspapers and journals. However, what distinguished this expedition from traditional field trips was that its task was to collect both old and new folklore. Proponents of Soviet folklore were involved in a process of what Eric Hobsbawm calls the invention of tradition.[93] The Soviet government encouraged the creation of *noviny*—contemporary Soviet folklore that borrowed the style of *byliny* but addressed modern-day themes and glorified socialist construction (e.g. these *noviny* could describe a "miracle" of the five-year plan). Combined with socialist content (secular modernity), Soviet folklore displays a peculiar blend of archaic and modern elements. This temporal coexistence functioned as an enabling condition of socialism. The line between true folklore and folk stylization was completely blurred in Stalinist culture. Reciters of oral epic (*baxshis*, *ashugs*, *akyns*) and their creations were essentially invented by the state; *noviny* was thus largely *fakelore*.[94]

This fictional-documentary tension, inherent to Soviet fakelore, strongly reverberates in *Three Songs of Lenin*. Remarkably, Vertov's "folkloric" songs derive from previously transcribed fieldwork material, as his archive establishes.[95] At the beginning of his work on the film, Vertov was given a compilation of folkloric material that had been transcribed and printed. This set includes typescripts and manuscripts of Azeri verses written by different hands (pages 46–52), translated poems that had already appeared in print in *Pravda* in the 1920s (page 14), and even some pages from a poetry compilation by Nikolai Aseev (pages 64–68).[96] In a 1936 diary account, Vertov maintains that some of the songs were recorded in situ while he was working on the text of other songs. (He does not mention if these were transcriptions made by others or by himself.)[97] Thus, the texts' actual provenance is difficult to trace but the fact remains that the written component played a significant role.

A section of the first song derives from the poem "The Death of Lenin" (Smert' Lenina), allegedly composed by the "Komsomol member Atabaev" and written down in Konibodom, Tajikistan, in March 1925.[98] The last stanza of the poem in Vertov's archive reads:

> We never saw him,
> We never heard his voice,
> But he is dear to us, like a father.
> Even more so—for not a single father
> Will do as much for his children
> As Lenin has done for us.[99]

The rather naïve verse, which differs only slightly (and insignificantly) from the actual titles appearing in the film,[100] nevertheless accomplishes the same operation that lies at the core of *Three Songs of Lenin*: it takes Lenin's absence and turns it into a meaningful presence. "Atabaev," as a young ethnic member of the Soviet communist party, establishes an ideological kinship with someone whose political stance he also shares and represents.

The beginning of the second song, accompanied by European-style classical music,[101] is borrowed from the middle section of the verse "On the Square Stands a Tent" (Na ploshchadi stoit kibitka), which was recorded in 1926 in a Kyrgyz settlement in Fergana:[102]

Verses in *Three Songs of Lenin*:

We loved him as we love our steppes,
No—even more than that!
We would give all our tents and steppes,
We would give our life
Just to have him back.

Verses in Vertov's archive:

We love Lenin like we love our steppes,
No—even more: we would give
All of our tents and steppes,
All camels, wives, and children,
To have him back.
But he is in a dark, terrifying, unknown . . .
Where shall we find him?[103]

The fact that Vertov omits the eccentric and controversial part of the transcribed version in which the supposedly male singers are ready to sacrifice "all camels, wives, and children" (sic) for Lenin's sake and replaces it with "our life" is significant. The radical sacrificial urge to expunge something very specific in the name and life of the ideal is replaced with a more abstract and, at the same time, more absolute conception of life. Furthermore, Vertov omits the ominous concluding line of the stanza invoking the "dark, terrifying, unknown" space of death.[104] This quotational palimpsest is an evocative case of the domestication of orality—the unmediated "folkloric" tradition undergoes a process of cultured revision and rearrangement. The material accomplishes a shift from the oral to the written domain and reaches its apotheosis as intertitles (projected writing).

Moreover, while the music accompaniment of the second song continues, another set of "verses" appears: ". . . he founded our party of steel . . . / . . . he built it from year to year . . . / . . . he edified and tempered it in a relentless tenacious struggle . . ." This time the source is not an instance of peoples' art but a quotation from the appeal titled "To the Party. To All Working People," made by the Central Committee of the Communist Party of the Soviet Union immediately after Lenin's death: "A man has passed who founded our party of steel, built it from year to year, led it under the blows of tsarism, edified and tempered it in a vehement struggle against traitors to the working class, against the undecided, the hesitating, against defectors."[105]

The seamless conflation of the primordial folkloric voice with political discourse is very pronounced. The "alleged" voice is delivered through writing (titles appearing on the screen) and originates from an official printed declaration—a textual monument on its own. The textual-discursive provenance of Vertov's "folkloric song" is a striking multimedia palimpsest: the voice of the peripheral people is comprised of texts solicited by the mediators-ethnographers and political ideologues.

Finally, the third song of the documentary, which is sung in Kyrgyz (with titles in Russian) by a female choir with piano accompaniment (yet another act of Westernization/domestication) is the beginning of the same poem "On the Square Stands a Tent" that was used in the second song:

Verses in *Three Songs of Lenin*	Verses in Vertov's archive
…In Moscow…in the great city of stone…on the square stands a tent…and Lenin lies in it…	In Moscow, in the great city of stone Where all representatives of the people gathered, On the square stands a tent, And Lenin lies in it.
…and if you have immense grief……go to this tent and look at Lenin	If you have immense grief And nothing consoles you, Go to this tent And look at Lenin.
and your sorrow will dissolve as in water…	And your sorrow will dissolve as in water And your grief will swim away, like leaves in a torrent And new quiet grief will embrace you, When you will see the one, who was the father of the country And who was pierced by death's sting.[106]

Vertov accomplishes a reinvention of the invented tradition: he works with the quasi-folklore material and adjusts it to his own specific artistic needs. The *aryk* water of the poem is transformed into the hydroelectric power of the Soviet industrialization project—a favorite object of visualization for avant-gardists. The primordial folkloric word enters the late modernist culture of the Soviet state. This incongruous combination is intensified with the persistent motifs of reading and literacy that permeate the film: ethnic women and children read books about Lenin and learn newly modernized alphabets (in one scene, a woman reads the history of the Communist Party of the Soviet Union, designed by Rodchenko).

The clash between the oral and written was a constant refrain of Vertov's career. The director consistently refused to write film scripts for his documentaries, rejecting the urge to frame reality artificially and in advance before it had revealed itself. This refusal resulted in his dismissal from Sovkino in 1927 and his relocation to Kyiv. Instead, he insisted on the use of thematic, calendar, and itinerary plans as his guiding paperwork—they were "*a plan of action for the movie camera* to reveal the given theme in life, but not a *plan for staging* the same theme."[107] He did not record life but uncovered and revealed it. *Three Songs of Lenin* was Vertov's first film with a "literary film script."[108] Vertov, however, treated his initially scripted libretto not as a confining arrangement but as a dynamic and mutable plan. As he writes to a production unit: "A documentary film plan is not something rigid. It's a plan in action."[109]

Nevertheless, in a rather confusing manner, the written word precedes the documentary about the spoken word. This is evident even in Vertov's account of his intense work on the film: "I had to write poems and short stories, dry reports, travel sketches, dramatic episodes, trans-sense word-collages; I had to make schemata and diagrams—and all this to achieve the graphic, crystalline composition of a given series of shots."[110] Everything written, from dry reports to trans-sense wordplay, sparks the creation of image. Vertov, as a master of the documentary image freed from literature, inadvertently declares that "in the beginning was the Word."

THE DEATH OF LENIN AND THE BIRTH OF LENINISM

Vertov's signature documentary—*Man with a Movie Camera*—was overshadowed during his lifetime by the success of *Three Songs of Lenin*. Although the first version of *Three Songs* was supposed to have premiered at the Bolshoi Theater on January 21, 1934, the anniversary of Lenin's death, it was instead released in November 1934 and simultaneously exhibited in over forty cities.[111] On November 10, 1934, as *Pravda* commented on its "triumphant" screening in New

York, prominent figures of the Bolshevik political establishment such as Nikolai Bukharin and Karl Radek applauded the film as the most significant achievement of Soviet cinematography.[112]

Although Stalin also initially praised it, he later changed his public stance and claimed that the documentary created an ideologically incorrect impression: "Lenin is portrayed only using material from Central Asia. This produces a completely misleading emphasis on Lenin as the leader and standard-bearer solely of the East, merely the 'leader of the Asiatics,' which is profoundly mistaken."[113] Stalin's stance was echoed in the press and in *Cinematograph of the Millions* by Boris Shumiatsky, the head of the Soviet film industry from 1930 to 1937 and a former member of the Central Asian Bureau.[114] The alleged Eastern bias of the film functioned as an obstacle to the international appeal of Leninism. While the fringes of the USSR, the farthest outposts of the country, played an important constructive role in the process of building socialism in one country, they could not have constituted a focal point. The margins simply could not take the role of the center.

As a result of these ideological pressures, *Three Songs of Lenin* was taken out of distribution, and in 1938 Vertov produced two new versions with approximately one-sixth of the film consisting of brand new footage: the 64-minute sound version and the 52-minute silent version, both of which remain the earliest surviving "authorized" versions of the film.[115] The changes were made to the original negatives, though the first two reels of the film remained largely untouched.[116] As a result, the reedited film became dominated by the "internationalist" agenda that presumed the Russian proletariat's vanguard role. The new 1938 version, according to the director's own 1952 account, included more recent documentary material. It incorporated footage that was not ethnically marked, but rather presented European Soviet material, passing it off as universal: documentary footage featuring Aleksei Stakhanov and the Moscow-Volga Canal, and, most notably, Stalin's speech made to his electoral district in Moscow in 1937 in which the leader urged voters to "keep before them the great image of the great Lenin and imitate Lenin in all things."[117] Mimicry becomes a key tool of ideological incorporation—one has to contemplate the "image" of the dead leader to comply with the reality of Stalinism. In the same 1952 account, Vertov presents a discourse of succession-continuity by quoting Henri Barbusse's famous laconic statement: "Stalin is Lenin today."[118] Stalin functions as an anchor of the present—a guarantor of the continuity of (socialist) life.

In 1970 Elizaveta Svilova, Vertov's widow and longtime editor, together with the director Ilya Kopalin and the editor and director Semiramida Pumpianskaia, reedited and prepared a restored version of the film with a re-recorded

FIG. 3.2 Dziga Vertov, Stills from *Three Songs of Lenin*, 1938.

music soundtrack. This posthumous 1970 reconstruction sought to align with the original 1934 version. For instance, Svilova restored the footage containing images of repressed or out-of-favor individuals such as Anatolii Lunacharsky and Nadezhda Krupskaia and removed several sequences with Stalin. However, it seems that the film's new editors left the Eastern material as subdued as it had become in 1938.

Leninism knew no borders; however, its Russian roots were carefully conserved. The recurring sequence depicting Gorki, a country estate where Lenin spent the last months of his life, is essential for the ideological coordinates *Three Songs of Lenin* tries to establish. The film opens with an emphatically tilted-angle shot of trees in a park. A remnant of the old avant-garde days, this upward-directed Rodchenko-like shot performs the function of supplication—it seeks comfort after the leader's departure. Organicity prevails through a series of peaceful shots of nature, which are accompanied by lyrical European music. A shot of an empty bench on which Lenin was famously photographed is a culmination of this sequence. It is notable, however, that in the 1938 edit, the shot with the empty bench is preceded by a photograph of Lenin and Stalin sitting on chairs in Gorki in the summer of 1922, followed by a blurred shot of the bench from a distance. The removal of the shot with the photograph in the 1970 edit signifies a post-Khrushchev revision of historical progression and power succession: the seat of power had to remain open—empty.

The trope of absence played an important role in the genesis of the film. In his 1946 diary, Vertov writes:

> I took one shot, the bench in Gorki, for instance, and carefully looked at it. I "bombarded" the shot with particles from my brain and the shot was transfigured. A seated Lenin appeared on the bench. A gigantic panoramic view of the country emerged. The Kara-Kum desert was silent. An emancipated woman was singing a song about Lenin.
>
> ... By releasing the energy of the "bench in Gorki" shot, I unfolded for the viewer-listener a documentary song that would be comprehensible to all nations.[119]

Vertov operates within mythographic categories when he invokes the "energy" of the shot. Once freed by means of "brain particle bombardment," this energy prompts a transformation—an emergence of other images. The art of filming ceases to be a process of passive vision, instead becoming an active force that molds and expands reality. The procedure undermines the conventional notions of spatial singularity and homogeneity: the space of the empty bench, located close to the metropolitan center and the ultimate seat of power (Moscow) releases the peripheral topoi. Gorki evolves into a cosmological center of the Soviet universe—everything takes its roots in, expands, and accelerates from it. Finally, this space prompts the appearance of the documentary song, which transcends linguistic boundaries.

The organic idyll of Gorki is supplanted by the industrial verticality of the final part of the film. *Three Songs of Lenin* concludes with Lenin's petrification—his eleven-meter monument by Ivan Shadr (erected in 1927 on the site of the hydroelectric station in Mtskheta, Georgia) that is also shot using an avant-garde *rakurs*. This time, the camera's upward gaze is not beseeching; it has found its terrestrial "idol." The organic natural beauty of swaying trees is replaced with the pure, laconic forms of the towering monument. The cessation of Lenin's physical existence and the construction of a spiritual ideology/mythology simultaneously elevate and undermine Lenin as a corporeal entity. The film's overall discursive movement reflects this progression: Lenin as a ray of light enlightens the women of the East in the first song fades with his death in the second song, but then finally transforms into the industrial, empowering *energiia* of the third song. The trajectory culminates with the ossified but literally electrified image of the leader. The emancipatory urge of the Bolshevik project comes to a climax with Leninism.

The discourse of succession-continuity is also evident on another level of the film. The tripartite structure of *Three Songs of Lenin* mirrors the "Issue XXI" of *Kino-Pravda* (Leninskaia kino-pravda, 1925), dedicated to Lenin. The early experimental documentary was also split into three parts, depicting various stages of Lenin's life and afterlife: 1. Lenin's leadership during the Civil War; 2. Lenin's illness, death, and funeral (which included a subsection titled "Lenin, but not moving"); 3. Lenin's legacy.[120] The concluding subsection of the last part ("Along the rails of Leninism") showed how Lenin's image continued to live on in the hearts of the international proletariat. Vertov basically recycles his avant-garde experience with *Kino-Pravda*.

However, what *Three Songs of Lenin* introduces is a pronounced modernizing aspect that was muted in the "Issue XXI" of *Kino-Pravda*. The theme of the transformation of the Soviet land is further developed in the discursive emergence of Lenin's project of electrification, as manifested by the Dnieper hydroelectric dam and "Il'ich's bulb" that delivers the spiritual energy of the Soviet Union. In his early "WE" manifesto, Vertov writes that "our path leads *through the poetry of machines, from the bungling citizen to the perfect electric man.*"[121] As Aleksandr Deriabin argues, *Three Songs of Lenin* was the culmination of Vertov's theoretical search for a "synthetic Adam," for he had finally found an image of the perfect man.¹²² The film reaches its pinnacle with the appearance of Lenin's profile composed of electric bulbs—the *vozhd'* as "the light of truth," the light that cannot be physically contained.

The final four minutes of the 1970 version, which follow the visual display of industrial achievements, are quite remarkable in the sense that they depict a transference of power. The sequence starts with a conveyor belt with various folios of Lenin's works in different languages rotating on a pulley. The process of spinning signifies transformation: the physical body turns into text, and Lenin morphs into Leninism. This is the culmination of a visual motif that permeates the film—various books with Lenin's name or his portrait on bindings, with women and children reading them herald the arrival of textual Leninism. The conveyor belt of Leninism is then superseded by a monument to international workers prominently featuring a black man raising a flag of the borderless proletarian movement.

The internationalism of Lenin's legacy is further amplified in parade and march sequences taking place in different locales: starting in Red Square with the mausoleum in the background and then transferring to Germany, England, China, and Spain. These international displays of loyalty are brought back to the center in an aerial shot of a parade in Red Square. Importantly, it is Stalin who stands on the Mausoleum's tribune (the "grave" with Lenin's physical body) and receives the parade as the leader's reincarnation. The symbolic transmission of power is followed by the spiraling text of Lenin's "Stand fast!" speech, which had been prominently featured in the middle of the film with Lenin's recorded voice. However, this time Lenin's voice is missing, and the viewer sees only the text. The voice of Lenin as a speaking subject is muted and turned into the printed text of Leninism, accompanied by a heroic choir. Lenin's "electrified" profile is then superimposed on the Mausoleum and thus accomplishes an act of ultimate monumentalization.

The very final images of the film have also a textual provenance—they comprise a quotation from the anonymous Tajik folk song "We Will Not Forget the Name of Lenin" (Ne zabudem my imeni Lenina). Once again, the song was not folkloric material collected by Vertov since it was published in the 1920s, before the director found himself in Central Asia. The text reads: "Centuries will pass with an iron gait, / and people will forget the names of the countries in which their ancestors lived before / people will forget the language of their ancestors / but they will never forget the name Lenin."¹²³ The concluding text of the film proclaims an expansive internationalist rhetoric: the passage from ethnic particularity to international universality. It does so by mirroring and mimicking

Lenin's speech, which ascends upward from the lower left corner at the same time as the concluding text spirals upward from the lower right corner. The two texts—a political speech and a folkloric hymn glorifying the political leader—twist and tighten the nuts and bolts of Soviet political discourse.

The ending of *Three Songs of Lenin* signifies the discursive arrival of Stalinism that appropriates the textual legacy of Lenin. The text begins its ideological reign. This turn toward the textual reflects the dramatic change that was taking place at the time—an amplified tension between such categories as word-deed and reflection-action. In a famous passage in his *Literature and Revolution* (1924), Trotsky attacks formalism on the grounds of its disconnection from social and historical reality and claims that its proponents indulge themselves in "the superstition of the word": "The formalist school represents an abortive idealism applied to the question of art. The formalists show a fast-ripening religiousness. They are followers of Saint John. They believe that 'In the beginning was the Word.' But we believe that in the beginning was the deed. The word followed, as its phonetic shadow."[124] One year before this, Bronisław Malinowski published an article in which he claimed that oral cultures tend to perceive language as a mode of action and not merely as an instrument of reflection.[125] The situational and operational frames of reference of this word stay within the bounds of real life. For Trotsky as well, words have great power, and this power is transformative, not contemplative. Words acquire meaning only when they leave the space of dictionaries and participate in "real life" events.

This living, human lifeworld of the Bolsheviks evolves into a completely different entity once Stalin, Trotsky's chief opponent, assumes power. To establish the Soviet mythology of Leninism, Stalin invested great energy into the enforcement of formulaic repetitions of certain dictums while action as such became of secondary importance. It represented an evident borrowing from the oral tradition, which transmits knowledge by means of repetition, since something that is not repeated aloud soon disappears. Walter Ong, in one of his influential monographs, identifies a tendency to aggregate as a key characteristic of orally based thought and extrapolates it onto the Soviet context. The given aggregative quality, as opposed to an analytic one, manifests in the use of epithets and other formulary types of expression that appear to be redundant when written:

> The clichés in political denunciations in many low-technology, developing cultures—enemy of the people, capitalist war-mongers—that strike high literates as mindless are residual formulary essentials of oral thought processes. One of the many indications of a high, if subsiding, oral residue in the culture of the

Soviet Union is... the insistence on speaking there always of "the Glorious Revolution of October 26"—the epithetic formula here is obligatory stabilization, as were Homeric epithetic formulas "wise Nestor" or "clever Odysseus"...[126]

Vertov's oriental "songs" can be seen as an enactment of prescribed dictums—these were refrains or variations of the ultimate canonical song of Stalinism. The words of the songs do not merely describe reality, they shape it. Vertov's folklore, thus, shares with totalitarian *sociolects* a tendency not to name entities but to create them by means of performative utterance. Language creates reality. Moreover, the epithetic essence of Stalinism tries to transmit the collective will: "the individual's reaction is not expressed as simply individual or 'subjective' but rather as encased in the communal reaction, the communal 'soul.'"[127] Knowledge and history are conceptualized as fixed and definite, and the given state of certainty does not tolerate semantic discrepancies that can be produced by individual consciousness.

The discourse of archaization, the return to the primordial word with its ability to transform the world, marked and defined Stalinist modernity. It actively incorporated various elements present in every oral tradition and used them to create a socialist mythological consciousness. The presence of divine inspiration or even supernatural frenzy was one of these key elements. According to Zhirmunsky, many Central Asian epic singers were, according to their own accounts, urged to sing by some divine force or old masters who visited them in their sleep (the tradition dates back to Caedmon).[128] This comprised a truly otherworldly impetus that is translated into the notion of *enthusiasm*, a labor frenzy that, in Stalinist culture, performs the function of the enabling condition of socialist construction.

The phenomenon of Stalinist socialist enthusiasm resonates with the figure of the ecstatic *rhapsode* famously addressed in Plato's *Ion*. Distinguished by ecstasy that impedes any critical reflection, the rhapsode has no real artistic skill and is reminiscent of a soothsayer in being divinely possessed. The Stalinist rhapsode delivers a formulaic repetition of certain dictums that are supposed to create a discursive frenzy, transmitting the energy of the repressive cult. This is clearly illustrated in one of the interviews in *Three Songs of Lenin*. A director of a kolkhoz named after Lenin appears to be on the verge of ecstatic breakdown when she utters the following words in her dialectal specificity:

> And I feel where I've come to and what our leaders are saying. Those are nevertheless golden words they are saying. You should write them down and put them

in your head and when you get back home, you've got to tell them . . . And you want to do as the leaders say, you want to get things organized in the *kolkhoz*. And you think to yourself . . . you remember what's behind you, but the Bolsheviks say don't turn back. Forget the hard times you've gone through and march ahead! You think that it's like that, but maybe it's . . . You need to live through it yet, you need to achieve it yet, you need to figure out how to approach it . . . And here is the question. You get all that into your head, and tears well up all by themselves.

The woman commences by stating that she "feels" where she has arrived and what the leaders say. Sensation, as a bodily experience, replaces analytic faculty. Critical reflection is supplanted by corporeal reaction. She must inscribe the words of the leaders into her brain—no interpretative "deviation" is allowed. She also appears to reflect on some traumatic experience but then instantaneously discards the memory—she must stride forward, as commanded. Consequently, her speech breaks down grammatically. The verb of critical reflection (to think) is paired with those of ideological commotion (to get things organized, to march ahead, to make the right approach). When she finally attempts critical reflection ("and here is the question . . ."), she breaks down in tears. The enthusiasm overwhelms her and hinders her reasoning.

The voice finds itself at the intersection of body and language: Vertov was aware of this displaced topology. The director's early conceptualization of language in cinema, where he downplays the semantic component and amplifies the sound element, rather unexpectedly finds a correlation with the verbalism of Stalinism. The performance of folkloric songs, where the very act of performance overshadows the content of the song as such, somehow corresponds to the Stalinist power of speech—acts of utterance of hackneyed slogans to display unconditional loyalty to the big political Other. It is no coincidence that the director relies on songs and speeches in *Three Songs of Lenin*—the two vococentric phenomena are involved in the constitution of the political. The divide between *phone* and *logos* is no longer valid, and the mid-1930s Soviet culture amalgamates the two. However, the conundrum of Stalinism lies in the fact that it absolutely depends on the fundamentals of written culture. Orality is legitimized only if it is conceived within the premises of the "high" culture of writing. The spoken word must be transcribed to become semantically stable and serviceable for political discourse. There is no authority of the voice as such, only the authority of the collective in the name of which the word is uttered and then petrified by means of transcription. Uncannily, this procedure mirrors the textual provenance of *Three Songs of Lenin*.

ORALITY AS DEVICE

In 1941 Vertov was evacuated to Alma-Ata, the capital of the Kazakh SSR—the city to which the two leading Soviet film studios, Mosfilm and Lenfilm, had been relocated. The unified studio produced 80 percent of the Soviet films during the war and it was here where Vertov made his penultimate film, *The Front, to You!*[129] Upon its completion in 1942, the film was subjected to several drastic alterations, received a low distribution category, and was never screened outside of Kazakhstan, with the authorities banning the film's screening in Moscow altogether.[130] This was a rather unspectacular denouement for one of the cinema's most influential innovators. The film nevertheless reveals the director's evolution as a late modernist documentary visionary who worked creatively within the restraining tenets of military propaganda.

The Front, to You! is the most scripted and staged film in Vertov's oeuvre. Though, Vertov claimed that he employed nonprofessional actors, scenes involving them are staged and have a fictional film sensibility. The uncompromising incompatibility of documentary and staged material, which had marked his theory and practice from the very beginning, now evolves into a complex, theoretically construed symbiosis of the real and fictional planes. The "archaic" oral tradition again played a constructive role in this process.

The Front, to You! announces the complete advent of the modern Soviet epic. The film, like *Three Songs of Lenin*, is a blend of ethnic folklore and the discourse of socialist construction that Vertov describes in similar terms, as "national in form and socialist in content."[131] However, the abstract and distant capitalist foe of the 1934 documentary is replaced with a very concrete adversary—Nazi Germany. Moreover, *The Front, to You!* presents the harmonious and total integration of ethnically diverse socialist subjects through the practice of labor and warfare. It is constructed as a heroic tale, glorifying the labor exploits of the young woman Saule, who works in a lead mine, and the war exploits of her husband Dzhamil, who fights the Nazis at the front. Over eight years, the newly liberated woman of the East presented in *Three Songs of Lenin* had evolved into an almost ethnically neutral image of a completely emancipated Soviet shock worker from Kazakhstan—a key home front space of the country during World War II. Over 450,000 Kazakhs were mobilized for military service during World War II, and this created a severe drain of manpower in the republic. By 1945 nearly 80 percent of all agricultural workers were women. This was a case of involuntary emancipation: women had to take on jobs such as agronomist and tractor driver, technical and mechanical positions that had formerly been all-male.[132]

The film reflects the wartime reality. Titles announce that Saule has just seen her husband off to the front. They are superseded by a pastoral scene in which the woman is standing on a hill and waving a head scarf to bid farewell to her husband galloping on a horse through a canyon—her headscarf, a former attribute of religious submission, turns into a secular garment. The scene is then followed by a series of images of workers walking toward a mine in Ridder, a small mountain town in Kazakhstan. After a few seconds the miners emerge from a shaft, the entrance of which is decorated with Stalin's portrait, and among them is Saule. Outside the shaft, a female radio broadcaster solemnly announces Dzhamil's feat for which he has received a military decoration, and Saule's co-workers congratulate her. The happy woman walks back home where she writes Dzhamil a letter in which she says that she hopes that the lead she has extracted was in the bullet that killed the enemy (Kazakhstan produced 85 percent of all Soviet lead). This is followed by a series of documentary images, which are presumably "seen" by Dzhamil after receiving the letter. They show various industries (lead and coal mining, fishing, oil) of Kazakhstan with a narrator explaining in voiceover their significance for the front. A rhythmical "labor" song follows the industrial display, with predominantly female workers in agricultural fields harvesting grain, beets, rice, and cotton. The collective song is followed by Dzhamil reading Saule's letter, in which she announces her intention to break the mining record he had previously set. Saule is then shown drilling boreholes down in the shaft and producing about two hundred tons of lead. She victoriously emerges from the mine surrounded by her coworkers congratulating her on a new record. After a sequence with piles of ore, the product of Saule's labor, the woman is shown walking back home in a light summer dress. At home, she looks at Dzhamil's photograph and the shot/reverse-shot technique connects the husband and wife. The film concludes after their gazes seem to "meet."

The film's prologue, which precedes the farewell scene, performs a very significant function—it is the only sequence of the film where the ethnic oral tradition plays a structural role. The film opens with a traditional Kazakh folk singer (*akyn*) sitting solemnly, like a statue, on a felt carpet and holding a traditional Kazakh two-stringed instrument, the *dombra*.[133] The *akyn* is played by real-life singer Nurpeis Baiganin (1860–1945), who was a late arrival to the pantheon of Soviet folksingers—his works started to be transcribed only in 1938. He was famous for performances of traditional epic military tales and for composing *noviny* about World War II heroes. Baiganin's fame was certainly eclipsed by the stardom of Dzhambul Dzhabayev (1846–1945), one of the icons of Stalinist culture, who was supposed to have played a role in the film but failed to do so, probably due to health issues.

The *akyn* is used as a framing device in the film: his presence is crucial, for he is presented here as a mediator who oversees the narrative progression from the very beginning. Baiganin hears the cacophonous sounds of war while the camera gets closer and closer to his face. Before he commences his song in Kazakh, intertitles in Russian start rendering his yet silent voice: "Today, when my motherland Kazakhstan, together with the other republics of the Soviet Union, applies all efforts to crush the enemy of humanity—bloody Hitler—how can I not sing to you about young Saule." The *akyn* then proceeds with his song and Russian titles appear over the entire frame, overpowering the barely heard voice: "Far from the front, in one of the picturesque corners of Soviet Kazakhstan, in a workers' settlement, surrounded by mountains rich in lead, lives the young and hardworking Saule."

The *akyn*'s voice does not deliver meaning but emanates as a semantically free phonic substance. The meaning is conveyed by titles. Rodchenko's mobile constructivist intertitles that had been used in Vertov's 1920s experiments are replaced with rather conventional and abundant italic titles that perform a translating function in *The Front, to You!* As a result, the text simultaneously dominates and frames the image. The written language seems to enter the formerly archaic space of Central Asia as a manifestation of modernity. Indeed, the pan-Soviet project of Cyrillization had been completed in 1941, drawing the Soviet Orient into the sphere of influence of the Russian tradition.

Importantly, the sung text absolutely does not correspond to the titles. The actual words the akyn sings in Kazakh are:

> In the land of Kazakhstan,
> In my boundless country,
> The best of all countries,
> In the land shaken by the enemy,
> Between Aityr and Balkhash,
> Lead is smelt.
> Having such weaponry,
> Deliver death to the enemies!
> People of Kazakhstan!
> Destroy as many enemies as possible
> On the adversary's frontlines!

This non-correspondence between the actual song, which delineates the spatial coordinates of the republic and calls for a general resistance, and the titles, which provide a more specific introduction to the character of Saule, is striking.

FIG. 3.3 Dziga Vertov, Stills from *The Front, To You!*, 1942.

The Kazakh oral "tradition" is in discord with Russian written culture. The sung words are reduced to their sonorous materiality and Vertov concentrates on the vocal and ignores the semantic. As in *Three Songs of Lenin*, the actual words of the song seem to play a secondary role—the very (documentary) fact of performance as an acoustic phenomenon is more important. The sound document overpowers the literary text.

Moreover, Vertov likely took Dzhambul's published song "To Moscow" (Moskve, 1941)[134] as the discursive core of his film, for the similarities are too evident. Once again, the domesticated transcribed folkloric material performs the function of an original oral source. Dzhambul's song, also translated into Russian, glorifies Kazakhstan as a home front space that helped in the defense of Moscow and highlights the Kazakh industrial centers' production of bullets and coal that were used to fight the enemy (he recounts Shymkent, Aral, Balkhash and Ridder—the same *topoi* that prominently feature in Vertov's film). Moscow and Kazakhstan comprise a singular whole, like integral parts of a human body—the internalized colonial subjugation produces an image of the inextricable co-existence of the metropolitan center and its raw material appendage.

This textual origin of the whole film project can be partially explained by developments surrounding the script production. At an early stage, Vertov employed a group of leading Soviet Kazakh writers—Mukhtar Auezov[135] (1897–1961), Gabit Musrepov[136] (1902–1985) and Sabit Mukanov (1900–1973)—together with Shklovsky. The artistic collective functioned in a rather colonial manner: the Kazakh writers, as subordinate subjects in relation to the metropolitan emissaries, were expected to provide ethnically specific material, while the renowned Moscow artists were supposed to give it a proper aesthetic form. The names of the local writers thus are not to be found in the titles of the film, a radical departure from the original film script.

The initial proposal was based around a competition between five or six *akyns* (*sostiazanie akynov*, known in Kazakh as *aitys*) that was referred to as "an argument between mountains and rivers" (i.e., different parts of Kazakhstan).[137] The singers glorified their respective regions by highlighting which natural resources (cotton, meat, lead, or coal) they provide for the front. Their respective songs were supposed to call into cinematic being individual shock workers who distinguished themselves in their respective industries. The planned version of the film was supposed to conclude with a verbal confrontation between Hitler and Dzhambul (!). Hitler calls on his troops, who have been slowed down by winter conditions, to turn the Soviet land into a desert when the weather gets warmer.[138] Images of blooming spring are then shown with Dzhambul uttering the following words: "Yes, spring—this is our spring. This is our sun, and we will proceed as it does: from East to West. Spring is power and naissance. Sing about how close-knit and strong we are, Nurpeis."[139] Hitler's plan for extermination is countered by nature, which is "owned" by the ethnically Kazakh Soviet citizens—spring stands for life, not death. The Chancellor of the Third Reich is not the Führer by virtue (or vice) of his political and administrative regalia; rather, as Mladen Dolar puts it, "it is the relationship of the voice which makes him the Führer, and the tie that links the subjects to him is enacted as a vocal tie."[140] His voice is endowed with a legislative function; it generates and also suspends the law. Yet Hitler's voice as the (supra)-law is directly challenged by the Soviet folkloric singer's voice. The clash of antagonistic political discourses is turned into a vocal battle.

Interestingly, the oral clash was a point of contestation between Shklovsky and Vertov. The ending includes Shklovsky's note of disagreement with the proposed narrative strategy: "I'd do it differently here. I'd put spring first, then Hitler would talk and then Dzhambul would respond right away. But I can't get past a certain fibrous substance—the cotton wool of Vertov's resistance. Let everything happen the way this man—so accustomed to himself—wants."[141] Shklovsky terse prose reveals irritation with Vertov's obstinate position. He does not want springtime to be a temporal divide between the two antagonistic spaces (Germany and the USSR), but instead a common "reservoir" of time where the contestation takes place. Nature's temperate season, which traditionally stands for rebirth, rejuvenation, renewal, resurrection, and regrowth, allows the battle of two politically appropriated oral traditions to unfold.

However, the scene did not make it into the final cut in any form. *The Front, to You!* accommodates a different type of oral contestation: the *akyn* competes with the voice-over of the Russian narrator for discursive authority. The *akyn*'s singing voice, neutralized by the written word of the intertitles, is then superseded by that of the narrator, a voice that possesses true power to generate meaning. The *akyn* is subjugated by the impersonal and ubiquitous authority of the "voice of God" commentary. Hence, his role as a mediator can only be speculated about, for he makes an appearance only in the beginning and then completely vanishes from the narrative structure of the film. However, according to the literary script, he was supposed to conclude the film with a song after Saule broke the record. The text of the song reads: "This unity of the front and home front, the unity of the peoples of the Soviet land—this helped our leader, the great Stalin, to free humanity from Hitler, the cannibal."[142] The song, a celebration of the friendship of the Soviet peoples, is replaced with nondiegetic orchestral music with a choir singing a *vocalise* song (i.e., a vocal passage consisting of a melody without words).[143] Stalinism finds its discursive affirmation in a mere enthusiastic melody—words, in any language, are no longer required.

The disembodied voice of authority, a narrator's voice—had been actively resisted by Vertov during his work on *Three Songs of Lenin*. Retrospectively, in

1944, Vertov reflected yet one more time on his experience of making the 1934 documentary.[144] He claims that the film was capable of transmitting thoughts from the screen directly, without having to be translated into words. Meaning is being delivered by audiovisual means:

> *Three Songs of Lenin* did not require a narrator. If you did add one, the screen would speak through words. Thoughts on the screen would not strike the viewer's brain directly. The narrator would be a translator, and the film would not be understood in the same way, it would take the direction of a radio monologue in words. All the richness of the film would go into the accompaniment. The diversity of perception would be stifled and channeled within a verbal flow. The author of the text would bind his thoughts into sentences. The narrator, remaining invisible, would speak those sentences. The viewer would become a listener. And, in taking in these sentences, would retranslate them into thoughts . . .[145]

The Front, to You! appears to integrate every formal aspect that this passage contests. It neutralizes the singing-speaking subject of the Soviet land (*akyn*) and elevates the narrator, who performs the function of the omnipresent and all-knowing agent delivering an authoritative commentary. The latter also clearly becomes a translator—he interprets the locally specific Kazakh material for the Russified Soviet citizen. This is what Michel Chion refers to as *acousmatic voice*, a voice without an origin and an identifiable source, for there is no body to which it can be assigned.[146] It possesses four ultimate powers—ubiquity, panopticism, omniscience, and omnipotence—and disrupts the seamless diegetic flow of the audible and visual elements.[147] The narrator of *The Front, to You!* indeed appears to have the ability to be everywhere, to see all, to know all, and to have complete power over the narrative.

However, the film still does not fully submit to the power of the *acousmatic* voice and accomplishes something more complex than a mere translation of the visual into the verbal. The narrator's somewhat detached manner of speech creates an effect of moderated pathos—he does not deliver ultimate meaning to the viewer but rather appears to engage with visual sequences that prompt his appearance and disappearance in various episodes. He initially enters the narrative structure of the film not as an otherworldly and all-knowing commentator but as a disembodied voice that verbalizes and responds to Dzhamil's thoughts (the protagonist envisions the expanse of his motherland as part of the home front). This comprises a rather nuanced and somewhat "natural" interaction of the visual and the aural, wherein the authority of the disembodied voice is not fully domineering.

This coexistence of audiovisual elements was inherent in the film's initial conception. The director, for instance, insists on the "organic" character of *The Front, to You!* where sound and picture are interdependent: "Content proceeds simultaneously within the music, in the word, in dialogue, titles, image.... A voluminous crystal form.... Not an amorphous amalgamation, accompanied by the narrator's text.... An organic confluence of all components."[148]

Terms such as organicity and harmony enter Vertov's theoretical vocabulary during this period. A crystal—a highly ordered structure providing for the organic convergence of all elements—replaces the factual thingness of the *kino-thing* as a central metaphor. This synergy is evident in the three "constructions" (*konstruktsii*, fig. 3.4) that the director drew during an early stage of work on the film.[149] Each comprises a circle, the most "harmonious" of the simple shapes, with additional layers added on top and bottom. The diagrams depict an image-sound relationship where the two elements are presented as separate (different semicircles) and equal at the same time (the two form a complete circle). Image is placed in the left-hand column, and sound in the right-hand one. The diagrams, meticulously enumerating all visual-sound components, include a substantial amount of the material that did not make it to the final cut (especially the episode with the Panfilov Division's twenty-eight guardsmen that will be discussed below). However, the displayed unity of image and sound is central to the film's structure.[150]

The formal unity of image and sound, as it appears in the "constructions," evolves into one of the major themes in the film, which complicates officially endorsed discourse contrasting the "high" culture of writing to archaic orality. Indeed, Soviet folklore consisted of a peculiar blend of oral and written traditions: it completely displaced the improvisatory nature of the epic song, which is never repeated word for word, by relying on fixed, written texts that nevertheless retained the form and structure of the oral epic. Variation and improvisation, key aspects of oral epic performance, completely vanish once they are "transcribed" onto paper or recorded. Real performance must be witnessed and lived through. In oral epic, the poem is composed during the performance—there is no division between the "text" and its enactment. As Walter Ong puts it, writing "is a particularly pre-emptive and imperialist activity" and it "tyrannically locks [words] into a visual field forever."[151]

Instead of granting folklore its own oral domain, Stalinist culture made a substantial discursive effort to identify folklore with literature so that it could view the oral tradition from the premises of written culture. Gorky claimed written culture's direct dependence on folklore: all great works of literature relied on folkloric narratives.[152] A politically "reoriented" Vladimir Propp echoes this stance by forthrightly pronouncing that "[once] written down, folklore is the beginning of literature."[153]

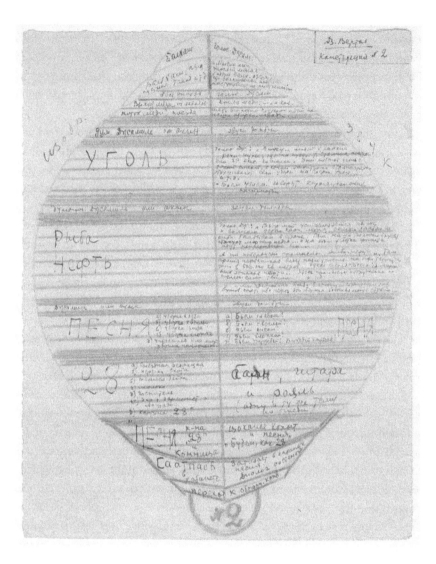

FIG. 3.4 Dziga Vertov, "Construction No. 2" for *The Front, to You!*. Collection Dziga Vertov / Austrian Film Museum, Vienna.

The given "imperial" vision of orality was also popularized among local experts. Esmagambet Ismailov, a prominent folklorist of Kazakh origin, wrote an authoritative monograph on *akyns* that was translated into Russian in 1957 in which he acknowledges the fact that written culture influenced the art of folk singers and vice versa. However, the wording he chooses valorizes the "high" culture of writing: the *akyns* could reach the level of "representatives of written poetry."[154]

The glorification of Soviet folklore as literature reached its pinnacle in Iurii Sokolov's influential 1938 textbook *Russian Folklore*, in which the author asserts: "If the term 'literature' is employed not in its literal sense (written materials), but more widely; that is if we understand by it not only written artistic creations, but oral artistic productions in general, then folklore is a special branch of literature, and folkloristics thus is seen to be a part of literary scholarship."[155] The folkloric storyteller, according to Sokolov's interpretation, gains the authority of the literary author since he or she is not a mere transmitter of tradition but essentially a creative contributor to it: every performer of oral poetic works "is at the same time, to a considerable degree, their creator and author."[156]

However, Nikolai Andreev, in his largely favorable review of the textbook, challenges Sokolov's identification of folklore with literature: even the work of a very creative narrator-interpreter retains a stronger dependence on the rigid tradition than does a writer. This criticism was a sign of a significant change in the official view of folkloric authorship: the replacement of the author-storyteller by collective creative authorship. The individuality of literary authorship was contested and the stance that "under socialism, the whole nation is the creator of folklore" became formulaic.[157] Andreev posits that the collective character of folklore manifests itself in the collective possession, coauthorship, and reflection of popular ideas and moods.[158] This standpoint was also echoed in various contemporaneous attempts to conceptualize folklore. Following Gorky's classic definition, Vladimir Chicherov, for instance, defines folklore as the proletariat's collective art: "the collective creation of the masses of working people, which has an artistic value."[159] This blend of literary and oral traditions comprises a key characteristic of Soviet culture: "The collective poetic work of the masses is created in our time both in writing and orally. Their combination is in principle the new feature of contemporary mass art."[160] As a result, high literary culture, fused with its popular counterpart—folklore—created essential socialist realism with its insistence on clarity, popular appeal, and rootedness in reality.

The clash between the oral tradition and the practice of writing punctuates the narrative structure of *The Front, to You!*. The spoken word, which manifests itself in the *akyn*'s song, the radio broadcast, the "folk" labor song, and the voice-over narration, is counterpoised by the written word that finds its expression in the abundant titles and, more notably, in the letters exchanged by the protagonists. The narrative line takes shape only when the couple—Saule and Dzhamil—exchange letters. The words written by Saule urge Dzhamil to imagine the riches of his country that literally fuel his struggle with the adversary. Writing instigates action. Together with the intertitles, the letters establish *written* language as an essential discursive component of the film. For Vertov, who had famously used intertitles in Esperanto, language always performs an ambivalent and, at times, ambiguous function. However, in *The Front, to You!*, he appears to have accomplished a passage from orality to writing. The written exchange between Saule and Dzhamil takes place again at the end of the film: the couple, after describing their respective exploits, exchange glances and eventually are brought together into an imaginary proximity using a shot/reverse-shot technique.[161] The word of the letter unites the two.

While the two protagonists appear to function as transmitters of written culture as they abandon their oral past, their ontological position in the film as semi-documentary entities is noteworthy. The two nonprofessional actors appear to transcend human subjectivity as such. In his handwritten notes for the film (made on a narrow piece of paper and written in a stanza-like manner), Vertov presents Saule's image as someone who collapses the limit between subject and object, between the physical world and ideology. Further, this *outsideness*, her overcoming of spatial-bodily identity, is unambiguously connected with the artistic strategy of documentary filmmaking:

> Saule is documentary in the same way that images of folk art are documentary. The *akyn* sings about Saule while implying the home front. And he sings about the home front while envisioning Saule. Saule is many Saules. Saule is not a singular but a plural form. That is why it's pointless to argue about her. As a plural form, she is documentary. To indicate her surname, address, the mine where she worked—that is, to do what would be useful for a newsreel or an event-centered film—is useless and harmful for a synthetic film. This would turn Saule into a particular case, into a singular form. Whereas Saule is a generalization.[162]

The documentary image, as a singular original fact, transforms into a synthetic generalization. Vertov accomplishes a leap from the domain of individual subjectivity to the realm of the collective. Saule, as a concrete individual working in a particular mine, is transcended in favor of a condensed but extensive image. For Vertov, this ontological profusion is inspired by the oral tradition, with its tendency for abstraction:

> If we are not discussing newsreels or an event-centered film, but rather a summarizing, synthetic film rooted in images of folklore art, then the very question of the degree of chronicle quality in the figure of Saule cannot and should not be posed. Saule is not shock worker so-and-so, but one among many who accomplished a certain amount of work on a given day in a particular mine. It suffices that she is not an actress but a kolkhoz woman who was mobilized for the

FIG. 3.5 Dziga Vertov, Stills from *The Front, To You!*, 1942.

work in the mine and who then entered the movie camera's field of vision for the first time. Saule's behavior is the behavior of the many. The decision about Saule's quest being a "close-up" not of a single woman but of the many women on the home front, was in all ways reasonable and precisely corresponded to the author's design, the *akyn*'s story and [unintelligible] of the approved script.[163]

Shklovsky famously challenged Vertov for leaving the realm of the real in his documentaries. In his article titled "Where Is Dziga Vertov Striding?" he insists that *fact* loses its essence when it is "unsigned," not properly attributed: "the newsreel material that has been worked over by Vertov has been deprived of its soul, its documentary quality. Newsreel needs a signature, a date.... Dziga Vertov cuts up newsreel. In this respect, his work is not artistically progressive.... I want to know the number of the steam engine lying on its side in Vertov's film."[164] That is, Vertov deprives the documentary material of its historicity—the mark of time evaporates. Consequently, "the thing has lost its thingness and has begun to show through [*skvozit'*], like a symbolist work of art."[165] *The Front, to You!* directly responds to Shklovsky's concerns. However, the newsreel practice of specific dating and classification (time, name, place) does not define the documentary image as such for the late Vertov. Ontology precedes denomination.

In her ontological profusion, Saule, can in fact be perceived almost as a metonymic extension of her motherland—the Kazakh Soviet Socialist Republic. The region's newly acquired republican status, together with its internationalist aspirations, combines with a celebration of its ethnic particularism and with traces of a new mode of Soviet colonialism. Indeed, an earlier version of the script had the *akyns* singing about the rich fairytale underworld of the country: the Kazakh people, although "aware of these riches, could not get hold of them."[166] In keeping with classic orientalist practices of representation, Kazakhstan is presented primarily as a vast reservoir of natural resources. The narrator affectedly announces the republic's role as a rich natural addendum to the chain of Soviet production: "Is there any metal that does not exist in the Kazakh earth? Is there any mineral that cannot be extracted from the bowels of her soil?" he asks rhetorically. Lead, coal, copper, zinc, molybdenum, chrome, and oil are all prominently celebrated throughout the film—and so, metonymically, is the land of Kazakhstan. While *Three Songs of Lenin* is dominated by aerial shots, *The Front, to You!* is a celebration of the downward verticality that reveals the bowels of the country. Indeed, as the literary script posits, "the October Revolution and Stalinist Five-Year Plans opened up the bowels of Kazakhstan and uncovered treasures that are scarce on our planet."[167]

One of the earlier versions of the script was even more pronouncedly orientalist and revealed a tension between the cultured metropolitan center (Moscow) and the empty periphery, abundant in natural resources. It starts with the Kazakh geologist academician Kanysh Satpaev attending a Bolshoi performance of Mikhail Glinka's *A Life for the Tsar* (a nationalistic and imperial tale about resistance to foreign invasion, known during the Soviet era under the name *Ivan Susanin*), which is interrupted by a Nazi air raid.[168] Satpaev finds himself in the Moscow underground, which functions as an air raid shelter, with Maksim Mikhailov, the production's lead singer. During the raid, the rather hapless Kazakh geologist tries to run outside when he sees and hears the firebombs but is prevented from doing so by a policeman. Satpaev sees only the material aspects of warfare—everything is reduced to the raw material from which it is made: "This is aluminum, magnesium, fulminating mercury, oil, coal."[169] The fact that the conversation about the bowels of the Kazakh land takes place in the Moscow underground—a landmark of Stalinism—is no coincidence. Verticality permeates *The Front, to You!*, with up-and-down movement largely defining the film's spatial coordinates. The means of resistance are to be found deep down in the earth:

The metro tunnel. The firing of antiaircraft guns is audible.
– Our antiaircraft guns will not be worn out, says Satpaev. There is molybdenum in their steel. The Germans will not break through our armor. There is molybdenum and tungsten in it. Our tanks' chassis will not be worn down. They contain niobium. They contain chrome, nickel, vanadium. All the elements of victory are ours.[170]

The formalist-modernist overcoming of the raw material of life evolves here into the late modernist treatment of matter: raw material does not transform into an artifact to create a moment of cognitive illumination, but is instead celebrated as a useful substance from which real products can emerge. The latter strategy carries the potential to be even more radical than Vertov's cinematic theory of the 1920s, which celebrated real facets of existence that were objectively perceptible only to the cinematic apparatus. The presence of real matter in the Soviet documentary discourse of the late 1930s and early 1940s is overwhelming to the extent that it resists the need to construct a synthetic view from various perspectives of reality. *The Front, to You!* contains a remarkable episode—upon receiving a letter from Saule, Dzhamil imagines his motherland as a map and then this cartographic image is followed by a succession of close-ups of different minerals, found in its bowels.

During a discussion of the film proposal, Vertov made a very remarkable statement that illuminates the episode celebrating raw materials: "I get the impression that the mountains, with all their riches, moved toward the front, while herds followed [them], clothing the Red Army soldiers. I see, for instance, metal being poured, or perhaps lead melting like soup cooked in a big pot. I know that I have to refine it, but it becomes clearer if I have it firing [see it in action] straight away."[171]

Here, matter defies artifice. Raw materials, without being processed, reach the frontline. Utility undermines aesthetic appreciation altogether. The given artistic strategy contrasts sharply with Vertov's early experiments. In *Cine-Eye* (Kinoglaz, 1924), reverse motion is used to reveal what Vertov called "the origins of objects"—the kino-eye provided provenance for commodities such as bread and meat. In the same manner, *A Sixth Part of the World* (Shestaia chast' mira, 1926) attempts to demystify the commodity by revealing the relations of production and the mechanisms behind its reification, so a worker can overcome the alienation of capitalist private property. But in *The Front, to You!*, commodity enters a mythological realm. Industrial processes that exposed the construction of commodities are now presented as participating in the epic clash of evil and goodness. The economic relations of interdependence and the social relations they create are downplayed in favor of epic confrontation.

Vertov's intricate statement about raw material moving towards the front found a more conventional rendering in the film, in the guise of a feature song—"We're reaping the harvest for the battle" (My dlia bitvy zhatvu zhnem). The tone of jubilation in the collective Russian song completely overpowers the voice of the *akyn* heard in the beginning. It "neutralizes" the declared in the beginning Kazakh orientation of the film. The song's appearance is preceded by scenes of idyllic landscapes featuring geese, chickens, horses, ducks, and swimming children, all announcing a discursive switch to agriculture. The song itself is performed by a female choir, which provides a challenge to the male "voice of God" narration: the exultant melodious jubilation contrasts with an almost dry analytic narration. This division can be explained by the symbolic patriarchal order's tendency to privilege the semantic (the sphere of reason) over the vocal (the bodily sphere). As Adriana Cavarero observes, "voice becomes secondary, ephemeral, and inessential—reserved for women."[172] Vertov appears to uncritically reinforce the gender dynamics in which "woman sings, man thinks."[173]

The initial design of the soundtrack, however, was drastically different.[174] The final song was supposed to be that of the *akyn*, with Nurpeis glorifying Soviet achievements by singing about how the desert, "where a turtle used to hide in sands," was being transformed into fertile soil. The camera was supposed to show fields of cotton with women of different nationalities (Kazakhs, Ukrainians, Belarusians, Russians, and Uzbeks) joining Nurpeis in song, in their respective languages. This was to be an ultimate display of the Soviet "friendship of the

FIG. 3.6 Dziga Vertov, Stills from *The Front, To You!*, 1942

peoples"—unity through diversity. However, the song ends up being sung in Russian—the lingua franca of Stalinism.

The song that appears in the film is a folkloric stylization composed by Gavriil Popov, a professional composer famous for his score for *Chapayev*. More importantly, Popov was assisted by Vasilii Velikanov, a musicologist born and educated in Petersburg. Velikanov had traveled to Kazakhstan in 1936 to collect folklore material and remained in the republic for the rest of his life, creating relatively canonical pseudo-folkloric operas and ballets based on Kazakh myths and legends. The song's lyrics were not the product of national lore but were written by Vladimir Lugovskoi—a prominent Soviet poet, a former constructivist who had evolved into a rather successful cultural official in the 1930s. The song in Russian, accompanied by bold titles, glorifies the practice of agricultural labor and assigns it a function of resistance to the Nazi invasion. The filmed workers, mostly Central Asian, sing about products of their labor, such as wheat, beets, or cotton, which directly contribute to the forthcoming victory over Hitler. Every grain and every cotton bud turns into a metaphorical bullet that will strike a Nazi invader. Labor becomes violence.

The fusion of labor and violence appears in the film as an intertext. Lugovskoi's stylized song derives from a textual source found in Vertov's folkloric material that he had used for *Three Songs of Lenin*: the poem "Laughing Fields" (Smeiushchiesia polia) about the cotton harvest. One stanza stands out in particular as a possible source for the main song *The Front, to You!*—the collective song glorifying labor. The similarities are striking:

"Laughing fields."	"We're reaping the harvest for the battle."
We're cultivating white gold	We're reaping the harvest for the battle
Every stem of which is a bullet for the enemy	We hit the Nazis with bread
His back will be wounded	Every grain is a bullet
He will withdraw from us grousing in vexation and resenting.[175]	Well-aimed, it hits the enemy
	Every ear [*kolos*] is dear to us
	It brings destruction to the enemies.

Violence and mythology also converge in one of the key unfilmed episodes of *The Front, to You!*: the Panfilov Division's twenty-eight guardsmen. The Twenty-Eight was a group of soldiers from the Red Army's 316th Rifle Division that took part in the defense of Moscow during World War II. According to an official Soviet historical account, they were all killed in action on November 16,

1941, after a fierce battle during which they destroyed eighteen German tanks. All twenty-eight soldiers were collectively endowed with the title Hero of the Soviet Union. However, according to an investigation by military prosecutor Afanas'ev, the story of the Twenty-Eight was a fabrication invented by correspondents and editors of *Krasnaia Zvezda*—a main news outlet of the Ministry of Defense of the Soviet Union.[176]

From a very early stage, the film relied heavily on the "feat" of the twenty-eight guardsmen of the Panfilov division. A monument to the Twenty-Eight—a pyramid made of ice on one of the mountain peaks in Kazakhstan with the twenty-eight names inscribed on its surface—played an important narrative role: it was observed by Dzhambul and Nurpeis and prompted the whole resistance narrative to unfold in the form of a song.[177] This was a natural monument, commemorating a fake military feat. The episode of the Twenty-Eight also played a crucial role in reinforcing the "friendship of the peoples" trope. In one of the renderings, Nikolai Shvernik, the chairman of the Nationalities Council of the Supreme Soviet of the Soviet Union, was shown giving a speech in London about the Twenty-Eight's "feat" and his speech was then broadcast to the United States, China, and Lebanon.[178]

In the Soviet wartime heroic narrative, the "feat" of the Panfilov Division's twenty-eight guardsmen occupied a special place as the ultimate manifestation of national unity through diversity. The division, formed by ethnic Kazakh, Kyrgyz, Ukrainian, and Russian soldiers, defended Moscow—the capital of the first socialist society. According to the infamous article in *Krasnaia Zvezda*, the last words of the division's political commissar Vasilii Klochkov were "Russia is a vast land, yet there is nowhere to retreat—Moscow is behind us!" Moscow, as the universal center, could not capitulate. The war, an attempt to disrupt the historical continuum of socialism, is defied by an image of the unified collective future—the trope of the "friendship of the nations."[179] However, the two tropes—the "feat" of the twenty-eight guardsmen and the "friendship of the nations"—remained in the domain of mythology.

THE END OF DOCUMENTARY?

At the beginning of his cinematic career, Vertov had combined theoretical inquiry with artistic innovation. As a result of this combination, he developed a set of anti-illusionist and self-reflexive techniques that largely came to define the documentary genre. In the 1920s, he insisted that the people should temporarily stop being the focus of filming since they are unable to control their movements.[180] The path of the kino-eye is a passage "from the bungling citizen to the perfect electric man":[181] "I am kino-eye. From one person I take the hands, the strongest and most dexterous; from another I take the legs, the swiftest and most shapely; from a third, the most beautiful and expressive head—and through montage I create a new, perfect man."[182] This was a cinematic Narcissus, constructed in the mold of Frankenstein, conceived as a vehicle through which space and movement were explored.

Vertov's radical early deviation from a conventional, character-centered mode of narration resulted in the fetishization of the cinematic apparatus. The fact that the field of vision of the camera was not defined by any character's psychology was crucial for the director. This was a guarantor of ultimate objectivity since the image is withdrawn from the subjective domain. Vertov's self-proclaimed direct and unmediated access to reality was provided by the kino-eye's inherent objectivity—deficiencies of the human eye are neutralized by the camera's capacity to observe things as they really are.

Gilles Deleuze was among the chief advocates of Vertov's material-mechanistic suprahuman cinematic eye. In his view, the human eye's relative immobility and optical constraints were surmounted by the kino-eye.[183] Such techniques as looping, acceleration, deceleration, image granulation, miniaturization, inversion, and double exposure expanded the human receptive organ's abilities. Since each of these techniques involves montage, Deleuze insists that the kino-eye itself equals montage. For John MacKay, however, Vertov's early theory and practice did not constitute a purely post-human mode of perception. As he puts it, Vertov regarded cinema as offering "a new means of appropriating and redistributing perception . . . through an expansion of perception's purview and a de-privatizing (i.e., de-narrativizing in terms of 'characters') of its channels."[184] Thus, perception is decentered and the ontological authenticity of the cinematic image, which is not shaped solely by the human vision, is achieved.

A nonanthropocentric, or de-privatized, mode of perception permeated Vertov's films up to *Enthusiasm*. However, the director's animus toward character-centered narration gradually gives way to a celebration of human subjectivity. As Elizabeth Papazian puts it, "the tension in Vertov's work between the illusory objectivity of documentary modes and the opacity of poetry makes space for the subject."[185] Instead of a human figure produced through the artificial re-assemblage of montage, the late modernist Vertov presents an allegedly "organic" integral human being who possesses a certain vision of the world. The human is presented not as an integral part of production processes but as a biopolitical constituent, an ideological element of a larger (and more abstract) sociopolitical system. In his diary of 1932, Vertov writes:

> It is important not to repeat the mistakes in the sound shooting of people that were pointed to during the discussion of *Symphony of Donbass*: 1) shock workers do not appear as distinct one from another (one needs to overcome the schematism that leads to obliteration of personality); 2) [the way I] show a human [does not draw attention to something] fundamental about them (one needs to select situations that fundamentally characterize a human). One needs to shoot and record people in a moment when they cease to react to the apparatus, when they no longer notice it. Then we have on the screen "a non-acting human" . . . Here lies an aspiration to show people without a mask, without acting, an aspiration to shoot people in such a way that they don't notice the process of shooting, an aspiration to read on their faces the thoughts exposed by kino-eye.[186]

The process of overcoming "schematic mechanicalness" led to experiments with character psychology. At the end of 1933, Stalin issued a directive to prevent overloading documentary chronicles with "superfluous" details.[187] Documentary films, according to him, should not follow the convention of fictional cinema where the presence of details is counterbalanced by acting. Instead, they should be laconic and "compact," revealing only the typical (*tipicheskoe*) and most important aspects of social phenomena. Stalin underlines the amalgamated nature of a film character:

> an artist creates character types mainly through creative imagination and not by a simple transfer of them into his work [from reality]. Gogol was certainly capable of creating images and types that have become classic these days—the eyebrow, nose, gait, habits of one man; the actions and other characteristic traits of another—and by intermixing these traits, by combining the most typical ones, he could create his images, which have become classics. Our contemporary artists can do the same.[188]

What Stalin describes is a montage of character traits, a *typical* Soviet "Adam," who contrasted with Vertov's *exceptional* cinematic man constituted of different physical parts. The Soviet ideologue appropriates the chief principle of the montage method and extrapolates it onto human appearance and interiority. Stalin's "creative physiology and psychology" replaces the "creative geography" of the avant-garde cinema. Sensory encounter with the outside world is replaced with characters' internal psychology and their relationship with the outside world. Human interiority, of course, was a component pertinent to the content of a work of art and not its formal aspects. Individual psychology, completely indoctrinated by the discourse of Stalinism, reigns supreme while the spectrum of emotional experiences is reduced to two emotive states: positive exultation and indignant anger, both of which are preconditions for the Stalinist conception of human agency.

Because of this discursive shift from the objective fact of the social environment to the subjective realm of individual (albeit typical) psychology, the documentary genre gradually introduced more and more fictional elements. The unpredictability and irregularity surrounding an ordinary event were surmounted by the ritualistic treatment of the documentary image—it gradually became part of Stalinist "theater" where facts are staged and scripted, and people-actors are invented. Vertov's theoretical and practical stances were attacked exactly from these positions. In 1935, an influential Soviet documentary film critic argued that proponents of the kino-eye viewed the dynamics of life as chaotic, composed of discrete facts perceived as stationary and lying beyond the dialectic continuum.[189] What his films needed was historic dynamism and deep human psychology.

As the epistemic coordinates of the Soviet cultural discourse began to shift, Vertov's own aesthetic vision underwent a reorientation. He insisted that the documentary genre was constantly evolving and his late interest in semifictional "film-portraits" followed this evolution. The genre of film-portrait allows the director "to limit space and prolong time, necessary for a deeper presentation of plenitude within the small."[190] Human psychology reveals itself only from within a temporal continuum. The camera no longer creates but observes. Vertov's disregard for forms of mimetic figuration is gradually replaced with a careful appropriation of mimetic practices, and thus the primacy of the factual is replaced with the emergence of the fictional. The eschewal of the detailed script, the avoidance of acting, and the reliance on unstaged material are all modified into a hybrid treatment of the documentary image. What emerged was a "living human being," organically incorporated into the premises of Stalinist culture.

The Front, to You! is Vertov's pinnacle achievement in the aesthetics of the "living human being," the discursive grounds of which had already been prepared in *Three Songs of Lenin*.[191] The living *observed* gains more significance than the *observer* (the mechanical kino-eye). The country's leading film journal, *Iskusstvo kino*, published Vertov's 1940 interview "On Love for the Living Man" as late as 1958—after his death and at a time when his legacy had become nearly irrelevant in the Soviet Union. This article contained a notable rhetorical shift.[192] Vertov surveys his oeuvre from a different vantage point, undermining the epistemic powers of the kino-eye:

Essentially, everything I have done in cinema was directly or tangentially connected with my persistent attempt to uncover the mindset of "the living human being." Sometimes this human being was a not-revealed-on-the-screen author—the director of the film. Sometimes this image of "the living human being" contained within itself various aspects not of a single concrete human being but of several, or even many, correspondingly selected people.

The mother gently rocking her baby to sleep in *Lullaby*, from whose point of view the film is ostensibly being narrated, turns into a Spanish, a Ukrainian, a Russian, and an Uzbek mother over the course of the action's development. Nevertheless, there is only one mother in the film, as it were. The image of the mother is distributed among several persons. The image of the girl is also constituted by images of several persons. In front of us stands not a mother but the Mother, not a girl but the Girl. As you see, it is quite difficult to explain. An understanding of this is only achieved directly from the screen.[193]

This is Vertov's retrospective and essentially late modernist attempt to theorize the place of the human subject in his oeuvre. He establishes a continuity between his early avant-garde experiments, which undermined the anthropocentrism of human perception, and the later search for the organic human subject. The retroactive procedure culminates in the pronouncement that a singular entity in fact stands for a collective. The "living being" is stripped of her physiological essence and evolves into a supra-corporeal collective entity. Hence, a single individual can conceal ethnic diversity within herself and can become Spanish, Ukrainian, Russian, or Uzbek. Nevertheless, the diversity of subjectivities appears in the form of an "amalgamating" individual. A mother becomes the Mother, and a girl becomes the Girl. This ontological substitution culminates in the creation of an ideal late Stalinist subject—typical but essentially deprived of facticity and human agency. It is noteworthy that the phrase "living human being" appears inside quotation marks in the published 1958 journal article, while it remains unmarked in the original.[194] Vertov seemed to maintain his utopian belief in a real living human being free of any quotation marks.

In 1940, Semen Ginzburg, an editor of *Iskusstvo kino*, wrote a largely positive article about Vertov. He emphasized, however, that the director, despite his substantial contribution to the aesthetics of documentary cinema, "had not yet understood—and, unfortunately, it is unlikely that he has fully understood it even now—that it is not fiction [*vymysel*] that is essentially bad, but untruthful fiction. He had not understood that genuinely artistic fiction conveys the truth of life."[195] It was a rather difficult task to implement the prescribed formula. The dividing line between the fact of life and its fictional rendering was no longer maintained. "The living human being," with her dialectic contradictions and incongruities, represented the only discursive way out for the director. He had to put her in quotation marks.

A Sixth Part of the World was Vertov's early avant-garde attempt to provide a vision of proletarian and ethnic unity. The cinematic catalog of nations explores the global trade system and attempts to envision the Soviet economy in the context of *international* trade—the country exports natural resources (grain, oil, fur) and imports industrial equipment. By bringing together various topoi of the Soviet borderlands and the peoples who inhabit them, the film creates a vision of the socialist future without the center as a dominant locale—geographical and cultural heterogeneity prevails. The Orient, nevertheless, undergoes a process of dissolution during the film: the space ultimately gets integrated into the homogenous Soviet collective, thus constituting, in Walter Benjamin's words, a "filmic colonization of Russia."[196] The film concludes with Stalin's speech at the Fourteenth Congress of the Communist Party in December 1925, in which he announced the possibility of building socialism in one country. The boundary-traversing ambitions of the kino-eye had to be contained and channeled into a boundary-enforcing celebration of internal diversity.

Vertov projected modernist cultural forms onto the site of the Soviet Orient once again in 1934 but this time they were inflected by an emerging preoccupation with the human subject, in line with late modernist trends. The sound experiment of *Enthusiasm* continued and expanded the ontologically filmic kino-eye experiment while opening new possibilities to render human subjectivity. Language, as a sound phenomenon, fully enters Vertov's aesthetic domain with *Three Songs of Lenin*. The international appeal of the silent cinema was superseded by the Soviet intranational celebration of folklore—the Soviet people's creative voice. The technical advancement of sound technology in film was crucial for recording examples of contemporary epics, usually emanating from the Eastern fringes of the country.

However, folklore's discursive premises underwent drastic reformulations that were reflected in Vertov's films. The debates of the 1930s reconsidered the notion of authorship in the oral tradition and folklore's general relationship with written culture. The oral word was consequently appropriated for socialist construction. Yet it also had to be "tamed," mediated through practices of transcription and translation. Vertov's *The Front, to You!* demonstrates further evolution in this context. Folklore as a document of reality evolves into folklore as a mythic entity: the main heroine of the film is stripped of human subjectivity and endowed with the ability to stand in for the collective. Consequently, the heroics of labor, together with the glorification of its products, replace human qualities and the heroine becomes a pure ideological incarnation.

Over a period of thirteen years (1930–1942), Vertov's sound theory and practice underwent drastic reformulation—from the concrete industrial noises of *Enthusiasm* to the recorded documentary folkloric material of heterogeneous Turkic peoples in *Three Songs of Lenin*, to their culmination in the invented *fakeloric*, studio-recorded Russian songs of *The Front, to You!*. In a truly dialectic manner, the aspiration to merge with the real tasks of Soviet life and with reality as such is displaced by mythic epic elements. This is why the archaism of Vertov's oriental documentaries can be seen as part of a dialectic late modernist continuum, linking his avant-garde notion of the mechanical kino-eye and its demystification of the filmic image with the unveiling of documentary truth. The films are actively involved in the process of mythmaking, and the poetic potential of the folklore of the Soviet East came to play an important role in the creation of Soviet reality, with its own myth of socialist labor. As a result, Vertov's oriental documentaries register a gradual move toward fictional abstraction—a paradoxical development that played out against the backdrop of his early avant-garde theories.

CHAPTER 4

SOCIALIST TIME

Sergei Eisenstein

The collection of the Museum of Cinema in Moscow features a copy of the small booklet *On the Film 'Bezhin Meadow' by Eisenstein* (*O fil'me 'Bezhin lug' Eizenshteina*) from Eisenstein's private library. The booklet, subtitled "Against Formalism in Cinematic Art," describes the unfinished 1936 feature film as an "ideological failure." It includes several critical articles and the director's repentance, "Mistakes of *Bezhin Meadow*" (Oshibki 'Bezhina luga'). Eisenstein's copy of the low-budget booklet is adorned with a laconic inscription-dedication: "To the idiot! [Dure!]." The "idiot" in question is Pera Atasheva (1900–1965), Eisenstein's longtime assistant, close friend, and eventual wife. Atasheva had warned Eisenstein that he was setting down a dangerous path in agreeing to make a film about Pavlik Morozov, a newly sanctified hero of the emerging Stalinist canon, famous for having denounced his kulak father and subsequently dying at the hands of his family. Eisenstein allegedly told Atasheva that her concerns were unfounded and that she was acting like an idiot. To this Atasheva reportedly responded: "I may be an idiot, but I'm right."[1] And she was indeed right. The inscription thus acknowledges Eisenstein's "ideological mistakes" in an ironic and laconic manner. To have engaged with the officially endorsed myth in a manner unconstrained by strict political conventions was, to put it simply, a poor choice.

Bezhin Meadow (*Bezhin lug*, 1936) was a watershed event for Eisenstein—it was his first project upon his return to the Soviet Union from a multi-year trip to Europe, the United States, and Mexico. More significantly, it was his first attempt to contribute to the cultural milieu of the Stalinist state—a radically different country from the one the director had left in 1928, shortly after his encounter with Alfred Barr. But Eisenstein's attempt to reenter the Soviet cultural scene was doomed. After several cost overruns, missed deadlines, and two radically different versions of the film, *Bezhin Meadow* was ultimately pronounced an artistic and ideological failure. Its production was halted, and it was eventually suppressed and destroyed.[2] Publication of the booklet was a pointed act of public (self-)flagellation: it was intended as a headstone to mark the grave of formalism.

In the booklet's opening article, Boris Shumiatsky emphasizes that Eisenstein viewed his work on *Bezhin Meadow* as an opportunity to reform himself and to make his art integral to the process of socialist construction after a long period of physical absence and artistic "silence."[3] Shumiatsky identifies a "pathos of the socialist restructuring of agriculture" as the desired discursive core of the film.[4] However, Eisenstein delivered a different kind of pathos—a "pathos of spontaneous destruction"[5]—as the actors representing kolkhoz workers in fact looked as though they belonged to a biblical or a mythological plane. The film as whole was a manifestation of harmful "remnants of formalism."[6]

Eisenstein was expected to deliver a secular story of the emerging socialist subjectivity that elevated ideological obligations above family kinship. But religious symbolism predominates in *Bezhin Meadow*: the prototypical figures of Abraham and Isaac or Rostam and Sohrab from Ferdowsi's *Shāhnāmeh* clearly function as an inspiration. As a result, a tragic socialist tale was infused with clear Oedipal undertones. Indeed, Svetlana Boym identifies the whole real-life saga of Pavlik Morozov as "the Soviet version of the Oedipal myth par excellence—only secrets, blindness, and the metaphysical conversation with the sphinx are lacking."[7]

Eisenstein's leap into the archaic domain was consistent with his theorization of art as a dialectic interplay between regressive and progressive elements that gained momentum after the completion of the 1925 film *Battleship Potemkin* (*Bronenosets Potemkin*). As Naum Kleiman highlights, the thematic conflict between father and son shapes the overall structure of the 1936 film—the archaic father dwells in a pre-class milieu while his son is a herald of the future post-class society.[8] Thus the film's narrative relies on tension between the two consciousnesses emanating from two drastically different temporal frameworks: the fundamentally backward peasants, manifested in the image of the father, face the vanguard of the new socialist reality in the image of the son.

The leap into the archaic did not conform with the future-oriented epic of socialist construction. Ilya Vaisfel'd, a young opponent of Eisenstein, admonishes the director for his temporal "muddle": "it is incorrect to seek a source of artistic form for socialist realist art in the primitive mind."[9] He further challenges both the avant-garde Eisenstein of the 1920s, where the idea of intellectual montage that defied "real" human emotions predominated, and the late modernist Eisenstein of the 1930s, who saw regress as a constructive element of art.[10]

The official legitimization of folkloric and epic narratives in the Soviet arts, which were lionized by Gorky in 1934, did not give license to an ideologically free engagement with mythology. Such engagement still had to be framed by the pathos of historical progression and oriented toward a bright socialist future; myth had to serve the socialist realist narrative. Evgenii Veisman, another critical voice in the booklet, refers to Stalin's rendering of the myth of Antaeus as an exemplary allegory for the relationship between the Party and the people it represented: the Greek hero remained invincible as long as he was physically linked with the earth that had given birth to him.[11] Indeed, Stalin is convinced that the Bolsheviks, "like Antaeus, are strong because they maintain a connection with their mother, the masses, who gave birth to them, suckled them and reared them. And as long as they maintain the connection with their mother, with the people, they have every chance of remaining invincible."[12]

Ironically, Eisenstein also engaged with the myth of Antaeus in his writings, but this engagement, of course, was marked by his idiosyncratic theoretical vision. For him, the earth that gave Antaeus his invincible indestructibility stands for something else: the source of all power lies not in the proximity to the populus but in the knowledge of "the laws of the movement and formation of the universe."[13] The earth of the Greek myth provides nature's fundamental laws and thus sets a morphological standard. The myth, for Eisenstein, points to the question of (aesthetic) form.

In the mid-1930s, however, detachment from the masses was a cardinal sin of formalism, and Eisenstein clearly understood this. He begins his repentance in 'Mistakes of *Bezhin Meadow*' by acknowledging the main mistake: "The mistake is rooted in a certain deeply individualistic illusion of the intelligentsia: . . . in the illusion that it is possible to pursue a revolutionary cause 'at one's own risk and peril' and not in the *thickness of the collective* . . ."[14] He proceeds further by referring to the key dichotomy of Soviet ideology—the passage from spontaneity (*stikhiinost'*) to consciousness (*soznatel'nost'*):

> Spontaneous revolutionism is where the Bolshevik consciousness and the disciplining of that consciousness should have established themselves long ago—therein lies the origin of the errors. . . .
>
> In my own stylistic aspirations and inclinations, I have an immense attraction to the general [*obshchemu*], the generalized [*obobshchennomu*], the generalization [*obobshcheniiu*]. But is this generality [*obobshchennost'*] that same "general" [*obshchee*], the understanding of which the Marxist doctrine of realism teaches us? No. Because generalization in my work devours particularity. Instead of emanating through the concrete particular, generalization scatters into disengaged abstractedness.[15]

The tension between the particular and the general, captured here in intricate wordplay comparable to that of Shklovsky's "Error" essay, was one of the key theoretical issues that Eisenstein tackled in late texts. For him, all great works of art must elevate a particular phenomenon to the level of generalization. The two are interdependent and the "right" balance between the two (equality and equivalence) is essential to the realist tradition of representation: "Greatness and immortality start from the moment when this or some similar situation is fitted onto the shoe-block of generalization. That is, when the generalized General begins to shine through the Particular of a particular case."[16]

But in his repentance of 1937, Eisenstein realizes that his general theory of art has come dangerously close to the realm of abstraction. The tragic story of Pavlik Morozov is elevated to a level of generalization that fails to deliver an ideologically unambiguous and edifying message. Instead of providing an illuminating saga of the triumph of the advanced socialist consciousness over backward spontaneity, the film delivered an abstruse message about the human condition in general and the "dark" primordial forces that govern it. The heroic death of Pavlik Morozov does not amount to socialist redemption, as it does not deliver a sense of ideological closure in line with a teleological vision of history's moving forces. Instead, it represents a manifestation of this ethereally elusive mythological event, one recurring in time.

Eisenstein's vision of time and history was highly problematic for Soviet ideologues, as it downplayed the conclusiveness of revolutionary force and, instead, emphasized a continuous unity across historical periods. It appears that after the failure of *Bezhin Meadow*, the director's energy for theorizing found creative release in engaging with the persistent continuity of national artistic forms within the bounds of the Soviet Union. His work on *The Great Fergana Canal* and his subsequent evacuation to Alma-Ata in 1941, during which he revisited his concept of history, allowed him to explore traditional arts of Central Asia, the "primitive" aspect of which, according to Eisenstein, "hides the whole syntax of the language of the forms of art."[17] Thus, *national form* as such was the domain that allowed Eisenstein to engage with both regressive and progressive elements of art. It legitimized his theoretical inquiry into the synthetic unity of artistic practices rooted in a universal human experience. *Aleksandr Nevsky* (1938) and both parts of *Ivan the Terrible* (1944, 1945), Eisenstein's late masterpieces, can also be interpreted as projects dealing with the *vernacular*—in this case, Russian national form.[18]

The structure of the present chapter reveals Eisenstein's unrelenting interest in the category of national form. It commences with a discussion of the late 1943 essay "On the Question of: 'National in Form, Socialist in Content' (Catholicism and Paganism, Remy de Gourmont, Elizabethan Ballads)," which asserts the continuity of aesthetic forms. The chapter further establishes that this theory of general aesthetic continuity was conceived in Mexico in the early 1930s. *¡Que viva México!* was Eisenstein's earliest attempt to engage with distinctly national forms that nevertheless speak of a universal human experience. The "Desert of Fergana" section explores how the engagement with the ethnic other in revolutionary Mexico was transplanted to the Soviet Orient. To enforce the heroics of the socialist present (the construction of the Great Fergana Canal in 1939), the director leaps into the region's distant and recent past (the epochs of Tamerlane and of Russian imperial dominance). The subsequent section examines Eisenstein's innovative attempts to provide an equivalent to the perspectival "distortions" of Eastern miniatures, a distinct national formal feature, on the cinematic screen. Finally, "Ornament as a National Form" provides an analysis of Eisenstein's 1941–42 series of drawings inspired by Kazakh folklore. The formal structure of the drawings is informed by the director's investigation into the sphere of ornament and line and allowed him to articulate an immanent tension between nationally specific material and universal formal devices.

PREHISTORY OF NATIONAL FORM

On February 23, 1943, as part of his grand *Method* project, Sergei Eisenstein wrote the essay "On the Question of: 'National in Form, Socialist in Content' (Catholicism and Paganism, Remy de Gourmont, Elizabethan Ballads)."[19] Typically multilingual and eclectic, this represented a rather belated reflection on Stalin's famous definition of Soviet culture as "national in form, socialist in content." Writing from Alma-Ata, the capital of the Kazakh USSR and the Oriental home front, Eisenstein witnessed the consequences of drastic changes in the Soviet nationality policy in the late 1930s that intensified Russocentric discourses, which were further strengthened by patriotic sentiments during World War II. Thus, Eisenstein's engagement with the formula, which idiosyncratically propagated national diversity, is both strange and pivotal.

The short essay marks a pinnacle in Eisenstein's inquiry into the issue of content and form. It is noteworthy that the essay began with an error: in his manuscript, instead of "national in form" he initially wrote "national in content."[20] This slip of the director's pen points to a very important aspect of his conceptualization of the form-content dichotomy: for Eisenstein, form and content were always symbiotic. As early as 1925, in "The Problem of the Materialist Approach to Form," he argued that form produces meaning—making the delivery of content efficient. Moreover, any work of art can be identified as revolutionary if its form is defined by the revolutionary material with which it engages.[21] The presumed unity of form and content is amplified even further in one of the key essays, "Perspectives," which summarizes the director's theoretical views of the 1920s. There, Eisenstein writes:

> How many bayonets have, for instance, been broken on the question of "form and content"!
> All because the dynamic, active and effective act of "content" [*soderzhanie*] as "containing within oneself" [*sderzhivanie mezhdu soboi*] has been replaced by an amorphous, static and passive understanding of "content" as "contents" [*soderzhimoe*].
> How much inky blood has been spilled because of the persistent desire to understand *form* only as deriving from the Greek *phormos* or wicker basket—with all the "organizational conclusions" that flow from that!
> A wicker basket where those same unhappy "contents" bob about on the inky floods of the polemic.[22]

Eisenstein replaces the passivity of form as a container and content as the filling with a distinct dynamism wherein the two interact with each other. Through a maze of lexicographic and etymological twists and turns, he arrives at the conclusion that the task of *form* is disclosure [*obnaruzhenie*]—it is not a static containment but is always an active process of uncovering:

> "Disclosure" [*obnaruzhenie*] characterizes image from a different, socially active standpoint: it "discloses," i.e., establishes the social link between a particular phenomenon and its surroundings.
> . . . "content" [*soderzhanie*]—the act of containing [*sderzhivanie*]—is an *organizational principle*.
> The principle of the organization of thinking is in actual fact the "content" of a work.
> A principle that materializes in the sum total of socio-physiological stimulants and for which form serves as a means of *disclosure*.[23]

This stance seemingly challenges Stalin's prescriptive understanding of national form as a passive vessel, replacing it with an active dialectical tension between form and content. National as an essence-free form is replaced with a dynamic understanding of formal function—form not only holds content but discloses it. Content itself is endowed with an active function. In another essay, "In the Interests of Form," he takes on the concept of content by also animating it and reaffirming it as a proactive entity. This is accomplished by a reference to a definition of the word *idea* in a Greek-Russian dictionary: "'ἰδέα Ionic. (1) appearance, exterior; (2) image, type, method, feature, quality . . .; especially: method of exposition, form, and type of speech; (3) idea, prototype, ideal.'. . . These three points are the three mammoths of cinema."[24]

The second meaning of idea-content, as a method of exposition, is crucial for Eisenstein, in that it provides a necessary juncture with *form*; the two comprise a dynamic pair. The theoretical line of demarcation between the two entities is completely erased—they become an interdependent set, and Eisenstein finds the root of this interdependence with the help of a lexicographic reference. Similarly, in the essay "Circus Mystery Play" he forcibly argues that there is no division between form and content: plot cannot be conceived solely as an element of content for it is one of the stages in the process of the formal arrangement of the material according to its ideological vector, while, on the other hand, the rhythmic distinctiveness of a work of art reveals the tension between conflicting themes, that is, it enters the domain of content.[25] He continues by arguing that certain themes that are not presented in a fixed way, but instead are characterized by their dynamic qualities of becoming (*stanovlenie*), are mainly reflected in the formal structure of the work of art.[26] Becoming, endurance in time (or evolution, the term Eisenstein would later prefer) would eventually develop into a central category that would help him formulate his key theoretical principles and understanding of art beyond cinema.

The director's investment in the formal intricacies of montage never receded, even at the height of the attacks on formalism. In the article "'Eh!' On the Purity of Film Language," written in 1934 as a response to Gorky's call for linguistic conservatism, Eisenstein conceptualizes a fashion for Russian montage in the West in colonial terms. This fashion is compared to the exoticism of "negro" plasticity and "Polynesian masks."[27] But fashions pass while *culture* remains, the director concludes. What is needed is a deep understanding of the structure of editing procedures. He then continues to argue that one cannot equate montage with "the left deviation in formalism" and identifies montage as "the most powerful compositional means of realizing plot," as "the syntax for the correct construction of each particular fragment of a film," and, finally, as "simply the elementary rules of cinema orthography."[28] This stance challenges official discourses aimed at undermining any innovative engagement with form by arguing for the indivisible form-content interrelationship. Form, as an active constituent, continues to matter while the official stance that content plays a "leading role" in relation to form, as articulated in the definition of "form and content" in the *Literary Encyclopedia*, is challenged.

Nevertheless, "On the Question of: 'National in Form, Socialist in Content'" brings to light a new set of challenges that were not boldly stated in the early essays.

The 1943 text makes a rather remarkable rhetorical turn by evoking Catholicism and sixteenth-century songwriting. The essay was a reassertion of the form and content unity that challenged the dispensability and variability of the Stalinist national form and reestablished its dialectic link with content. In it, Eisenstein argues that the discursive tension between form and content was always characteristic of epochs in which cardinal ideological changes occurred, with the October Revolution being one of the greatest.[29] He then proceeds to discuss how Christianity (Catholicism) utilized pagan forms for its own needs and adapted them to deliver new "ideological" content. His discussion revolves around two essays by the French Symbolist poet, novelist, and influential critic Remy de Gourmont: "A Religion of Art" ("Une religion d'art, 1898) and "The Psychology of Paganism" ("Psychologie du paganisme," 1900).[30] De Gourmont argues that Catholicism is a paganized form of Christianity, fusing the eternal with the transient and the cerebral with the sensuous. It also borrows its aesthetic sensitivity from the pagan tradition.[31] Eisenstein succinctly renders this as: "The idea in Catholic art comes from Christianity, while its formal rendering (*figuration*) comes from paganism."[32]

Insisting on the inherent adaptability of formal devices, Eisenstein dedicates the second half of his essay to Elizabethan ballads, a genre typified by the transformation of secular, often crude love songs into spiritual hymns.[33] Again, an old form delivers new content and breaks down the hierarchy of genres. He observes a similar tendency in the poetics of Aleksandr Blok, who used Roma songs and other vernacular forms to deliver his own set of (revolutionary) themes. Regardless of epochs and geographical locations, art presents a continual flow of aesthetic evolution where high and low genres intermingle. Immersion in the vernacular of popular forms becomes a necessity while historical continuity evolves into a trope that renegotiates differences (high and low, familiar and alien).

This continuity is dialectically balanced by a still-productive concept of rupture in the social domain. A dynamic steadiness of the flow of time is enabled by constant and inevitable social upheavals. Thus, the discursive kernel of the essay lies in Eisenstein's conceptualization of rupture in historical time, be it the emergence of Christianity or the October Revolution, through the prism of continuity. It is always possible, or even necessary, to deliver a new message by acknowledging past achievements in the formal domain. This was a truly idiosyncratic take on the socialist realist premise of artistic continuity with a rather substantial set of differences: the official artistic method disdained the immediately preceding avant-garde tradition as an "unproductive leftist deviation" and saw itself as the ultimate pinnacle of artistic development. For Eisenstein, however, art finds itself on an infinite developmental spiral with significant historical cataclysms and disruptions providing mere convolutions.

FROM THE TROPICS OF TEHUANTEPEC

Eisenstein's 1943 vision of national form and socialist content was deeply rooted in several of the director's incomplete projects and his consistent theoretical inquiries of the 1930s. Visiting Mexico in 1931 was a defining moment of his career. While the other protagonists of this book traveled to Central Asia or actively engaged with the "national form" on "native" Soviet soil, Eisenstein found himself on a different continent. Accompanied by his close associates Grigorii Aleksandrov and Eduard Tisse, he made a long journey to North America via Europe, where he stopped for numerous lectures, screenings, and conferences. At Hollywood, his initial destination, Eisenstein was supposed to explore innovative sound technologies; he also made consistent attempts to secure funding for his newly conceived American films. After several projects failed, he conceived a film about revolutionary Mexico and received financial backing from the left-leaning American writer Upton Sinclair. Instead of learning about ultramodern sound technologies, he ended up exploring "archaic" indigenous Mexican cultures. The exposure to the radically "alien" civilizations was a personal and professional watershed for the director.[34] Mexico became Eisenstein's own Orient.

The simultaneous coexistence of different layers of time in one space was a defining component of *¡Que viva México!* (1931–32), the Mexican film he had envisaged. The unfinished film presents a vision of cultures at different stages of development in one geographical space. This is accomplished by means of dividing the film into several novellas. As Eisenstein explains:

> The cohesion of the novellas was maintained by several traversing lines. Their consecutiveness stretched along according to a historical characteristic. Not according to historical epochs, but to geographical zones. This is because the culture of Mexico's epochs looks like a fan, spread out on the surface of its land, [if viewed] from the vertical column of history. Its dispersed parts are preserved in that everyday cultural appearance transmitted by the country as a whole in specific historical stages of its development. It seems that you move not in space but in time while traveling from Yucatán to the tropics of Tehuantepec, from the tropics to the central plateau, to the fields of the Civil War in the North, or to an absolutely modern Mexico City. The social systems, appearances, cultures, and customs of these divergent parts of the federation appear to belong to prehistoric times, the pre-Columbian epoch, the epoch of Cortés, the period of Hispanic feudal domination, and the years of struggle for independence.[35]

In Eisenstein's cinematic conception, various regions of Mexico presented a stratified cultural landscape and reflected traces of different historical epochs: the pre-Columbian indigenous civilizations of Aztec, Maya, Huichol, and Olmec; the Catholicism imposed by the Spanish conquistadores; the regime of Porfirio Diaz (1876–1910), and the Civil War (1910–1920). Eisenstein's attempt to spatialize time, using the "spread-out fan" metaphor, is a defining conceptual move, for it is essentially dialectical. Present and past concurrently coexist and this temporal amalgamation profoundly defined the director's creative engagement with the Mexican material. His filmic and theoretical work resounded with, in Masha Salazkina's words, "the distinctly modernist conceptions of nonlinear temporalities as alternative genealogies, altering our understanding of historical temporality by means of an art that absorbed the real temporal dislocations in society brought about by technology."[36]

The influence of the French sociologist and ethnologist Lucien Lévy-Bruhl on Eisenstein was crucial. The director read *La mentalité primitive* (1922) in Paris before his trip to the United States and Mexico. The stance that collective pra-logical mental structures, particularly manifesting themselves in religious practices, shape "primitive" societies fascinated him. According to Lévy-Bruhl, the "primitive" mind does not recognize the contradictions that govern logic— it does not differentiate between the natural and the supernatural.[37] Thus, the neutralization of the principle of noncontradiction using a return to primitive, sensuous thinking was a novel take on the principle of dialectics.[38] Undermining the structure of difference was key to Eisenstein's late understanding of dialectics as a synthetic procedure. The interplay between progress and regress was framed through the prism of dialectics, which itself evolves into a synthetic category mitigating the tension of opposites. More importantly, the unity achieved by tension was extrapolated from the key notions of form and content.

Dialectics, of course, was a cornerstone of Eisenstein's artistry. As Shklovsky put it in his monograph about the director, "Eisenstein's thinking is dialectic. He saw everything in its past and future; for him, the static does not exist: he reveals inexhaustible stages of becoming in it."[39] Deleuze, in his turn, identified Eisenstein simply as "a cinematographic Hegel."[40] It is evident, however, that there was an evolution in the director's understanding of dialectics, if not a drastic shift in his understanding of it through the course of his career as a filmmaker and theorist. The Eisenstein of the 1920s had seen *conflict* as the central kernel of the dialectical process: collision on various levels (volume, color, motion) never really finds complete resolution, perpetuating a permanent dynamic conflict and imposing arbitrary meaning.[41] This is what Leonid Kozlov, the late Soviet film critic, calls the aesthetics of "montage extremism."[42] Eisenstein's late modernist understanding of dialectics, on the other hand, was permeated with the notion of synthesis in such contradictory tendencies and in sets of oppositions. More radically, the late modernist Eisenstein conceives the montage principle as a "reconstruction of laws [that govern] the thought process."[43]

David Bordwell sees in Eisenstein's varied approaches to dialectics a schism between two radically different epistemological positions.[44] The later 1930s stance, marked by "the relapse into Romanticism," professes a different kind of montage procedure, where "parts of the art work will be arranged not to collide but to commingle; the goal is not friction but fusion, not analysis but synthesis."[45] Mikhail Iampolsky, however, convincingly argues that there is no epistemological rupture in Eisenstein's theoretical work and sees his 1920s texts, where disparate fragments or montage cells played a key role, as a preparatory stage for the final synthetic fusion.[46] The productive tension of fragments professed in the 1920s undergoes a process of synthetic unification in the 1930s and is infused by such discourses as *pra-logical* forms of thinking or *regress*, both of which operate as a challenge to formal principles of reasoning.

Eisenstein's understanding of dialectics in the 1930s knew no conceptual borders. As noted by Oksana Bulgakowa, he endowed dialectics with pronounced corporeal features by directly connecting it with the antagonistic clash of conscious and unconscious drives in psychoanalysis; he conceived art as a dynamic orgiastic unity (*ex-stasis*).[47] Ecstatic experience, according to the director, is a gateway to achieving a synthetic tandem between mythological thinking and modern logical consciousness. Consequently, dialectic materialism, as an ideological concept, was pushed into a corporeal realm and connected with bisexuality and all kinds of mystical experiences, even those stimulated by drugs and alcohol, which Eisenstein saw as providing access to a nondifferentiated state.

The shift in Eisenstein's understanding of dialectics (from conflict to synthesis) and of totality (from formalist constructedness to organicity) resulted in a profound engagement with foreign cultures. In *Method*, he argues that his interest in different epochs (XIII, XVI, or XX centuries) and in different nations (Russia, Mexico, Uzbekistan, USA) was motivated by a conviction that all social processes and changes are but different guises of the same countenance (*lik*) and that "this countenance consists of the incarnation of the ultimate idea—an attainment of unity."[48] Organic totality is the key principle while the given structure of difference is its necessary prerequisite.

Eisenstein's preoccupation with various "temporally retrograde" concepts such as regress, pra-logical forms of thinking, or primitive communism could be traced in 1920s texts. As early as 1926, in his article "The Five Epochs," published in *Pravda*, he tried to argue for a productive coexistence of different historical layers as a condition that enabled socialism.[49] *Mnogoukladnost'*, the coexistence of "multiple" (*mnogo*) different socio-economical "structures/forms" (uklad) was a phenomenon that arose from different historical stratifications and was, according to Lenin, a specific condition of Russian society that, while still allowing for the revolution, would eventually give way to a homogenous social order—socialism. For Eisenstein, on the other hand, the coexistence of different socio-economic structures would not necessarily culminate and resolve itself in a homogenous state. He insisted on the possibility, if not the necessity, of the continuing simultaneity, the dialectical interpenetration of archaic and novel forms of being.[50] He did not suggest, however, that the human civilization should accomplish a "return to the primitive," but rather it should function as a synthetic amalgamation of all present stages of development:

> But of principal interest in all this matter is the fact that not only does the process of development itself not proceed in a straight line, . . . but that it marches by continual shifts backwards and forwards, independently of whether it be progressively (the movement of backward peoples towards the higher achievements of culture under a socialist regime), or retrogressively (the regress of spiritual super-structures under the heel of national-socialism). This continual sliding from level to level, forwards and backwards, now to the higher forms of an intellectual order, now to the earlier forms of sensual thinking, occurs also at each point once reached and temporarily stable as a phase in development.[51]

This stance resonates with Soviet modernity's vision of a socialist future for its "underdeveloped" territories as a form of reconstructed past—the classless paradise of primitive communism. It also points to Lenin's vision of backwardness as an enabling precondition of socialism. In this way, primitive thinking was infused with progressive traits.

In "The Content of Form," while analyzing Marx's Preface for *The Communist Manifesto*, Eisenstein investigates primitive communism as a social system devoid of class antagonism:

> The reflection of this social order in consciousness determined those particular traits of consciousness which we call pre-logical, pra-logical in their historical features, or sensuous, complex, undifferentiated, diffuse in their qualitative features.
>
> And a distinguishing aspect of this type of consciousness is therefore *the absence of the antagonistic principle, the absence of contradictions.*[52]

The absence of contradiction, an idea that strongly echoes Lévy-Bruhl's argument, leads to a productive co-existence, a dialectical principle in action. Moreover, archaic and modern aspects of life are both essential in shaping the ontological human condition. Artists simply must acknowledge this. And Eisenstein did exactly this—his preoccupation with "pra-logical" forms of thinking permeated his theoretical vision throughout the 1930s with a renewed force. The main thesis of his book *Method*, being written at the time and conceived as an "autobiographical novel of ideas,"[53] was that every artistic expression in any media obtains an emotional force by resuscitating innate "lower" strata of consciousness.

Eisenstein confesses that in Mexico and more intensely after his return to the USSR he realized that "engagement with art leads the viewer into the realm of cultural regress," for "the mechanism of art is refined as a means to lead people away from rational logic, 'to immerse' them in sensuous thinking and by that very action to trigger in them an emotional-sensuous effect, emotional upsurges."[54] The Mexican experience was the director's personal "way of regress." The ultimate otherness of the country, its unprecedented fusion of modern and archaic modes of being prompted a qualitative change in the director's aesthetic vision: his early avant-garde cerebral radicalism was dialectically imbued with primordial organicity and corporeality, which would begin to prevail in the 1930s. The structures of difference in Mexico enacted a mechanism that revealed a primal, natural state. The figure of the "primitive," a possessor of pra-logical thinking, emerges and evolves into a dominant force in the director's later theoretical investigations.

As Antonio Somaini notes, the Mexican project represents a turning point in the director's life and work and its impact can be observed in Eisenstein's enormous late project *A General History of Cinema*: the director "believed that all the historical strata that coexist in the present are accessible in the same way to the historian and to the artist, because both are capable of moving freely, up and down, across the different 'layers' of culture and of consciousness."[55] Indeed, in his *Notes for a General History of Cinema*, Eisenstein presents a view of cinema as a "synthesis of the arts." He also conceived montage as a historical tool—it is supposed to rearrange historical phenomena to produce new connections and thus expose morphological analogies between seemingly heterogeneous forms from different spatial and temporal points. Cinema's ability, as one of the ultimate art forms of modernity—"the heir of all artistic cultures," to invert the flow of time, to reach out to the past, is inherently linked with the importance of the dyadic tension between regress and progress.

This rhetorical sequence, emphasizing the constructive nature of "archaic" forms, shaped the director's address at the All-Union Creative Conference of Soviet Filmworkers in January 1935. Eisenstein's most important public speech was supposed to celebrate the progressive aspects of Soviet cinematic art, but it forcibly delivered a radically controversial argument by providing numerous examples of "pra-logical" (*pralogicheskoe*) and "sensuous" (*chuvstvennoe*) thinking exercised by children and "primitive" tribes. He acknowledged the colonial and racist underpinning of many anthropological attempts to conceptualize "primitive" consciousness, including those of Lévy-Bruhl.[56] Nevertheless, Eisenstein presented his alternate take on the presumed radical divergence between the "primitive" and modern mind by insisting that the two are linked by means of stadial succession (*stadial'nost'*, stage-like development, or stadialism). Thus, an emotionally engaging work of art has always had to balance between *regress* and *progress*, or rather enact a dyadic tension between the two:

> art is nothing other than an artificial psychical regression to the forms of earlier emotional thinking; in other words, a phenomenon identical with any form of intoxicant, alcohol, shamanism, religion and so on!. . . .
>
> The dialectic of a work of art is constructed upon a most interesting "dyad." The effect of a work of art is built upon the fact that two processes are taking place within it simultaneously. There is a determined progressive ascent towards ideas at the highest peaks of consciousness and at the same time there is a penetration through the structure of form into the deepest layer of emotional thinking. The polarity between these two tendencies creates the remarkable tension of the unity of form and content that distinguishes genuine works.[57]

Eisenstein concludes this section of his address by directly connecting the dynamism of rational and pra-logical forms of thinking with the dualism of form and content. The dialectic tension between sharply contrasting archaic and modern elements emanates as a dynamic co-existence, akin to the one that exists between *form* and *content*:

> a work of art loses its integrity if one or other element prevails. If the balance tips in favor of logic and theme, the work will be dry, rational, and didactic. . . . But to err on the side of emotional forms of thinking, regardless of logic and theme, is equally fatal for the work, which is then doomed to be emotionally chaotic, wild, and delirious. Only the "dyadic" interpenetration of these tendencies can maintain a genuine tension, a unity of form and content.[58]

As with the categories of time and space, *form* and *content* are brought together by the creative vision underpinning *¡Que viva México!*, the project Eisenstein worked on immediately before his return to the Soviet Union and the ensuing

Congress. This exposure to such radically alien vernacular forms had powerfully shaped his theoretical outlook and given him the courage thereafter not to follow any prescribed theoretical path. *Form* and *content* featured prominently in the document titled "Rough Outline of the Mexican Picture," written in English for potential financial backers in the United States.[59] Eisenstein started this by suggesting that the *sarape*, a blanket worn as a cloak by people in Latin America, could be a potent symbol of Mexico in his film:

> So striped and violently contrasting are the cultures in Mexico running close to each other and being centuries far away. No plot, no whole story could run through this sarape without being false or artificial. And we took the contrasting independent closeness of its violent colors as the motif for constructing our film: six episodes running one after another—different in character, different in people, different in animals, trees, and flowers. And still held together by [the] unity of the weave—the rhythmic and musical construction and the unrolling of the Mexican spirit and character.[60]

There is no homogenous content that could provide a unifying element for different historical temporalities. Instead, the director suggested that *form*—a structure made of the divergent stripes of a *sarape*—should serve the unifying function. The contrasting synthesis of the "unity of the weave" becomes a core formal device that merges divergent elements while still preserving their inherent difference.

More importantly, a few pages later Eisenstein alludes to the practice that imperial Spain and the Roman Catholic Church had of appropriating Aztec art and architecture. He writes: "Statues of saints that arose on the spots of pagan altars.... Catholicism and paganism. The Virgin of Guadalupe worshipped by wild dances and bloody bullfights."[61] The quotation distinctly resonates with the general argument of Anita Brenner's book *Idols Behind Altars* (1929), which argued for a similar amalgamation of the pre-Columbian and modern cultures and which Eisenstein had read attentively just before he arrived in Mexico. This artistic continuity, manifest in the conversion to Christianity without abandonment of past pagan deities—an unexpected synthesis—evolves into a more general understanding of the uninterrupted continuity of *form*. Content can be new, but forms are everlasting. Soon after his return from Mexico, Eisenstein recorded the following entry in his diary:

> Form as a phase of content—one of the best propositions.
> It contains a conclusion, made previously: that form is an idea, but expressed by way of atavistic methods and by means of reasoning.

FIG. 4.1 Sergei Eisenstein, Stills from *¡Que viva México!*, 1931–32.

Let art be . . . a synthesis.

A complete triad.

Thesis—common sense. . . .

Antithesis—a step backward in terms of phase of reasoning.

And synthesis: a marriage of the sharpest consciousness with the full-bloodedness of the primitive.

This is, of course, the alpha and omega of what can be said and done about art.

The concept of the idea and form as stages is astoundingly lucid and complete in its harmony.[62]

Here, Eisenstein brings together the entirety of his conceptual constellation: stadialism, synthesis, primitivism, and, of course, the form and content dichotomy. Together, they form a harmonious vision of art, and all would feature prominently in his late theoretical speculations. Later the same day, he resolves to begin working on his "general method," referred to as "a system" at this time: "I have everything. I can create a system in its entirety. *And I ought to*."[63] The crux of Eisenstein's 1943 essay "On the Question of: 'National in Form, Socialist in Content,'" which would develop this idea of the continuity of form, was grounded in his Mexican experience. The national form of socialist art knew no borders and its conceptual core was identified here in a different space, with the clash of diverging temporalities in Aztec and Catholic cultures. This was a true internationalism that Stalin's formula would forever postpone.

TO THE DESERT OF FERGANA

After the purges of 1937 and the March 1938 show trial, Akmal Ikramov and Faizulla Khodzhaev, both of whom were defamed in Rodchenko and Stepanova's copy of *Ten Years of Soviet Uzbekistan*, were convicted as "enemies of the people." Their management of the irrigation sector and cotton production in Uzbekistan were characterized as inefficient.[64] The purges of Ikramov and Khodzhaev marked the advent of *narodnye stroiki* (people's construction projects), "voluntary" mass-scale irrigation projects that were supervised by Usman Yusupov, who succeeded Ikramov. Yusupov's signature initiative was the construction of the Great Fergana Canal in 1939.[65] Large-scale irrigation projects comprised a key constituent of the Soviet modernization policies in the republic. The Uzbek population was clustered around ancient oases and along rivers and canals. These spaces relied on ancient irrigation systems, and access to water was key for survival and prosperity in the semi-arid and arid climate of Central Asia.

In May 1939, Petr Pavlenko, who cowrote the script for *Alexander Nevsky*, alerted Eisenstein to plans by Uzbek and Tajik kolkhoz workers to build an irrigation canal in the span of one month.[66] The canal, which was eventually built in forty-five days under oppressive desert conditions, was a true miracle of socialist modernity. Coordinated mass construction started on August 1, 1939, and quickly became a feat of labor highly publicized in the Soviet press. On June 18, 1939, Eisenstein set out on a trip to the region with his cameraman Eduard Tisse and Pavlenko to film the process of construction for *The Great Fergana Canal*, conceived as a semi-documentary and semi-fictional project. On August 16, Tisse reported that he had finished location shooting on several of the canal's construction sites—Uch-Kurgan, Izbaskent, and sites where Tajik and Uzbek farmers worked together.[67]

The symbiosis of Mexico's mythological past and revolutionary present was further developed in *The Great Fergana Canal*, for which the theme of *progress-regress* was extrapolated from Mexico onto the Soviet Orient. The convergence of divergent temporalities, the figure of the "primitive," and pra-logical forms of thinking all regained discursive significance through the prism of socialist modernity in the Uzbek project.[68] This tackled, in the director's own words, "the theme of tomorrow that has become today."[69] As Eisenstein wrote for *Pravda*, "working on this film, you are participating physically in one of the most striking episodes of creative reconstruction in the history of mankind," for these one hundred and fifty miles "are not just the route of the canal: they have separated the people from perspectives that previously only the bravest imagination dared to envisage."[70] Space and time converge: the project was not merely a case of the radical transformation of space: it was also a feat of overcoming the trauma of a colonial past with the "backwardness" and "stagnation" that accompanied it—it was a quest to deliver the progressive socialist "now."

Eisenstein outlined a temporal triptych in *The Great Fergana Canal*: first, a fourteenth-century feudal prologue, in which Tamerlane's Mongol forces invade the medieval city of Urgench, would be followed first by a prerevolutionary drama depicting the confrontation between poor peasants and usurers who sell water at high prices, then a heroic contemporary tale of the construction of the 150-mile-long Fergana Canal by 160,000 Soviet Central Asian peasants. While water functions as a means of warfare in the prologue, it becomes a point of contestation in the colonial section and ultimately evolves into a symbol of prosperity and a channel for friendship among the peoples.[71] Historical flashbacks would culminate in the very act of construction in the present. "Organic" connection is crucial for how the film would establish continuity: "Here, from our Soviet land, from the peak of social development achieved by humanity, we were preoccupied with something else: not with a picture of disintegration but with one of the connectedness of time. [This comprised] a picture of the blood circulation of epochs, their connections, their transition from one to another, a picture of successions and co-existences."[72] The statement resonates strongly with Eisenstein's conceptualization of national form as an entity that functions as a guarantor of historical continuity. Time, then, serves as an animating force behind social progress and aesthetics.

On July 22, 1939, Eisenstein made a simple drawing depicting "the structure" for the planned film; it showed three towers of different heights.[73] The two tallest ones, representing the medieval and socialist periods, were connected by the shorter imperial one. The significance of the first and third parts lies in them being united thematically by the redirection of rivers, although this redirection had diametrically opposite intentions. The middle episode, set in the recent colonial past, was meant to be a limbo in which the people fell victim both to nature and to the evil exploiters who used water as the means of their manipulation. Accordingly, the film was intended to open with a scene of mass murder. Tamerlane's army built a dam and deprived the city of its water source. The ensuing drought killed almost all the inhabitants of Urgench, until a few stonemasons took revenge on the invaders by unleashing the obstructed water onto them and forcing them to retreat. This temporary dam functioned as a deadly force and its lethal essence was supposed to be dialectically balanced by a life-affirming act—the construction of the Fergana Canal centuries later, a wellspring of life and prosperity in the Soviet land.

In October 1939 the Fergana film project was abruptly halted after Eisenstein was forced to abandon the historical portion of the scenario (the prologue) due to the pressure "from above."[74] He fiercely defended the three-part structure and even received support from Usman Iusupov, the First Secretary of the Central Committee of the Communist Party of Uzbekistan. Iusupov wrote a letter to Zhdanov in which he passionately argued for the necessity of having all three parts in place and emphasized that this integrity would preserve "the monumentality of the film's concept."[75] However, the powerful patron's support was not enough, and Eisenstein lost the bureaucratic battle. The structure of *The Great Fergana Canal* could no longer hold. The three-part division of the film, extending back to the region's historical past, was of the utmost significance to the filmmaker. For the Soviet ideologues based in Moscow, however, the coexistence of these different temporalities was simply problematic.[76]

However, the unfinished project's importance should not be underestimated. It represents one of the most creative engagements with the Oriental fringes of the Soviet Union and vividly reveals the attempt by a key avant-gardist to push into the terrain of late modernism. The republic becomes a reservoir for defamiliarizing experiences—its inherent difference is enhanced through radical transformation. As Eisenstein puts it in his *Pravda* article, "Everything here is unusual. The land has become unrecognizable. For days, for weeks, in even less than a month, the area where the canal is being built has been transformed. It is not melancholy for the past, but pride and rapture that this unusual land evokes: its name is Fergana."[77] "Unusual" is a significant modifier in this short text—the Uzbek land becomes a marvel of the socialist project. Orientalist exoticism is replaced with a socially progressive fascination. However, it is curious that Eisenstein conceives of the project using a rather standard "we vs. the Other" colonial dichotomy. As he probably unconsciously expresses it, the kernel of the film is to show how the future is revealed through the present, but "the theme of our tomorrow organically arises from the past of the peoples of the East in the same manner that a truthful understanding of the future emerges from a deep understanding of the past"[78] "Our tomorrow" is counterposed by "their Oriental past." The project of radical emancipation is conceived using the rhetoric of exclusivity.

Nevertheless, the film's orientalism is discursively ambiguous. The central exotic aspect of *The Great Fergana Canal* is the figure of Tokhtasyn, a fictional epic Uzbek singer who supposedly oversees the narrative progression, like Nurpeis in Vertov's 1942 feature. He functions as Eisenstein's Oriental Virgil, guiding the viewer through a prerevolutionary feudal and colonized Inferno toward the constructed classless Paradiso of socialist Uzbekistan. The epic singer preserves his "primordial roots" into the socialist present as a possessor and guarantor of the "authentic" national heritage.

It is important to note that folklore for Eisenstein, in contrast to Vertov, was not always an important formal and thematic element. He confessed that he "remained stubbornly 'unmoved' by the unquantifiable abundance of images from folklore" throughout the years;[79] and that he was only able to approach folkloric material through his exposure to "low-stratum" deviations from the standards of literary language—"Paris argot, London cockney and later American slang"[80]—"dialects *of* modernism." What attracted him was the way these linguistic "deviations" could deliver the "sensual charm of an image."[81] Folklore starts to matter when he conceives of it as belonging to the realm of sensuous, pra-logical thought. It reveals the structure of human reasoning in its primeval glory.

For the director, Tokhtasyn is a medium that provides access to the sensuous past. His "primordial roots" endowed him with an authority that let him deliver the medieval prologue as an epic song in the film.[82] According to the initial plan, Tokhtasyn would sing the first song about the siege by Tamerlane's troops, then tell his own story in the second song set in the recent colonial past, and finally in the third song, he would "directly enter the action and act independently."[83] This was a movement away from historical reflection toward modern action, with the first and third parts truly epic in form.

In the second part, when he is forced to trade his young daughters to a moneylender in exchange for limited access to water for his dried-up field, Tokhtasyn features as a character endowed with agency. He challenges the moneylender after his allotted half-hour of irrigation expires and gets involved in a spontaneous riot when paupers break the dam and flood the streets of the settlement. Tokhtasyn barely survives the lynching, while his son, referred to in the script as Tokhtasynov—the Russified surname form of the name Tokhtasyn—escapes to participate in an anti-colonial rebellion in Andizhan, and later, during Soviet times, becomes one of the leading engineers of the Great Fergana Canal. The singer, who remembers the conflicts of the past and had himself experienced colonial oppression then becomes the witness of a modern heroic tale, the conquest of nature's blind forces. Reunited with his son at the construction site, he is given the privilege of opening the dam in a ceremony that will unleash torrents of water. The old man, however, chooses to give this privilege back to his son. One of the most bizarre sequences in the film—a so-called "prayer" for Stalin—would follow this scene. Tokhtasyn kneels, raises his hands upwards, and utters the following words: "May the name of the man who has brought us together be blessed, and may his happiness be greater than ours. . . . May his heart be with us forever. . . . His name is the symbol of happiness!"[84]

Stalin is the gatherer of the people, who perform the feat of labor. The trope of friendship between the peoples, a Russocentric form of interethnic unity, would be the key discursive plane of the film. Uzbek, Tajik, Kazakh, Kyrgyz, Turkmen, Russian, and Armenian peasants are shown all working together on the construction site. Towards the end, during a collective feast, they enjoy performances by Khalima Nasyrova, an Uzbek soprano, and Tamara Khanum, née Petrosian, a Fergana-born singer and dancer of Armenian extraction. This leads to the final scene, in which Tokhtasyn is given the privilege of "hand[ing] the water over" to the Tajiks: he eventually cuts the ceremonial ribbon across the canal, marking the border between the Uzbek and Tajik republics, with a single knife blow. In this jubilant ending, water would unite nations and erase borders.

The figure of Tokhtasyn also proves to be essential for the general formal design of *The Great Fergana Canal*. In his commentaries for the script, Eisenstein extensively discusses the narrative aspects of the film and especially the problem of how to present a smooth transition from the pre-revolutionary episode to the 1939 construction of the canal. Remarkably, the filmmaker resolves the narrative knot by engaging with a classical formalist text through *reversal*:

"A reverse Kholstomer"—appears on a piece of paper with my scrawlings at the moment when a little book on Tolstoy accidentally turned up and [helped me] to resolve, at one stroke, both impediments that had hindered the movement of the narrative line [*siuzhet*] from the second theme to the third.[85]

The little book in question is Shklovsky's *Theory of Prose* (1929), which discusses the function of *ostranenie* while using examples from Tolstoy's story "Kholstomer" and novella *Khadzhi-Murat*. Eisenstein takes one of the key formalist devices and appropriates it by means of (formalist) *reversal*. Tolstoy chooses an animal consciousness to challenge the presumed values of a bourgeois society—a horse naturally fails to understand the ontological underpinnings of the notion of *private property*. Eisenstein, in his turn, decides to depict an epoch that transcends the concept of private property altogether—the socialist present, marked by collective ownership. He does so through a consciousness that fails to comprehend this social model, free of private property, upon his first encounter with it: Tokhtasyn fails to understand how 160,000 people mobilized themselves and collectively built the irrigation canal. The singer's "backwardness" evolves into a device that propels the plot. As Eisenstein explains, "one has to take someone's pre-revolutionary or even better pre-war consciousness, to isolate it for about thirty years and then suddenly to make it collide with the stage of that new socialist sweep, which our country achieves in a phenomenon like the construction of the Fergana canal."[86] The thirty-three-year gap, between Tokhtasyn's conflict with the moneylender and his reunion with his son at the construction site, becomes a narrative necessity: "From *incomprehension* of the phenomenon step by step to its *acceptance*.... From the status of the *most backward*, step by step, to the position of the *most advanced*. . . . *From the most backward* to the position of the *one who leads* the movement."[87]

Backwardness acquires progressive qualities. The singer makes a dramatic leap in terms of his ideological outlook—from a retrograde onlooker to a leader of the vanguard. Moreover, this transition is further projected onto whole Uzbekistan as the figure of Tokhtasyn evolves into a metonymic extension of his own motherland:

But the matter is even broader: isn't all of Uzbekistan embodied here in Tokhtasyn?
 Impoverished and enslaved under Tsarism. A slave of water and a slave of the *bai* [feudal lord], backward and held back in his development, does he not now find himself ahead of everyone, being the first, through the powerful upsurge of the creative will of its sons, to accomplish a leap into those realms of the history of future socialist labor, which we, thanks to it, can call those of today.[88]

The amalgamation of individual consciousness with the geographical space of the Soviet Orient, resonating with Vertov's conceptualization of the figure of Saule in *The Front, to You!*, is striking. The two characters undergo a process of radical transformation, and their backwardness is conceived as an enabling condition. The past of the region acquires its validity only because of its ability to transform itself into the progressive Soviet present. But Eisenstein does not stop here. He also reflects on Tokhtasyn's craft—the ancient oral tradition of epic singers—and argues that its ability to unite the disparate elements of the past into a cohesive image (*edinyi obraz*) is comparable to the general principles of montage, which produces a unified vision out of unrelated fragments of filmic material.[89] Eisenstein ponders: "How did this unexpected junction of ancient epic song structure [stroia] with the ultra-cinematic device of montage and filming occur? Only because the image of every work of art, since ancient times, is constructed in a "montage" way."[90]

The case of Tokhtasyn establishes the centrality of montage. Epic tradition is uninterruptedly linked with the ultra-modern aesthetic practice. As a method of transforming raw filmic material to create an impression of reality from smaller units, montage provides a universal artistic procedure to enable independent meaning. As if echoing Eisenstein, Shklovsky writes in his monograph about the director: "Human culture is 'montage-like'. The past does not disappear. Reassessed, it enters the present. But a concept created by the past combines with new images and serves other people."[91] Montage, for the two renowned avant-gardists, becomes a formal method that enables the continuity of culture; it is also an indispensable epistemic tool in which tradition plays a key role. This also registers an important shift from avant-garde fragmentation to epic continuity of late modernism.

FRAMING NATIONAL FORM

Work on *The Great Fergana Canal* had a profound effect on Eisenstein the theorist. Shortly before the Uzbek project was halted, he made an important set of notes in his diary while still in Tashkent. Written on October 1, 1939, they comprise the director's earliest systematic theoretical attempt to engage with the formula "national in form, socialist in content." Eisenstein begins with a bold statement that the notion of the "truthful image" [*istinnyi obraz*], arguably the fundamental operative principle of his aesthetics, is inherently linked with the discourse of national form. He writes:

Toward the question: *Of representation* [izobrazhenie] *and generalized image* [obobshchennyi obraz] <and their unity in the "truthful" image [istinnyi obraz]>

It's essential to say that on the highest *social-stylistic level* of the problem, this interrelationship is completely encompassed in the formula: national in form and socialist in content.[92]

The interplay between "representation" (a mere pictorial fact) and "generalized image" (an analytic artistic impression) is paramount. As Eisenstein argues in *Montage 1938*, aesthetic synthesis is a procedure in which separate static and factual *representations*, gathered in the artist's mind and vision, evolve into an emotionally arresting *generalized image*—an analytic and logical comprehension of a set of representations that reveals the permanence of a broader phenomenon.[93] That is, the *generalized image* turns multifarious aspects of the world into its self-revealing image. Using the figure of Tokhtasyn, the director shows how the singer also produces a *generalized image* as his epic craft transforms a mere fact into a profound impression of reality:

> Tokhtasyn's song is not a scientific treatise, it is not a historical chronicle with word-for-word commentary that documents every detail. Tokhtasyn's song is almost a legend, it is a popular epos, it is a popular *skaz*. And, as such, it carries its strength not in a meticulous documentalism but in that *general image*, which amalgamates the views and fates of many cities ... of the East into a unitary tragedy of sands and waters that have been unleashed by wicked human will and the hatred of different peoples toward one another.[94]

Eisenstein argues that his film will engage fully with the epic genre, with song as a key narrative component, and form a respectful tribute to it. By recollecting the dramatic past and conflating it with the socialist present, Tokhtasyn elevates the region's natural condition (its lack of water) to the level of the human condition. Centuries of conflict reach their climax in a feat of collective labor that overcomes antagonistic nature and celebrates the Soviet friendship among peoples. Epic tradition materializes in the epic construction effort.

However, according to his theoretical notes, the synergistic clash of *representations* and *image* culminates in something qualitatively different—the *"truthful" image* (*"istinnyi" obraz*). The word "truthful" always appears in quotation marks, which indicates that Eisenstein realizes the word is not being used in its commonly accepted sense. One might speculate that the symbiotic tension between factual *representations* and a fictional *artistic image* results in a *"truthful" image* that can aspire to transcend this very reality-fiction dichotomy—it enters the realm of ultimate truth, a reconciliation of logical rationality with pra-logical sensuality.

Transcendence is accomplished again by means of a symbiotic tension between form and content. According to Eisenstein, national form belongs to the domain of the sensuous (a pra-logical stage), while content dwells on the analytic, cerebral level. The two can provide a higher symbiosis as the *"truthful" image*:

> the same formula "national in form, socialist in content" encompasses the whole basic scheme of the dynamism of the artistic image, that is, of the phenomenon of art itself.
>
> The national as a more ancient stage of the socialist. Form as an earlier stage of cognition—*sensuous* in relation to content—a stage of cognition—of the cerebral...[95]

For Eisenstein, national consciousness, as a reaction to colonial rule, functions as a precondition for a revolution that, in turn, leads toward a classless socialist society—a more progressive state.[96] Thus the national, as a state or stage, precedes and leads up to its socialist counterpart. Form, in turn, becomes a subsidiary entity in relation to content. Form is thus a sensory-emotional rendering of content. This line of reasoning corresponds to Stalin's early (1906) reading of Marx's political economy: he first argues that "the material side, the external conditions, [and] being" comprise the *content*, while "the ideal side, [and] consciousness" comprise the *form*; he then emphasizes that "in the process of development content precedes form, form lags behind content."[97]

National form, as an engagement with the epic genre in *The Great Fergana Canal*, together with its socialist content—the material construction effort itself—will produce the *ultimate truth*, which exists in a post-logical category. As Eisenstein concludes in his notes: "The formula, as we may see, is entirely constructed according to the same unity and mutual interpenetration of the pictorial [*izobrazitel'nogo*] and the figural-abstracted [*obrazno-abstragirovannogo*], becoming amalgamated in the truthful-figural [*istinno-obraznom*], and manifests itself as the highest point on this path: the point of *style* [*tochkoi stilia*]."[98] This rather convoluted fragment seems to deliver a simple message: to achieve the final (but unclarified) "point of style," nations and forms have to undergo a "stadial" development.

Stadial succession is crucial for Eisenstein's theory at large. The importance of this concept emerges from a text written a year after the Tashkent notes—the "spherical book," sketched in 1940. One of the earliest structures of the director's grand theoretical treatise *Method* outlined three key parts: "I. On Montage," "II.

On Composition," "III. Summation [*itogi*]."⁹⁹ The final part, a set of ultimate theoretical conclusions, was preceded by a still unpublished *Einführung*—German for "introduction," the term Eisenstein preferred to the Russian *vvedenie*. What is striking is that this text, which summarizes the key aesthetic principles of filmmaking, is dedicated *exclusively* to the question of national form.

In this *Einführung*, Eisenstein sets out on a quest to unpack the theoretical potential of Stalin's "national in form, socialist in content," which constitutes for the director nothing less than "the most profound thing of all that has been said concerning the nature of art," because it "contains the entire basic dynamics of interrelation within art as a process, [as well as] within the work of art as an organism."¹⁰⁰ To be more precise, its importance lies in alluding to a complex interaction between form and content. National form thus evolves into a key point for reorientation, as such operative principles as *stadialism, regress, bi-sex*—the core of Eisenstein's late theoretical lexicon—are directly linked with it.¹⁰¹

Eisenstein starts, as if mirroring his 1939 notes, by stating that national consciousness is the first stage of human development with socialist consciousness being the highest.¹⁰² The continuity between the two signals their interdependence, for they each represent separate points on the continuum of historical development. He elaborates: "from the sense of self of the family derives the self-consciousness of the clan; from it emerges national consciousness; from a reconsideration of the nation, from the class point of view, grows the highest self-consciousness, that of the international unity, of working people in their struggle with capitalism, a socialist consciousness emerging in national forms."¹⁰³ National form is framed not as a mere aesthetic category, but as an enabling component of social development—it is present in its nascent "form" at every level of the social-relational structure.

Moreover, Eisenstein once again relates this progression to the relationship between form and content—the former precedes the latter, and the two are placed on the continuum of evolution: "Thus, socialism is somewhat in advance in relation to the national, and through this, the formula tells us something very important regarding the interrelation between form and content. ~~Form is also content~~ Form is older than content by one cycle . . ."¹⁰⁴ Yet again, a slip of the writer's hand establishes an equivalence between form and content that is later replaced by a stadial relationship. Form precedes content. A few sentences later, Eisenstein elaborates further: "In its unformed state content is a formulation; while form is content that is articulated one step *backwards* in relation to a formulation, which is undeniably the most progressive "form" of the "formulation" of thought, that is, it is stadially connected [with] but is of a different degree of adequacy than content."¹⁰⁵

This dense wordplay creates a maze of reflexive interrelationships and symmetric interdependences. Stadial succession concurrently facilitates procedures of both correspondence and difference. Form simultaneously is and is not content (and vice versa). This is a significant reevaluation of the form-content dynamic pairing in that it completely undermines the hierarchical correlation that marked the official Soviet definition and even Eisenstein's early attempts at theorization of the form and content interrelationship.

Such theoretical "vagueness" is intensified even further at the end of the *Einführung*. Eisenstein concludes it with a certain rhetorical openness:

> According to the Stalinist formula, we know one thing: form is one step behind in relation to the formulation of content.
>
> That is, the same stage, verbalized in a language that is one phase earlier than the logical language that formulates the thesis.
>
> What kind of language is it? Where should it be found? How to discover it?
>
> Here the formula does not provide a further answer. One must go through a diversity of real practice, so one can practically arrive at the same position in its analysis: in a theoretical summary, in a theoretical generalization [one must] once again ascend toward and encounter this primary and foundational formula, which was grasped and articulated in the short thesis: national in form, socialist in content.[106]

To return to the context of *Fergana*, it can be posited that Eisenstein's practical application of such theoretical elaborations comprised an attempt to find a cinematic equivalent to the aesthetic structure of the Persian-style miniature. This was a hands-on task that followed complex theoretical elaborations. In a note written in July 1939 at his dacha in Kratovo, near Moscow, before starting to film material for *Fergana*, he recalled an earlier "Persian" project. In 1933, after his return from Mexico, he had expressed an interest in adapting Ferdowsi's epic poem *Shāhnāmeh*, seeing the text as an "abreaction" to the unfinished *¡Que viva México!*—it was supposed to be a release of the previously repressed "national" Mexican material. Since it would most likely have required another trip abroad, when the director's talent was desperately needed in his native land, the head of the State Cinema Organization, Boris Shumiatsky, personally intervened to veto the project.

Unable to adapt Ferdowsi for Soviet viewers, Eisenstein did not abandon his interest in Persian miniature style and its cinematic equivalence. While teaching at the State Institute of Cinematography in 1934, he delivered a lecture on this subject. The lecture began by addressing various unsuccessful attempts to extrapolate mechanically new content on old forms, such as Palekh lacquer painting or embroidery (traditional Russian crafts) depicting contemporary industrial scenes.[107] He also referred to Spanish Catholicism, Diego Rivera's use of religious composition in his frescoes of proletarian life, and his own engagement with Golgotha and St Sebastian iconography.[108] Clearly, the realization that came to him in Mexico—that aesthetic forms endure and new content can be delivered through them—continued to shape his vision and theoretical concerns.

What interested Eisenstein in Persian art was related primarily to *perspective*, as traditional miniaturists did not use foreshortening. Classical Persian miniatures present a system of so-called *vertical* (or isometric) perspective that displays figures as overlapping each other, while elements of the exterior or interior setting, such as lakes or carpets, appear flat on the page. Consequently, "nearer" figures are shown below larger figures, and the only way to indicate the relative position of elements in the composition was by overlaying them. The Latin word *perspicere* means "to see through," whereas the Persian miniature presented a multiplicity of kaleidoscopic gazes directed at the world—an inherently distinctive way of looking.

In a 1934 lecture, Eisenstein argued that filmmakers can create the same effect as a Persian miniature by introducing two distinct vanishing points within a shot. His basic idea is to adapt mattes, used in special effects filmmaking, to combine two image elements (usually foreground and background) into a single, final image. But by filming the background from a radically vertical point of view, Eisenstein could create an illusion of two incongruent perspectives.[109]

The Fergana project led Eisenstein to return to this earlier attempt to conceptualize a "Persian-style shot" that would reproduce the basic stylistic features of Persian miniatures on the film screen. In 1939 diary notes on the question of national form, he considers illustrating his theoretical elaborations: "*How it ought to be* {illustrations: a foray into examples of resolutions [in the sphere of] plasticity [by means of] the 'Eastern' composition of the Uzbek film material}."[110] This novel way of (re)presenting reality, corresponding to established "Oriental" visual practices, was a practical demonstration of the inherent adaptability of formal devices with their ability to travel throughout different times and locations. The stylistic form of the Persian miniature, which had historically influenced certain artistic practices found in the territory of contemporary Uzbekistan, finds its renewed life in a different medium and with a different content.

A set of drawings in the Eisenstein archive presents different visual styles for the three parts of *The Great Fergana Canal*.[111] "Eastern" style images dominate the first part, involving several palace interiors that invite this kind of mode of representation. Figures in most of these images are placed at different levels (two, three, and even four) and the director proposed several solutions for how to achieve the effect of a vertical perspective. An interplay of different visual and spatial scales is one of the solutions that Eisenstein discusses extensively and visualizes in his sketches. For some exterior scenes in the first part, he suggests making an intentionally small waterfall, which would create the effect of spatial incongruity; he also suggests setting the camera's field of vision at a wide angle, so that the horizon is not visible and the vanishing point is not easily located.[112] The inversion of Shklovsky's treatment of "Kholstomer" becomes a literal inversion of perspective in Eisenstein's treatment of the film's visual design.

Eisenstein's engagement with "Oriental" visual culture was not a mere episode in his rich artistic biography. It is inherently interconnected with broader aesthetic discourses and remained continuously present throughout the 1930s and until his death in 1948. In 1940, for instance, in a speech at the Creative Conference on Problems of Historical and Historical-Revolutionary Film, he argued that historical landscape should be shot as if from a distance, and should include only representative, generalized (*obobshchennye*) features. Reality, however, should not be arbitrarily distorted by artists. Generalization, as a mode of abstraction, replaces the procedure of defamiliarization. To illustrate his point, Eisenstein recollected his visit to Uzbekistan, when he realized that the nonnaturalistic perspective of Persian-style miniatures derives from real experiences of space in which objects are arranged in certain ways:

> If you go to an old, good teashop, and drink tea on the fourth platform up, then you will be able to see all the figures arranged in the same way as is sharply defined in the miniature.
>
> If you walk through the paddy fields, which are also arranged in terraces, you will get the same impression.
>
> We are all used to the stylized forms of trees in miniatures—circular, oval, and so on. But if you walk past mulberry trees at the appropriate period, you will see that they have all been pruned in just that way....
>
> In this way, the miniaturists, who had not ruined their eyes on other types of painting, were able to look at the special features of the points of view that were formed around them.[113]

Stylized ways of representing reality, he argues, are deeply rooted in the real experience of space and of the natural environment. Here, the avant-garde finally reconciles itself with "reality," and the *generalization* of key aspects of the latter replaces its *distortion*. However, the modernist inclination to self-consciously contest representational limits is preserved through *abstraction*. Hence, modernist strangeness acquires a new set of discursive connotations: difference is conceptualized through generalization.

ORNAMENT AS NATIONAL FORM

In late 1941, immediately upon Eisenstein's evacuation to Kazakhstan, Atasheva became involved in a project based on the medieval Kazakh epic tale of Kozy Korpesh and Baian Sulu. The cinematic adaptation, entitled *The Steppe Warrior* (*Stepnoi batyr*), was supposed to be directed by Eisenstein's VGIK students Valentin Kadochnikov (1911–1942) and Fedor Filippov (1911–1988).[114] However, the production of the film was halted after Kadochnikov's premature death, and no surviving scripts have yet been identified. Only a few sporadic discussions of the film's general conception are available in the correspondence between Atasheva and Kadochnikov.[115]

On January 4, 1942, Eisenstein created the "Koshma" series of drawings that were likely produced to help Atasheva and his students find a stylistic key for their treatment of the story, a peculiarly localized oriental version of *Romeo and Juliet*. Eisenstein's drawings engage with the nationally specific narrative and invoke nationally specific materiality. Koshma is a commonly used felt fabric among nomadic peoples of Central Asia. It is made of camel or sheep wool by means of kneading and compression that inextricably entangle fibers. Decorated with interwoven ornamental patterns, it is used as an effective insulation in yurts as well as a decorative object. Eisenstein creates an artistic rendering of the ancient craft by creating six banners that present the lovers' tragic story. The Central Asian republic, a temporary home for the major Soviet film studios, provided the locally specific material as inspiration, to be woven into the fabric of socialist culture by the "metropolitan" cultural agent.

Eisenstein's engagement with the epic tale took place only a few years after its reemergence in the 1930s. A transcribed text of the epos in its "classic" rendering was introduced to the Soviet audience in 1936 by Mukhtar Auezov, who published the tale of Kozy Korpesh and Baian Sulu as performed by prominent epic singer Zhanak (1770–1856).[116] Three years later, Auezov, together with Leonid Sobolev, wrote an article "Epos and Folklore of the Kazakh People" (Epos i fol'klor kazakhskogo naroda), commissioned by *The Literary Critic*.[117] Written in sync with the ideological preoccupations of the time, it establishes the Kazakh folk tradition as relevant to the Soviet reader and prominently features a synopsis of the story of Kozy Korpesh and Baian Sulu. A betrothed couple from birth, the two were separated after the death of Kozy's father. The estranged young people search for each other, but Kozy dies at the traitorous hands of Kodar, a giant shepherd who earlier saved the cattle of Baian's father. Baian, bequeathed to be buried next to her lover, kills Kodar before stabbing herself with a knife next to Kozy's dead body. But this tragic end does not deliver closure: Kodar's relatives separate the lovers' graves by burying Kodar between them. Thus, a briar bush that sprouts on Kodar's grave becomes a natural fence separating the flowers that blossom on the two lovers' graves. The flowers ultimately overcome the obstacle, and the lovers find their reunion in death in another form of life.[118]

Eisenstein's "Koshma" series consists of six drawings that are adorned with the "AA" ideogram, enacting an amalgamation of two key topoi for Eisenstein in the early 1940s—Alma-Ata and Moscow. The drawings are marked by variations in the couple's gestures and appearances and provide an idiosyncratic take on the Kazakh epic tale. The first drawing (fig. 4.2, *top*) is likely to be a preliminary sketch, for it is distinctly different in style from the other five. It is rendered in graphite pencil (the other five are in two colors of crayon) and presents the lovers holding hands while facing different directions. The plant-like representation of the traditional Kazakh ram's horn ornament (*koshkar muyiz*) envelops and provides the base for the couple. Their reproductive organs are covered by ornamental branches. Kozy's slanted eyes give him a reptilian appearance, and Baian likewise has pronouncedly animalistic traits—she has hoops instead of feet, and her nose resembles a pig snout. However, she wears nuptial jewelry on her forehead and earrings that "domesticate" her. The couple's proximity to the natural world is also enhanced by the presence of various animals that are formally rendered as ornament. A rampant lion in the lower right-hand corner stands erect on one hind leg with forepaws and the other hind leg raised to strike while a heron- or swan-like bird emerges from its gaping jaws. The bird, in turn, overlaps with Baian's raised left arm, while a second bird hovers in the air on the bridegroom's side, overlapping with Kozy's right arm. The fluid continuity between plants, animals, and humans is pronounced.

The second drawing (fig. 4.2, *bottom*) prominently features a rhythmic linear pattern of scroll-like foliage that verges on the abstract.[119] The intricate ornamental lace lacks volume but its spiraling stems create a more dynamic composition by delicately enveloping the couple as they hold hands. Zoomorphic ornamental patterns are completely absent in this foliate visualization of the epic tale. Nevertheless, the man and woman are depicted as an inherent part of the fecund natural world that surrounds them.

The four remaining drawings are stylistically unified. It seems that Eisenstein identified a representational key: accomplished in red and blue crayons, two primary colors of the Kazakh decorative tradition, they present Kozy and Baian as a proto-couple. The colors enact a binary tension: the man's red contour adjoins the woman's blue figure, immersing the couple in synthetic unity with the surrounding red and blue ornament. The movement of the hands, the turn of the torsos, and the curves of the lovers' necks are all rendered using uninterrupted

FIG. 4.2 Sergei Eisenstein, "Kozy-Korpesh and Baian-Sulu [1, 2]," 1942, RGALI.

contour. The rhythmic basis of the drawings, achieved by means of economy of line, is very prominent. The couple seem to have merged into a single body in the third drawing (fig. 4.3, *top*), where their contiguous legs (the man's left and the woman's right leg) disappear under a palmette. Baian gently leans on Kozy, whose right leg stands firmly on what appears to be a koshma. The stylized carpet functions as a stable marker of gravity from which the aerial dynamism of the ornament emanates. The scrolled foliage of the lower section of the ornament emphasizes the lyricism of the lovers' embrace and seems to enter the couple's lower bodies to emerge from their heads as swan-like patterns.

The fourth drawing (fig. 4.3, bottom), which has the subtitle "Erotic Koshma" (*erotichnaia koshma*), also features an ornamented carpet on which the man stands, and the woman kneels. The position of the lovers' bodies and the exposure of their lower strata (though their reproductive organs are not depicted) provide the erotic tension. Kozy's left-hand holds the kneeling Baian's plait while his right hand extends toward the sky—a possibly ecstatic gesture prompted by the sexual act. Bird-like ornamental patterns also assume phallic shapes above the couple.

The fifth and the sixth drawings (fig. 4.4) place the epic heroes on a horizontal plane with a pronounced zoomorphic pattern (ornamental swans folding their necks together) that completely dominates the visual field. The drawings resonate with the narrative, which recounts the protagonists' posthumous transformation into two trees with branches interwoven at their highest point. The gestural relationship between the two signals a continuation of life, albeit in a different form. At the same time, all four horizontal drawings seem to represent the couple as Adam and Eve (nota bene: *adam* means human in Kazakh) merged with the natural world while the two vertical drawings represent the lovers through the prominent presence of koshma, a domestic item of culturally specific "material."

Multiple interpretative variations on a single theme are one of Eisenstein's signature devices. A central theme of the "Koshma" series is, clearly, the interdependence of living organisms. The drawings posit that man is an inseparable part of nature, as the two human figures are interwoven into a complex web of interrelations, which extend not only to animate organisms but to inanimate matter (such as minerals) as well. This stance was crucial for Eisenstein the theorist; his drawings, as observed by Kleiman, very often comprise an intermediary link between directing and theoretical works.[120] Indeed, the production of the "Koshma" drawings coincided with the director's intense work on his grand treatise *Method*.

In "Three Kingdoms" (Tri tsarstva), a fragment from *Method* that remains unpublished, Eisenstein expands his synthetic vision of artistic forms and extrapolates it to biological forms of life. Yet again, the director commences by invoking the "national in form, socialist in content" formula wherein form and content

FIG. 4.3 Sergei Eisenstein, "Kozy-Korpesh and Baian-Sulu [4, 5]," 1942, RGALI.

are *stadially* linked—that is, national consciousness, as a stage, precedes and leads to the universal socialist counterpart.[121] The thesis that the category of national, in an evolutionary sense, is one step behind the socialist ideal, but that the two together constitute "an organic wholeness,"[122] is crucial for Eisenstein. It allows him to integrate such notions as backwardness and regress into the modern fabric of the advanced socialist vision. The director identifies this stadial interdependence as a universal law and illustrates this imperative by how an artist artistically renders [*oformliaet*] individual elements of various kingdoms of nature: specifically, minerals, plants, and animals.

In his classification, Eisenstein relies on the work of Carl Linnaeus (1707–1778), who laid the foundations for modern biological nomenclature. The natural scientist distinguished two kingdoms of living things: Regnum Animale (the animal kingdom) and Regnum Vegetabile (the vegetable kingdom, for plants). He also identified minerals as a third inanimate kingdom, Regnum Lapideum. Eisenstein employs this classification system to reveal a formal interdependence between the three domains:

> In order to "be formed" [*oformit'sia*] into a work of art, a representative of each "kingdom" has to take form [*prinimat' formu*] that is inherent to a representative of a "preceding" kingdom!
>
> In order to enter [the domain of] art, that is, to acquire an artistic image [quality], in order to acquire form and style,
>
> > the plant borrows the structural principle of the mineral;
> > the animal—of the plant;
> > man—of the animal;
> > divinity—the form of man![123]

Eisenstein maintains that the process of artistic rendering [*oformlenie*] takes place by way of *stylization*—an appropriation of the formal structure of the preceding (stadially lower) domain: plants assume a geometric mineral structure, animals take on botanical forms, while humans undergo a zoomorphic transformation.[124] To put it in bolder terms, the entry into the artistic sphere takes place through (formal) regress.

The link between ornament and regress, as manifested in "primitive" cultures, was too obvious for Eisenstein to miss. The director's deeply engaged interest in regressive aspects of "primitive" cultures allowed him to explore the structure of ornament and to identify its relevance to his theoretical endeavors. However, this celebration of ornament was clearly at odds with the avant-garde's

FIG. 4.4 Sergei Eisenstein, "Kozy-Korpesh and Baian-Sulu [3, 6]," 1942, RGALI.

tendency toward ardent de-ornamentation, which very often was accompanied by a supercilious colonial stance. Indeed, Adolf Loos's statement that the "*evolution of culture is synonymous with the removal of ornament from utilitarian objects*,"[125] quoted above, is preceded by a classical colonial sentiment that counterpoises nature and modernity. Loos writes: "what is natural to the Papuan and the child is a symptom of degeneracy in the modern adult."[126] The racialized (and gendered) history of ornament and its alleged "fall" from the steamship of modernity reached its culmination in Loos's text. Traditionally, the question of ornament prompts animated debates that enact discursive tensions between such categories as excrescence and essence, surface and interiority, peripheral and central, femininity and masculinity, utility and decoration, and finally, in Anne Anlin Cheng's words, between "Western discipline and Oriental excess."[127] As a result, ornament's articulation of the "primitive" and the "Oriental" shapes how we conceive "the denuded modern surface and modern personhood itself."[128]

For Eisenstein, however, ornament was the gateway to a general system of representation. The director reclaims ornament, understood by most fellow modernists as a superfluous, anachronistic, and decorative entity, and refashions it as a dynamic formal structure. In "Notes on Line and Ornament," written in 1940, Eisenstein identifies three essential constituents of *image* (*obraz*): "representation" (*izobrazhenie*, a pictorial fact); "generalized image" (*obobshchennyi obraz*, an analytic artistic impression); and recurrence (*povtor*). Eisenstein emphasizes that the three form a triad that always interpenetrate one another in what he deems a perfect work of art. *Representation*, as a mode of automatic or "naturalistic" reproduction, undergoes a fusion with *generalized image*, an analytic impression; *recurrence*, as a pure manifestation of movement and rhythm, animates the two. In their pure form, however, the three comprise the following triad: 1) naturalism; 2) geometric schema; 3) ornament.[129]

Representation, a naturalistic imprint of the material realm, is balanced by the abstraction of a geometric schema of *generalized image*. The two then are counterpoised by the dynamism of ornament as *recurrence*. More importantly, the ornament's *recurrence* is distinguished by a pronounced connection with the corporeal-sensuous realm. As Eisenstein succinctly puts it, "recurrence of the ornament as a [recurrence] of respiration, heartbeat, or peristalsis of the intestines."[130] This corporeal link thus makes ornament distinct from the stasis and sterility of a geometric schema—it animates the whole process of representation by providing access to the sensuous realm. Eisenstein challenges the avant-garde rejection of the organic ornament in favor of "the abstraction of the wire-like bodies of constructivism."[131] Ornament is rhythm while rhythm is an ultimate manifestation of nature. Eisenstein considered this distinction to be his own theoretical discovery:

"'The geometricity of ornament' . . . comprises a primary synthesis, wherein the pure "intellectualism" of the given stage—geometrism—relates to utmost sensuality (regressive even for pra-logic!) [and with] recurrence as an element of a purely physiological phenomenon (that is, even lower than pra-logic)."[132]

Eisenstein knew no restraints in his theoretical endeavors. Thus, elaborating on the same subject in 1943, he alludes to "the rhythmic precision of the articulation of Stalin's oath"[133] before turning to the phenomenon of ornament in his discussion of rhythm and recurrence: "Meanwhile, approaching rhythmicality and especially the primary and primordial rhythm is, at the same time, a return to forms that are the most primary, the earliest, [and] not only primeval but even the animal [or] vegetative."[134] The connection between ornament and the physical realm is further elaborated in an extensive quotation from a Russian translation of Ernst Kretschmer's *Medizinische Psychologie* (*Medical Psychology*, 1922). Eisenstein highlights several passages on rhythmic movement patterns found in single-celled protozoa and multicellular eukaryotic organisms.[135] He appears to be fascinated by the fact that these "primitive" rhythmic patterns also manifest themselves in the human organism. They are not governed by psychic impulses of the central nervous system—they lead "their own relatively independent protozoan-metazoan life."[136] Eisenstein further proceeds to highlight Kretschmer's argument that all forms of organic life are inherently linked with patterns of movement found in the kingdom Plantae—"vegetative forms of movement," as he defined them, permeate everything.

The interconnection between man and nature and its impact on artistic representation is further explored in another set of drawings made in Alma-Ata. A few days before making the "Koshma" series, the director produced a set of drawings that stylistically resonate with his Mexican period, in that they are arresting in their firm and confident lines and overall laconism. The three drawings— "Totem," "In Memory of Mountain Goat Hunters" (Pamiati okhotnikov na gornykh kozlov), and "The Bird Hunt" (Okhota na ptits)—loosely revolve around the theme of the hunt.[137] The hunt is rendered as an intricate conflation of vertical and horizontal planes and reveals a dynamic interaction between celestial prey and the terrestrial hunter (the dominions of life and death). Eclectic in nature, they do not display a unified stylistic key. However, they certainly echo decorative objects found in Scythian cultures of nomadic tribes roaming in Central Asia and parts of Eastern Europe. Scythian art, which flourished in the Iron Age, is dominated by predation scenes, and its conventional subject matter enacts a tension between the wild domain and its domestic or docile counterpart.

Scythian artifacts were prominently displayed in the Hermitage's permanent collection throughout the 1920–30s and must have been known to Eisenstein, who famously did on-location shooting at the Winter Palace for his film *October* in 1927.[138] Almost immediately upon his arrival in Alma-Ata, the evacuated director ordered several book titles that reference Scythian art from his private library in Moscow.[139] Among them was Dmitrii Eding's 1940 monograph *Carved Sculpture of the Urals* (*Reznaia skul'ptura Urala*), which is exclusively dedicated to the style of Scythian animal depictions. Eding attempts to identify local, as opposed to "external," Byzantine, or Western, aesthetic influences on medieval Eastern European art and finds them through the animal style of Scythian art.[140] He claims that the ancient artistic practices of Central Eurasia profoundly impacted the course of the region's aesthetic development. They constituted Slavic tribes' internal "oriental" inspiration, and this stance resonated with Eisenstein during his evacuation in Alma-Ata.

Yet again Eisenstein elaborates his aesthetic vision of human embeddedness within nature's domain. The animals and the hunter have undergone a process of aesthetic framing—they are all represented resting on plinths. These plinths perform an important function, as they are located inside the field of representation. That is, in Eisenstein's drawings, the represented object is a drawn sculpture on a pedestal, which itself is engaged in an intricate process of representation. The double frame allows the director to establish and, at the same time, disrupt the otherworldliness of the mythological realm. By aesthetically engaging the process of framing, Eisenstein inadvertently contributes to twentieth-century aesthetic discourses that challenge the notion of aesthetic framing as auxiliary in nature. Jacques Derrida, for instance, influentially contests Kant's evaluation of picture frames and sculptural pedestals as mere ornamentation (*parergon*) to the artwork proper. For Kant, as noted in his *Critique of Judgment*, the frame performs a secondary task; it does not take attention away from the pure beauty of form, which always resides in a great object of art.[141] The Kantian frame establishes and safeguards the pure aesthetic realm as transcending meager reality. For Derrida, however, the frame makes the difference between the outside and the inside only seem natural.[142] The frame is liminal in all senses—its inner and outer limits are difficult, if not impossible, to define. Therefore, it is a challenge to distinguish between the intrinsic and the extrinsic. Eisenstein's drawings appear to enact this very uncertainty.

The animal on "Totem" (fig. 4.5) is a hybrid entity with various features borrowed from at least three different animals. It features a goat's tail and cloven hooves, a stag's horns and muzzle, and a horse's mane. The animal is rendered in a crouching position, with legs folded beneath its body and antlers streaming above and across its back—easily recognizable motifs of Scythian art. However, instead of traditional looped antlers that can assume zoomorphic forms,

FIG. 4.5 Sergei Eisenstein, "Totem," 1941, RGALI.

Eisenstein presents a tree of life emerging directly from the animal's head. However complex these eclectic elements are, they fuse into a single entity of compelling force and beauty.

The central theme of the drawing is the continuity of life, for the composition centers on two fetuses passing through the birth canal. The lower fetus seems to be undergoing a process of birth for there is a protuberance in the tree of life's trunk next to it that is ready to evolve into a fully-fledged branch. The upper fetus, for its part, reveals the dynamics of birth. It is depicted as if emanating from three hypostases of womanhood, flanked by two male figures. The child is thus conceived at the intersection of female and male "streams."

Eisenstein's attention to various elements of national clothing in the drawing is simply astounding. Headwear in traditional Kazakh society prescribes strictly defined social roles, and the drawing enacts these conventions. The old man in the left corner wears a *malakhai*, a tapered fur hat with ear flaps, and holds a traditional whip (*komcha*)—a phallic symbol of power. The hunter of the lower branch wears an *aiyr kalpak*, a pointed, upturned cap usually worn by representatives of the upper class. He is depicted holding a bow and an arrow—likewise, locally recognizable symbols of male potency, which were indeed identified as such by Herodotus.[143] This vision of patriarchy animates the allegorical vision depicted in the drawing. The two male figures occupy the lower branches of the tree of life while framing the three hypostases of womanhood on the top.

The young girl wears a small hat adorned with owl feathers, a socially prescribed piece of headwear for unmarried young women.[144] She appears to hold her own braid decorated with a *shashbau*—a jewelry item weaved into woman's braids that was usually made of silver geometric plates, semi-precious stones, and coins. The piece traditionally signified that the wearer had reached sexual maturity.[145] The matriarch in the middle is wrapped in *kimeshek*, the traditional headwear of married old women that covers the head and neck. *Kimesheks*, made of white cloth adorned with lace patterns, indicated that the wearer had reached menopause. The third woman wears a cone-like headdress—*saukele*—a bridal attribute. For her wedding, a bride was to wear all the jewelry that she possessed, as each piece carried its own symbolic import. The *saukele* itself had many implicit mythological symbols, and it was often adorned with depictions of the tree of life.[146]

This complex and meticulous engagement with attributes of Kazakh national clothing is balanced by the universal vision of the *tree of life*, connecting all forms of creation found in cultures throughout the world.[147] For Vladimir Toporov, the *tree of life* is a variation of the *world tree* that models cosmic relations: the tree usually depicts a circulation of "vital energy" from plants via animals to humans.[148] Furthermore, J. H. Philpot, whose book on sacred tree imagery is quoted by Eisenstein,[149] suggests that individual births are "represented as taking place directly from a tree"[150] in origin myths.

The concept of the mythical tree was central to Eisenstein in his adaptation of *Die Walküre* in 1940.[151] The opera commenced with a prologue that revealed the unity of plants, animals, and humans by featuring Yggdrasil—an immense mythical ash tree that plays a central role in Norse cosmology. The tree branches, which took up the entire expanse of the stage, were inhabited by animals and people. Among several creatures that live within Yggdrasil are four stags who crane their necks upward to chomp at the branches. In Eisenstein's words:

> With the gradual convergence of the music and the lyrical tension of the duet, the tree grew, became covered with young foliage, and came alive with flowers. Beasts and birds darted through its luscious greenery; by the end, the tree was to have been encircled by a ring of entwined bodies of countless Siegmunds and Sieglindes, who had also experienced the languor, the thrill, and the triumph of love.[152]

"The triumph of love," however, is supplemented by the erasure of individual subjectivity, or rather its multiplication. At the end of Act I, the tree assumes the role of "a pantheistic emblem of the creation, as it appeared to primitive man."[153] The primitive totemism of hunting societies triumphantly concludes Eisenstein's adaptation.

The fusion of the animal and human domains is enacted differently in another drawing from the series, "In Memory of Mountain Goat Hunters" (fig. 4.6). The unity of life forms is replaced with their union in death: the wounded stag with an arrow piercing his back is depicted impaling the hunter on its horns.[154] The hunter's bow subsequently becomes his aureole and the two, animal and man, are posthumously amalgamated into a single image in the act of mutual interpenetration. The goat is traditionally associated with masculinity and the reproductive powers of the sun, as the depicted luminous radiance clearly enacts.[155] The horns, which sprout into the tree of life in the "Totem" drawing, stand here as pillars of death. Furthermore, while the Kazakh folkloric tradition seems to be downplayed in "In Memory of Mountain Goat Hunters," the drawing can still be considered a loose interpretation of the Kazakh folk legend of Aksak-kulan (the lame onager).[156] According to the legend, Jochi, Genghis Khan's eldest son, died during an onager hunt. The young prince was killed during a pursuit when a lame onager suddenly turned and attacked him.

The laconism of the drawing is what makes it stand out in the series. The hunter is presented in a radically stylized manner: his extremities are barely pronounced, and his facial features are reduced to three circular openings standing for two eyes and a mouth. The dynamism of the simple line manifests itself in a pure outline without any trace of shading, thus creating an illusion of solidity. In general, Eisenstein's drawings characterize themselves by an economy of line that both exudes expressive sensualism and strives ever toward abstraction. In the 1946 text "How I Learned to Draw (A Chapter about My Dancing Lessons)," a

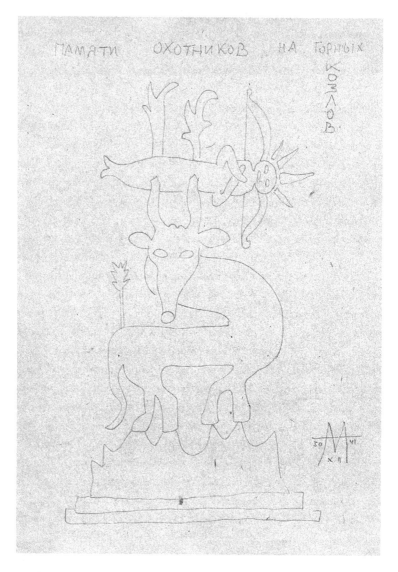

FIG. 4.6 Sergei Eisenstein, "In Memory of Mountain Goat Hunters," 1941, RGALI.

part of his memoirs, Eisenstein provides an extensive treatment of his lifelong, though intermittent, obsession with the process of drawing. The experience in Mexico yet again proves to be formative:

> It was in Mexico that my drawing underwent an internal catharsis, striving for mathematical abstraction and purity of line.

The effect was considerably enhanced when this abstract, "intellectualized" line was used for drawing especially sensual relationships between human figures, usually in especially complicated and random situations![157]

In Mexico, various objects of "primitive" art played a pivotal role for Eisenstein. In a similar manner to his conceptualization of national form, an "incongruous" amalgamation of strikingly different traditions creates an enticing work of art. The ancient pagan tradition of *corrida de toros* merges with Christian iconography in one image depicting a crucified bull pierced with arrows like St. Sebastian. Mexico was again a place of cultural metamorphosis and continuity: "in one element of the Resurrection festival they mix the blood of Christ from the morning mass in the cathedral with the streams of bulls' blood in the afternoon corrida in the city's arena."[158]

The linear drawing delivers the asceticism of form. But it also enacts the perpetually unresolved dichotomy between the abstraction of intellect and the sensibility of intuition and irrationality. Geometrical purity is almost absent in Eisenstein's drawings, and this asceticism still bears "sensuous" marks that deliver pictorial expressivity. *Kinesis* of the pure line produces an emotional impulse that leads to *ekstasis*.

Upon his return from Mexico, Eisenstein experienced yet another crucial realization through the practice of drawing that would be essential for his later theoretical investigations. In September of 1932, he wonders:

> Why do my drawings, despite the total absence of anatomic qualities, [prompt] human-like physiological agitation for the observer?....
>
> The thing is that the drawings are *protoplasmic avant tout*. And they're spontaneous [*stikhiiny*] because they cover a process between primary protoplasm and a formed person.
>
> A truly appealing theme of my drawings is the *emergence* [*stanovlenie*] from plasma of the person being formed [*oformliaiushchegosia*]...[159]

Protoplasm derives from the Greek *protos* for "first," and *plasma* for "thing formed." Being the primordial *formed* entity or rather *nondifferentiated* primary matter, jelly-like protoplasm for Eisenstein is the beginning of all life forms. Through various transformations, it can evolve into higher animal and human forms, but it is also a bold reminder of the "lower" foundation of life as such. Fetal protoplasmic beginnings of human life are a testimony to this, and Eisenstein's drawings find themselves on the evolutionary continuum: the graphic line functions as a basis for the dynamic process of composition, and this dynamism is achieved through elastic curves of the protoplasm-like "fluid solidity," which marks all forms of life. As Luka Arsenjuk perceptively observes, his drawings resist being identified as substantial and stable forms: "Eisenstein asks us to imagine a figure marked by a movement that exceeds the limits of figurative imagination, a certain *what* that has lost the stability or substantiality of its own contours in the wake of absolute movement."[160]

The dynamic mutability of forms is consequently developed into a theory of "plasmaticity," which Eisenstein identifies as a foundational principle of Walt Disney's work. Disney, as Eisenstein puts it in his notes, "makes the line run—he emancipates the sleeping beauty (not only the partner of the seven gnomes), but also the sleeping beauty Line."[161] The shape-shifting character of Disney's cartoons, in which the contours of bodies and objects undergo a process of constant fluctuation by means of extraction and compression, ascertains that matter is free to "take on any form dynamically."[162] The perpetual formal oscillation—the "return to a world of complete freedom"[163]—again points to nature and its origins. As Eisenstein puts it, Mickey Mouse, the first factual dynamic drawing, possess this *plasmaticity par excellence*: "this is the very foundation of that which I reduced to plant vegetatism (as a plant) within Kretschmerian bounds.... This is the *plasmaticity* of solid objects: extension of necks, legs, rhythmical oscillation of trees, of solid figures, etc."[164]

Disney's protean forms and metamorphic transformations point to earlier forms of life. Similarly to Kretschmer's "vegetative forms of movement," they undermine the anthropocentric stability of forms and create a dynamic and interfusing vision of the world. "The Bird Hunt" (fig. 4.7), the third and final drawing in the series, celebrates this dynamism. It boldly enacts the contrast between the high and low planes by means of the hunting trope. The hunter and his game meet in the intermediate space, and all are captured in vigorous and dynamic poses. The compositional "tension" also prompts a reading of the scene as a continuous narrative: one bird is startled by the arrow about to be shot; the second one is pierced by an arrow and appears to be ready to plummet; and, finally, the third bird falls dead downward from the skies in the lower right. The birds thus stretch the space, as their motion vectors point in three different directions. Each of the three birds is on the cusp of a dramatic event (being shot, falling, or hitting the ground).

The shape-shifting and writhing birds are clearly Disneyesque in their plasticity. Their curved necks and bent wings overcome solidity of shape. Instead, dynamism reigns supreme. Eisenstein was clearly inspired by cartoon drawings that he first saw in 1929–30 in Europe and America and that he continued to engage with until his death. For instance, the dynamism of the three birds in "The Bird Hunt" resonates with Disney's 1931 cartoon "Birds of a Feather," the

FIG. 4.7 Sergei Eisenstein, "The Bird Hunt," 1941, RGALI.

story of a joyful flock of birds attacked by a hawk that steals one of the birds' baby chicks. After a collective chase and a dramatic fight, the little bird is eventually rescued. The air fight between the flock and the hawk, during which smaller birds bravely attack the predator from different angles, corresponds to the multi-vector dynamism presented in Eisenstein's drawing. Furthermore, the hunter's dynamic masculinity shares common visual properties with Popeye the

Sailor—a fictional muscular American cartoon character. Created by Elzie Crisler Segar in 1929, Popeye became a hero of popular theatrical cartoon shorts in the 1930s. His signature boxer's pose is emulated in the depiction of the hunter, who is dressed in a tunic and wears an *aiyr kalpak*. The man, who has just fired an arrow, freezes in a pose full of dynamism. A simple contour line renders movement as a visible pronounced trace.

Eisenstein's engagement with the infinite plasticity of American cartoon characters is consistent with his preoccupation with the underlying discourse of *regress*, for Disney's narrative themes and aesthetic devices point, according to him, to "pra-logical" and "sensuous" forms of thinking.[165] In November 1941, he wrote "Animal Epic" (Zverinyi epos) as part of his larger Disney study, in which he theorized the relationship between form and content in the light of the progressive function of regressive elements. According to archival documents, Eisenstein relied heavily on the work of Aleksandr Veselovsky. The Disney research was supposed to be illustrated with examples taken from Veselovsky's *Historical Poetics*.[166]

Eisenstein purchased *Historical Poetics* in Alma-Ata on November 13, 1941.[167] The 650-page volume, which appeared for the first time in Veselovsky's *Collected Works* in 1913, was released with great pomp in 1940 to celebrate (belatedly) the literary critic's centenary. The publication comprised his resurrection from relative discursive oblivion. Veselovsky's historicity of literature and form-oriented approach to art resonated with Eisenstein's theoretical precepts at the time: cultural continuity and change were essential elements for their respective attempts to concoct a universal aesthetic vision.

The modern notion of literature, for Veselovsky, evolved from a divorce from the original *syncretism*—an indiscriminate amalgamation of epic, lyric, and dramatic genres. Syncretism stood for the ultimate cosmic unity between the human figure and the world that surrounded it, and Veselovsky provides various origin myths that connect humans with trees and other manifestations of nature.[168] However, this connection was loosened with the development of human agency and self-consciousness: "The more he [man] cognized himself, the more the border between him and the surrounding nature was revealed and the idea of identity was replaced by the idea of divergence. Ancient syncretism was waning before the dissecting exploits of knowledge: equations [such as] lightning–bird [or] man–tree were replaced by *comparisons*: lightning as a bird, man like a tree, etc."[169] The individual voice of the poet gains its full power in individualistic modernity once the primitive totemism of hunting societies wanes.

In general, Veselovsky contends that poetics cannot be defined by terms that rely on "the abstract concept of beauty," and it should be seen as a correlation of aesthetic forms with the systemically changing social ideals and affective-behavioral schemata.[170] These forms easily traverse geographical boundaries and survive historical cataclysms. Veselovsky's *historical poetics* thus postulates an idea of the unity and regularity of the development process of universal aesthetic production and argues for this process' embeddedness in the flow of history. As Veselovsky writes, literary history is "the history of social thought in its imagistic-poetic survival [*perezhivanie*] and in the forms that express this sedimentation."[171] *Perezhivanie*, which can be translated as a "survival" and as an "emotional experience," refers to a tradition that continues its existence and, at the same time, possesses an affective power—it prompts an emotional response to a work of art. The historically rooted experience comprises a site where cultural forms are reappropriated and perpetuated. The persistence and longevity of various genres, plots, or types thus mark the process of literary evolution.

Veselovsky's cross-cultural and cross-historical comparative intervention resulted in a direct correlation between social and literary history: poetic form is a mediated response to historical processes, and it should be seen as essentially *recursive*. This very recursive temporality of culture is the point of convergence between Veselovsky's evolutionary vision of culture as a succession of forms and Eisenstein's conception of the continuity of forms. Historical poetics perceives culture as thriving through cross-pollination with foreign cultural elements and the resurrection of faded aesthetic forms. Analogous to Eisenstein's remarks about pagan elements in Catholicism, Veselovsky highlights a coexistence of Christian and pagan elements in Russian culture—a pagan-driven folkloric tradition is "balanced" by the Orthodox Church "behind which stood the poetic as well as the philosophical tradition of Greek culture."[172] Veselovsky's historical poetics presents a post-Hegelian understanding of the universal and unilinear course of history that inevitably leads to the realization of human freedom.

However, Eisenstein supplements the unilinear temporality of the post-Hegelian conception of history with a *non-synchronous* vision of modernity. Two days after he purchased Veselovsky's volume, he wrote a series of notes on plot construction entitled "Plot in the General System of Form. Plot as a Form of Realization of Idea" (Siuzhet v obshchei sisteme formy. Siuzhet kak forma voploshcheniia idei). Here, Eisenstein makes an important observation:

> Veselovsky justly writes: "There are new [*novoiavlennye*] plots, suggested by the growing demands of life, that bring in new situations and types from everyday life, and there are plots that respond to the eternal demands of thought unexhausted over the course of human history. Somewhere, by someone, these plots were given a fortuitous expression, or formula, sufficiently flexible to encompass not new content but a new interpretation of the association-rich plot, and so

the formula remains. People will return to it, changing its sense, widening its meaning, and modifying it. As the stylistic formula "desire" has recurred and continues to recur, so, for example, do the plots of Don Juan and Faust recur throughout the centuries . . ."[173] Beginning with "somewhere, by someone" the idea is substantially debased: it is not a matter of someone discovering "a fortuitous expression," but rather that only a scheme, taken from the relations and the thought of tribal [social] structure, can have a sensuous effect. Veselovsky himself deals with it!

But Veselovsky doesn't say and apparently doesn't know the main thing. Genuine works of art are only those that unite both provisions in a mutual interpenetration: the "new" [*novoiavlennoe*] and the "everlasting" [*vekovechnoe*].

That is why he is preoccupied with the less interesting [aspects]: examining plots, correctly taken from situations, that are typical for the tribal [social] structure, but [he] demonstrates them with epic, that is, earlier and almost synchronous stages of artistic practice, which solidified and reflected this set of relations. However, they are interesting not because of these [aspects]. They are interesting as a kernel for later and contemporary plot constructions.

A sensuous capture [*zakhvat*], that is, a "great" work of art, will not emerge until contemporary material is threaded on the core of the tribal (pra-logical) situation.[174]

This rhetorical move resonates with the formalists' stance regarding historical poetics in general. In 1925, Boris Eikhenbaum summarized the formalists' contentious departure from Veselovsky's vision of literary evolution. The latter was too reliant on tradition, and the argument that "the new form makes its appearance to express a new content" was replaced by Shklovsky's assertion that "the new form makes its appearance [in order] to replace an old form that has already outlived its artistic usefulness, to replace an old form that has already lost its artistic viability."[175] The interplay between old and new, so cherished by Eisenstein, animates the formalist project that valorizes perception as such and tackles the problem of content by formal means.

The director, however, emphasizes the relevance of the old and archaic as such—these elements function as a constructive core on the level of both form and content. For Eisenstein, a work of art born in individualistic modernity acquires its ability to impact *only* if it engages with poetic formulas found in primitive collectivity. Veselovsky's "paleontology of plots," in Zhirmunsky's apt description,[176] is useful for him if it reveals ancient plots and motifs' interaction with contemporary material. Indeed, in the remaining pages of the short essay, he proceeds to demonstrate the prolonged and deformed life of the father–son conflict throughout the centuries and in his script for *Ivan the Terrible*—the film on which he was intensively working at the time. Eisenstein turns Veselovsky's survival and persistence of forms into their endurance and utmost relevance to the contemporary situation. The new and everlasting are interlocked on the continuum of history.

During the anti-cosmopolitan campaign, Veselovsky, who died in 1906, was identified as a source of inspiration for both formalist and "cosmopolitan" trends in literary studies.[177] *Historical Poetics* was one of the earliest attempts to introduce a comparative approach in literature by systematizing aesthetic form through disparate spaces and times. The primacy of form led to anti-formalist accusations that the category of content had become redundant. As Soviet critics claimed, Veselovsky's theory suggests that "ideas perish, only forms are eternal."[178]

Veselovsky's vision of boundless world culture, which influenced and inspired Eisenstein, became deeply problematic for the boundary-enforcing culture of Stalinism. The spatial interconnectedness of diverse cultures, for Veselovsky, was supplemented by the linearity of historical development—the interplay between historical *longue durée* structures and conjunctural *événements*.[179] Consequently, he was condemned for disparaging Russian cultural achievements by highlighting their borrowed essence. Russian culture, per Veselovsky's narrative, displays a complex interplay between borrowed and inherited cultural elements that betray its historical role as a middle ground between East and West. The Mongol invasion further amplified the migration and dispersal of legends and stories from East to West.[180] Ultimately, the assimilation of foreign material functions as an impetus for the Russian nation's cultural development in general.

Indeed, Viktor Zhirmunsky argues in the introduction to the 1940 republication of *Historical Poetics* that artistic *borrowing* [zaimstvovanie] is Veselovsky's principal historical category, which is reflective of the sociopolitical reality of any given epoch.[181] Popular consciousness (*narodnost'*) is enabled by a complex process of cultural cross-pollination, wherein foreign elements are gradually appropriated and thus enter the domain of the familiar.[182] Vladimir Shishmarev, Veselovsky's pupil and the director of the Institute of World Literature at the time, attempted to make the theory of borrowing palatable to late Stalinism and its understanding of modernity:

> Veselovsky's whole work, in essence, could be seen as an attempt to identify causes and ways by which the alien [*chuzhoe*] is converted into one's own [*svoe*] or the old was renewed; that is, to identify those *qualitative* changes that the process of

assimilation introduced to the assimilated [material].... Imperialism is a natural stage of capitalism; Russia learned from Europe in the past, now Europe and America learn much from us. What is important is the qualitative aspect, that is, the individualization of all these intersections, mutual borrowings, etc., [in] the formation of so-called national cultures, literatures, and languages, those currents that, at some point, will merge in the single sea of humanity.[183]

Shishmarev positions Veselovsky's historical poetics as an ideologically neutral critical concept and states that its comparative approach can be appropriated for a study of cultural cross-pollination within the Soviet Union. However, late Stalinist modernity insisted on the purity and exceptionality of the Russian cultural paradigm. It was not an opportune occasion to advance the study of difference and the ways it infiltrates the realm of the familiar.

Viktor Shklovsky, who critically engaged with Veselovsky's ideas in the 1929 edition of *Theory of Prose*, became his fierce defender in 1947. Echoing Shishmarev, Shklovsky attempts to reclaim *Historical Poetics* from the accusation of cosmopolitanism by emphasizing its truly international agenda. He even seems to project his own "erroneous" but truthful scientific quest on Veselovsky: "He was guilty of a mistake, although he spoke about the right thing. He was a genius, who might have been able to create a 'historical poetics,' a genius whose work we cannot ignore; we cannot proceed without that work. But we must say that there is no repetition in art—there is only seeming repetition."[184] Furthermore, Shklovsky claims that Veselovsky relies on a conviction that all nations are equal and provides a challenge to the domineering colonial cultural paradigm. The already familiar trope of *winding road* that permeated Shklovsky's account of reorientation emerges in his defense of Veselovsky, a fragment of which was partially quoted in the Introduction:

There is an old proverb that all roads lead to Rome. This is the proverb of colonizers, who dragged everything to Rome. This proverb is false. Great cultures were created beyond Rome, great roads crossed our country and existed for us, not for Rome. But this proverb lived on, cheating the world, and depriving nations of history. Veselovsky, apart from the material of Slavic nations, used folklore material from all the peoples of Russia.

Veselovsky's works showed that there are different roads—that, beyond old Roman roads, there are the green roads of the Serbian epos and the roads of the Old Russian oral epic poem, which bear the dust of a distant imminent enemy who must be fought.[185]

Shklovsky's 1947 defense of Veselovsky is full of the rhetorical tropes and stylistic features of "A Monument to a Scholarly Error." It also echoes *Turksib* and *Marco Polo*, texts that overlay the geographical boundaries of the Soviet state onto the fluid spatial network of the Silk Road—trade routes, as previously mentioned, that connected the East and the West. However, a sense of movement—whether back to Rome or away toward the periphery—is discursively contained within the passage, which abruptly ends on a combative note that resonates in tone with the anti-cosmopolitan campaign and gestures toward Slavic epic traditions. This militarism derived from the late-Stalinist conviction that all roads had to lead to the reconstructed Stalinist Moscow: the new "socialist Rome."

Nevertheless, Shklovsky's defense of Veselovsky and Eisenstein's extensive engagement with the pioneer of comparative literary studies taking place at the moment of their discursive purge comprised a deep conviction that the continuity of artistic forms defines the cultural process at large. *Historical Poetics* contends that aesthetic development is conditioned by a dynamic conflation of new (strange) and conventional (familiar) elements. This stance acutely resonated with the former avant-gardists as they tried to establish evolution and historicism as animating forces of aesthetic form in the late modernist period—a movement, of course, compelled by the ideological pressures of socialist realism.

The historical continuity and the co-existence of archaic and modern ways of life that Eisenstein witnessed in Mexico and later theorized with Veselovsky's help created an unexpected juncture between the main aesthetic categories of form and content and established a new theoretical avenue of his *Method*. The concepts of stadialism, synthesis, primitivism, and the reimagined form–content interrelationship shape his theoretical system, which was developed during the late modernist period. Engagement with the question of national form (and socialist content) evolved into one of the persistent refrains of his post-Mexico theoretical explorations. The Veselovskian sense of historical continuity, rootedness in the incessant flow of time, was crucial for Eisenstein in the 1930s, and it culminated in the conviction that new messages could be delivered in archaic forms. New ideas and old forms could now dialectically co-exist, and regress could come to play a progressive role.

This consequently led to the director's gradual legitimization of folklore for the socialist present—a cultural medium comprised of an inexhaustible reservoir of national forms. As with the universal communist project, this engagement with folkloric material was not to be restrained by concrete national borders. Eisenstein writes:

> A people's genius nourishes art. Genuinely great creations rest upon a national, collective genius. And only an art whose roots penetrate deep into the people can endure the centuries.
>
> That is why we hold epic works in such profound reverence, especially those that fully embody the spirit of the nations who populate our Union: Igor's Host, David of Sasun, Dzhangar, Manas, and works by Rustaveli, Alisher Navoi, Nizami...
>
> But our interest in the national epic is still broader: it spills over our country's borders, and we can admire epic poetry created by the genius of foreign peoples.[186]

National epic narratives, in this sense, would structure and concretize late Eisenstein's theoretical abstractedness. As he puts it in his 1937 repentance, discussed at the beginning of the chapter, his principal "formalist" mistake, similar to Shklovsky's, lies in the fact that *generalization* in his work devours *particularity*: "Instead of emanating through the concrete particular, generalization scatters into disengaged abstractedness."[187] The director's exploration of various manifestations of national form, whether it is the vertical perspective of Uzbek art or a Kazakh ram's horn ornament, serves as one instance of the indispensable *particular*.

This conviction was further solidified by Eisenstein's meticulous engagement with Veselovsky's *Historical Poetics* in the fall and winter of 1941–42. The author, for Veselovsky, is a historicized subject who finds his place in a complex interaction of evolving aesthetic forms—from the simplest forms of myth to the subsequent formal evolution of literary modes (rodov).[188] Eisenstein was clearly in agreement with the literary critic that narrative motifs and other structural components are constantly on the move from one culture to another, and are thus essentially mutable. However, Eisenstein emphasized the importance of the "simplest" archaic forms for modernity; the new and the everlasting are interlocked throughout the *longue durée* of historical progress. The archaic is not to be superseded and deposited in the archive of human civilization. Its persistent existence is a key component of the progressive socialist art.

This rendering of regress in progressive terms was a signature feature of Eisenstein's mature theoretical exploration. Indeed, one section of *Method*, entitled "Obsession (Idée fixe)," began with the claim that his discovery of the function of regress contributed to ending the delusion that *ostranenie* (defamiliarization) might help to reveal the "mystery of form."[189] Regress, along with all its interrelated concepts, becomes a key point of reorientation, moving the director and theorist from his earlier iconoclastic avant-garde convictions toward late modernist sensibilities. On April 14, 1940, Eisenstein reflects in his diary on the canonical futurist incantation "dyr-bul-shchyl" by Aleksei Kruchenykh as "primordial-sensuous sounds," which constitute "a *stenography of intonation* as such" that delivers an impact "not through a concrete-informative [soderzhatel'noe] image," but "simply from the inner recesses [as something] primordially impulsive."[190] Regress thus became a defamiliarized *ostranenie*. This was an ingenious attempt to reimagine the already defunct avant-garde practices and to inscribe them into the evolving late modernist framework that was part of the socialist culture of the time.

It is notable that Georg Lukács, with his skeptical vision of the ideological value of the 1920s, nevertheless argues that the avant-garde experiment was necessary for the formation of socialist culture and that "no analysis of socialist realism would be complete without a consideration of the reactionary, decadent elements in social and literary life which influenced it in its early stages."[191] The avant-garde experiment was not a mere fertilizer for the period that followed, however, as the four case studies have shown. Rather, it comprised an organic corpus of aesthetic convictions that continued their "belated" life, albeit in a refashioned and modulated way. It is essential that this was not even a Frankenstein of artificially transformed aesthetic persuasions and practices; it was a living and fully functional body. I therefore identify the life of this body as an instance of *late modernism*.

EPILOGUE

"END" POINTS

In 1938, during the height of Stalinist terror, Eisenstein recollects an encounter with a strange sea dweller: "In Mexico I angled a small four-eyed fish. Essentially, it consisted of two eyes each divided in two. One pair looks out above the water. One pair sees down below the water. And the fish glides on the mirror of the water, its exacting gaze aimed both out of the water and down below, into the underwater kingdom."[1] The fish Eisenstein saw was likely an Anableps, a species that inhabits the low-lying areas of southern Mexico and whose eyes are raised above the top of the head and divided into two different parts. It can indeed see above and below the water simultaneously, and this unusual ability is essential for its surface-dwelling lifestyle.

Eisenstein could certainly appreciate the Anableps with its dual perspective. For him and other late modernists, as heirs to the avant-gardes of the recent past, the process of reorientation was also conditioned by two planes—the bed of political reality and the upper limits of the aesthetic horizon. They assumed a multidirectional vantage not unlike that of the surface-dwelling fish to create nonlinear forms of affiliation with the reigning ideology. As a result, the combination of sociopolitical constraints and an urge to evolve aesthetically allowed the late modernists to navigate the murky waters of Stalinism. The "national in form, socialist in content" formula created a space for the formal experimentation of the avant-garde to continue into the Stalinist period, as it identified itself with otherized stylizations of Russia's colonial frontiers. This was modernism's belated life, albeit in a refashioned form.

The already-subdued historical avant-garde lost its radical edge after the Great Break of 1929. It was deprived of institutional support (*New Lef*, VKhUTEMAS, GAKhN, and INKhUK ceased to exist or were morphed into other institutions) and its aspiration to eradicate the division between art and life was no longer its prerogative. Instead, following the 1932 decree that disbanded all existing artistic groups and replaced them with unified associations of creative professions, the Stalinist state became the sole curator of life *and* art in the country. The nascent sociopolitical formation could not accommodate formal intricacy. The emancipatory and, to a certain extent, anarchic force of the avant-garde form suddenly became redundant. Even the utilitarian form of constructivism and productivism was disregarded, as it followed *function* that derived from a leftist ideological "deviation." But although "reckless" formal experimentation was halted, the historical avant-garde found a possibility to evolve elsewhere: in *national form*.

National particularity was construed as a temporary and necessary stepping-stone to socialist assimilation. The *particular* was thus never supposed to acquire a legitimate identity, but was instead to be used as a means to attain the *universal*. In this role as a subordinate to socialist universal content, national form structured representational practices in the 1930s. Suspended between two philosophical definitions of the notion of form—immaterial idea in Plato and material shape in Aristotle—it became the only discursive category that allowed for acceptable variety and that invited heterogeneity under the aegis of the prohibitive totalitarian state. Consequently, the mode of making things strange (*ostranenie*) evolved into a preoccupation with strange and unfamiliar ethnic cultures; these cultures, while preserving an element of exoticism, were presented as comprehensible, clearly defined, and striving toward the universal proletarian ideal.

While colonial experience confined native cultures to a distant past, the socialist project made them contemporaneous and bestowed on them an ability to change and advance within their specific national frameworks. Thus, in contrast to European modernism's general fixation on the "primitivism" or "foreignness" of the other, socialist orientalism was preoccupied with the other's ability to *transform itself*. The Soviet orientalist project was not a mere "strategy of representational containment," to use Jameson's formulation;[2] rather, it was a concerted effort in the name of radical transformation, the total erasure of cultural difference being its promise and its objective. While late Soviet modernists tended to view national form within the framework of modernist non-synchronicity, the officially endorsed Soviet national form was inscribed into a unilinear progression of universal history. The "avant-garde" vision of Soviet culture as a radically novel sociopolitical formation lost its appeal in the 1930s. It was replaced by a belief in a developmental historicity of national cultures and their primordial roots as reflected in preceding artistic traditions.

As the gaze of the avant-garde experimenters turned—or rather, was reoriented—eastward, Central Asia emerged as an important topos for articulating key ideological precepts. It was an essentially heterogeneous and dynamic geographical region, which invited the radical transformation of physical and social space—from industry and infrastructure to language and literary canons. The Soviet Orient was a malleable political construct, a form of institutionalized ethnic heterogeneity that reflected the presence of the country's rigid borders while still preserving the borderless aspiration of the Soviet internationalist project.[3] But it also provided a space for a defamiliarizing experience—one analogous to forms of existence that lie at the core of modernist aesthetics. While Stalin's conception of transient national form functioned as a discursive smokescreen, the representatives of the Soviet avant-garde, who were proactively involved in the process of *formal* experimentation in the illustrious 1920s, made an intellectual effort to turn national form into a functional aesthetic category. Their visual and literary artifacts attest to the idea that creativity can be *situational*—emerging from opportunities inherent in a certain cultural context at a given time, and in this case, from the contradictory nature of Soviet orientalism itself.

The concept of alterity marked Russia's modernist movement from the beginning. Early modernists, the representatives of the Russian Silver Age, tended to *stylize* ethnic heterogeneity with modern effects (e.g. the symbolists' synthesis of modern and archaic elements, as in Viacheslav Ivanov's "myth-creation").[4] They extensively explored what Michael Kunichika referred to as "indigenous antiquity."[5] This fascination with unearthing and reclaiming the past revealed a somewhat fetishistic fixation on ethnic material. The avant-gardists, in contrast, *formally interrogated* alterity as such (e.g., Natalia Goncharova's Neo-Primitivism or Velimir Khlebnikov's "word-creation"). The ethnic material of the avant-garde underwent a process of formal restructuring, resulting in the emergence of an original and future-oriented artifact. The late modernists, in turn, wove alterity into the fabric of the Stalinist state; there are echoes of both *stylization* and *formal interrogation* in their body of work. The shifting Soviet political horizon offered a corrective to modernist exoticism through the universal socialist project.

The late Soviet modernists reshaped and even manipulated sets of local cultural forms. Their aesthetic visions provided a critical interface between the politics of alterity and supranational Soviet subjectivity. Eventually, these reimagined forms were presented as both locally rooted (national) and transcending their origins—that is, aspiring toward socialist ideals of community. This approach resulted in several cross-cultural mishaps that violated the specificity and originality of given cultural forms: Shklovsky's confluence of Kazakh and Kyrgyz identities in *Turksib*, Rodchenko and Stepanova's passing off of Turkmen carpet as Uzbek in *Ten Years of Soviet Uzbekistan*, Vertov's "translation" of the *akyn*'s song that did not even remotely correspond to the actual words (*The Front, to You!*), and Eisenstein's awkward attempts to elevate the genre of the Persian miniature in Uzbek national arts. The late modernists inadvertently highlight the supposed generic essence of the Soviet Orient. National form was in fact replaceable and variable.

Thus, "reorientalist" modernity reveals the gradual process of the homogenization of cultural difference. Official Soviet culture elaborated its vision of internal ethnic diversity and internationalism: cultural specificity and locality played an essential role as a pathway toward the universal ideals of the communist project. However, the form–content division was not equally balanced, with greater value placed on the latter. Late Stalinism boasted of attending to national forms, even as it tried to define all national forms through the prism of socialist content. The singularity of "content" thus enfolded the dissipating variety of national forms and enabled sociopolitical centralization. It is precisely in the centralizing folds of Stalinism that the notion of *socialist alterity* is articulated. Paradoxically, however, this type of identity model *contained*, in both senses of the word, the notion of *heterogeneity*. In other words, the official Soviet ideology, while directly invoking the constructive role of otherness, simultaneously relegated it to the cultural periphery and so subordinated difference in its various forms to the singularity of acceptable content.

Evgeny Dobrenko accurately renders the imperial inclinations of late Stalinism as the reaction of a patriarchal society to the process of modernization, which manifested itself in "the Russian national form of a universal phenomenon."[6] However, his rendering of a new *imperial* culture as "internationalist in form and *nationalist* in content" is incorrect:[7] the realm of content in late Stalinism came fully under the auspices of the socialist ideological framework—there could be only *socialist* content, "translated" and distributed in a variety of national forms. The universal socialist essence enabled international appeal and ostensibly maintained a diversity of forms. However, the Russian national form assumed the role of the vanguard (*avangard*), one that sought to deliver the ultimate socialist content.

The 1935 concept of the *friendship of the peoples*, rendered as a bond of reciprocated ideological affection, provided the diminished Stalinist alternative to socialist internationalism that established a hierarchy of forms. The concept's inherent claim to egalitarianism, which professes the horizontality of power or authority, was undercut by the special status assigned to the Russian nation—*primus inter pares*. The Latin phrase describes someone who is formally equal to other members of their group but is accorded unofficial privilege. This resulted in a *hierarchical* approach to a supposedly egalitarian view of difference.[8]

Victory in World War II brought further sweeping cultural changes through isolationist nationalism. The internationalist drive of the early Soviet project dwindled in prominence, to the point where it became associated with the pejorative category of cosmopolitanism. The pathos of the unconditional, boundary-traversing internationalism of the 1920s unexpectedly became a "cosmopolitan deviation." The anti-cosmopolitan campaign, which unfurled between 1948 and 1953, was the last act of Stalinism that was consequently repressed in the official historiography—it was not discussed in print in the USSR until 1989.[9] Late Stalinist modernity, galvanized by the victory in World War II, found itself facing a threat in the form of Western cultural expansion, fueled by American-led postwar reconstruction efforts.[10]

The anti-cosmopolitan campaign was sustained, above all, by the fear of an external and ideologically hostile enemy. Thus, one of its key ambitions was to eliminate acts of "kowtowing to the West" (*nizkopoklonstvo pered zapadom*) in Soviet culture. As a result, the Soviet Union withdrew from participation in international art fairs, such as the Venice Biennale, and suspended nearly all international alliances in the cultural and scholarly spheres. Whole disciplines, among them genetics and quantum mechanics, were deemed ideologically inappropriate. Einstein's theory of relativity also came under ideological siege as "reactionary and idealist."[11] The 1949 *Dictionary of Russian Language* was criticized for incorporating too many foreign words and established literary terms such as *akrostikh* (acrostic) and *alliteratsiia* (alliteration) were among "problematic" entries.[12]

The attack on all foreign cultural influences endowed the Russian national form with unbounded international potential. Allusions to almost all external cultural liaisons and impulses, be they Byronic echoes in Pushkin's lyric poetry or the influence of the classical Viennese style on nineteenth-century Russian opera, were framed as slanderous and threatening to Russians' uniquely "progressive" culture—the alleged frontline of the universal socialist movement. Russian national form assumed a primary cultural role, analogous to the role of the Communist Party as a vanguard in cultivating progressive consciousness among its followers. Thus, Russia was identified as "the most prominent nation among all the nations that comprise the Soviet Union."[13] As the backbone of Soviet society, it purportedly helped the national forms of its "brother" nations to advance toward the socialist ideal.

The newly uncritical celebration of all dimensions of Russian culture and the emergence of the Russocentric form of etatism caught Isaak Nusinov, the author of the *Literary Encyclopedia* article on "national literature," off guard. He became a prominent target of the anti-cosmopolitan campaign, which resulted in his arrest and eventual death. Nusinov's 1941 monograph *Pushkin and World Literature* (Pushkin i mirovaia literatura) was belatedly criticized, six years after its publication, for emphasizing the influence of Western writers on Pushkin. The book was blamed for suggesting that Russian literature in its entirety amounted to little more than a supplement to its Western counterpart.[14]

The case of Nusinov, as with those of many other Soviet critics of Jewish origin, bears testimony to the fact that the anti-cosmopolitan campaign displayed anti-Semitic features. Soviet Jews were attacked for their alleged cosmopolitan affiliations, with professional critics and scholars often singled out.[15] However, the campaign extended beyond its blatant anti-Semitism. Frank Grüner describes the anti-cosmopolitan paradigm as a "conceptualization of *the* Jew as *the* antipode of the Russian or Soviet citizen."[16] As the antipode, Jews were often targeted as the "last" among equals. At the same time, the "negative" focus of the campaign, negating the Jew, opened the way for a "positive" aspect as well: the elevation of Russian culture and, by denying possibilities for difference, the conflation of Russian and Soviet identities. The only Soviet nationality that had a "right" to essentialize itself and claim its international appeal was the Russian.[17] Any similar claims that encompassed non-Russian identities posed a threat to the Soviet social hierarchy.

The pinnacle of the anti-cosmopolitan campaign was the article "On One Antipatriotic Group of Theatre Critics," published in *Pravda* on January 28, 1949. It identified socialist realism as an aesthetic method expressive of patriotic feelings and branded formalism as an abstract cosmopolitan framework.[18] However, the main purpose of this article was to defend Russian culture from "slanderous" critical evaluations. For instance, Abram Gurvich, a prominent literary critic of Jewish origin, was accused of smearing the Russian national character: his literary criticism was described as "a slander of the *Russian Soviet* person ... we cannot but condemn this attempt to disgrace the Soviet national character."[19] The next day, *Literaturnaia gazeta* commenced its condemnation with the following sentence: "Cosmopolitanism is alien to the life and historical purpose of one's own people, a lackey-like adoration of the bourgeois culture of the West and an equally servile failure to understand the great value of the powerful Russian national culture and the cultures of the other brotherly nations of the USSR."[20] The "powerful" Russian national form is commended while the Soviet multicultural plurality ("the cultures of the other brotherly nations") is reduced to the domain of *et cetera*.

The new (anti-cosmopolitan) vision of interethnic relations was marked by the special status of the Russian nation, which began to be viewed as the "state-bearing people" with an international appeal within the Soviet Union's borders and beyond. The new Soviet national anthem (1943) placed Russians squarely at the head of the Soviet family of nations: "The unbreakable union of free republics was welded forever by Great Rus'." On May 24, 1945, during a Kremlin reception to celebrate victory in World War II, Stalin famously toasted the Russian people as "the most prominent nation among all the nations that comprise the Soviet Union."[21] In the words of Aleksandr Poskrebyshev, a confidant of Stalin, Russians in the USSR were the Soviet society's "cementing force, strengthening the friendship of the peoples."[22] This launched an all-encompassing conflation of Russian and Soviet identities that has endured, albeit in different manifestations, well beyond the collapse of the country in 1991.

Viktor Vinogradov, who effectively presided over Soviet linguistics after World War II, wrote a celebratory treatise dedicated to the Russian language in 1945. Succinctly titled *The Great Russian Language* (Velikii russkii iazyk), it pronounced Russian an "international language" whose mediatory and emancipatory role would be crucial for the development of a future international language:[23]

> In the new governmental context, the Russian language has undertaken an important mission—it serves as an ideological leader. It is developing not only as the native language of the Russian people but also as the international language of socialist culture and Soviet statehood. Thus, not only national principles and premises, but also universal ones, are becoming all the deeper and more ingrained in the structure of Russian.[24]

Vinogradov articulated the pan-Soviet claim in favor of the Russian language: it is presented as a neutral *lingua franca*, but with a clear set of features that are representative of a domineering *lingua imperii*. There is an attempt to preserve the international appeal of the socialist project through sustained rhetorical efforts to essentialize Russian culture and portray it as the vanguard of the international socialist movement. In reality, of course, Vinogradov's treatise was a blatant rejection of the truly internationalist appeal of socialism.

It is confusingly emblematic that Vano Muradeli's opera *The Great Friendship* (Velikaia druzhba, 1947) was chosen as a focal point of the anti-cosmopolitan campaign. The opera's action revolves around the political activities of Sergo Ordzhonikidze, a prominent Soviet commissar of Georgian descent who contributed to the consolidation of the Soviet multiethnic state and who died in 1937, possibly at his own hand and out of fear of repressions. Allegedly, the opera presented a distorted vision of early Soviet interethnic alliances and tensions. However, this was not the most significant point of criticism. The tone of the attack in the pages of *Pravda* was identical to that of the 1936 anti-Formalist campaign that targeted Shostakovich. Yet again the problem lay in the formalist "muddle instead of music." Muradeli's opera was characterized in a manner that mirrored the 1936 attack: "it is muddled and disharmonious, built on continuous dissonances, on combinations of sounds that grate on one's ears. Individual lines and scenes that are nearly melodious are suddenly interrupted by discordant noise, which is outright bizarre to the normal human ear and is depressing for listeners."[25] But a novel rhetorical component also appeared: the

Russian operatic tradition was presented as a role model for the Soviet present. The nineteenth-century tradition, despite the obvious imperial connections, was described as "distinguished by its meaningful content, the richness of its melodies and its wide range, its popular nature [*narodnost'*], its elegant, beautiful and clear musical form, [all of which made] Russian opera the world's greatest opera tradition, and a genre of music loved by and accessible to the population at large."[26]

As this book has argued, the political implications of aesthetic form are difficult to overestimate. Indeed, the Stalinist cultural paradigm consistently concerned itself with the notion of form: the 1936 campaign against formalism was accompanied by an active endorsement of national forms. The conflation of the notion of aesthetic form with the concept of national identity was thoroughly and intentionally articulated. The anti-cosmopolitan campaign, which included a distinct anti-formalist component, solidified a radical transformation of Soviet internationalism: it resulted in the exultation of the Russian national form. National forms, which were eventually supposed to dissipate, were instead reinforced by the project of Soviet modernity. One of these—the Russian national form—was reinforced with even greater impetus. Through an identification with otherness in the form of stylized portrayals of Russia's colonial frontiers, the anti-cosmopolitan campaign thus negated the possibility of modernism's evolution. The growing postwar Russophile tendencies prompted a radical change: the Russian national heritage became an integral and domineering part of the Soviet cultural paradigm.

Paradoxically, the Stalinist vision of Soviet internationalism, articulated alongside the anti-cosmopolitan campaign, denied any form of external cultural influence in relation to Russian culture—the core of the Soviet state paradigm. It celebrated diversity while preserving essentialist "purity." In a new post-1948 vision of the ethnic diversity of the Soviet state, the Russian national form prevailed, as it was conceived as a *privileged form of particularity* that had immediate access to the *universal*. This process resulted in the eventual homogenization of difference: other Soviet national forms, led by the Russian vanguard, aspired to the eventual eradication of difference (and the emergence of universal proletarian culture). Instead of treating difference as divergence, late Stalinist ideologues conceptualized difference as undergoing a gradual process of homogenization. Consequently, ethnic difference was rendered through the prism of ideological sameness.

This new elevation of Soviet internationalism received its most vivid material rendering in the "Friendship of the Peoples" fountain, built in 1954 at the All-Union Agricultural Exhibition (VSKhV), which was renamed the Exhibition of Achievements of the National Economy (VDNKh) in 1959. The multiple designs and redesigns of VSKhV (1937, 1939, 1948–1954) reveal the complex genealogy of

Stalinist culture and delineate its cultural contours. VSKhV was a site where the gradual stylistic shift played out in material form, from the active engagement with international styles (e.g., Art Deco) in the late 1930s to the appropriation of the classical tradition (specifically, Russian Neoclassicism of the eighteenth and early nineteenth centuries) and the active endorsement of vernacular decorative forms in the early 1950s.

One of the key principles of VSKhV was a demonstration of the socialist economy's material abundance and the cultural and sociopolitical achievements of the young Soviet state. World exhibitions in general, as Walter Benjamin observed, are "places of pilgrimage to the commodity fetish"[27] where assemblages (of objects and peoples) promote consumption. The Soviet exposition followed suit by giving material form to Stalin's notorious 1935 pronouncement: "Life has become better! Life has become happier!" Yet this dictum radically diverged from the harsh reality of near-universal poverty. The USSR saw a withdrawal from the rationing system that covered basic food items such as sugar, meat, and vegetables as late as October 1, 1935. Cornucopias overflowing with produce and flowers, which were employed as a persistent decorative motif throughout the exposition, simply did not have a real referent.

The VSKhV site was, in short, a ritual display of the desired and imagined socialist reality. It lay claim to wealth in its various societal manifestations—agricultural bounty, technological and industrial supremacy—in a kaleidoscopic display. As material signifiers of the alleged progress of the command economy, the VSKhV images telegraphed Stalinism's limitless authority. Material "prosperity" usually manifested itself in the form of stylized garlands of flowers and baskets of fruit with sculptural carvings projecting out from the plane of the wall in a neo-Baroque manner. Abundance was rendered through aesthetic excess. Soviet artists were encouraged to unleash "life-affirming" strategies of beautification. Overloaded with decoration, the pavilions comprised a vision of surplus whose ornamentation was expressive of alleged prosperity. As the renowned sculptor Vera Mukhina wrote, "the art of our future is not the art of single individuals with their narrow horizons; it is the art of the very broadest horizons. And of no small importance to that art is its decorative nature—not as embellishment [*ukrashatel'stvo*], but as an element of direct, forceful, joyful impact."[28]

With pronounced theatricality, the exhibition presented Soviet ethnic minorities as subjects and objects of power, fully inscribed into a vision of socialist modernity.[29] Musicians and dancers, dressed in stylized ornamental garments, welcomed visitors. The Uzbek pavilion featured an open rotunda with a small fountain inside, a dodecagonal structure that resembled an ornament enlarged and transformed into an architectural element. By engaging tropes of Islamic exoticism such as calligraphy and arabesque, the pavilion presented them as fully domesticated and inscribed into the socialist vision, intelligible and ready for consumption.

VSKhV justified the sociopolitical status quo in the Soviet Union as natural and inevitable, perpetual, and beneficial for the proletariat. The regime secured widespread belief in its legitimacy in the wake of World War II; the style of the exposition, termed "Victory style" (*stil' "Pobeda"*) in Russian scholarship, reflects this historical moment.[30] The key characteristic of this style is an amalgamation of Russian-inspired ornamentation and classical architectural elements. At the exposition, the facades of the exhibition halls featured the lush extravagance of ornamental patterns blended with socialist heraldry, and were designed with a clear awareness of grand historical architectural styles. The mannerist refinement of the style was overwhelming.

Irina Belintseva argues that "popular taste" manifested itself not in imaginative appropriation of village architecture or artistic craftsmanship, but rather in a general appeal for floweriness, for an abundance of details, and ostentatious "intricacy"—aspects that corresponded to the popular understanding of revelry, riches, luxury.[31] In "Avant-Garde and Kitsch," written as the first VSKhV was under construction, Clement Greenberg conceives of kitsch as a productive tool for sociopolitical indoctrinations:

> The encouragement of kitsch is merely another of the inexpensive ways in which totalitarian regimes seek to ingratiate themselves with their subjects. Since these regimes cannot raise the cultural level of the masses . . . by anything short of a surrender to international socialism, they will flatter the masses by bringing all culture down to their level. It is for this reason that the avant-garde is outlawed, and not so much because a superior culture is inherently a more critical culture. . . . As a matter of fact, the main trouble with avant-garde art and literature, from the point of view of fascists and Stalinists, is not that they are too critical, but that they are too "innocent," that it is too difficult to inject effective propaganda into them, that kitsch is more pliable to this end. Kitsch keeps a dictator in closer contact with the "soul" of the people. Should the official culture be one superior to the general mass-level, there would be a danger of isolation.[32]

The construction of the audaciously decorative "Friendship of the Peoples" fountain at the redesigned VSKhV was Stalinism's last contact with the "soul" of the Soviet people. Here, political indoctrination took a material form in line with the popular understanding of beauty as excess; through unrestrained floweriness and ostentatious intricacy, it achieved "spectacular" impact. Designed by Konstantin Topuridze and Grigorii Konstantinovsky (relatively unknown architects) and erected between November 1952 and July 1954, the fountain was the largest aquatic installation in the country at the time:[33] it occupies a 1,312-square-foot granite basin and propels about eight hundred jets of water some seventy feet into the air, with 250 light projectors creating an intricate interplay of water and light. This grandeur, almost rococo in its decorative excess, certainly reflected the Stalinist fixation with hydraulic culture and lavish ornamentation. With Stalin's death in 1953, the fountain also marked a posthumous commemoration of this vision. Its placement was both strategic and symbolic: the "Friendship of the Peoples" was built in place of the 1939 main pavilion and positioned right on the intersection of the two main axes of the 1954 exhibition complex.[34] According to 1952 plans, a new monument to Stalin was supposed to be placed next to the fountain and the chief architect explicitly argued that the two were to function as stylistically paired highlights of Kolkhoz square.[35]

The fountain is an allegorical rendering of Stalin's concept of the "friendship of the peoples" in material form, and its political symbolism is evident. The "friendship" concept accomplished discursive "leveling" that enabled horizontality, in accord with Stalin's discourse on "leveling the plane" of nationalisms in the 1930s in which the nationalism of the dominant nation was equated with local, often anti-imperial, nationalisms of the oppressed. The supposed equality of national forms took on an imposing material presence. On a more subtle level, the fountain gave material form to yet another ideological construct of Stalinism—the metaphor of the *flowering* (*rastsvet*) of cultures in relation to national forms.[36] It found its roots in Tugendkhol'd's early conceptualization of the arts of different nationalities as flowers at different stages of blooming. Stalin's construct extended this concept further: the "blossoms" of national culture, after blooming and withering, were destined to deliver the ultimate fruit of socialist universalism—a unified world culture that would be socialist in both form and content. The process of "blossoming" emphasized the naturalized life of the nation.[37] But the primordialization of ethnicity did not undermine the state's aspirations in the sphere of social engineering. Multiple Soviet national "flowers" were subject to political "gardening"—they were on their way toward ideological sameness.

The process of the flowering of individual nations is realized through the vision of domestication: taming their nature through tropes of cultivation. Twenty-five-foot-tall sheaves of wheat, hemp, and sunflower—three key agricultural plants in the Soviet Union at the time—were stacked in a towering arrangement that constituted a static core of the fountain (sculpted by Zoia Ryleeva).[38] The process of the adaptation of plants to cultivation is identified as a potent symbol of the "flowering" Soviet nations. Nations are placed around a single sheaf; "natural" aspects of national identity are reclaimed by socialist modernity by means of domestication. The sheaf itself pointed to the Soviet coat of arms, which featured the globe with a superimposed hammer and sickle, the rising sun of the new socialist era, and a five-pointed star. The composition is flanked by wheat sheaves bound with a continuous red ribbon that renders Marx's appeal "Workers of the world, unite!" in the fifteen national languages of the country but with the Russian inscription placed right in the center.

The centerpiece, in its florid opulence, is surrounded by sixteen sculptured figures floating on islands of granite around the sheaf and projecting forward from the fountain. These allegorical female statues representing the sixteen republics of the Soviet Union were produced by three different sculptors,[39] the most renowned of whom was Iosif Chaikov (1888–1979). Born in Kyiv, he graduated from the École nationale supérieure des arts décoratifs in Paris, taught at VKhUTEMAS, and headed the Society of Russian Sculptors. It was Chaikov who was commissioned to produce a figure representing Russia, the most important element of the sculptural ensemble.[40] His treatment of the human figure aspired to classicism, and the sculptures are marked by subtle contrapposto.

Aleksei Teneta (1899–1972), born in Warsaw but raised and educated in Moscow, was another prominent sculptor of the time commissioned to create statuary for the fountain. A VKhUTEMAS graduate, he had been deeply influenced by the work of the renowned sculptor Ivan Shadr. Teneta rose to prominence with a body of work dedicated to the Stakhanovite movement and visual themes of World War II memorialization. His later work, characterized by epic qualities, conflated Russian and Soviet identities.[41] Teneta's four fountain figures achieved their vibrant expressiveness through a nearly identical pose: each wielded a prop in her right hand while keeping the left arm lowered; fluttering skirts rounded out the dramatic dynamism. He also reinforced the bases of the sculptures with decorative floral elements.

The third sculptor, Zinaida Bazhenova (1905–1987), was the youngest of the three. Born in Tomsk, she graduated from an art college in Yekaterinburg before receiving training in monumental sculpture in Mukhina's workshop at VKhUTEIN. Bazhenova was traditionalist in her approach, and her work was marked by well-defined decorative qualities.[42] Before her apprenticeship with Mukhina, she studied gemstone cutting at an applied arts college. But a two-year evacuation to Uzbekistan in 1941 transformed Bazhenova's artistic sensibility; she began to work with ceramics and her color palette expanded radically under the influence of the opulent mosaics of medieval mosques. The 1961 monograph dedicated to her work emphasizes "decorative opulence [nariadnost']" and "keen engagement with color" as signature aesthetic virtues of her artistic practice.[43] Bazhenova's sculptures appear more static and archaic than those by Chaikov and Teneta. They feature modern stylization and rely on a fundamentally conventional aesthetic conception of decorative art. Here, alterity assumes an exterior role, providing access to the essence of the work (its socialist content) while nevertheless remaining surface-bound.

The three sculptors, each with a different aesthetic take on Soviet ethnic alterity, were required to negotiate the stylistic demands of the fountain's sculptural ensemble while presenting a vision of ethnic difference constrained by ideological uniformity. The formulaic personification of the Soviet republics as women enacts Stalin's pervasive rhetoric of ethnic difference with the Soviet leader himself cast as gardener of the nations. Representational rigidity is achieved by the static nature of the women's poses, their lack of emotional expression, their strictly regular placement around the giant sheaf, and the uniformity of the gilded surface. There is not much variation in the postures and gestures, and it is difficult to disentangle the figures one from another: each woman holds a bouquet of flowers or a fruit branch and wears a stylized national costume whose distinctive features are nearly invisible, obscured by the texture of the gold coating.[44]

The placement of the sixteen sculptures in a circle is infused with popular symbolism. The figures enact a *khorovod*, a Slavic pagan circle dance during which participants hold each other's hands while moving in a circle, imitating movement around the sun and symbolizing unity and friendship. The *khorovodnitsa*, usually a more experienced woman, is the dance's principal leader, directing the flow of movement and initiating changes in dance patterns. The statue representing the Russian woman is positioned at the center of the composition (from the main pavilion's perspective), and has her hand outstretched in a hailing gesture while holding a sheaf of wheat that resonates with the core of the fountain. She is the *khorovodnitsa*, and the other fifteen figures surrounding her are arranged in an order that reflects the population figures of the individual republics.[45] Our Russian *khorovodnitsa*'s ethnic attributes, as if aspiring to universality, are muted—perhaps even neutral. Unexpectedly, her costume does not include a *kokoshnik* (a traditional Russian headdress); she wears a "universal" flower wreath instead. Her special role was even more prominent at an earlier design stage where she appeared holding only the hammer and sickle (fig. 5.1), tools of industrialization and cultivation, the official symbol of solidarity between the urban proletariat and rural peasants.[46]

The Slavic representational orientation of the fountain is reinforced by its geography: it faces the 1954 main pavilion and shows its back to both the "Stone Flower," the second major fountain of the exposition, and the pavilion of the Ukrainian Soviet Socialist Republic behind it. Like the "Friendship of the Peoples" fountain, the "Stone Flower" fountain was also designed by Topuridze and

EPILOGUE

FIG. 5.1 Konstantin Topuridze, "Friendship of the Peoples" sketch, 1952, Archive and Library Fund of the VDNKh.

Konstantinovsky, and they have a direct originary connection. The initial plan presented the "Stone Flower" as a centerpiece of the "Friendship of the Peoples" (the two cores have an identical structural design) instead of the present giant sheaves of wheat. It was named and designed after the eponymous flower from Pavel Bazhov's "Uralic" fairy tale "The Stone Flower" (Kamennyi tsvetok, 1938).

The tale, Russophile "fakelore," was "transcribed from memory" by the author at the height of Stalinist terror.[47] It is a bizarre amalgamation of folk and modern traditions, infused with the working-class argot; one critic described it as "secretive tales of Ural workers."[48] Its material rendering was supposed to be the core of the aquatic structure, surrounded by the sixteen statues representing the sixteen Soviet republics. Bazhov's tale openly channeled the Russocentric tendency of late Stalinist policy on nationalities.[49] However, "The Stone Flower" was eventually built as a stand-alone fountain and the 25-foot-tall sheaves of wheat, hemp, and sunflower became the core of the "Friendship of the Peoples."

The two aquatic structures comprised an elaborate *allegorical* treatment of interethnic relations in the Soviet Union. Their excessive aggregation of signs, an amalgamation of (pseudo-)mythical and agricultural paraphernalia, follows the conventions of the allegorical mode of expression. Allegorical representation challenges a realistic one, for the world in allegory ceases to be purely physical and becomes an enigmatic accretion of signs. Walter Benjamin, in his influential work *The Origin of German Tragic Drama*, posits that allegory is an experience that arises from a vision of the world as transient, an intimation of mortality. Ruin, which reveals the dialectic tension between history and nature, becomes its preferred site: "In the ruin history has physically merged into the setting. And in this guise history does not assume the form of the process of an eternal life so much as that of irresistible decay. Allegory thereby declares itself to be beyond beauty."[50]

In fact, the "Friendship of the Peoples" quickly became a cultural ruin that embodied the process of decay of Stalinist aesthetics. The allegorical rendering of the diversity of the Soviet Union collapsed under the weight of its decorative excessiveness. On November 19, 1954, a year and a half after Stalin's death and less than four months after the pompous opening ceremony, the Moscow branch of the Union of Soviet Artists organized a discussion of the work that had been done at the VSKhV. The practical working group discussion quickly evolved into a fundamental debate about decorative arts. Vladimir Tolstoy, an emerging authority on monumental and decorative arts, delivered the keynote speech in which he noted a tendency toward excessive pomp (*pyshnost'*) and decorativeness (*ukrashatel'stvo*).[51] He claimed that "this tendency to adorn without an attempt to find a solution in terms of architectural plasticity has led to somewhat monotonous artistic decisions."[52] The gold coating of the bronze statues undermined their plasticity and expressiveness; uninhibited ornamentation was a sign of artistic weakness—mere filler that failed to translate into figurative expression. Nikolai Sobolevsky, a leading art historian specializing in decorative and plastic arts, was more uncompromising—he referred to the gilded fountain as a "petty merchant's shoddy thing" (kupetskaia [sic.] deshevka) surrounded by sixteen "samovars."[53]

EPILOGUE

In short, the VSKhV was a fiasco. An All-Union conference of construction workers that took place in early December 1954 pronounced the "aesthetic excesses" of the main Soviet exhibition to be economically harmful. In the same year, Georgii Gradov, a leading member of the Academy of Architecture of the USSR, submitted a letter to the Central Committee of the Communist Party of the Soviet Union in which he condemned decoratively archaic tendencies in Soviet architecture.[54] Gradov was consequently invited to share his concerns and became part of the working group that produced the famous resolution "On the Elimination of Excesses in Design and Construction," which cleared the way for the return of modernism and marked the beginning of the construction of panel housing in the Soviet Union.[55]

The aesthetics of Stalinism itself were removed as nonessential, superfluous decorations. Enabled by a swath of Khruschevian reforms and decrees in 1955 (shortly preceding his campaign against Stalin's cult of personality), the anachronistic approach was pronounced *excessive* and neutralized by a rebirth of architectural modernism. As the incipient critic of Stalinism succinctly put it, "we're not against beauty, but against excesses."[56] After 1955, the belated life of late modernism was prolonged even further. The return of modernism in Soviet architecture, enabled by the de-Stalinization reforms, reconfirmed the complex entanglement of the artistic sphere with sociopolitical practices. Though the doctrine of socialist realism was still in place, the Soviet Union essentially returned to the mainstream of international aesthetic development. This change was personified by Alfred Barr in several triumphant trips of cultural diplomacy to the Soviet Union in 1956 and 1959, during which he delivered a series of lectures dedicated to the MoMA permanent collection to audiences in Leningrad, Moscow, Tbilisi, and Yerevan. Presenting the contemporary American art scene, Barr included a screening of a documentary on abstract painter Jackson Pollock—an event that would have been inconceivable just a few years before. International alliances in the cultural and scholarly spheres were thus restored, and modernism, yet again, was identified as an expressive framework of socialist modernity. As Yuri Tynianov put it, "there are no dead ends in history. There are only interludes."[57]

NOTES

PREFACE

1. Alfred H. Barr, *Cubism and Abstract Art* (MoMA, 1936), 18.
2. Barr acknowledges that "movements confined in their influence to a single country have not been included." Barr, *Cubism and Abstract Art*, 9.
3. Retrospectively, this marker did not register the continuous evolution of surrealism and Bauhaus into the 1930s and beyond while modern architecture (as a broader phenomenon) was just gaining momentum in 1925.
4. Alfred H. Barr, "Russian Diary 1927–28," *October* 7 (1978): 12–13.
5. Barr, "Russian Diary 1927–28," 11, 18.
6. A. N-k, "Vystavki 'setsessionistov' v Berline i Vene," *Mir Iskusstva* 15 (1899): 15–16. However, the journal gradually changed its position and one of its late issues prominently featured Olbrich's work displayed at the Moscow Architectural Exhibition of 1903. *Mir Iskusstva*, no. 3 (1903): 118–20.
7. Mikhail Men'shikov, "Sredi dekadentov," in *Vyshe svobody* (Sovremennyi pisatel', 1998), 344.
8. A. Savina (ed.), *Vrubel': Perepiska. Vospominaniia o khudozhnike* (Iskusstvo, 1963), 109.
9. Men'shikov, "Sredi dekadentov," 343–44.
10. Mark Bassin, "Asia," in Nicholas Rzhevsky, ed., *The Cambridge Companion to Modern Russian Culture* (Cambridge University Press, 2012), 58.
11. Petr Pertsov, "Zheltye ili belye?," *Novyi put'*, no. 2 (1904): 277.
12. Frederick Engels, "The Turkish Question," in *Collected Works*, vol. 12, *Marx and Engels, 1853–54* (Lawrence & Wishart, 2010), 23.
13. Vladimir Lenin, "The Autocracy Is Wavering...," in *Collected Works*, vol. 6 (Progress, 1961), 349.
14. Leah Feldman, "Orientalism on the Threshold: Reorienting Heroism in Late Imperial Russia," *boundary 2* 39, no. 2 (2012): 180.

INTRODUCTION: POINTS OF REORIENTATION

1. Viktor Shklovskii, "Aleksandr Veselovskii—istorik i teoretik," *Oktiabr'*, no. 12 (1947): 177.
2. Viktor Shklovskii, *O teorii prozy* (Sovetskii pisatel', 1983), 163.
3. Shklovskii, *O teorii prozy*, 165.

4. Shklovskii, *O teorii prozy*, 165.
5. The focal point of this book is Russian/Soviet "metropolitan" modernism and its consequent dislocation. A separate case is made for "indigenous" modernist traditions, remotely situated from the Russian centers of modernity, that forcibly claimed cross-cultural differentiation and political self-determination. Harsha Ram, for instance, convincingly establishes the case of Georgian modernism, which "evolved against the backdrop of socialist revolution, anti-colonial nationalism, and a local context of astonishing cultural diversity" and "experienced a contracted and accelerated pattern of development that collapsed many of the distinctions of periodization and of theory." Harsha Ram, "Decadent Nationalism, 'Peripheral' Modernism: The Georgian Literary Manifesto Between Symbolism and the Avant-Garde," *Modernism/modernity* 21, no. 1 (2014): 345, 343. A similar case is made for Azerbaijan by Leah Feldman, who addresses how the space "was reimagined through writings across radically disparate linguistic, cultural, and disciplinary conventions." Leah Feldman, *On the Threshold of Eurasia: Revolutionary Poetics in the Caucasus* (Cornell University Press, 2018), 35. The war in Ukraine boosted scholarship on the distinctiveness of Ukrainian modernism, and its contours continue to be reinforced. See Konstantin Akinsha et al., eds., *In the Eye of the Storm: Modernism in Ukraine, 1900–1930s* (Thames & Hudson, 2022). While similar cases can be made for other constituent republics of the Soviet Union, the Baltic states, annexed in 1940, had distinctive modernist traditions oriented beyond the Slavic cultural paradigm. See Serge Fauchereau, *Art of the Baltic States: Modernism, Freedom and Identity 1900–1950* (Thames & Hudson, 2022); and Steven Mansbach, "Capital Modernism in the Baltic Republics: Kaunas, Tallinn, and Riga," in *Races to Modernity: Metropolitan Aspirations in Eastern Europe, 1890–1940*, ed. Jan Behrends and Martin Kohlrausch (Central European University Press, 2014), 235–66.
6. William Phillips, "Our Country and Our Culture: A Symposium (III)," *Partisan Review* 19, no. 5 (1952): 589.
7. Sergey Abashin and Andrew Jenks, "Soviet Central Asia on the Periphery," *Kritika: Explorations in Russian and Eurasian History* 16, no. 2 (2015): 361.
8. Steven Lee's analysis posits that "from the alignment of art and revolution emerged many striking, eccentric ways of expressing cultural difference—visions of political and artistic vanguardism that deepened rather than erased ethnic particularism; visions of world revolution in which the ethnic Other took the lead." Steven Lee, *The Ethnic Avant-Garde: Minority Cultures and World Revolution* (Columbia University Press, 2015), 2.
9. Transcaucasia shaped the nineteenth-century Russian orientalist imagination, and it continued to be a prominent "source" of otherness for twentieth-century modernists such as Osip Mandelstam, Boris Pasternak, and Iurii Tynianov. However, the Christianization of Armenia and Georgia, Transcaucasia's proximity to Europe, and its prominent political representation among the Soviet elites made the wider geographical region, from the point of view of Moscow, more familiar. Central Asia was the "vanguard" of underdevelopment in the twentieth century.
10. Joseph Stalin, "The Political Tasks of the University of the Peoples of the East," in *Works*, vol. 7, *1925* (OGIZ, 1947), 140.
11. Raymond Williams, *The Politics of Modernism: Against the New Conformists* (Verso, 1989), 79.
12. See Vladimir Lenin, "On the Significance of Militant Materialism," in *Collected Works*, vol. 33, August 1921–March 1923 (Progress, 1973), 227.
13. Andrei Bely, for instance, referred to "vexatious, dummy [*dosadnyi, manekennyi*] modernism" that conflicted with "true symbolism." Andrei Belyi, "Chekhov," *Vesy* 8 (1904): 5. Vsevolod Meyerhold invoked "cheap modernism" in theater. Vsevolod Meyerhold, "Iz pisem o teatre," *Vesy* 6 (1907): 98. Additionally, *stil' modern* (modern style), a Russian equivalent to art nouveau, and "sovremennoe iskusstvo" (modern art) were possible locutions at this period.
14. Astradur Eysteinsson, *The Concept of Modernism* (Cornell University Press, 1992), 8, 52.
15. Timothy J. Clark, *Farewell to an Idea: Episodes from a History of Modernism* (Yale University Press, 1999), 7.

INTRODUCTION ♣ 267

16. Clement Greenberg, "Modernist Painting," in *Clement Greenberg: The Collected Essays and Criticism*, vol. 4, ed. John O'Brian (University of Chicago Press, 1986), 85–93; Harold Rosenberg, *The Tradition of the New* (Horizon Press, 1959).
17. Theodor W. Adorno, "Culture Industry Reconsidered," in *The Culture Industry: Selected Essays on Mass Culture*, ed. J. M. Bernstein (Routledge, 1991), 98–106.
18. Renato Poggioli, *The Theory of the Avant-Garde* (Harvard University Press, 1968), 9
19. Peter Bürger, *Theory of the Avant-Garde* (University of Minnesota Press, 1984), xv.
20. Georg Lukács, "Realism in the Balance," in Theodor Adorno et al., *Aesthetics and Politics*, Radical Thinkers 19 (Verso, 2010), 36–37.
21. Georg Lukács, *The Meaning of Contemporary Realism* (Merlin Press, 1963), 25.
22. Clement Greenberg, "Avant-Garde and Kitsch," in *Clement Greenberg: The Collected Essays and Criticism*, vol. 1, *Perceptions and Judgments, 1939–1944*, ed. John O'Brian (University of Chicago Press, 1986), 8.
23. Greenberg, "Modernist Painting," 92.
24. Robert Russell, "The Modernist Tradition," in *The Cambridge Companion to the Classic Russian Novel*, ed. Malcolm Jones and Robin Feuer Miller (Cambridge University Press, 1998), 210. See also Donald Fanger, "City of Russian Modernist Fiction," in *Modernism, 1890–1930*, ed. Malcolm Bradbury and James McFarlane (Penguin, 1976), 468, 479; and Emily Finer, "Russian Modernism," in *The Oxford Handbook of Modernisms*, ed. Peter Brooker et al. (Oxford University Press, 2010), 838. Victor Erlich concurs with the traditional view of the chronological scope of Russian/Soviet modernism (1910–1935) and the argument that "the modernist ferment was abruptly discontinued by bureaucratic fiat," but nevertheless suggests that "the full reach of the term may properly encompass a larger sequence, extending from the turn of the century to the immediate aftermath of the Second World War." He does not elaborate further. See Victor Erlich, *Modernism and Revolution: Russian Literature in Transition* (Harvard University Press, 1994), 1–2.
25. Charles Jencks, *Late-Modern Architecture and Other Essays* (Rizzoli, 1980), 10.
26. Fredric Jameson, *Postmodernism, or, the Cultural Logic of Late Capitalism* (University of North Carolina Press, 1991), 305.
27. Tyrus Miller, *Late Modernism: Politics, Fictions, and the Arts between the World Wars* (University of California Press, 1999), 13.
28. Miller, *Late Modernism*, 13.
29. Miller, *Late Modernism*, 19, 20.
30. Selim Khan-Magomedov, *Il'ia Golosov* (Stroiizdat, 1988), 196.
31. Selim Khan-Magomedov, *Konstruktivizm: kontseptsiia formoobrazovaniia* (Stroiizdat, 2003), 537.
32. Leonid Livak, *In Search of Russian Modernism* (Johns Hopkins University Press, 2018), 113.
33. Livak, *In Search of Russian Modernism*, 149, 132, 127.
34. Marshall Berman, *All That Is Solid Melts Into Air: The Experience of Modernity* (Penguin, 1988), 235–36.
35. Sheila Fitzpatrick, *The Russian Revolution* (Oxford University Press, 2017), 3.
36. Stephen Kotkin, *Magnetic Mountain: Stalinism as a Civilization* (University of California Press, 1997).
37. Devin Fore, *Realism after Modernism: The Rehumanization of Art and Literature* (MIT Press, 2012), 6.
38. Vladimir Paperny, *Architecture in the Age of Stalin: Culture Two* (Cambridge University Press, 2002). The claims that socialist realism remained the only aesthetic framework in high and late Stalinism follow this conventional binary-based understanding of the period (avant-garde vs. socialist realism); see Evgeny Dobrenko, *Late Stalinism: The Aesthetics of Politics* (Yale University Press, 2020), 24. The binary vision of Soviet culture, with a clear line of demarcation between the 1920s and the 1930s, was first articulated by Nicholas Timasheff in his influential 1946 monograph *The Great Retreat: The Growth and Decline of Communism in Russia* (Arno Press, 1972). There is much debate over this view of Soviet culture in recent historical scholarship: see David Hoffmann, "Was There a 'Great Retreat'

from Soviet Socialism? Stalinist Culture Reconsidered," *Kritika: Explorations in Russian and Eurasian History* 5, no. 4, (2004): 651–74; Kotkin, *Magnetic Mountain*, 3–6, 355–61; Matthew Lenoe, "In Defense of Timasheff's Great Retreat," *Kritika: Explorations in Russian and Eurasian History* 5, no. 4 (2004): 721–30; and Terry Martin, *The Affirmative Action Empire: Nations and Nationalism in the Soviet Union, 1923–1929* (Cornell University Press, 2001), 414–30.

39. Boris Groys, *The Total Art of Stalinism: Avant-garde, Aesthetic Dictatorship, and Beyond* (Princeton University Press, 1992), 44.

40. Boris Groys, "A Style and a Half: Socialist Realism between Modernism and Postmodernism," in *Socialist Realism Without Shores*, ed. Thomas Lahusen and Evgeny Dobrenko (Duke University Press, 1997), 83. Groys also directly invokes Stalin's formula "national in form, socialist in content" in another essay, using it as a platform for a peculiar rhetorical somersault that will probably puzzle most scholars of the avant-garde: "Socialist Realism is usually defined as art [that is] 'socialist in content and national in form,' but this also signifies 'avant-garde in content and eclectic in form,' since 'national' denotes everything 'popular' and 'progressive' throughout the entire history of the nation. Avant-garde purity of style is, in fact, the result of the still unconquered attitude of the artist toward what he produces as an 'original work,' corresponding to the 'unique individuality' of the artist. In this sense, the eclectic may be regarded as the faithful expression in art of a truly collectivist principle." See Boris Groys, "The Birth of Socialist Realism from the Spirit of the Russian Avant-Garde," in *The Russian Avant-Garde and Radical Modernism: An Introductory Reader*, ed. Dennis Ioffe and Frederick White (Academic Studies Press, 2012), 274.

41. Edward Said, *Orientalism* (Penguin, 2003), 17, 26. The question as to whether or not the Soviet Union can be classified as a modern colonial empire continues to challenge scholars. The definitional elusiveness of the Soviet Union can be traced back to the status of the Russian Empire—the state structure that preceded the USSR—in which blurred racial boundaries, a cosmopolitan ruling elite, ambiguous strategies for managing difference, and high-visibility instances of colonists "going native" or conforming to local culture (as opposed to the broad cultural assimilation of native culture itself) all add to the confusion. Some historians and literary scholars have identified certain traits of the political structure of the USSR as inherently imperial and in sync with the conventional colonial practices of the Habsburgs and the Ottomans. Others have emphasized various manifestations of difference, rather than similarity, between the Soviet project and imperial traditions. See Francine Hirsch, *Empire of Nations: Ethnographic Knowledge and the Making of the Soviet Union* (Cornell University Press, 2005); Adeeb Khalid, "Russian History and the Debate over Orientalism," *Kritika: Explorations in Russian and Eurasian History* 1, no. 4 (2000): 691–99; Martin, *The Affirmative Action Empire*; Paula Michaels, *Curative Powers: Medicine and Empire in Stalin's Central Asia* (University of Pittsburgh Press, 2003); Douglas Northrop, *Veiled Empire: Gender and Power in Stalinist Central Asia* (Cornell University Press, 2004); Yuri Slezkine, "Imperialism as the Highest Stage of Socialism," *Russian Review* 59, no. 2 (2000): 217–34; Yuri Slezkine, "The USSR as a Communal Apartment, or How a Socialist State Promoted Ethnic Particularism," *Slavic Review* 53, no. 2 (1994): 414–52; and Ronald Grigor Suny, "The Empire Strikes Out: Imperial Russia, 'National' Identity, and Theories of Empire," in *A State of Nations: Empire and Nation-Making in the Age of Lenin and Stalin*, ed. Ronald Grigor Suny and Terry Martin (Oxford University Press, 2001), 23–66.

42. Vera Tolz, *Russia's Own Orient: The Politics of Identity and Oriental Studies in the Late Imperial and Early Soviet Periods* (Oxford University Press, 2011), 100–101.

43. "Vostokovedenie (inache orientalistika)," in *Bol'shaia sovetskaia entsiklopediia*, vol. 9 (Sovetskaia Entsiklopediia, 1951), 193–202.

44. See for instance Sergei Ol'denburg, "Sovetskoe vostokovedenie," *Front nauki i tekhniki*, nos. 7–8 (1931), 64–66.

45. Anouar Abdel-Malek, "Orientalism in Crisis," *Diogenes* 44 (1963), 103–40.

46. Edward Said, *Culture and Imperialism* (Knopf, 1993), 97.

47. Said, *Culture and Imperialism*, xxiii.
48. Homi Bhabha, *The Location of Culture* (Routledge, 1994), 2.
49. Ernst Bloch, *Heritage of Our Times* (Polity Press, 1991), 97.
50. Said, *Culture and Imperialism*, 51.
51. Douglas Mao and Rebecca Walkowitz, "The New Modernist Studies," *PMLA* 123, no. 3 (2008): 738.
52. Jessica Berman, *Modernist Fiction, Cosmopolitanism, and the Politics of Community* (Cambridge University Press, 2001), 3. This broad shift toward understanding modernism as shaped by sociopolitical, material, and economic structures within a globally conceived modernity is a product of "new modernist studies," a field that challenges a vision of modernism as a purely aesthetic concept committed to apolitical and ahistorical formal experimentation. This "new" trend resulted in "weakening" the very term *modernism*. See Paul Saint-Amour, "Weak Theory, Weak Modernism," *Modernism/modernity* 25, no. 3 (2018): 437–59.
53. Susan Stanford Friedman, *Planetary Modernisms: Provocations on Modernity Across Time* (Columbia University Press, 2015), 80.
54. Andreas Huyssen, "Geographies of Modernism in a Globalizing World," in *Geographies of Modernism: Literatures, Cultures, Spaces*, ed. Peter Brooker and Andrew Thacker (Routledge, 2005), 7.
55. Elleke Boehmer and Steven Matthews, "Modernism and Colonialism," in *The Cambridge Companion to Modernism*, ed. Michael Levenson (Cambridge University Press, 2011), 286.
56. Boehmer and Matthews, "Modernism and Colonialism," 288.
57. Williams, *The Politics of Modernism*, 44.
58. Fredric Jameson, *The Political Unconscious: Narrative as a Socially Symbolic Act* (Routledge, 2002), 194–270.
59. Fredric Jameson, "Modernism and Imperialism" in *Nationalism, Colonialism, and Literature*, ed. Terry Eagleton et al. (University of Minnesota Press, 1990), 50–51.
60. Terry Eagleton, *Exiles and Émigrés: Studies in Modern Literature* (Schocken, 1970).
61. Jahan Ramazani, *A Transnational Poetics* (The University of Chicago Press, 2009), xii, xi.
62. Michael North, *The Dialect of Modernism: Race, Language, and Twentieth-Century Literature* (Oxford University Press, 1994).
63. John Bowlt and Matthew Drutt, eds., *Amazons of the Avant-Garde: Alexandra Exter, Natalia Goncharova, Liubov Popova, Olga Rozanova, Varvara Stepanova, and Nadezhda Udaltsova* (Deutsche Guggenheim, 1999), 314.
64. Benedikt Livshits, "My i Zapad," in *Terent'evskii sbornik. Vypusk 1* (Gileia, 1996), 256.
65. Jane Sharp, *Russian Modernism Between East and West: Natal'ia Goncharova and the Moscow Avant-Garde, 1905–1914* (Cambridge University Press, 2006), 7. See also Andrei Kovalev, "Russkaia zhivopis' i Vostok: desiatye gody XX veka," in *Nauchnye soobshcheniia. Gosudarstvennyi muzei iskusstva narodov vostoka. Vypusk XIII* (Moscow, 1980), 22–47; Harsha Ram, "Spatializing the Sign: The Futurist Eurasianism of Roman Jakobson and Velimir Khlebnikov," in *Between Europe and Asia: The Origins, Theories, and Legacies of Russian Eurasianism*, ed. Mark Bassin et al. (University of Pittsburgh Press, 2015), 137–49.
66. Harsha Ram, "World Literature as World Revolution: Velimir Khlebnikov's *Zangezi* and the Utopian Geopoetics of the Russian Avant-Garde," in *Comintern Aesthetics*, ed. Amelia Glaser and Steven Lee (University of Toronto Press, 2020), 31–80.
67. Emma Widdis, *Socialist Senses: Film, Feeling, and the Soviet Subject, 1917–1940* (Indiana University Press, 2017), 167.
68. Widdis, *Socialist Senses*, 168.
69. Said, *Orientalism*, 3.
70. Contrast this with Katerina Clark's insistence that the concepts of national and *inter-* or *trans-national* cannot be seen as rigidly binary opposites, especially in the context of the Soviet Union of the 1930s; see Katerina Clark, *Moscow, the Fourth Rome: Stalinism, Cosmopolitanism, and the Evolution*

of Soviet Culture, 1931–1941 (Harvard University Press, 2011), 9. In her most recent book, Clark extends her argument by engaging a broader cultural space of Eurasia that was subject to leftist political and cultural molding. She considers Comintern-sponsored international literature as "the beginnings of a world literature" and an attempt "to establish symbolic hegemony as a 'soft' route to ideological hegemony"; see Katerina Clark, *Eurasia without Borders: The Dream of a Leftist Literary Commons, 1919–1943* (Harvard University Press, 2021), 9, 15. However, by largely accepting Soviet self-proclaimed emancipatory discourses of internationalism and anti-colonialism, Clark's two monographs also tend to downplay the socio-political and cultural effects of Russification in the late 1930s.

71. Vasilii Kliuchevskii, *Sochineniia v deviati tomakh. Tom IX* (Mysl', 1990), 385.
72. Yuri Tynianov, *Poetika. Istoriia literatury. Kino* (Nauka, 1977), 257.
73. Mikhail Bakhtin, *Author and Hero in Aesthetic Activity*, in *Art and Answerability: Early Philosophical Essays by M.M. Bakhtin*, ed. Michael Holquist and Vadim Liapunov, trans. Vadim Liapunov (University of Texas Press, 1990), 85.
74. Stalin, "The Foundations of Leninism," in *Works. Volume 6* (Moscow: OGIZ, 1953), 79–80.
75. See Richard Pipes, "The Establishment of the Union of Soviet Socialist Republics," in Rachel Denber (ed.), *The Soviet Nationality Reader: The Disintegration in Context* (Boulder: Westview Press, 1992), 35–86.
76. See Erik Van Ree, "Socialism in One Country: A Reassessment," *Studies in East European Thought* 50, no. 2 (1998): 77–117.
77. Stressing its underdeveloped character, Viatcheslav Morozov identifies Russia as a subaltern empire: "Russia can and must be seen as a subaltern, as an object of external colonization that was integrated into the capitalist world-system on unequal terms." Viatcheslav Morozov, *Russia's Postcolonial Identity: A Subaltern Empire in a Eurocentric World* (New York: Palgrave Macmillan, 2015), 31.
78. Vladimir Lenin, *Imperialism, the Highest Stage of Capitalism* in *Collected Works. Volume 22* (Moscow: Progress, 1964), 185–304.
79. 85 percent of the Russian population in 1917 was rural. Peasants displayed aspects of cultural backwardness and were largely indifferent to the urban class struggle. This disproportional schism between educated elites, a small fraction of urban workers, and the vast peasantry allowed Alvin Gouldner to define Stalinism as "an internal colonialism mobilizing its state power against colonial tributaries in rural territories." "Internal colonialism meant," Gouldner argues, "that the peasants were the raw material of socialism, not the object of its emancipation." He concludes with a bold claim that "Stalinism developed as an internal colonialism." Alvin Gouldner, "Stalinism: A Study of Internal Colonialism," *Telos*, no. 34 (1978): 13, 28, 41. Aleksandr Etkind extends temporal boundaries of the concept of *internal colonization* by arguing that it fully emerged with the rule of Peter the Great and the birth of the Russian Empire in 1721. Alexander Etkind, *Internal Colonization: Russia's Imperial Experience* (Cambridge: Polity, 2011), 102. However, "internal colonialism," if it is indeed a Russian imperial stratagem, does differ across different parts of the Soviet "periphery" and its "oriental" areas should be treated as distinctive. Alexander Morrison justifiably notes the concept's failure to grasp the pronounced multi-ethnic composition of the Russian empire: "where does the boundary run? Is the Volga region, with its large (and surviving) Turkic population, an example of 'internal' colonization while the Asian steppe is 'external?' Or does internal colonization only refer to Russians, wherever they might happen to be?" Alexander Morrison, "*Internal Colonization. Russia's Imperial Experience* by Alexander Etkind (review)," *Ab Imperio*, 3 (2013): 456.
80. This sentiment was shared by Leon Trotsky for whom "the privilege of historic backwardness" was an enabling condition for the revolutionary movement. Leon Trotsky, *The History of the Russian Revolution* (Chicago: Haymarket Books, 2008), 4.
81. Vladimir Lenin, *What Is to Be Done? Burning Questions of Our Movement* (New York: International Publishers, 1969), 78.

INTRODUCTION ♣ 271

82. Immanuel Wallerstein, "Social Science and the Communist Interlude, or Interpretations of Contemporary History," in *The Essential Wallerstein* (New York: The New Press, 2000), 380.
83. Mary Louise Pratt, "Arts of the Contact Zone," *Profession* (1991): 37.
84. Joseph Stalin, "National Factors in Party and State Affairs," in *Works*, vol. 5, *1921–1923* (OGIZ, 1953), 190–91, my emphasis. However, the "underdeveloped" constituents of the Soviet Union comprised a rather heterogeneous space. Transcaucasia was a melting pot of cultures and divergent political affiliations. While Armenia and Georgia had their own literary traditions even before Russia received its own alphabet, Azerbaijan was an important cultural hub with a pronounced influence of Persian and Ottoman cultures. On the other hand, autonomous republics and national formations within the Russian Soviet Federative Socialist Republic (RSFSR), including Chechnya, Tatarstan, Chuvashia, Bashkiria, Tuva, and the Siberian territories of Yakutia and Buryatia, had a completely different (and "regional") status within the USSR. Although they were labeled as "underdeveloped" along with their republican counterparts, they did not receive the same amount of funding and were not subjected to large-scale transformative projects (such as establishing literary canons, literary languages, etc.).
85. Marlene Laruelle, *Central Peripheries: Nationhood in Central Asia* (UCL Press, 2021), 17.
86. Terry Martin, "Modernization or Neo-Traditionalism? Ascribed Nationality and Soviet Primordialism," in *Stalinism: New Directions*, ed. Sheila Fitzpatrick (Routledge, 2000), 354.
87. Slezkine, "The USSR as a Communal Apartment," 414.
88. Cloé Drieu, *Cinema, Nation, and Empire in Uzbekistan, 1919–1937* (Indiana University Press, 2019), 8.
89. However, national delimitation and the emancipatory project of socialist modernity created another dichotomy. Soviet Orientalists started to distinguish between the "Soviet Orient" (Central Asia, the Caucasus, the Volga-Urals and Siberia) and the "Foreign Orient." This same distinction was reflected in the way research institutions were structured throughout the country. Scholars of the Soviet "internal" Orient consistently presented the territory as a symbol of successful socialist development whose "backwardness" belonged to the past, while the "Foreign Orient" was considered still in the process of struggling with capitalist powers. Alfrid Bustanov, *Soviet Orientalism and the Creation of Central Asian Nations* (Routledge, 2016), xx, xiii.
90. Georges Bataille, *The Accursed Share: An Essay on General Economy*, vol. 1, *Consumption* (Zone, 1998), 151.
91. Karl Marx, *A Contribution to the Critique of Political Economy* (International Publishers, 1970), 21.
92. In 1929, before he had become a disillusioned Marxist, Wittfogel published a two-part article on geopolitics in the Soviet journal *Under the Banner of Marxism*; see Karl Wittfogel, "Geopolitika, geograficheskii materializm i marksizm," *Pod znamenem marksizma*, nos. 2–3 (1929): 16–42 and no. 6 (1929): 1–29.
93. Karl Wittfogel, *Oriental Despotism: A Comparative Study of Total Power* (Yale University Press, 1957), iii.
94. Wittfogel, *Oriental Despotism*, 136.
95. Gayatri Chakravorty Spivak, *A Critique of Postcolonial Reason: Toward a History of the Vanishing Present* (Harvard University Press, 1999), 72. Interestingly, the Asiatic Mode of Production (AMP) concept is a glaring omission in Edward Said's work; he did not extend his discussion of orientalist discourse to include any writings on AMP, though its relevance is obvious for cultural and historiographic purposes. However, Bryan S. Turner's work, published in the same year as Said's monograph, does address the notion of AMP as evidence that "Marxism itself contains a heavy dosage of Orientalism," which manifests itself in "the view of history as an unfolding essence and by the specification of the static nature of 'Asiatic society.'" For Turner, AMP reflects Eurocentric prejudices about Asia; see Bryan Turner, *Marx and the End of Orientalism* (Routledge, 1978), 82.
96. Spivak, *A Critique of Postcolonial Reason*, 79.
97. Lajos Magyar, a Hungarian émigré also known by his Russified name Liudvig Mad'iar, was a key proponent of AMP in the Soviet Union. From 1926–1927 he served in the Soviet embassy in China;

he then worked for the Oriental Secretariat of the Comintern from 1929 until 1934 when he was purged. Magyar's published study of agricultural practices in China, which opened with a reflection on AMP and imperialism, prompted fierce debates in the late 1920s and the early 1930s; see Lajos Magyar, *Ekonomika sel'skogo khoziaistva v Kitae* (Moscow: Gosudarstvennoe izdatel'stvo, 1928), 5–22. He argues for the universality of AMP and identifies it as a necessary pre-capitalist stage which all peoples must undergo. The Asiatic element thus is not a geographically specific concept. Sergei Dubrovskii was Magyar's key opponent. In his 1929 monograph, he basically argues that AMP is a mere Asiatic variant of feudalism or slave society, and it does not comprise a stage. Sergei Dubrovskii, *K voprosu o sushchnosti "aziatskogo" sposoba proizvodstva, feodalizma, krepostnichestva i torgovogo kapitala* (Nauchnaia assotsiatsiia vostokovedeniia, 1929). The pinnacle of the AMP debate came when the two views clashed at a conference in Leningrad in February 1931. Mikhail Godes, a keynote speaker, confirmed the vision of AMP as a form of feudalism; one of the respondents countered that it dangerously undermines the Comintern's efforts to incite revolutionary struggle among the world's colonial peoples because of geographical specificity and particularism; see *Diskussiia ob aziatskom sposobe proizvodstva. Po dokladu M. Godesa* (GSEI, 1931), 27, 74. They also vehemently rejected the supposition that a bureaucratic apparatus could function as a ruling class. The conference effectively dismantled AMP as a discursive category, and over time it became politically unacceptable.

98. Vasilii Struve, "Problema zarozhdeniia, razvitiia i upadka rabovladel'cheskikh obshchestv drevnego Vostoka," in *Izvestiia Gosudarstvennoi akademii istorii material'noi kul'tury. Vypusk 77* (OGIZ, 1934), 32–111.
99. TSK KPSS [Commission of the Central Committee of the CPSU(B)], *The History of the Communist Party of the Soviet Union (Bolsheviks): A Short Course* (International Publishers, 1939), 123.
100. Wittfogel, *Oriental Despotism*, 408.
101. TSK KPSS, *The History of the Communist Party of the Soviet Union (Bolsheviks)*, 118.
102. Etienne Balibar, "The Nation Form: History and Ideology," *Review (Fernand Braudel Center)* 13, no. 3 (1990): 346.
103. Rogers Brubaker, *Nationalism Reframed: Nationhood and the National Question in the New Europe* (Cambridge University Press, 1996), 18.
104. According to Dobrenko, the Stalinist literary machine looked obsessively toward the East for inspiration and substantiation of its aesthetic and ideological ambitions, and folklore, as the archaic voice of the people, served this purpose perfectly. Dobrenko reduces the notion of national form to language (and grammar), specific to a given nation. Evgeny Dobrenko, "Total'naia lingvistika: Vlast' grammatiki i grammatika vlasti," *Russian Literature* 63, nos. 2–4 (2008): 586.
105. David Brandenberger, *National Bolshevism: Stalinist Mass Culture and the Formation of Modern Russian National Identity, 1931–1956* (Harvard University Press, 2002), 93.
106. Cf. Sergei Abashin, "Sovetskaia vlast' i uzbekskaia makhallia," *Neprikosnovennyi zapas* 78, no. 4 (2011): 95–97; Dobrenko, "Total'naia lingvistika," 586; Ilya Kalinin, "USSR: The Union of National Form and Socialist Content," *Russian Studies in Philosophy* 60, no. 5 (2022): 382–94; Martin, *The Affirmative Action Empire*, 12–13; Slezkine, "The USSR as a Communal Apartment," 418; and Michael G. Smith, "The Tenacity of Forms: Language, Nation, Stalin," in *Politics and the Theory of Language in the USSR 1917–1938: The Birth of Sociological Linguistics*, ed. Craig Brandist and Katya Chown (Anthem Press, 2010), 112. Zaal Andronikashvili's recent article is a rare exception, but the discussion is limited to the Georgian "national form," and he primarily addresses "practical" aspects of its application; see Zaal Andronikashvili, "National Form: The Evolution of Georgian Socialist Realism," *Slavic Review* 81, no. 4, (2022): 914–35.
107. Stalin, "The Political Tasks of the University of the Peoples of the East," 141.
108. Caroline Levine, *Forms: Whole, Rhythm, Hierarchy, Network* (Princeton University Press, 2015), 3. Harsha Ram is another of the very few scholars who see a productive nexus of political and aesthetic

realms in the category of form. As Ram perceptively notes, "the category of the *national* in Soviet cultural politics was as instrumentalized but also as potentially volatile as the category of *form* in Soviet aesthetics: when subordinated to the unifying force of socialist ideology, they played an essential but subordinate role; when released from this constraint, they engendered the literary heresy of formalism and the political heresy of nationalism: both involved the fragmentation of the whole (be it the Soviet Union or the work of art) and the fetishization of parts." Harsha Ram, "National Mythopoesis: Georgian Symbolism, the National Question, and Socialist Realism," unpublished paper.

109. Otto Bauer, "The Nation," in *Mapping the Nation*, ed. Gopal Balakrishnan (Verso, 2012), 39–77.
110. Bauer, "The Nation," 61.
111. Bauer, "The Nation," 52.
112. Bauer, "The Nation," 49.
113. Benedict Anderson, "Introduction," in *Mapping the Nation*, ed. Gopal Balakrishnan (Verso, 2012), 5.
114. Joseph Stalin, "Marxism and the National Question," in *Works*, vol. 2, *February 1907–February 1913* (OGIZ, 1946), 311–12.
115. Stalin, "Marxism and the National Question," 308.
116. Stalin, "Marxism and the National Question," 307.
117. Stalin, "Marxism and the National Question," 307. My reading has been informed by Samuel Coggeshall's analysis of the polemics between Bauer and Stalin. See Samuel Coggeshall, "Stalin, 'National Content,' and National Destiny," unpublished paper.
118. Stalin, "The Political Tasks of the University of the Peoples of the East," 140.
119. Joseph Stalin, "Political Report of the Central Committee to the Sixteenth Congress of the C.P.S.U.(B.), June 27, 1930," in *Works*, vol. 12, *April 1929–June 1930* (OGIZ, 1949), 380.
120. Irina Sandomirskaia, "*One Sixth of the World*: Avant-garde Film, the Revolution of Vision, and the Colonization of the USSR Periphery during the 1920s (Towards a Postcolonial Deconstruction of the Soviet Hegemony)," in *From Orientalism to Postcoloniality*, ed. Kerstin Olofsson (Södertörns högskola, 2008), 9.
121. See, for example, Stalin, "Political Report of the Central Committee to the Sixteenth Congress of the C.P.S.U.(B.), June 27, 1930," 379, 380, 381.
122. See Elitza Dulguerova, "Introduction to Iakov Tugendkhol'd, 'In the Iron Dead-end' (1915)," *Modernism/modernity* 17, no. 4 (2010): 899–903.
123. Iakov Tugendkhol'd, "Sovremennoe iskusstvo i narodnost'," *Severnye zapiski*, no. 11 (1913): 154–55.
124. Iakov Tugendkhol'd, "K voprosu o natsional'nosti v iskusstve," *Natsional'nye problemy*, no. 2 (1915): 23.
125. Iakov Tugendkhol'd, "K izucheniiu izobrazitel'nogo iskusstva SSSR," *Iskusstvo narodov SSSR. Vypusk 1* (GAKhN, 1927), 48. In the same publication, Lunacharsky also used a metaphor of blossoming (*tsvetenie*) in his discussion of national forms; see Anatolii Lunacharskii, "Khudozhestvennoe tvorchestvo natsional'nostei SSSR," in *Iskusstvo narodov SSSR. Vypusk 1*, 15.
126. Iakov Tugendkhol'd, "Iskusstvo narodov SSSR," in *Iskusstvo oktiabr'skoi epokhi* (Akademiia, 1930), 96.
127. Tugendkhol'd, "Iskusstvo narodov SSSR," 87.
128. "Primitivism" was originally used in the specific context of art history. See William Rubin, ed., *"Primitivism" in Twentieth-Century Art: Affinity of the Tribal and the Modern*, vol. 1 (MoMA, 1984).
129. Iakov Tugendkhol'd, "Iskusstvo SSSR i natsional'nyi element," *Novyi mir*, no. 8 (1925): 120.
130. Tugendkhol'd, "K voprosu o natsional'nosti v iskusstve," 23.
131. Tugendkhol'd, "Iskusstvo SSSR i natsional'nyi element," 121.
132. Tugendkhol'd, "Iskusstvo SSSR i natsional'nyi element," 121.
133. Vladimir Lenin, "Critical Remarks on the National Question," in *Collected Works*, vol. 20, *December 1913–August 1914* (Progress, 1964), 24.
134. Lenin, "Critical Remarks on the National Question," 24.
135. Vladimir Lenin, "How Does Bishop Nikon Defend the Ukrainians?" in *Collected Works*, vol. 19, *1913* (Progress, 1977), 380–81.

136. Karl Marx and Frederick Engels, *Manifesto of the Communist Party*, in *Collected Works*, vol. 6 *Marx and Engels, 1845–48* (Lawrence & Wishart, 2010), 502.
137. Sergo Amaglobeli, *Iskusstvo narodov SSSR* (Uchpedgiz, 1932), 16–17.
138. Amaglobeli, *Iskusstvo narodov SSSR*, 17.
139. In an article written a year before, however, Rempel' views national form in a classical Leninist manner; see Lazar' Rempel', "O natsional'nom iskusstve," *Brigada khudozhnikov*, no. 7 (1931): 2.
140. Lazar' Rempel', *Zhivopis' sovetskogo Zakavkaz'ia* (OGIZ-IZOGIZ, 1932), 8.
141. Rempel', *Zhivopis' sovetskogo Zakavkaz'ia*, 8.
142. Rempel', *Zhivopis' sovetskogo Zakavkaz'ia*, 8
143. Isaak Nusinov, "Natsional'naia literatura," in *Literaturnaia entsiklopediia*, vol. 7 (OGIZ, 1934), 639.
144. Nusinov, "Natsional'naia literatura," 639.
145. As Kathryn Schild observes, "At the first plenum, Uzbek delegate Majidi criticized Russian literature set in Uzbekistan, which consisted almost exclusively of ethnographic sketches. This literature, he complained, reproduced the stereotype of the Sarts, Central Asian city dwellers, 'who love above all to sit in a tea-house and drink green tea.'" Kathryn Douglas Schild, *Between Moscow and Baku: National Literatures at the 1934 Congress of Soviet Writers* (PhD diss., University of California, Berkeley, 2010), 47.
146. RGALI, f. 631, op. 1, d. 12, l. 61–2. Régine Robin is one of very few scholars to critically engage with the way the national question was conceived at the Congress. She posits that an interest in "the other" "made it possible to organize a truly pan-national Congress in 1934, one that attested both to the cultural diversity of the Soviet Union and to the constitution of a Soviet culture"; see Régine Robin, *Socialist Realism: An Impossible Aesthetic* (Stanford University Press, 1992), 32.
147. Evgeny Dobrenko, *Political Economy of Socialist Realism* (Yale University Press, 2007), 6.
148. The emancipatory policies of indigenization of the early 1920s continued into the 1930s, though they were primarily implemented in the newly established union republics and were not as heavily publicized.
149. See Isabelle Kaplan, "Comrades in Arts: The Soviet Dekada of National Art and the Friendship of Peoples," *RUDN Journal of Russian History* 19, no. 1 (2020): 78–94.
150. Peter Blitstein, "Cultural Diversity and the Interwar Conjuncture: Soviet Nationality Policy in Its Comparative Context," *Slavic Review* 65, no. 2 (2006): 291.
151. Osip Mandel'shtam, *Puteshestvie v Armeniiu*, in *Sobranie sochinenii v chetyrekh tomakh. Tom 3. Stikhi i proza, 1930–1937* (Art-Bizness Tsentr, 1994), 184.
152. Martin, *The Affirmative Action Empire*, 432.
153. David Brandenberger, "Global and Transnational in Form, Soviet in Content: The Changing Semantics of Internationalism in Official Soviet Discourse, 1917–1991," *The Russian Review* 80 (2021): 569.
154. Iu. Pavlov [Georgii Frantsev], "Kosmopolitizm—ideologicheskoe oruzhie amerikanskoi reaktsii," *Pravda* (April 7, 1949): 3.
155. Joseph Stalin, "Speech at a Conference of the Foremost Collective Farmers of Tajikistan and Turkmenistan," in *Works*, vol. 14, *July 1934–March 1939* (Red Star Press, 1978), 124–25.
156. This instance of discursive manipulation is reflective of Stalin's political thinking in general, which was marked by *retroactive* and *retrospective* rhetorical modes. As Erik van Ree argues, Stalin's political thought was "first, a justification after the deed instead of a source of inspiration for the deed; and, second, as a justification it was often even fundamentally at odds with reality, ideally deforming rather than reflecting it." See Erik van Ree, *The Political Thought of Joseph Stalin: A Study in Twentieth-Century Revolutionary Patriotism* (Routledge, 2002), 3.
157. [Editorial], "RSFSR," *Pravda* (February 1, 1936): 1.
158. Most representatives of the Soviet historical avant-garde who remained in Russia in the late 1930s and throughout the 1940s met with tragedy. Vladimir Maiakovsky committed suicide in 1930.

1. SOCIALIST MATTER   275

Kazimir Malevich died from cancer in 1935, and El Lissitzky from tuberculosis in 1941. Sergei Tretiakov, for whom the East was an important locus of socialist revolution, and Aleksei Gan were prosecuted in 1937 and 1942 respectively. Osip Brik, Aleksei Kruchenykh, and Vladimir Tatlin, the three most prominent avant-garde representatives who survived the Stalinist repressions, lived on the margins of Soviet cultural life. The OBERIU (Union of Real Art) circle, which employed the futurist-dadaist model, was founded in 1928 and had already ceased to exist by the early 1930s. Its prominent representatives, such as Daniil Kharms, Alexander Vvedensky, and Nikolay Zabolotsky, were repressed between 1938 and 1941, while Konstantin Vaginov died from tuberculosis in 1934.

159. My argument is focused on the transformation experienced by the writers and artists of the left avant-garde. Of course, not all late modernist texts and visual artifacts were thematically connected to the eastward turn. Notable examples include those produced by Mikhail Zoshchenko and Anna Akhmatova, who were evacuated during the war to Alma-Ata and Tashkent, respectively. Both were targets of the 1946 attacks that launched the anti-cosmopolitan campaign. However, Akhmatova's *Poem Without a Hero* (Poema bez geroia), a great revision of the (imperial) Petersburg poetic tradition, was written in Uzbekistan and its latter sections explicitly thematize the geographical breadth of Soviet territory.

1. SOCIALIST MATTER: VIKTOR SHKLOVSKY

1. Viktor Shklovsky, *A Sentimental Journey: Memoirs, 1917–1922* (Cornell University Press, 1970), 169.
2. As Evgenii Toddes has convincingly shown, both accommodation and interiorization shaped Boris Eikhenbaum's texts from the 1930s. Evgenii Toddes, "B. M. Eikhenbaum v 30-50-e gody," in *Tynianovskii sbornik: Deviatye Tynianovskie chteniia* (OGI, 2002), 563–691.
3. Viktor Shklovsky, *Theory of Prose*, trans. Benjamin Sher (Dalkey Archive Press, 2009), 12.
4. Shklovsky, *Theory of Prose*, 13.
5. Viktor Shklovsky, *Bowstring: On the Dissimilarity of the Similar* (Dalkey Archive Press, 2011), 282–83, modified translation.
6. Viktor Shklovsky, "Ullya, Ullya, Martians," *Knight's Move*, trans. Richard Sheldon (Dalkey Archive Press, 2011), 22.
7. According to Aage Hansen-Löve's classic periodization, this was the third and final stage of development of the formalist method. Aage Hansen-Löve, *Russkii Formalizm: Metodologicheskaia rekonstruktsiia razvitiia na osnove printsipa ostraneniia* (Iazyki russkoi kul'tury, 2001), 357–410.
8. Shklovsky's texts from the 1930s and early 1940s are largely ignored in the scholarship on formalism. Major monographs by Victor Erlich and Peter Steiner barely reference them; see Victor Erlich, *Russian Formalism: History and Doctrine*, 3rd ed. (Yale University Press, 1981); Peter Steiner, *Russian Formalism: A Metapoetics* (Cornell University Press, 1984). Aage Hansen-Löve, in his influential monograph, consciously leaves out Shklovsky's post-1930s texts; see Hansen-Löve, *Russkii Formalizm*, 10. Among the rare exceptions are articles by Jan Levchenko, Anne Dwyer, and Anja Tippner; see Jan Levchenko, "Poslevkusie formalizma. Proliferatsiia teorii v tekstakh Viktora Shklovskogo 1930-kh godov," *Novoe Literaturnoe Obozrenie* 128, no. 4 (2014): 125–43; Anne Dwyer, "Standstill as Extinction: Viktor Shklovsky's Poetics and Politics of Movement in the 1920s and 1930s," *PMLA* 131, no. 2 (2016): 269–88; and Anja Tippner, "Viktor Shklovskii's *Marko Polo—Razvedchik*: Medieval History vs. Geopoetic Representation of Imperial Space," *Detskie chteniia* 6, no. 2 (2014): 102–11.
9. Viktor Shklovskii, *Gornaia Gruziia: Pshaviia. Khevsuretiia. Mukheviia* (Molodaia gvardiia, 1930), 39, 41.
10. Shklovskii, *Gornaia Gruziia*, 70.
11. Shklovskii, *Gornaia Gruziia*, 54.

12. Roman Iakobson, *Teksty, Dokumenty, Issledovaniia* (RGGI, 1999), 122.
13. Quoted in Iakobson, *Teksty, Dokumenty, Issledovaniia*, 124–25.
14. Viktor Shklovskii, "Pamiatnik nauchnoi oshibke," *Literaturnaia gazeta* (January 27, 1930): 1.
15. Shklovskii, "Pamiatnik nauchnoi oshibke," 1.
16. Levchenko, "Poslevkusie formalizma," 127–28.
17. Viktor Shklovsky, *Third Factory* (Dalkey Archive Press, 2002), 31, modified translation.
18. Shklovsky, *Theory of Prose*, 120.
19. Shklovskii, "Pamiatnik nauchnoi oshibke," 1.
20. Shklovskii, "Pamiatnik nauchnoi oshibke," 1, my emphasis.
21. Shklovskii, "Pamiatnik nauchnoi oshibke," 1.
22. In fact, in its second redaction, each section of "Monument to a Scholarly Error" is preceded by a lengthy quotation from an article by Tynianov and Jakobson that was published in the very last issue of *Novyi LEF* and revisited key Formalist stances. Their influence is certainly visible in Shklovsky's "repentance." See Viktor Shklovsky, "Pamiatnik nauchnoi oshibke [vtoraia redaktsiia]," *Novoe Literaturnoe Obozrenie* 44, no. 4 (2000): 154–58; Iurii Tynianov and Roman Jakobson, "Problemy izucheniia literatury i iazyka," *Novyi LEF*, no. 12 (1928): 35–37.
23. Aleksandr Galushkin, "[Razgovory s Viktorom Shklovskim]," *Novoe Literaturnoe Obozrenie* 131, no. 1 (2015): 232.
24. Mark Gel'fand, "Deklaratsiia tsaria Midasa, ili chto sluchilos' s Viktorom Shklovskim," *Literaturnaia gazeta* (March 13, 1930): 2. A similar assessment was given by Georgii Gorbachev, "My eshche ne nachinali drat'sia," *Zvezda*, no. 5 (1930): 124–25.
25. RGALI, f. 562, op. 1, d. 485, l. 19.
26. Viktor Shklovskii, *Za 60 let: Raboty o kino* (Iskusstvo, 1985), 115.
27. Gilles Deleuze, *The Fold. Leibniz and the Baroque*, trans. Tom Conley (University of Minnesota Press, 1993), 227.
28. Aleksandr Galushkin, "'Nastupaet nepreryvnoe iskusstvo . . .' V. B. Shklovskii o sud'be russkogo avangarda nachala 1930-kh," *De Visu*, no. 11 (1993): 25.
29. Heinrich Wölfflin, *Renaissance and Baroque*, trans. Kathrin Simon (Cornell University Press, 1966), 39.
30. RGALI, f. 674, op. 2, d. 11, l. 67.
31. Viktor Shklovsky, *A Hunt for Optimism*, trans. Shushan Avagyan (Dalkey Archive Press, 2012), 128.
32. RGALI, f. 562, op. 2, d. 87, l. 35.
33. Boris Ol'khovyi, "O prostote i poniatnosti," *Literaturnaia gazeta* (March 31, 1930): 2.
34. Maxim Gor'kii, "O iazyke," *Pravda* (March 18, 1934): 2; and in *Literaturnaia gazeta* (March 18, 1934): 1.
35. Gor'kii, "O iazyke," 1.
36. Viktor Shklovskii, "O liudiakh, kotorye idut po odnoi i toi zhe doroge i ob etom ne znaiut. Konets barokko," *Literaturnaia gazeta* (July 17, 1932): 4.
37. Viktor Shklovskii, "Prostota—zakonomernost'," *Literaturnaia gazeta* (June 5, 1933): 2.
38. RGALI, f. 562, op. 1, d. 50, l. 4.
39. Viktor Shklovskii, *Podenshchina* (Izdatel'stvo pisatelei v Leningrade, 1930), 186–92.
40. Viktor Shklovskii, "O kul'ture rechi," RGALI, f. 562, op. 1, d. 128, ll. 5–9.
41. RGALI, f. 562, op. 1, d. 128, l. 5.
42. RGALI, f. 562, op. 1, d. 128, l. 6.
43. RGALI, f. 562, op. 1, d. 128, l. 6.
44. RGALI, f. 562, op. 1, d. 128, l. 7.
45. Anonymous [allegedly written by David Zaslavskii and edited by Stalin], "Sumbur vmesto muzyki," *Pravda* (January 28, 1936): 3.
46. "Sumbur vmesto muzyki," 3.
47. Maksim Gor'kii, "O formalizme," *Literaturnaia gazeta* (March 27, 1936): 2.

1. SOCIALIST MATTER

48. Gor'kii, "O formalizme," 2.
49. Gor'kii, "O formalizme," 2.
50. Georg Lukács, *The Meaning of Contemporary Realism*, trans. John and Necke Mander (Merlin Press, 1963), 19.
51. Lukács, *Contemporary Realism*, 19.
52. Lukács, *Contemporary Realism*, 46.
53. Shklovsky, *Sentimental Journey*, 232.
54. Hansen-Löve, *Russkii Formalizm*, 181.
55. Shklovsky, *Theory of Prose*, 190.
56. During his speech at the First Soviet Writers' Congress, Gorky highlights that writers should work on developing their "cognitive ability" (poznavatel'nuiu sposobnost'). Maksim Gor'kii, "Za druzhnuiu tvorcheskuiu sredu," *Literaturnaia gazeta* (August 23, 1934): 3.
57. Published in *Literaturnyi Leningrad*, no. 20 (1936): 3. The original typescript is in Shklovsky's archive: RGALI, f. 562, op. 2, d. 87, ll. 33–39.
58. RGALI, f. 562, op. 2, d. 87, ll. 33–34.
59. RGALI, f. 562, op. 2, d. 87, l. 34.
60. RGALI, f. 562, op. 2, d. 87, l. 38.
61. RGALI, f. 562, op. 2, d. 87, l. 34.
62. Fredric Jameson, *The Prison-House of Language: A Critical Account of Structuralism and Russian Formalism* (Princeton University Press, 1975).
63. Shklovskii, *Podenshchina*, 7–8.
64. Elizabeth Astrid Papazian, *Manufacturing Truth: The Documentary Moment in Early Soviet Culture* (Northern Illinois University Press, 2009).
65. Nikolai Chuzhak, "Ob etoi knige i ob nas (Predislovie)," in *Literatura fakta: Pervyi sbornik materialov rabotnikov LEFa* (Federatsiia, 1929), 3.
66. Viktor Shklovsky, "Technique of Writing Craft," in *Viktor Shklovsky: A Reader*, ed. and trans. Alexandra Berlina (Bloomsbury Academic, 2017), 178.
67. Andrei Belyi et al., *Kak my pishem* (Kniga, 1930).
68. Viktor Shklovsky, "The Way I Write," in *Viktor Shklovsky: A Reader*, 210.
69. Viktor Shklovskii, "Kak ia pishu," in Viktor Shklovskii, *Gamburgskii schet: Stat'i, vospominaniia, esse* (Sovetskii pisatel', 1990), 424.
70. *Pervyi vsesoiuznyi s"ezd sovetskikh pisatelei 1934: Stenograficheskii otchet* (Khudozhestvennaia literatura, 1990), 607.
71. Shklovskii, "Kak ia pishu," 424–25.
72. RGALI, f. 562, op. 1, d. 216, l. 35.
73. Matthew J. Payne, *Stalin's Railroad: Turksib and the Building of Socialism* (University of Pittsburgh Press, 2001), 154.
74. Karin Lesnik-Oberstein, *Children's Literature: Criticism and the Fictional Child* (Clarendon Press, 1994).
75. Shklovskii, *Podenshchina*, 205–19.
76. Shklovskii, *Podenshchina*, 205.
77. Shklovskii, *Podenshchina*, 206.
78. Shklovskii, *Podenshchina*, 206.
79. Shklovskii, *Podenshchina*, 207.
80. *Pervyi vsesoiuznyi s"ezd sovetskikh pisatelei 1934*, 31.
81. Semyon Dimanshtein, "Rekonstruktivnyi period i rabota sredi natsional'nostei SSSR," *Revoliutsiia i natsional'nosti*, no. 1 (1930): 14.
82. Matthew Payne, "Viktor Turin's *Turksib* (1929) and Soviet Orientalism," *Historical Journal of Film, Radio and Television History* 21, no. 1 (2001): 57.

1. SOCIALIST MATTER

83. Karl Marx, *Capital: A Critique of Political Economy*, ed. Ernest Mandel, trans. Ben Fowkes and David Fernbach (Penguin Books, 1990), 1:163.
84. Shklovsky, *Podenshchina*, 19.
85. Shklovsky, *Podenshchina*, 19.
86. Maksim Gor'kii, "[Zametki o detskikh knigakh i igrakh]," in *Sobranie sochinenii v 30 tomakh. Tom 27* (GIKhL, 1953), 518.
87. Shklovskii, "O liudiakh, kotorye idut po odnoi i toi zhe doroge i ob etom ne znaiut," 4.
88. Shklovsky, *Theory of Prose*, 6.
89. RGALI, f. 562, op. 1, d. 216, l. 15.
90. Shklovskii, *Turksib*, 11.
91. This stance fully aligned with the official understanding of the economic rationale of the railway. See, for instance, Turar Ryskylov, "Turkestano-Sibirskaia zheleznaia doroga i ee znachenie dlia narodnogo khoziaistva SSSR," in *Turkestano-Sibirskaia Magistral'* (SNK RSFSR, 1929), 5–23.
92. Jameson, "Modernism and Imperialism," 50–51.
93. Karl Marx, *Grundrisse: Foundations of the Critique of Political Economy* (Penguin Books, 1993), 524.
94. Wolfgang Schivelbusch, *The Railway Journey: The Industrialization of Time and Space in the 19th Century* (The University of California Press, 1986), 35.
95. Viktor Shklovskii, *Turksib* (Gosudarstvennoe izdatel'stvo, 1930), 32.
96. Shklovskii, *Podenshchina*, 30.
97. Shklovskii, *Podenshchina*, 36–37.
98. Shklovskii, *Turksib*, 12.
99. Shklovskii, *Turksib*, 30.
100. Shklovskii, *Turksib*, 19.
101. H. G. Wells, *Anticipations: Of the Reaction of Mechanical and Scientific Progress Upon Human Life and Thought* (Chapman and Hall, 1901), ii.
102. Shklovskii, *Turksib*, 30.
103. Shklovskii, *Turksib*, 14.
104. See Anne Dwyer's very apt analysis of the cover: "Starting from the lower left corner and moving up to the center, a steam train charges ahead. On the top, occupying a narrow strip and sloping downward, a caravan of camels traverses a background of sand dunes—an iconic representation of nomadic life. The two lines are destined to meet somewhere to the right of the cover; the curious will have to open the book to discover what this collision will entail." Dwyer, "Standstill as Extinction," 278. However, I would like to dispute the claim that the caravan and the locomotive are "destined to meet somewhere to the right of the cover." Their trajectories in fact will not allow them to collide—the caravan is directed slightly toward the viewer while the locomotive's angle is more dramatic, almost aimed at the viewer. The train of modernity is rushing onward and the herd of animals cannot draw near it.
105. Viktor Shklovskii, *Zhili-byli: Vospominaniia. Memuarnye zapisi* (Sovetskii pisatel', 1966), 126.
106. Robert Tucker, *Stalin in Power: The Revolution from Above, 1928–1941* (Norton, 1990), 607–609.
107. Ernst Bloch, *Heritage of Our Times*, trans. Neville and Stephen Plaice (Polity, 1991), 97.
108. Karl Marx, *Capital: A Critique of Political Economy*, ed. Ernest Mandel, trans. Ben Fowkes and David Fernback (Penguin Books, 1991), 3:1038.
109. Yuri Slezkine, "Primitive Communism and the Other Way Around," in *Socialist Realism Without Shores*, ed. Lahusen and Dobrenko, 329.
110. As Alfrid Bustanov notes, the general attitude toward nomadic people was always shaped by the historical studies of the Golden Horde civilization: "The Golden Horde had been viewed as a union of barbarian bands with rulers that despotically suppressed settled peoples such as the medieval Christian Russians." Bustanov, *Soviet Orientalism and the Creation of Central Asian Nations* (Routledge, 2016), 39.

1. SOCIALIST MATTER   279

111. Martha Brill Olcott, *The Kazakhs*, rev. ed. (Stanford University Press, 1994), 183.
112. Francine Hirsch, *Empire of Nations: Ethnographic Knowledge and the Making of the Soviet Union* (Cornell University Press, 2005), 7.
113. Adalis, "Osedaiut kochevniki," *Nashi dostizheniia*, no. 9 (1931): 50.
114. Paperny, *Architecture in the Age of Stalin: Culture Two*, 36.
115. Viktor Shklovskii, *Marko Polo, razvedchik* (OGIZ, 1931), 5.
116. Shklovskii, *Marko Polo, razvedchik*, 12.
117. Shklovskii, *Marko Polo, razvedchik*, 38.
118. Tippner, "Viktor Shklovskii's *Marko Polo—Razvedchik*," 107.
119. Shklovskii, *Marko Polo, razvedchik*, 29–30.
120. It was again revised in 1969: Viktor Shklovskii, *Zemli razvedchik: Istoricheskaia povest'* (Molodaiia gvardiia, 1969).
121. Viktor Shklovskii, *Marko Polo* (Zhurnal'no-gazetnoe ob"edinenie, 1936), 290.
122. Shklovskii, *Marko Polo*, 59–60.
123. Dwyer, "Standstill as Extinction," 284.
124. Shklovskii, *Turksib*, 7.
125. Shklovsky, *Third Factory*, 78.
126. Andrei Platonov and Viktor Shklovskii, "Peschanaia uchitel'nitsa. Libretto," Gosfil'mofond, f. 2, op. 1, d. 7, ll. 133–62. The final version of the script was written by Mariia Smirnova.
127. Andrei Platonov, "Peschanaia uchitel'nitsa," in *Sobranie. Usomnivshiisia Makar: Rasskazy 1920-kh godov. Stikhotvoreniia* (Vremia, 2011), 87.
128. Viktor Shklovsky, *Zoo, or Letters Not about Love* (Dalkey Archive Press, 2001), 31, modified translation.
129. Shklovskii, *Marko Polo, razvedchik*, 4.
130. Iurii Tynianov, "Literaturnyi fakt," in *Poetika. Istoriia literatury. Kino*, 257.
131. Iurii Tynianov, "O literaturnoi evoliutsii," in *Poetika. Istoriia literatury. Kino*, 270.
132. Iurii Tynianov, "Tiutchev i Geine," in *Poetika. Istoriia literatury. Kino*, 387.
133. Pavel Medvedev and Mikhail Bakhtin, *The Formal Method in Literary Scholarship: A Critical Introduction to Sociological Poetics* (The Johns Hopkins University Press, 1978), 37, 171.
134. Stephen Lovell, "Tynianov as Sociologist of Literature," *The Slavonic and East European Review* 79, no. 3 (2001): 419.
135. Viktor Shklovskii, "Retsenziia na knigu Georgiia Lukacha 'Istoricheskii roman'," RGALI, f. 562, op. 1, d. 126, ll. 1–8. As Galin Tihanov puts it, Shklovsky's "unreserved ahistoricism" was replaced with "a demonstrative immersion in history in the 1930s." Galin Tihanov, "Viktor Shklovskii and Georg Lukács in the 1930s," *The Slavonic and East European Review* 78, no. 1 (2000): 49.
136. Viktor Shklovskii, "O literature Tadzhikistana (Po materialam poezdki v Tadzhikistan. Otchet) 27–28 maiia 1934," RGALI, f. 562, op. 1, d. 92, ll. 1–39.
137. Shklovskii, "O literature Tadzhikistana," l. 5.
138. Shklovskii, "O literature Tadzhikistana," l. 19.
139. Shklovskii, "O literature Tadzhikistana," 20.
140. Jessica Merrill, "Fol'kloristicheskie osnovaniia knigi Viktora Shklovskogo 'O teorii prozy'," *Novoe Literaturnoe Obozrenie* 133, no. 3 (2015): 198.
141. Shklovskii, *Dnevnik*, 154.
142. Il'ia Kalinin, "Viktor Shklovskii, ili prevrashchenie literaturnogo priema v literaturnyi fakt," *Zvezda*, no. 7 (2014): 198–221.
143. Shklovskii, *Dnevnik*, 120.
144. Shklovskii, *Dnevnik*, 120.
145. Shklovskii, *Dnevnik*, 121.
146. Shklovskii, *Dnevnik*, 120.

147. Kazimir Malevich, "From Cubism and Futurism to Suprematism: The New Painterly Realism," in *Russian Art of the Avant-Garde Theory and Criticism, 1902–1934*, ed. John Bowlt (The Viking Press, 1976), 119.
148. One of Shklovsky's earliest surviving manuscripts, produced at some point between 1915 and 1918 for the Reserve Armored Car Division of the Socialist Revolutionary Party, is a twelve-page manual on how to exploit different (armored) car models. RGALI, f. 562, op. 1, d. 809, ll. 1–12.
149. *Pervyi vsesoiuznyi s"ezd sovetskikh pisatelei 1934*, 155.
150. RGALI, f. 562, op. 1, d. 380, l. 1.
151. RGALI, f. 562, op. 1, d. 380, l. 2.
152. Shklovsky, *Theory of Prose*, 5.
153. RGALI, f. 562, op. 1, d. 380, l. 2.
154. RGALI, f. 562, op. 1, d. 380, l. 2.

2. SOCIALIST VISION: ALEKSANDR RODCHENKO AND VARVARA STEPANOVA

1. Aleksandr Rodchenko, *Stat'i. Vospominaniia. Avtobiograficheskie zapiski. Pis'ma* (Sovetskii khudozhnik, 1982), 95–96.
2. Christina Kiaer, *Imagine No Possessions: The Socialist Objects of Russian Constructivism* (MIT Press, 2005), 1.
3. Joseph Stalin, "Light from the East," in *Works*, vol. 4 (OGIZ, 1947), 181. See for comparison Stalin's other articles where "the East" occupies a central role but now as an East in relation to Western Russia: "Don't forget the East" (1918) and "Our Tasks in the East" (1919).
4. Stalin, "Light from the East," 185.
5. Stalin, "Light from the East," 186.
6. Francine Hirsch, "Getting to Know 'The Peoples of the USSR': Ethnographic Exhibits as Soviet Virtual Tourism, 1923–1934," *Slavic Review* 62, no. 4 (2000): 683–709.
7. Mikhail Karasik highlights "historical paradox that the formal methods and practices of Constructivist art were not only deemed suitable but were in demand for official books." Mikhail Karasik and Manfred Heiting, eds., *The Soviet Photobook, 1920–1941* (Steidl, 2015), 11.
8. Dmitrii Ushakov, *Tolkovyi slovar' russkogo iazyka* (OGIZ, 1935), 1117.
9. Christina Lodder, *Russian Constructivism* (Yale University Press, 1983), 1.
10. Alexander Lavrentiev, ed., *Alexander Rodchenko. Experiments for the Future: Diaries, Essays, Letters and Other Writings* (MoMA, 2005), 111. From 1922 to 1930, as a professor at VKhUTEMAS (Higher Art and Technical Studios), Rodchenko taught the design of transformable, multifunctional everyday utensils in the metalworking department. Julia Vaingurt asserts that the constructivists' narrow principle of utility was gradually replaced with a more complex vision reminiscent of the Greek *techne*, as a "contemplation of a particular instance of 'coming-to-be,'" or as a "mode of cognition through making." Julia Vaingurt, *Wonderlands of the Avant-Garde: Technology and the Arts in Russia of the 1920s* (Northwestern University Press, 2013), 5, 6.
11. Lodder, *Russian Constructivism*, 180.
12. Selim Khan-Magomedov, *Rodchenko: The Complete Work*, ed. Vieri Quilici (MIT Press, 1987), 115.
13. Shklovskii, *Gamburgskii schet*, 100.
14. Aleksei Gan, *Constructivism* (Tenov Books, 2014), 62.
15. Gan, *Constructivism*, 62. Maria Gough's analysis suggests that the constructivist notion of *faktura* underwent a transformation from an anti-authorial "materiological determination" to a more conventional functionalism. Material ceased to determine form and evolved into a practical entity:

"Faktura as a principle of materiological determination (form follows material) was replaced by a nascent functionalism (form follows function)." Maria Gough, "Faktura: The Making of the Russian Avant-Garde," *RES* 36 (1999): 58. Emma Widdis, in turn, convincingly links the notion of *faktura* with *ostranenie* if the latter is understood as a process of "rediscovering the sensory plenitude of experience, through the body." See Emma Widdis, *Socialist Senses: Film, Feeling, and the Soviet Subject, 1917–1940* (Indiana University Press, 2017), 29.

16. Varvara Stepanova, "On Facture," in Varvara Stepanova, *The Complete Work*, ed. and trans. John E. Bowlt (MIT Press, 1988), 176.
17. Varvara Stepanova, *Chelovek ne mozhet zhit' bez chuda* (Grant, 1994), 77.
18. Stepanova, *Chelovek ne mozhet zhit' bez chuda*, 77. Concurrently with Stepanova, Rodchenko elaborates the distinction between *depiction* and *painterliness* in his 1921 text "Line," where he argues that the appearance of an "abstracted" element in painting was crucial for the development of art: "'painterliness,' the texture of the surface, various open spaces, varnish, underpainting, and so on; in other words, what appeared was a painterly approach to the picture. Since then, the picture has ceased being itself, it became a painting or a thing." Aleksandr Rodchenko, "Line," in Lavrentiev, *Experiments for the Future*, 111.
19. Varvara Stepanova, "O vystavlennykh grafikakh," in *Chelovek ne mozhet zhit' bez chuda*, 41.
20. Aleksandr Lavrentiev, *Varvara Stepanova* (Russkii avangard, 2009), 48, 50.
21. Stepanova, "On Facture," 176.
22. In her 1921 report "On Constructivism," Stepanova argues that constructivism is not an artistic movement but a form of ideology. "Intellectual production," superseding contemplative art, was supposed to utilize its experience in formal experimentation (non-figurative art and abstract constructions in three dimensions) with real material production infused with Marxist ideological standpoints. See Varvara Stepanova, "On Constructivism," in Stepanova, *The Complete Work*, 173. This contrasts with Maria Gough's argument that the Constructivists' preoccupation with form is never singular: "it is never a preoccupation with *making* at the expense of the ideological meaning of that which is made." Thus, impersonal form and ideological radicalism are brought together. See Maria Gough, *The Artist as Producer: Russian Constructivism in Revolution* (University of California Press, 2005), 14.
23. Stepanova, "On Constructivism," 174.
24. Lodder sees the failure of Constructivism to transform the human habitat in a radical manner (for their designed objects did not enter mass production due to material scarcities) as a main factor forcing them to reorient their creative impulse toward smaller-scale typographical, poster, and exhibition design tasks. Lodder does note, however, that "the term 'constructivist graphic design' seems to be somewhat contradictory." Lodder, *Russian Constructivism*, 181, 204. In a more recent article, Lodder directly links constructivist engineering with sociopolitical engineering: "artistic construction was a metaphor for, and indeed a stimulus to, reconstruction in the broadest possible sense." Christina Lodder, "Art into Life: International Constructivism in Central and Eastern Europe," in *Central European Avant Gardes: Exchange and Transformation 1910–1930*, ed. Timothy Benson (MIT Press, 2002), 173. Alexander Lavrentiev also claims that Rodchenko and Stepanova's work in the sphere of book design, which started as early as 1923, derived from the constructivist urge to "enter life." Aleksandr Lavrentiev, "Vstuplenie," in Aleksandr Rodchenko and Varvara Stepanova, *Al'bom* (Kniga, 1989), 5.
25. Benjamin Buchloh, "From Faktura to Factography," *October* 30 (1984): 99.
26. Varvara Stepanova, "Photomontage," in Stepanova, *The Complete Work*, 178.
27. Stepanova, "Photomontage," 178.
28. Quoted in L. Volkov-Lannit, *Aleksandr Rodchenko risuet, fotografiruet, sporit* (Iskusstvo, 1968), 55.
29. Stepanova, "Photomontage," 178.
30. Stepanova, "Photomontage," 178.
31. Stepanova, "Photomontage," 178.
32. Lodder, *Russian Constructivism*, 181.

33. Buchloh, "From Faktura to Factography," 103.
34. Aleksandr Rodchenko, "The Paths of Contemporary Photography," in Lavrientiev, *Experiments for the Future*, 212, modified translation. Bottom-up and top-down perspectives are also referred to as the worm's-eye and bird's-eye views in the critical literature.
35. The Russian word *rakurs* derives from French *raccourci*, meaning shortcut. The modern pronunciation of *rákurs*, with the stress on the first syllable, differs from *rakúrs*, the one used during Rodchenko's time.
36. Sergei Morozov, *Sovetskaia khudozhestvennaia fotografiia* (Iskusstvo, 1958), 60.
37. Rodchenko, "The Paths of Contemporary Photography," 211.
38. "*Lef* i kino. Stenogramma soveshchaniia," *Novyi Lef*, nos. 11–12 (1927): 67.
39. Aleksandr Rodchenko, "*LEF* Notebook," in Lavrientiev, *Experiments for the Future*, 199.
40. Boris Kushner, "Otkrytoe pis'mo," *Novyi Lef*, no. 8 (1928): 38–40.
41. Rodchenko, "The Paths of Contemporary Photography," 211.
42. Rodchenko, "The Paths of Contemporary Photography," 208.
43. Osip Brik, "Ot kartiny k foto," *Novyi Lef*, no. 3 (1928): 31.
44. Brik, "Ot kartiny k foto," 33.
45. Alexander Rodchenko, "Against the Synthetic Portrait for the Snapshot (1928)," in *Photography in the Modern Era: European Documents and Critical Writings, 1913–1940*, ed. Christopher Philips (MoMA, 1989), 242, modified translation.
46. Rodchenko, "Against the Synthetic Portrait for the Snapshot (1928)," 240–41, modified translation.
47. "Deklaratsiia ob"edineniia 'Oktiabr'," *Pravda* (June 3, 1928): 7.
48. *Bor'ba za klassovye proletarskie pozitsii na fronte prostranstvennykh iskusstv* (IZOGIZ, 1931), 9.
49. *Bor'ba za klassovye*, 9.
50. Pavel Novitskii, ed., *Izofront: Klassovaia bor'ba na fronte prostranstvennykh iskusstv. Sbornik statei ob"edineniia "Oktiabr'"* (OGIZ–IZOGIZ, 1931), 135–36.
51. Novitskii, *Izofront*, 138.
52. Novitskii, *Izofront*, 138.
53. Novitskii, *Izofront*, 143.
54. Novitskii, *Izofront*, 143.
55. Novitskii, *Izofront*, 147.
56. Lazar' Rempel', "O natsional'nom iskusstve," *Brigada khudozhnikov*, no. 7 (1931): 2.
57. Ivan Matsa [János Mácza], "Vstupitel'noe slovo," in *Za bol'shevistskii plakat* (OGIZ–IZOGIZ, 1932), 16.
58. Matsa, "Vstupitel'noe slovo," 17.
59. Matsa, "Vstupitel'noe slovo," 17.
60. [Editorial], "Za konsolidatsiiu sil. Za sozdanie proletarskoi fotografii. Deklaratsiia initsiativnoi gruppy ROPF," *Proletarskoe foto*, no. 2 (1931): 14–15.
61. [Editorial], "Za konsolidatsiiu sil," 15.
62. Leonid Mezhericher, "Segodniashnii den' sovetskogo fotoreportazha," *Proletarskoe foto*, no. 1 (1931): 10.
63. Semyon Fridliand, "Zametki o tvorcheskoi praktike: k publikuemym rabotam gruppy ROPF," *Proletarskoe foto*, no. 2 (1931): 16.
64. [Unsigned], "Na pervom etape tvorcheskoi diskussii," *Proletarskoe foto*, no. 1 (1932): 12.
65. [Editorial board of] "Pionerskaia pravda," "K svedeniiu svobodnykh khudozhnikov," *Proletarskoe foto*, no. 1 (1932): 13.
66. Il'ia Sosfenov, "Dva fronta. Zametki ob osnovakh tvorcheskikh ustanovok," *Proletarskoe foto*, no. 5 (1932): 16.
67. Boris Ignatovich et al., "Otkrytoe pis'mo gruppy 'Oktiabr'' v redaktsiiu 'Proletarskoe foto'," *Proletarskoe foto*, no. 2 (1932): 3.
68. Boris Ignatovich, "Po tvorcheskim gruppirovkam," *Proletarskoe foto*, no. 3 (1932): 27.

69. A few years later, the problem of linear perspective was addressed in a 1937 issue of *Soviet Photo*, immediately after the first furious wave of anti-formalist attacks. It was the ultimate burial stone for *rakurs*. Sergei Morozov identifies foreshortening as an artificial "cerebral" point of view that is not inherent to the "natural" direction of human vision. Its danger lies in the fact that if it is not justified by a "thematic task," or content, it becomes an end in itself—a formalist trick. Sergei Morozov, "Lineinoe postroenie kadra," *Sovetskoe foto*, no. 9 (1937): 7.
70. Lavrentiev, *Rakursy Rodchenko*, 169. Izogiz, which was responsible for several high-profile publications such as *USSR in Construction*, underwent a drastic restructuring in 1932 after being accused of producing anti-Soviet propaganda.
71. Rodchenko, "Reconstructing the Artist," in Lavrentiev, *Experiments for the Future*, 298.
72. Rodchenko, "Reconstructing the Artist," 299.
73. Rodchenko, "Reconstructing the Artist," 209–304.
74. Rodchenko, "Reconstructing the Artist," 304.
75. Rodchenko, "Reconstructing the Artist," 298.
76. Rodchenko, "Reconstructing the Artist," 298.
77. *USSR in Construction*, no. 12 (1933). Belomor plays an important role in the history of Soviet culture since its construction prompted the publication of the mammoth volume *The Stalin White Sea-Baltic Canal: History of the Construction Project* in Gorky's *History of the Factory* series in 1934. Edited by Viktor Shklovsky and illustrated with Rodchenko's images, the book was a true collective effort. Gorky argues that the work on the book convinced him that it was an educational experience for fellow-traveler writers who can now ponder "more deeply the meaning of created reality [tvorimaia deistvitel'nost']" T. Dubinskaia-Dzhalilova and A. Chernev (eds.), "Perepiska M. Gor'kogo i I.V. Stalina," *Novoe Literaturnoe Obozrenie* 40, no. 6 (1999): 256.
78. For Khan-Magomedov, constructivism found the utmost expression of its convictions in two domains: architecture and graphic design. The latter, due to its expediency and relatively low-cost efficiency, was even more developed and predominant. Khan-Magomedov, *Konstruktivizm*, 401.
79. Similarly, Leah Dickerman notes that Rodchenko employs both a modernist oblique perspective that calls attention to the disparateness of their different elements while also muting a disjuncture between component parts "through retouching, and through a staggering of scale relationships to follow roughly the rules of perspectival recession." Leah Dickerman, "The Propagandizing of Things," in *Aleksandr Rodchenko*, ed. Magdalena Dabrowski, Leah Dickerman, and Peter Galassi (MoMA, 1998), 93.
80. Lavrentiev, *Rakursy Rodchenko*, 171.
81. L. Kristi, "Zametki o 'SSR na stroike,'" *Sovetskoe foto*, no. 2 (1940): 9.
82. Maks Al'pert, "Sotsializm pereplavliaet cheloveka," *Proletarskoe foto*, nos. 7–8 (1932): 8
83. Leonid Mezhericher, "Veshch' gromadnoi vospitatel'noi sily," *Proletarskoe foto*, nos. 7–8 (1932): 10.
84. Mezhericher, "Veshch' gromadnoi vospitatel'noi sily," 9.
85. B. Zherebtsov, "Montazh fotograficheskoi serii: O serii "Sem'ia Filippovykh," *Proletarskoe foto*, no. 9 (1932): 6.
86. Kristi, "Zametki o 'SSSR na stroike,'" 9.
87. Arkadii Shaikhet and Maks Al'pert, "Kak my snimali Filippovykh," *Proletarskoe foto*, no. 4 (1931): 46.
88. Sergei Tret'iakov, "Ot fotoserii k dlitel'nomu fotonabliudeniiu," *Proletarskoe foto*, no. 4 (1931): 20, 45.
89. Tret'iakov, "Ot fotoserii k dlitel'nomu fotonabliudeniiu," 45.
90. Rodchenko, "Reconstructing the Artist," 298.
91. Aleksandr Rodchenko, "Master i kritika. Nechitannoe vystuplenie," *Sovetskoe foto*, no. 9 (1935): 4.
92. Helena Holzberger, "National in front of the Camera, Soviet Behind It: Central Asia in Press Photography, 1925–1937," *Journal of Modern European History* 16, no. 4 (2018): 506.
93. *USSR in Construction [Fifteen Years of Kazakhstan]*, no. 11 (1935). As Anja Burghardt argues, the journal used non-Russian ethnicities and remote geographies "to show the progress and modernizing

development of the USSR. This modernization allows individuals to become integrated into a Soviet society in which ethnic and cultural differences are declared irrelevant." Anja Burghardt, "Picturing Non-Russian Ethnicities in the Journals *Sovetskoe foto* and *SSSR na stroike* (1920s–1930s)," *Russian Literature* 103–105 (2019): 211.

94. Timothy Nunan, "Soviet Nationalities Policy, *USSR in Construction*, and Soviet Documentary Photography in Comparative Context, 1931–1937," *Ab Imperio* 2 (2010): 71.
95. Several subsequent issues of *USSR in Construction*, designed by Rodchenko and Stepanova, are dedicated to raw materials such as timber (1936) and gold (1937).
96. *USSR in Construction*, no. 11 (1935): 34.
97. *USSR in Construction*, no. 11 (1935): 14.
98. Dobrenko, *Political Economy of Socialist Realism*, xx.
99. Galina Orlova, "'Voochiiu vidim': Fotografiia i sovetskii proekt v epokhu ikh tekhnicheskoi vosproizvodimosti," in Hans Günther and Sabine Hänsgen, eds., *Sovetskaia vlast' i media* (Akademicheskii proekt, 2006), 188.
100. *USSR in Construction*, no. 1 (1930): 3.
101. [Unsigned], "Lenin i fotografiia," *Sovetskoe foto*, no. 2 (1929): 33.
102. B. Zherebtsov, *Tekstovka k foto-snimku* (Biblioteka gazety Fotokor, 1932), 3.
103. Zherebtsov, *Tekstovka k foto-snimku*, 4.
104. *USSR in Construction*, no. 11 (1935): 15. Kuzembaev quickly rose through the official ranks of the Communist party but had to have a mediator (V. Sklepchuk) attached to him, allegedly so that he could improve his Russian language and technical skills.
105. *Proletarskoe foto*, no. 2 (1931): 43. Langman also exhibited his very radical object-free foreground shots into the mid-1930s; see "Kolkhoz Field" in *Sovetskoe foto*, no. 2 (1935): 26, and "Preparation of Soil for Cotton in Pakhta-Arapa" in *Sovetskoe foto*, no. 10 (1935): 10.
106. Boris Malkin, ed., *15 let Kazakhskoi ASSR* (Ogiz-Izogiz, 1936), 28 x 24 cm, print run of 3,000 copies. The work rivaled *Ten Years of Soviet Uzbekistan* in its use of non-standard materials.
107. The same shot of Kuzembaev appeared in *Sovetskoe foto*, no. 10 (1935): 15.
108. Rodchenko, "Reconstructing the Artist," 301.
109. Rodchenko, "Reconstructing the Artist," 301.
110. Eleazar Langman, "Tvorcheskie poiski," *Sovetskoe foto*, nos. 5–6 (1936): 28.
111. Eleazar Langman, "Moi universitet," *Sovetskoe foto*, no. 1 (1936): 26.
112. Langman, "Tvorcheskie poiski," 28.
113. Langman, "Tvorcheskie poiski," 28.
114. Langman, "Tvorcheskie poiski," 28.
115. Sergei Morozov, "Na putiakh k realizmu, k narodnosti," *Sovetskoe foto*, nos. 5–6 (1936): 9.
116. Morozov, "Na putiakh k realizmu, k narodnosti," 4.
117. Morozov, "Na putiakh k realizmu, k narodnosti," 4.
118. Among the techniques employed are intaglio, where the image is incised into a surface and the incised line holds the ink; letterpress, where copies are produced by repeated direct impression of an inked, raised surface against a sheet; and relief, where ink is applied to the original surface of the matrix.
119. M. Tursunkhodzhaev, ed., *10 let Uzbekistana* (Ogiz-Izogiz, 1934 and 1935), 29, 2 x 24.2 cm, print run of 2200 for the 1934 edition and 2000 for the 1935 edition.
120. The works include paintings and drawings by Usto Mumin, Dmitrii Moor, and Nikolai Karakhan and two canvases by Ural Tansykbayev.
121. L. R., "Zamechatel'naia rabota!," *Pravda* (December 21, 1934): 4. The work was also positively reviewed by El-Registan in *Izvestiia* (December 24, 1934): 4.
122. Vladimir Favorskii, "O sinteze iskusstv," in *Literaturno-teoreticheskoe nasledie* (Sovetskii khudozhnik, 1988), 398.
123. Favorskii, "O sinteze iskusstv," 398.

124. Aglaya Glebova, *Aleksandr Rodchenko: Photography in the Time of Stalin* (Yale University Press, 2022), 194.
125. Vladimir Favorskii, "O grafike kak ob osnove knizhnogo iskusstva," in *Literaturno-teoreticheskoe nasledie*, 322.
126. The avant-garde-inspired design finds its culmination on the infographics page, which is the most Constructivist in layout in the entire work. Iva Glisic explores the amalgamation of experimental and traditional techniques in other photobooks by Rodchenko and Stepanova and argues that they "point toward a new understanding of not just the resilience of avant-garde strategies throughout the Stalinist era, but also of the systematic synthesis of a range of different visual traditions undertaken by progressive artists in an effort to fashion a new vocabulary of design." Iva Glisic, "Terror and Dream: The Photobooks of Aleksandr Rodchenko and Varvara Stepanova, 1936–39," *Modernism/modernity* 28, no. 4 (2021): 730.
127. Julia Obertreis, *Imperial Desert Dreams: Cotton Growing and Irrigation in Central Asia, 1860–1991* (V&R unipress, 2017), 60.
128. Rodchenko, "Line," 113.
129. Astrakhan fur, luxurious and delicate yet with an intensified materiality befitting a capitalist paradigm, suddenly became identified with modern Soviet forms of material production. Its production, however, involves a very brutal process requiring the slaughter of a lamb just one to three days old. The harvested fur is exceptionally dense and has silky qualities.
130. Rodchenko and Stepanova, however, use two photographs of cotton and fur for the front and back endpapers of the luxury 1934 edition archived in Multimedia Art Museum, Moscow, MAMM, KPKP–1646/1.
131. Rodchenko, "Line," 113.
132. Aleksandr Rodchenko, "Working with Mayakovsky," in Lavrentiev, *Experiments for the Future*, 101.
133. Varvara Rodchenko, the couple's daughter, identifies two types of montage used by her celebrated parents: visible (a conventional technique in which several images are pasted onto a single plane and mixed with typographic material) and invisible (where the overall quality of a photograph is enhanced by replacing certain elements, such as the sky, with higher-quality ones). The invisible montage, employed here by Rodchenko, should be imperceptible and basically functions as retouching. Varvara Rodchenko, "Momenty tvorchestva," in Rodchenko and Stepanova, *Al'bom*, 141.
134. Leonid Mezhericher, "Tvorcheskie profili: Mnogogrannyi khudozhnik [Abram Shterenberg]," *Sovetskoe foto*, no. 1 (1934): 21.
135. The photograph "In the Garden of Kolkhoz 'Kommuna' of Alta-Aryk District," found on page 130 in *Ten Years of Soviet Uzbekistan*, also appeared as "Apricots in Bloom" in *Sovetskoe foto*, no. 3 (1934): 18. "Artisan Wood Cutter," on page 200 of *Ten Years of Soviet Uzbekistan*, is a version of "Work on Wood," published in *Sovetskoe foto*, no. 5 (1935): 35.
136. I would like to thank Aleksandr Lavrentiev for helping me with the photographs' attribution.
137. The photograph of marching athletes clearly resonates with Rodchenko's "Dynamo Marching Formation" photograph taken in 1935. The same aerial view of a turning formation making a circular shape dominates the composition.
138. Ekaterina Degot', *Russkoe iskusstvo XX veka* (Trilistnik, 2002), 115.
139. P. Krasnov, "A. M. Rodchenko (profili masterov)," *Sovetskoe foto*, no. 7 (1935): 25.
140. Sergei Morozov, *Fotoillustratsiia v gazete* (Goskinoizdat, 1939), 38–9.
141. Sergei Morozov, "Preodolenie ekzotiki," *Sovetskoe foto*, no. 6 (1933): 14.
142. Tansykbayev, whose name is misspelled in the caption, was an Uzbek painter of Kazakh descent. He studied with followers of the Wanderers and quickly came to be the most influential socialist realist artist in the republic.
143. But as Adeeb Khalid notes, "unveiling meant casting off the *paranji* and opening up the face; it did not necessarily mean donning European garb. Most women who unveiled replaced the *paranji* with a shawl or a headscarf." Furthermore, "as the campaign continued, the burden fell on male party

members to liberate 'their' women. The *hujum* became in many ways a site for the exercise of the power of men over women, often channeled through other men." Adeeb Khalid, *Making Uzbekistan: Nation, Empire, and Revolution in the Early USSR* (Cornell University Press, 2015), 355.

144. The blacked-out image is reproduced in David King, *The Commissar Vanishes: The Falsification of Photographs and Art in Stalin's Russia* (New York: Henry Holt, 1997), 133.

145. The copies are held at the Pushkin State Museum of Fine Arts (Pushkinskii muzei, GMII MLK GRP 36) and Multimedia Art Museum, Moscow (MAMM, KP–1646/1).

146. Leah Dickerman, "David King, *The Commissar Vanishes: The Falsification of Photographs and Art in Stalin's Russia*," *Art Bulletin* 80, no. 4 (1998): 756.

147. The two defaced local political leaders shown on the foldout are Akmal Ikramov, the first secretary of the Central Committee of the Communist Party of Uzbekistan from 1929 to 1937, and Faizulla Khodzhaev, the chairman of the Uzbek Council of People's Commissars. There is another defaced foldout on pages 88 and 89 of the 1934 edition of the *Ten Years of Soviet Uzbekistan*. The faces of the following politicians are blacked out: Jānis Rudzutaks, a prominent Latvian Communist revolutionary and a member of the Politburo; Abdulla Karimov, the deputy chairman of the Uzbek Council of People's Commissars; and Jēkabs Peters, a Latvian Communist revolutionary who played a part in the establishment of the Soviet Union and who, together with Felix Dzerzhinsky, was one of the founders and chiefs of the Cheka, the Soviet secret police.

148. Richard Brilliant, *Portraiture* (Reaktion Books, 1991), 7.

149. Aleksandr Rodchenko, "From the Diaries, 1934, 1936–1940," in Lavrentiev, *Experiments for the Future*, 328.

150. Kazimir Malevich, "Letter to Meyerhold," in *Art in Theory: 1900–1990. An Anthology of Changing Ideas*, ed. Charles Harrison and Paul Wood (Blackwell, 1992), 498.

151. Malevich, "Letter to Meyerhold," 498.

152. A. Vol'gemut, "Fotomontazh i fotopanno," *Sovetskoe foto*, no. 7 (1939): 4.

153. Vol'gemut, "Fotomontazh i fotopanno," 4.

154. V. Akhmet'ev and G. Volchek, "Fotografiia v glavnom pavil'one," *Sovetskoe foto*, no. 7 (1939): 9.

155. Buchloh, "From Faktura to Factography," 114.

156. Aleksandr Rodchenko, "O kompozitsii," in *Stat'i. Vospominaniia. Avtobiograficheskie zapiski. Pis'ma*, 112.

157. Roland Barthes, *Camera Lucida: Reflections of Photography*, trans. Richard Howard (Hill & Wang, 1982), 80.

158. L. Volkov-Lannit, "Problema skhodstva v fotoportrete," *Sovetskoe foto*, no. 9 (1940): 7.

159. Volkov-Lannit, *Aleksandr Rodchenko risuet, fotografiruet, sporit*, 60.

160. Boris Arvatov, *Iskusstvo i proizvodstvo* (Proletkul't, 1926), 127.

161. MAMM, KP–1496/4.

162. Tom Gunning, "What's the Point of an Index? or, Faking Photographs," in *Still Moving: Between Cinema and Photography*, ed. Karen Beckman and Jean Ma (Duke University Press, 2008), 28.

163. *Kazakhskii narodnyi ornament* (Iskusstvo, 1939).

164. Walter Benjamin, "Hashish, Beginning of March 1930," in *Selected Writings*, vol. 2, Part 1: 1927–1930, ed. Michael W. Jennings, Howard Eiland, and Gary Smith; trans. Rodney Livingstone (Belknap Press, 2005), 328.

165. Wilhelm Worringer, *Form Problems of the Gothic* (G. E. Stechert & Co., 1920), 46. Vladimir Stasov, an influential nineteenth-century Russian critic, similarly argued that there is not a single "idle [*prazdnoi*] line" in ornamental compositions and that every component is an expression of certain metaphysical preconceptions. Vladimir Stasov, *Russkii narodnyi ornament* (Obshchestvennaia pol'za, 1872), xvi.

166. John Ruskin, *The Seven Lamps of Architecture* (Wiley & Halsted, 1857), 144.

167. Alois Riegl, *Problems of Style: Foundations for a History of Ornament* (Princeton University Press, 1992), 64.

168. Gottfried Semper, *Style in the Technical and Tectonic Arts; or, Practical Aesthetics* (Getty Research Institute, 2004), 171.
169. Kristin Romberg, *Gan's Constructivism: Aesthetic Theory for an Embedded Modernism* (University of California Press, 2019), 92.
170. Vladimir Favorskii, "Ob ornamente," in *Literaturno-teoreticheskoe nasledie*, 240.
171. However, Natal'ia Goncharova was a notable exception. She, according to Jane Sharp, "was committed to translating form through ornament and recasting ornament as high art." Sharp, *Russian Modernism Between East and West*, 7.
172. Kenneth Lindsay and Peter Vergo, eds., *Kandinsky: Complete Writings on Art. Volume One (1901–1921)* (G. K. Hall & Co, 1982), 399.
173. Sergei Tret'iakov, "B'em trevogu," *Novy Lef*, no. 2 (1927): 3.
174. László Moholy-Nagy, *The New Vision and Abstract of an Artist* (Wittenborn, Schultz, Inc., 1947), 30.
175. Adolf Loos, "Ornament and Crime," in *Programs and Manifestoes on 20th-Century Architecture*, ed. Ulrich Conrads (MIT Press, 1975), 20.
176. Siegfried Kracauer, *The Mass Ornament: Weimar Essays* (Harvard University Press, 1995), 76.
177. Kracauer, *The Mass Ornament*, 75.
178. Kracauer, *The Mass Ornament*, 77.
179. Malte Rolf, *Soviet Mass Festivals, 1917–1991* (University of Pittsburgh Press, 2013), 156.
180. *Kazakhskii narodnyi ornament*, Fig. 45, Table XVIII.
181. Karasik and Heiting (eds.), *The Soviet Photobook, 1920–1941*, 12.
182. Aleksandr Rodchenko, "To the Newspaper *Sovetskoe iskusstvo*," in Lavrentiev, *Experiments for the Future*, 296.

3. SOCIALIST SOUND: DZIGA VERTOV

1. Mikhail Kaufman, "Poslednee interv'iu Mikhaila Kaufmana," *Kinovedcheskie zapiski*, no. 18 (1993): 143. According to other accounts, Dziga Vertov can be loosely translated from Ukrainian as "spinning top." Lev Roshal', "Stikhi kinopoeta," *Kinovedcheskie zapiski*, no. 21 (1994): 86.
2. Vertov was born David Abelevich Kaufman and later Russified his first name and patronymic.
3. Vertov, "Kino-Eye," in *Kino-Eye: The Writings of Dziga Vertov*, ed. Annette Michelson (University of California Press, 1984), 72.
4. Viktor Listov, *Istoriia smotrit v ob"ektiv* (Iskusstvo, 1973), 210.
5. Vertov, "To the Kinoks of the South," *Kino-Eye*, 50.
6. Roland Barthes, "Leaving the Movie Theater," in *The Rustle of Language*, trans. Richard Howard (Hill & Wang, 1986), 348.
7. Joseph Stalin, "Thirteenth Congress of the R.C.P.(B.). Organisational Report of the Central Committee, May 24, 1924," in *Works*, 6:227.
8. In Grigorii Boltianskii, *Lenin i kino* (Gosudarstvennoe izdatel'stvo, 1925), 19.
9. As John MacKay elegantly puts it, "Vertov" becomes "an ego-ideal who had done much in cinema but had to be projected outward, protected by personification." John MacKay, *Dziga Vertov: Life and Work*, vol. 1, *1896–1921* (Academic Studies Press, 2018), xx.
10. Vertov, "Kinoks: A Revolution," *Kino-Eye*, 15, modified translation.
11. Vertov, "Kinoks: A Revolution," 15. Vertov's skepticism about the capacity of human vision to provide us with genuine knowledge of reality resonates, as Malcolm Turvey persuasively shows, with the modernist film criticism of Jean Epstein, Béla Balázs, and Siegfried Kracauer. Malcolm Turvey, *Doubting Vision: Film and the Revelationist Tradition* (Oxford University Press, 2008), 11.
12. Vertov, "The Birth of Kino-Eye," *Kino-Eye*, 41.

13. Vertov, "*Three Songs of Lenin* and Kino-Eye," *Kino-Eye*, 124.
14. Lev Roshal', et. al., "'Pryzhok' Vertova," *Iskusstvo kino*, no. 11 (1992): 97.
15. I follow Jeremy Hicks in rendering Vertov's term *zhizn' vrasplokh*, long translated as "life caught unawares," as "life caught off guard" for it is a more literal translation from Russian that respects Vertov's distinction between filming people off guard and filming them with a hidden camera (unawares). Jeremy Hicks, *Dziga Vertov: Defining Documentary Film* (IB Tauris, 2007), 24.
16. Dziga Vertov, "Front kino-glaza," in *Iz Naslediia. Tom 2: Stat'i i Vystupleniia* (Eizenshtein-Tsentr, 2008), 108.
17. Vertov, "Kinoks: A Revolution," 16.
18. Vertov, "Kino-Eye," 67.
19. Vertov, "Kino-Eye," 61.
20. Vertov, "Kino-Eye," 66.
21. According to Latour, science, or any mode of objective representation, is not an impartial procedure or set of empirical principles; it should be considered a cultural phenomenon. Bruno Latour, *Science in Action: How to Follow Scientists and Engineers Through Society* (Harvard University Press, 1987).
22. Vertov, "Kinoks: A Revolution," 15–16.
23. Vertov, "'Kino-Glaz' i '11-i,'" *Iz Naslediia. Tom 2*, 135–37.
24. Vertov, "From Notebooks, Diaries," *Kino-Eye*, 162.
25. Karl Marx and Frederick Engels, *Collected Works*, vol. 5, *Marx and Engels 1845–47* (Lawrence & Wishart, 2010), 3.
26. Marx and Engels, *Collected Works*, 5:3.
27. [Editorial], "Sovetskaia kinematografiia v period rekonstruktsii. Zadachi assotsiatsii rabotnikov revoliutsionnoi kinemafotografii," *Kino* 331, no. 2 (January 11, 1930): 5.
28. Vertov, "[Protiv obvinenii v formalizme]," *Iz Naslediia. Tom 2*, 191.
29. Vertov, "[Protiv obvinenii v formalizme]," 191.
30. Masha Salazkina, "Introduction," in *Sound, Speech, Music in Soviet and Post-Soviet Cinema*, ed. Lilya Kaganovsky and Masha Salazkina (Indiana University Press, 2014), 6.
31. Viktor Shklovskii, *Ikh nastoiaschee* (Knigopechat', 1927), 21.
32. Sergei Eisenstein, Vsevolod Pudovkin and Grigorii Aleksandrov, "A Statement," in *Film Sound: Theory and Practice*, ed. Elisabeth Weis and John Belton (Columbia University Press, 1985), 84.
33. Eisenstein et al., "A Statement," 84.
34. Eisenstein et al., "A Statement," 84.
35. Vertov, "The Essence of Kino-Eye," *Kino-Eye*, 50.
36. Vertov, "K stat'e: 'Radio-glaz,'" *Iz Naslediia. Tom 2*, 402.
37. Vertov, "Mart 'Radio-glaza,'" *Iz Naslediia. Tom 2*, 198–99. According to Timothy Benson, the avant-garde's emphasis on communication that would cultivate both an internationalist social milieu and an elemental visual vocabulary capable of transcending national boundaries provided a risk of "its own deconstruction by the very recognition of the multiplicity of its transactions, the fracturing of its totality, and the dispersal of its assumed center." Timothy Benson, "Exchange and Transformation: The Internationalization of the Avant-Garde(s) in Central Europe," in *Central European Avant-Gardes: Exchange and Transformation, 1910–1930*, ed. Timothy Benson (MIT Press, 2002), 64.
38. Vertov, "Kak zarodilsia i razvivalsia kino-glaz," *Iz Naslediia. Tom 2*, 291.
39. Douglas Kahn, *Noise, Water, Meat: A History of Sound in the Arts* (MIT Press, 1999), 139.
40. Vertov, "Kak zarodilsia i razvivalsia kino-glaz," 292.
41. Vertov, "Zvukovoe kino u nas," *Iz Naslediia. Tom 2*, 186.
42. Vertov, "Vertov i kinoki," *Iz Naslediia. Tom 2*, 188.
43. Vertov, "Kak zarodilsia i razvivalsia kino-glaz," 290.
44. Vertov, "Mart 1930," *Iz Naslediia. Tom 2*, 227.
45. Vertov, "Entuziazm," *Iz Naslediia. Tom 2*, 230.

3. SOCIALIST SOUND   289

46. Aleksandr Shorin, *Kak ekran stal govoriashchim* (Moscow: Goskinoizdat, 1949), 87–90. V. P., "Zvukovaia produktsiia sovetskoi kinopromyshlennosti," *Proletarskoe kino*, no. 5 (1931): 12.
47. Ironically, the exploration of the industrial soundscape was preceded by tests of portable sound-recording equipment on Petersburg's Yelagin island, where Vertov attempted to record singing nightingales. The entry into factory cacophony was preceded by the effort to record a melodious tune in an organic setting. Shorin, *Kak ekran stal govoriashchim*, 90.
48. René Fülöp-Miller, *The Mind and Face of Bolshevism: An Examination of Cultural Life in Soviet Russia* (Harper & Row, 1962), 182.
49. Vertov, "Zvukovoi marsh (iz fil'ma 'Simfoniia Donbassa')," *Iz Naslediia. Tom 2*, 137.
50. RGALI, f. 2091, op. 2, d. 417, l. 59.
51. She is also shown later without earphones, sculpting a bust of Lenin.
52. Oksana Sarkisova, "Edges of Empire: Representations of Borderland Identities in Early Soviet Cinema," *Ab Imperio*, no. 1 (2000): 234.
53. Sergei Tret'iakov, "Kak desiatiletit'," *Novyi Lef*, no. 4 (1927): 35–36.
54. Boris Shumiatskii, "Stalin i kino," in *Kremlevskii kinoteatr. 1928–1953. Dokumenty*, ed. K. M. Anderson and L. V. Maksimenkov (ROSSPEN, 2005), 84.
55. Richard Taylor, "On Stalin's Watch: The Late-night Kremlin Screenings: May to October 1934," *Studies in Russian and Soviet Cinema* 7, no. 2 (2014): 252.
56. Mikhail Cheremukhin, "O narodnykh pesniakh sovetskikh fil'mov," *Iskusstvo kino*, no. 2 (1939): 54, 56.
57. V. Erofeev and Z. Zalkind, "Tekhnika zvukovoi kinoekspeditsii," *Proletarskoe kino*, no. 6 (1932): 43–48. In 1930, Vladimir Erofeev, one of the pioneers of the documentary expedition film genre, began filming an "ethnographic music film" based on Central Asian material. It is very likely that this experience, the first recording of ethnographic sound material with a mobile studio, influenced Vertov's then-forthcoming *Three Songs of Lenin*. V. P., "Zvukovaia produktsiia sovetskoi kinopromyshlennosti," 13.
58. I will refer to the 1970 edit of the film throughout the chapter unless otherwise indicated (see below for more on the differences between the 1934, 1938, and 1970 versions).
59. Vertov, "I Wish to Share My Experience," *Kino-Eye*, 120.
60. Vertov, "Simfoniia myslei," *Iz Naslediia. Tom 2*, 264.
61. Vertov, "From Notebooks, Diaries," 171.
62. Gul'nara Abikeyeva remarks on the manipulatory essence of Vertov's film: "In the opening sequence, we see a woman from Khiva against a background of the famous local architecture. She is in a completely enveloping veil (a burqa, known in Uzbekistan as a *paranja*). A few frames later, we see work on the railway line and we are shown a Turkmen woman; in her case only the lower part of her face is covered. In any event, this was in fact the local tradition. Finally, we see footage of a Kazakh woman, her face completely uncovered—but Kazakhs never wore the *paranja* in the first place. The end of this sequence shows Kazakh women picking tea and wearing only headscarves. By simplistically intercutting footage of women from a range of different countries and cultural traditions as though a chronological sequence were at stake, Vertov creates a myth: 'The Removal of the *Paranja*.'" Gul'nara Abikeyeva, "Central Asian Documentary Films of the Soviet Era as a Factor in the Formation of National Identity," http://www.kinokultura.com/2009/24-abikeeva.shtml, accessed January 27, 2018. The invention of the "generic Soviet East," which was created by filming in four republics, echoes the making of a "generic Soviet town," which entailed shooting *The Man with a Movie Camera* in several Soviet towns (I would like to thank Julian Graffy for drawing my attention to this point). This practice, in turn, strongly resonates with Kuleshov's conception of "created geography."
63. Vertov, "*Three Songs of Lenin* and Kino-Eye," 125.
64. Oksana Sarkisova, *Screening Soviet Nationalities: Kulturfilms from the Far North to Central Asia* (IB Tauris, 2017), 193.
65. Kristin Thompson, "Early Sound Counterpoint," *Yale French Studies*, no. 60 (1980): 138. Similarly, for Yuri Tsivian "these were not films made by a *kinok*, in the old sense." Yuri Tsivian, "Dziga Vertov

and His Time," in *Lines of Resistance: Dziga Vertov and the Twenties*, ed. Yuri Tsivian (Le Giornate del cinema muto, 2004), 25. Seth Feldman also argues that *Three Songs of Lenin* is "an example of the heavy hand of Socialist Realism methodically crushing Futurist and Formalist experimentation." Seth Feldman, "'Peace Between Man and Machine': Dziga Vertov's *The Man with a Movie Camera*," in *Documenting the Documentary: Close Readings of Documentary Film and Video*, ed. Barry Keith Grant and Jeanette Sloniowski (Wayne State University Press, 1998), 51. Other critics maintain that the film is in line with Vertov's experimental ethos since it does not follow the strict postulates of the socialist realist tradition, although they make this argument without analyzing the details of its sound design. See Vlada Petric, "Vertov, Lenin, and Perestroika: The Cinematic Transposition of Reality," *Historical Journal of Film, Radio, and Television* 15, no. 1 (1995): 4; Richard Taylor, *Film Propaganda: Soviet Russia and Nazi Germany* (IB Tauris, 1998), 76. John MacKay convincingly argues that Vertov's attention to individual experience and textual appeals to "folk sensibility" "enabled him to fit into the new discursive order while continuing to pursue his old avant-garde concern with the representation of sheer change and dynamism, with material process, and with cinema as a means of reconfiguring perception and spatial-temporal relations." John MacKay, "Allegory and Accommodation: Vertov's *Three Songs of Lenin* (1934) as a Stalinist Film," *Film History: An International Journal* 18, no. 4 (2006): 379. More recently, Lilya Kaganovsky has produced a detailed analysis of the film's sound design, though she barely discusses the Oriental songs themselves. Lilya Kaganovsky, *The Voice of Technology: Soviet Cinema's Transition to Sound, 1928–1935* (Indiana University Press, 2018), 178–226.

66. Oksana Bulgakova, *Sovetskii slukhoglaz: Kino i ego organy chuvstv* (NLO, 2010), 245.
67. Vertov, "Simfoniia myslei," *Iz Naslediia. Tom 2*, 264.
68. Vertov, "Kinonasledstvo o Lenine," in *Iz Naslediia. Tom 1: Dramaturgicheskie opyty* (Eizenshtein-Tsentr, 2004), 139–40.
69. Vertov, "Without Words," *Kino-Eye*, 118.
70. Vertov, "Without Words," 118.
71. Vertov, "*Three Songs of Lenin* and Kino-Eye," 124.
72. Elizaveta Vertova-Svilova, *Tri Pesni o Lenine* (Iskusstvo, 1972), 107.
73. Vertova-Svilova, *Tri Pesni o Lenine*, 107.
74. Vertov, "How We Made Our Film About Lenin," *Kino-Eye*, 117.
75. Emma Widdis, *Socialist Senses: Film, Feeling, and the Soviet Subject, 1917–1940* (Indiana University Press, 2017), 278.
76. Viktor Listov, "Mikhail Kol'tsov i 'Desiataia muza,'" *Kinovedcheskie zapiski*, no. 5 (1990): 50–51; Viktor Listov, "Vertov: odnazhdy i vsegda," *Kinovedcheskie zapiski*, no. 18 (1993): 128.
77. Mikhail Kol'tsov, "Poslednii reis," *Pravda*, no. 19 (January 24, 1924): 2.
78. As established by John MacKay. See MacKay, "Allegory and Accommodation," 382.
79. Dziga Vertov, *Stat'i. Dnevniki. Zamysly* (Iskusstvo, 1966), 196.
80. Vertov, "[Kinematografisty i kinoki]," *Iz Naslediia. Tom 2*, 57.
81. Vertov, "More on Mayakovsky," *Kino-Eye*, 187.
82. Editorial, "Pervye itogi obsuzhdeniia statei 'Pravdy,'" *Iskusstvo kino*, no. 4 (1936): 16.
83. Vertov, [O bor'be s formalizmom], *Iz Naslediia. Tom 2*, 301.
84. Mariano Prunes, "Dziga Vertov's *Three Songs of Lenin* (1934): A Visual Tour through the History of the Soviet Avant-Grade in the Interwar Years," *Criticism* 45, no. 2 (2003): 251–78.
85. D. Osipov, "Kinopoema o Lenine," *Pravda*, no. 201 (July 23, 1934): 4.
86. In Annette Michelson's words, the film's precise signifying function is revealed as "the process of historicization which transforms document into monument." Annette Michelson, "The Kinetic Icon in the Work of Mourning: Prolegomena to the Analysis of a Textual System," *October* 52 (1990): 38.
87. Viktor Zhirmunskii, *Fol'klor zapada i vostoka: Sravnitel'no-istoricheskie ocherki* (OGI, 2004), 40–41.
88. A. Astakhov, "Diskussiia o sushchnosti i zadachakh fol'klora v Leningradskom Institute rechevoi kul'tury (IRK), 11 iiunia 1931 g.," *Sovetskaia etnografiia*, nos. 3–4 (1931): 239.

89. Maxim Gorky, "Zakliuchitel'naia rech' na Pervom vsesoiuznom s"ezde sovetskikh pisatelei," *Sobranie sochinenii v tridtsati tomakh. Tom 27*, 342.
90. Gorky, "Zakliuchitel'naia ch'...," 342.
91. Ursula Iustus, "Vozvrashchenie v rai," in *Sotsrealisticheskii kanon*, ed. Khans Giunter [Hans Günther] and Evgenii Dobrenko (Akademicheskii proekt, 2000), 72. In 1938, a group of mostly illiterate singers were elected full members of the Union of Soviet Writers.
92. Katerina Clark, *The Soviet Novel: History as Ritual* (University of Chicago Press, 1981), 35.
93. Eric Hobsbawm and Terence Ranger, eds., *The Invention of Tradition* (Cambridge University Press, 1983).
94. This term was coined by Richard Dorson in his analysis of American folk legends and, according to his view, fakelore "falsifies the raw data of folklore by invention, selection, fabrication, and similar refining processes..." Richard Dorson, *American Folklore* (University of Chicago Press, 1977), 4.
95. RGALI, f. 2091, op. 2, d. 422, ll. 1–69.
96. The pages with Aseev's poetry are taken from Nikolai Aseev, *Rabota nad stikhom* (Priboi, 1929).
97. Vertova-Svilova, *Tri Pesni o Lenine*, 107.
98. RGALI, f. 2091, op. 2, d. 422, l. 14. The source of the first song was identified by John MacKay. See MacKay, "Allegory and Accommodation," 390.
99. RGALI, f. 2091, op. 2, d. 422, l. 14.
100. "But, all the same, he is dear to us all" is replaced with "but he was dear to all of us" and "even more so" is replaced with "moreover." RGALI, f. 2091, op. 2, d. 422, l. 14.
101. Hicks argues that the film "has a musical hierarchy in which the Western orchestral forms of Shaporin's music ultimately prevail." Hicks, *Dziga Vertov*, 97. In addition to Shaporin's original score ("March of the Shock Workers"), there are musical fragments from the Western canon: Wagner's *Twilight of the Gods*, Chopin's Piano Sonata No. 2 (*Funeral March*), Tchaikovsky's *Swan Lake*, and De Geyter's "The Internationale."
102. It is also remarkable that the *novina* "On the Square Stands a Tent" consequently appears in the lush folio *The Art of the Peoples of the USSR*, published in 1937 and edited by Gorky. See *Tvorchestvo narodov SSSR*, ed. Maxim Gorky et al. (Pravda, 1937), 81–82.
102. RGALI, f. 2091, op. 2, d. 422, l. 26.
103. RGALI, f. 2091, op. 2, d. 422, l. 26.
104. The subsequent line of the same song in the film, "... and neither we nor the grandchildren of our grandchildren will ever forget him!" is an unmodified quotation from the last stanza of the poem. RGALI, f. 2091, op. 2, d. 422, l. 26.
105. Tsentral'nyi Komitet RKP, "K partii. Ko vsem trudiashchimsia," *Pravda*, no. 19 (24 January, 1924): 1.
106. RGALI, f. 2091, op. 2, d. 422, l. 26.
107. Vertov, "On *The Eleventh Year*," *Kino-Eye*, 82, modified translation.
108. RGALI, f. 2091, op. 2, d. 49. However, despite the declared representational strategy, the director issued a small booklet accompanying the film that provided a literary synopsis of *Three Songs of Lenin*, together with various endorsements by Soviet and foreign luminaries. *Tri pesni o Lenine: Zvukovoi fil'm* (Mezhrabpomfil'm, 1934).
109. Vertov, "I Wish to Share My Experience," *Kino-Eye*, 122.
110. Vertov, "I Wish to Share My Experience," 122, modified translation.
111. It was followed by the 1935 silent version, produced specifically for provincial cinemas that still did not have equipment for sound projection.
112. L. V., "Na prosmotre fil'my 'Tri pesni o Lenine,'" *Kino*, no. 49 (28 October, 1934): 1.
113. Taylor, "On Stalin's Watch," 143.
114. Boris Shumiatskii, *Kinematografiia millionov. Opyt analiza* (Kinofotoizdat, 1935), 175. Editorial, "Pervye itogi obsuzhdeniia statei 'Pravdy,'" 17–18.

115. The two versions are available on the DVD released by the Austrian Film Institute: Dziga Vertov, *Tri pesni o Lenine*, ASIN 3958600867.
116. No original prints of the 1934/35 versions have been discovered to date. The Austrian Film Institute DVD booklet describes the changes made in the following way: "Significantly, a portrait of Lenin, which is mentioned in the documents but not described in any further detail, has been replaced by an iconic photo depicting Lenin and Stalin together. Vertov also removed some shots of Lenin at an appearance before the delegates of the Communist International (*Comintern*). In addition, he made some alterations to the film's soundtrack. The short monologue by a highly productive crude oil worker (*udarnik*), in which he recounts how he joined the party after Lenin's death, was cut out. In this sequence, the worker went on to mention that he was just one of over 100,000 workers to do so, leading the bay where they extracted millions of tons of crude oil every year to be rechristened 'Il'ich Bay.'"
117. Vertov, "Neskol'ko vospominanii," *Iz Naslediia*, 2:388.
118. Vertov, "Neskol'ko vospominanii," *Iz Naslediia*, 2:388. In 1934, Vertov stated that *Three Songs of Lenin* also included the song "A great pupil of great Lenin—Stalin—led us into battle," and then adds parenthetically "the song is given in sound and image." Vertov, "Kak my delali fil'm o Lenine," *Iz Naslediia*, 2:262.
119. Vertova-Svilova, *Tri Pesni o Lenine*, 114.
120. Vertov, "'Leninskaia kino-pravda.' Vmesto otvetov na voprosy," *Iz Naslediia*. 2:88.
121. Vertov, "We: Variant of a Manifesto," *Kino-Eye*, 8.
122. Aleksandr Deriabin, "Vvedenie v dramaturgiiu ego zhizni," *Iz Naslediia*, 1:20.
123. Quoted in Arshaluis Arsharuni, "Khudozhestvennaia literatura Srednei Azii," *Krasnaia niva* 16 (1929): 11.
124. Leon Trotsky, *Literature and Revolution*, trans. Max Eastman (Haymarket Books, 2005), 16.
125. Bronisław Malinowski, "The Problem of Meaning in Primitive Languages," in *The Meaning of Meaning: A Study of the Influence of Language Upon Thought and of the Science of Symbolism*, ed. C. K. Ogden and I. A. Richards (Harcourt, Brace & World, 1923), 312.
126. Walter Ong, *Orality and Literacy: The Technologizing of the Word* (Routledge, 2002), 38.
127. Ong, *Orality and Literacy*, 45.
128. Zhirmunskii, *Fol'klor zapada i vostoka*, 360–61. The irrational shamanic element always accompanied the image of the epic folk singer: *bakhshi*, for instance, has a double meaning in Uzbek culture (it is both sorcerer-shaman and epic storyteller), while Kazakhs distinguish between *baksy* and *zhyrshi-akyn*).
129. TsGAKZRK, f. 969, ed. khr. 1–4. The film is referred to as a "*kino-ocherk*" in the shot list held at the Central State Archive of the Republic of Kazakhstan. TsGARK, f. 969, "Montazhnye listy," l. 1.
130. Neia Zorkaia, "Veshchie sny Alma-Aty," *Iskusstvo kino*, no. 7 (1999): 131.
131. RGALI, f. 2091, op. 2, d. 98, l. 47.
132. Olcott, *The Kazakhs*, 188.
133. Österreichisches Filmmuseum V. 151. In one of the versions of the script, an *akyn* opening the film plays an accordion—a traditionally Russian instrument. Vertov, "'Kazakhstan—Fronty' [Variant stsenariia]," *Iz Naslediia. Tom 1*, 376.
134. Dzhambul Dzhabaev, *Izbrannye proizvedeniia* (Zhazushi, 1980), 327–30.
135. Auezov wrote the article "From Dombra to Opera, From the Legend to the Novel" that attempted to inscribe the Kazakh oral tradition into the Russified fabric of socialist modernity. Auezov Archive, f. KPR 1, op. 1, d. 239, ll. 42–53.
136. Musrepov wrote an article in Kazakh about Nurpeis Baiganin in 1941. Significantly, it uses Arabic script instead of Cyrillic. TsGARK, f. 1864, op. 1, d. 174, ll. 1–3.
137. Mukhtar Auezov, Gabit Musrepov, Sabit Mukanov, Viktor Shklovsky, and Dziga Vertov, "'Kazakhstan' (zametki k planu stsenariia)," *Iz Naslediia*, 1:395. Mukhtar Auezov et al., "'Kazakhstan' (plan libretto)," *Iz Naslediia*, 1:396.

138. Auezov et. al, "'Kazakhstan' (plan libretto)," 401.
139. Auezov et. al, "'Kazakhstan' (plan libretto)," 401.
140. Mladen Dolar, *A Voice and Nothing More* (MIT Press, 2006), 116.
141. Auezov et. al, "'Kazakhstan' (plan libretto)," 401.
142. Vertov, "'Kazakhstan—fronty' [Literaturnyi stsenarii]," *Iz Naslediia*, 1:410. Initially, a centenarian Dzhamil was the one meant to be singing the song about Saule. RGALI, f. 2091, op. 2, d. 985, l. 19.
143. But the *akyn*'s song in the script, nevertheless, was going to be drowned out by non-diegetic orchestral music with a choir accompanying his last words.
144. Vertov, *Stat'i. Dnevniki. Zamysly*, 257–58.
145. Vertov, *Kino-Eye*, 260.
146. Michel Chion, *The Voice in Cinema* (Columbia University Press, 1999), 21.
147. Chion, *The Voice in Cinema*, 24.
148. Vertov, *Stat'i. Dnevniki. Zamysly*, 242.
149. Österreichisches Filmmuseum V. 151 and RGALI, f. 2091, op. 2, d. 436, l. 39–40.
150. The clash between the spoken and the written shaped Vertov's project from the very beginning. The director makes a remarkable preamble before he commences on an actual description of his future film *The Front, to You!*: "The absence of a minimal set of oratorical skills and the manner I have of speaking in an unconfident voice about things in which I am profoundly confident deprive me of the opportunity to expound my project verbally. That is why I take refuge in written expression, which I am usually good at." RGALI, f. 2091, op. 2, d. 98, l. 2. Ironically, Vertov's attempt to glorify the oral tradition of the Soviet East is somewhat displaced by his very own lack of oratorical skills and his strong personal preference for the written mode of communication. His reluctance to engage in oral communication resonates on many levels with the general cultural trends of the time, with a historical transition from orality to writing being one of the principal tendencies.
151. Ong, *Orality and Literacy*, 10.
152. Gorky, "Zakliuchitel'naia rech'," 342.
153. Vladimir Propp, "Spetsifika fol'klora," in *Trudy iubileinoi nauchnoi sessii. Sektsiia filologicheskikh nauk*, ed. M. P. Alekseev et al. (LGU, 1946), 149.
154. Esmagambet Ismailov, *Akyny: Monografiia o tvorchestve Dzhambula i drugikh narodnykh akynov* (Kazakhskoe gosudarstvennoe izdatel'stvo khudozhestvennoi literatury, 1957), 22. Ismailov emphasizes that Dzhambul is an *akyn* of a new type, one who creatively reimagines the ancient folkloric tradition and is thus capable of depicting Soviet reality. He argues that Dzhambul's language and poetic devices were enriched by exposure to Soviet literature. Moreover, the scholar also highlights the general constructive role that Russian culture and language played in the formation of the Kazakh literary language in the second half of the nineteenth century and that this also "transformed the art of folk *akyns*." Literary language augmented the oral tradition. Ismailov, *Akyny*, 174, 312, 266.
155. Yurii Sokolov, *Russian Folklore* (Folklore Associates, 1966), 4.
156. Sokolov, *Russian Folklore*, 9.
157. Felix Oinas, *Essays on Russian Folklore and Mythology* (Slavica Publishers, Inc., 1985), 166.
158. Nikolai Andreev, "Russkii fol'klor," *Literaturnyi kritik*, nos. 10–11 (1939): 268.
159. Vladimir Chicherov, *Voprosy teorii i istorii narodnogo tvorchestva* (Sovetskii pisatel', 1959), 46.
160. Quoted in Oinas, *Essays on Russian Folklore and Mythology*, 167.
161. The document that details the final cut of the film is symbolically titled "The Word (Slovo)." RGALI, f. 2091, op. 2, d. 102, l. 2. However, there are still "oral" traces in the practice of writing in the film. Saule is reading her letter in Kazakh (with the voice over in Russian). There is also a dombra in her room, and before she starts writing, the viewer hears the instrument. A woman sings a song once Saule has finished writing her letter. It is also notable that the roles of Saule and Dzhamil were much more prominent in the original structure of the film.
162. RGALI, f. 2091, op. 2, d. 98, l. 58, 58 (reverse).

163. RGALI, f. 2091, op. 2, d. 98, l. 59.
164. Viktor Shklovsky, "Where Is Dziga Vertov Striding," in Tsivian (ed.), *Lines of Resistance*, 170.
165. Shklovskii, *Ikh nastoiaschee*, 64.
166. Auezov et. al, "'Kazakhstan' (plan libretto)," 397.
167. Vertov, "'Kazakhstan—fronty.' [Literaturnyi stsenarii]," 403.
168. Vertov, "'Kazakhstan—fronty.' Libretto," *Iz Naslediia*, 1:389.
169. Vertov, "'Kazakhstan—fronty.' Libretto," 390.
170. Vertov, "'Kazakhstan—fronty.' Libretto," 391.
171. Vertov, "[Iz stenogrammy obsuzhdeniia zaiavki na dokumental'nyi fil'm 'Tebe, front!']," *Iz Naslediia*, 2:342.
172. Adriana Cavarero, *For More than One Voice: Toward a Philosophy of Vocal Expression* (Stanford University Press, 2005), 6.
173. Cavarero, *For More than One Voice*, 6.
174. Vertov, "'Tebe, front!' [variant zaiavki]," *Iz Naslediia*, 1:372. In a version of the screenplay in Musrepov's archive, Nurpeis broadcasts his song from a radio station in Aktobe. TsGARK, f. 1864, op. 1, d. 113, l. 4.
175. RGALI, f. 2091, op. 2, d. 422, l. 36.
176. GARF, f. 8131, op. 37, d. 4041, ll. 306–20.
177. Vertov, "'Kazakhstan—fronty.' Libretto," 393. A preface in Auezov's archive identifies the twenty-eight guardsmen sequence as a narrative centerpiece of the film. See Mukhtar Auezov et al., "Predislovie k libretto," in *Neizvestnoe v naslediii Mukhtara Auezova: arkhivnye dokumenty* (Biblioteka Olzhasa, 2013), 283.
178. RGALI, f. 2091, op. 2, d. 985, l. 22 (verso).
179. In one of the literary renderings of the film, Dzhambul is shown sitting on an honorary chair at the presidium of the Academy of Sciences of the Kazakh SSR. The enormous map functions as a backdrop. He asks Nurpeis, his successor, to sing him a song about the great Soviet family. However, "we the peoples united by friendship" evolves into "we the family of the peoples united by Stalinist friendship." RGALI, f. 2091, op. 2, d. 985, l. 12.
180. Vertov, "We: Variant of a manifesto," 7.
181. Vertov, "We: Variant of a manifesto," 8.
182. Vertov, "Kinoks: A Revolution," 17.
183. Gilles Deleuze, *Cinema 1: The Movement-Image* (University of Minnesota Press, 1986), 84.
184. MacKay, *Dziga Vertov: Life and Work, Volume II*, tbc.
185. Elizabeth Astrid Papazian "Literacy or Legibility: The Trace of Subjectivity in Soviet Socialist Realism," in *The Oxford Handbook of Propaganda Studies*, ed. Jonathan Auerbach and Russ Castronovo (Oxford University Press, 2013), 80.
186. Vertova-Svilova, *Tri Pesni o Lenine*, 111.
187. Shumiatskii, "Stalin i kino," 86–87.
188. Shumiatskii, "Stalin i kino," 83.
189. R. Katsman, "Kinokhronika vchera i segodnia," *Sovetskoe kino*, no. 1 (1935): 69.
190. Sergei Drobashenko, "Teoreticheskie vzgliady Vertova," in Vertov, *Stat'i. Dnevniki. Zamysly*, 37.
191. *Lullaby* (Kolybel'naia, 1937) and *The Three Heroines* (Tri geroini, 1938)—two films originating in that decade—also contributed to the exploration of the "living human being." The former also productively engages with the ethnic particularism of the Soviet Union.
192. Vertov, "O liubvi k zhivomu cheloveku," *Iskusstvo kino*, no. 6 (1958): 95–99.
193. Vertov, "O moei liubvi k zhivomu cheloveku," *Iz Naslediia. Tom 2*, 329.
194. RGALI, f. 966, op. 1, d. 84, l. 1–12. Dziga Vertov, "O liubvi k zhivomu cheloveku," *Iskusstvo kino*, no. 6 (June 1958): 95–99. The title of the *Iskusstvo kino* article also lost the possessive pronoun "moei" (my).
195. S. Ginzburg, "Kino-Pravda," *Iskusstvo kino*, no. 1 (1940): 88.
196. Walter Benjamin, "On the Present Situation of Russian Film," in *Selected Writings. Volume 2, Part 1. 1927–1930*, 13.

4. SOCIALIST TIME: SERGEI EISENSTEIN

1. As reported in a private conversation by Naum Kleiman, who interviewed Atasheva in the 1960s.
2. Only several stills and partial prints from the first version survived and they were eventually published in the sixth volume of Eisenstein's *Collected Works* in 1971. See Sergei Eizenshtein, "Bezhin lug," in *Izbrannye proizvedeniia v shesti tomakh. Tom 6* (Iskusstvo, 1971), 129–52.
3. Boris Shumiatskii, "O fil'me 'Bezhin lug,'" in *O fil'me 'Bezhin lug' Eizenshteina* (Iskusstvo, 1937), 3.
4. Shumiatskii, "O fil'me 'Bezhin lug,'" 6.
5. Shumiatskii, "O fil'me 'Bezhin lug,'" 6–7.
6. Shumiatskii, "O fil'me 'Bezhin lug,'" 20.
7. Svetlana Boym, *Common Places: Mythologies of Everyday Life in Russia* (Harvard University Press, 1994), 91.
8. Naum Kleiman, "Formula finala," in *Formula finala: Stat'i, vystupleniia, besedy* (Eizenshtein-Tsentr, 2004), 71.
9. Il'ia Vaisfel'd, "Teoreticheskie oshibki Eizenshteina," in *O fil'me 'Bezhin lug' Eizenshteina*, 36.
10. Vaisfel'd, "Teoreticheskie oshibki Eizenshteina," 27, 34.
11. Evgenii Veisman, "Mify i zhizn'," in *O fil'me 'Bezhin lug' Eizenshteina*, 51.
12. A Commission of the Central Committee of the C.P.S.U.(B.), *The History of the Communist Party of the Soviet Union (Bolsheviks) [Short Course]* (International Publishers, 1939), 363.
13. Sergei Eisenstein, "Kangaroo," in *Nonindifferent Nature: Film and the Structure of Things*, intro. Herbert Eagle, trans. Herbert Marshall (Cambridge University Press, 1987), 199.
14. Sergei Eizenshtein, "Oshibki 'Bezhina luga,'" in *O fil'me 'Bezhin lug' Eizenshteina*, 52–53. My emphasis.
15. Eizenshtein, "Oshibki 'Bezhina luga,'" 53–54.
16. Sergei Eizenshtein, "Privlekatel'nost' 'intrigi' i magiia 'bessiuzhetnosti,'" in *Metod. Tom 1. Grundproblem* (Muzei kino, 2002), 261.
17. Eisenstein, "Kangaroo," 183.
18. In his notes, Eisenstein compares Urgench's multiculturalism to the diversity of medieval Novgorod, the main location of the Nevsky film. As he writes, "Kunia-Urgench, similar to Novgorod, should be variegated and polytypic." RGALI, f. 1923, op. 2, d. 199, l. 16.
19. Sergei Eizenshtein, "K voprosy 'Natsional'noe po forme, sotsialisticheskoe po soderzhaniiu' (katolitsizm i iazychestvo, Remy de Gourmont, Elizavetinskie ballady)," in *Metod. Tom 2. Tainy masterov* (Muzei kino, 2002), 374–77.
20. RGALI, f. 1923, op. 1, d. 1343, l. 19.
21. Sergei Eisenstein, "The Problem of the Materialist Approach to Form," in *S. M. Eisenstein*, vol. 1, *Writings, 1922–34*, ed. Richard Taylor (BFI, 1998), 60.
22. Sergei Eisenstein, "Perspectives," in *Writings, 1922–34*, 153–54.
23. Eisenstein, "Perspectives," 154.
24. Sergei Eisenstein, "In the Interests of Form," in *Writings, 1922–34*, 238.
25. Sergei Eizenshtein, "Misteriia tsirka," in *Metod. Tom 1. Grundproblem*, 437.
26. Eizenshtein, "Misteriia tsirka," 438.
27. Sergei Eisenstein, "'Eh!' On the Purity of Film Language," in *Writings, 1922–34*, 285.
28. Eisenstein, "Purity," 287.
29. Eizenshtein, "K voprosy 'Natsional'noe po forme,'" 374.
30. Remy de Gourmont, *La culture des idées* (Mercure de France, 1916), 131–97.
31. Eizenshtein, "K voprosy 'Natsional'noe po forme,'" 375.
32. Eizenshtein, "K voprosy 'Natsional'noe po forme,'" 376.
33. Eizenshtein, "K voprosy 'Natsional'noe po forme,'" 376–77.
34. The film's all-encompassing importance has been meticulously explored in the scholarship. See Anne Nesbet, *Savage Junctures: Sergei Eisenstein and the Shape of Thinking* (I. B. Tauris, 2003) and Masha Salazkina, *In Excess: Sergei Eisenstein's Mexico* (University of Chicago Press, 2009).

35. Sergei Eizenshtein, *Montazh* (Muzei kino, 2000), 92.
36. Salazkina, *In Excess*, 5.
37. Lucien Lévy-Bruhl, *Primitive Mentality* (Macmillan, 1975), 208.
38. Sergei Eizenshtein, "Soderzhanie formy (Zakliuchenie)," in *Metod. Tom 1. Grundproblem*, 440.
39. Viktor Shklovskii, *Eizenshtein* (Iskusstvo, 1976), 98.
40. Gilles Deleuze, *Cinema 2: The Time-Image*, trans. Hugh Tomlinson and Barbara Habberjam (University of Minnesota Press, 1997), 210.
41. This period is generally understood as that of a constructivist Eisenstein. See François Albera, *Eisenstein et le constructivisme russe: dramaturgie de la forme* (L'Age d'homme, 1990); and David Bordwell, *The Cinema of Eisenstein* (Harvard University Press, 1993), 195–98.
42. Leonid Kozlov, *Izobrazhenie i obraz: Ocherki po istoricheskoi poetike sovetskogo kino* (Iskusstvo, 1980), 99.
43. Sergei Eizenshtein, "Vnutrennii monolog," in *Metod. Tom 1. Grundproblem*, 108.
44. David Bordwell, "Eisenstein's Epistemological Shift," *Screen* 15, no. 4 (1974–75): 33.
45. Bordwell, "Eisenstein's Epistemological Shift," 41.
46. Mikhail Iampol'skii, "Eizenshteinovskii 'sintez,'" in *Uskol'zaiushchii kontekst: Russkaia filosofiia v postsovetskikh usloviiakh* (Ad Marginem, 2002), 87–88.
47. Oksana Bulgakowa, *Sergei Eisenstein. A Biography* (Potemkin Press, 2001), 170.
48. Sergei Eizenshtein, "Avtor i ego tema," in *Metod. Tom 1. Grundproblem*, 226.
49. Sergei Eizenshtein, "Piat' epokh," *Pravda* (July 6, 1926): 6. The unfinished *Moscow 800* film was even more daring in its attempt to amalgamate different historical layers—it was intended to employ a "jumping chronology" device—an organizational principle that places sequences according to thematic recurrences rather than the linear chronological order.
50. In 1939, Vsevolod Vishnevskii, in the first monograph dedicated to the director, interprets Eisenstein's experiments with *mnogoukladnost'* as failures, though necessary ones that consequently lead him to triumphant *simplicity*. Vsevolod Vishnevskii, *Eizenshtein* (Goskinoizdat, 1939), 32.
51. Sergei Eisenstein, *Film Form* (Harcourt Brace & World, 1949), 142–43.
52. Eizenshtein, "Soderzhanie formy (Zakliuchenie)," 442.
53. Naum Kleiman, "Problema Eizenshteina," in Eizenshtein, *Metod. Tom 1. Grundproblem*, 24.
54. Sergei Eizenshtein, "Vykhod iz krizisa," in *Metod. Tom 1. Grundproblem*, 131.
55. Antonio Somaini, "Cinema as 'Dynamic Mummification,' History as Montage: Eisenstein's Media Archaeology," in *Sergei M. Eisenstein: Notes for a General History of Cinema*, ed. Naum Kleiman and Antonio Somaini (Amsterdam University Press, 2016), 31.
56. Sergei Eisenstein, "Speeches to the All-Union Creative Conference of Soviet Filmworkers," in *S. M. Eisenstein: Selected Works*, vol. 3, *Writings, 1934–47*, ed. Richard Taylor (BFI, 1996), 36–37.
57. Eisenstein, "Speeches," 38.
58. Eisenstein, "Speeches," 38.
59. Museum of Modern Art (MoMA), Eisenstein Collection, folder A ("Que Viva México," manuscript text with drawings), l. 1.
60. MoMA, Eisenstein Collection, folder A ("Que Viva México," manuscript text with drawings), ll. 1–2.
61. MoMA, Eisenstein Collection, folder A, l. 8.
62. Sergei Eizenshtein, "[Moia sistema]," *Kinovedcheskie zapiski* 36/37 (1997–1998): 24.
63. Eizenshtein, "[Moia sistema]," 24–25.
64. For more details see Christian Teichmann, "Canals, Cotton, and the Limits of De-Colonization in Soviet Uzbekistan, 1924–1941," *Central Asian Survey* 26, no. 4 (2007): 499–519.
65. The canal construction was preceded by several scientific expeditions sent to the region to explore local practices of irrigation. A key expedition to Fergana took place in September–November 1934; it was initiated by the State Academy of History of Material Culture, which was headed by Nikolai Marr. IIMK, f. 2, op. 1, d. 219–221. A more general expedition took place from February 2 to November 2 1936 and it included an analysis of ancient documents pertaining to local irrigation practices. IIMK, f. 2, op. 1, d. 32.

4. SOCIALIST TIME   297

66. RGALI, f. 1923, op. 2, d. 202, l. 2.
67. Eduard Tisse, "Bol'shoi khudozhestvennyi fil'm o kanale," *Ferganskaia Pravda* (August 16, 1939): 1.
68. The Uzbek director Malik Kaiumov and his Moscow colleagues Leonid Varlamov and Boris Nebylitskii were also producing a film about the Fergana canal in the same year. The group managed to complete their film, and it was released under the title *The Mighty Flow* (*Moguchii potok*). The film resonates with Eisenstein's project on some level (for example, it concludes with a performance by Tamara Khanum for the kolkhoz workers). RGAKFD, 1-4209. Furthermore, some of Tisse's footage was likely used in the 77th issue of *The Cinema Journal of the Soviet Union* (Soiuzkinozhurnal). RGAKFD, 1-3101.
69. Sergei Eisenstein, "The Film About the Fergana Canal," *Studies in Russian and Soviet Cinema* 5, no. 1 (2011): 160.
70. Eisenstein, "The Film About the Fergana Canal," 157–58.
71. The water-sand dialectical tension was supposed to shape the film structure even at the level of the soundtrack. Sergei Prokofiev had been commissioned to compose a score for the film with two main themes—one for water and one for sand. Iu. Krasovskii, "Pis'ma S. M. Eizeinshteinu," *Iskusstvo kino*, no. 1 (1958): 96.
72. Sergei Eizenshtein, "Kommentarii k rezhisserskomu stsenariiu fil'ma o Ferganskom kanale," in I. V. Vaisfel'd, *Voprosy kinodramaturgii. Vypusk III. Sbornik statei* (Iskusstvo, 1959), 335.
73. RGALI, f. 1923, op. 1, d. 504, l. 2, and RGALI, f. 1923, op. 2, d. 199, l. 3.
74. He made the following note in his diary in 1940: "Ever since they 'cut Tamburlaine out of me'" (it sounds like appendicitis!) I have cooled toward it entirely." Eizenshtein, *Metod. Tom 2. Tainy masterov*, 472.
75. RGALI, f. 1923, op. 1, d. 520, l. 1 (verso). The Uzbek official, according to Eisenstein's notes, also made some concrete suggestions after reading the screenplay. One such note reads: "*Skipping the stage of capitalism*, Uzbekistan passed from semi-feudalism *straight* to socialism. *Show this.* This is thanks to the *Russian* proletariat." RGALI, f. 1923, op. 1, d. 519, l. 2.
76. As Naum Kleiman convincingly argues, "Without the first 'tower' the structure of the script would cease to be a fortress: a two-part structure would be converted into an '*izba* with a watchtower'—in other words, into a conventional agitational film about the 'cursed past' and the 'happy present.'" Naum Kleiman, "Fergana Canal and Tamburlaine's Tower," *Studies in Russian and Soviet Cinema* 5, no. 1 (2011): 107.
77. Sergei Eisenstein, "The Land Has Become Unrecognizable," *Studies in Russian and Soviet Cinema* 5, no. 1 (2011): 160.
78. Sergei Eizenshtein, "Fil'm o Ferganskom kanale," in *Izbrannye proizvedeniia v shesti tomakh. Tom 1* (Iskusstvo, 1964), 188.
79. Sergei Eisenstein, "On Folklore," in *S. M. Eisenstein: Selected Works*, vol. 4, *Beyond the Stars: The Memoirs of Sergei Eisenstein*, ed. Richard Taylor (BFI, 1995), 593.
80. Eisenstein, "On Folklore," 594.
81. Eisenstein, "On Folklore," 602.
82. Eizenshtein, "Kommentarii," 337.
83. Eizenshtein, "Kommentarii," 337.
84. Petr Pavlenko and Sergei Eisenstein, "The Great Fergana Canal," *Studies in Russian and Soviet Cinema* 5, no. 1 (2011): 153.
85. Eizenshtein, "Kommentarii," 339.
86. Eizenshtein, "Kommentarii," 340.
87. Eizenshtein, "Kommentarii," 340.
88. Eizenshtein, "Kommentarii," 341.
89. Eizenshtein, "Kommentarii," 352.
90. Eizenshtein, "Kommentarii," 352.
91. Shklovskii, *Eizenshtein*, 98.

92. RGALI, f. 1923, op. 2, d. 1160, l. 32.
93. Sergei Eizenshtein, "Montazh 1938," in *Neravnodushnaia priroda. Tom 1. Chuvstvo kino* (Muzei kino, 2004), 49.
94. Eizenshtein, "Kommentarii," 352, my emphasis.
95. RGALI, f. 1923, op. 2, d. 1160, l. 35.
96. RGALI, f. 1923, op. 2, d. 1160, l. 33.
97. Stalin, "Anarchism or Socialism?" in *Works* (OGIZ, 1946), 1:319.
98. RGALI, f. 1923, op. 2, d. 1160, l. 34.
99. Kleiman, "Problema Eizenshteina," 17.
100. RGALI, f. 1923, op. 2, d. 240, l. 3.
101. Eisenstein made a very graphic drawing "The Love Making Machine" (Le Machin à faire l'amour) on December 29, 1942 in Alma-Ata. It represents a hermaphrodite who displays both male and female reproductive organs and is depicted in the likeness of Tengu—a creature of Japanese folklore, part human, part bird. Hoover, John J. Stephan Collection, Box 4.
102. RGALI, f. 1923, op. 2, d. 240, l. 8.
103. RGALI, f. 1923, op. 2, d. 240, l. 10.
104. RGALI, f. 1923, op. 2, d. 240, l. 22.
105. RGALI, f. 1923, op. 2, d. 240, ll. 22–23.
106. RGALI, f. 1923, op. 2, d. 240, ll. 24–25.
107. RGALI, f. 1923, op. 2, d. 613, l. 28.
108. RGALI, f. 1923, op. 2, d. 613, ll. 27–30.
109. RGALI, f. 1923, op. 2, d. 613, ll. 33–34.
110. RGALI, f. 1923, op. 2, d. 1160, l. 34.
111. RGALI, f. 1923, op. 2, d. 198, ll. 1–42.
112. RGALI, f. 1923, op. 2, d. 198, l. 4.
113. Sergei Eisenstein, "The Problems of the Soviet Historical Film," in *Writings, 1934–47*, 136.
114. Sergei Eizenshtein, "Valia Kadochnikov," in *Izbrannye proizvedeniia v shesti tomakh. Tom 5* (Iskusstvo, 1968), 577.
115. RGALI, f. 1923, op. 2, d. 2404, ll. 1–17.
116. According to Auezov, there were more than sixteen versions of the epic tale with two radically different endings: a happy resolution in which the lovers marry and live a happy life, and a tragic conclusion where the two die. Mukhtar Auezov, "Kozy Korpesh i Baian Sulu," in *Mysli raznykh let. Po literaturnym tropam* (KGIKhL, 1961), 395.
117. Mukhtar Auezov and Leonid Sobolev, "Epos i fol'klor kazakhskogo naroda," *Literaturnyi kritik* 10/11 (1939): 210–33 and *Literaturnyi kritik* 1 (1940): 169–80. Auezov and Gabit Musrepov, both of whom worked with Vertov on *The Front, to You!* as consultants, were chief literary authorities on the Kazakh epos at the time. Musrepov adapted the story for his play *Kozy Korpesh and Baian Slu* [sic] in 1939. See Gabit Musrepov, *Kozy Korpesh and Baian Slu* (Iskusstvo, 1945).
118. Shklovsky discussed the story of Kozy Korpesh and Baian Sulu with Nurpeis himself (!), according to his 1966 memoirs. Shklovskii, *Zhili-byli*, 502.
119. Numbers written on the drawings do not match the archival nomenclature.
120. Naum Kleiman, "Pravila igry," in *Formula finala: Stat'i, vystupleniia, besedy*, 179.
121. RGALI, f. 1923, op. 2, d. 261, ll. 61–2.
122. RGALI, f. 1923, op. 2, d. 261, l. 62.
123. RGALI, f. 1923, op. 2, d. 261, l. 63.
124. RGALI, f. 1923, op. 2, d. 261, l. 64.
125. Adolf Loos, "Ornament and Crime," in *Programs and Manifestoes on 20th-Century Architecture*, ed. Ulrich Conrads (The MIT Press, 1975), 20.
126. Loos, "Ornament and Crime," 20.

4. SOCIALIST TIME

127. Anne Anlin Cheng, *Ornamentalism* (Oxford University Press, 2019), 16.
128. Cheng, *Ornamentalism*, 15.
129. Sergei Eizenshtein, "Zametki o linii i ornamente," in *Metod. Tom 2. Tainy masterov*, 430.
130. Eizenshtein, "Zametki o linii i ornamente," 430.
131. Eizenshtein, "Zametki o linii i ornamente," 445.
132. Eizenshtein, "Zametki o linii i ornamente," 435.
133. Sergei Eizenshtein, "Puti 'regressa,'" in *Metod. Tom 1. Grundproblem*, 195.
134. Eizenshtein, "Puti 'regressa,'" 195.
135. Eizenshtein, "Puti 'regressa,'" 196.
136. Eizenshtein, "Puti 'regressa,'" 196.
137. There is one additional drawing in the series: a sketch for "Totem." RGALI, f. 1923, op. 2, d. 1405, l. 3.
138. On Scythianism in early Soviet culture see Michael Kunichika, *"Our Native Antiquity": Archaeology and Aesthetics in the Culture of Russian Modernism* (Academic Studies Press, 2015), 217–22, 243–79.
139. Another recalled book was Aleksandr Miller's study of primitive art that includes a discussion of movement dynamics in Scythian artifacts. Aleksandr Miller, *Istoriia iskusstv vsekh vvremen i narodov. Kniga 1-a. Pervobytnoe iskusstvo* (P. P. Soikin, 1929), 28.
140. Dmitrii Eding, *Reznaia skul'ptura Urala. Iz istorii zverinogo stilia* (GIM, 1940), 5.
141. Immanuel Kant, *The Critique of Judgement* (Oxford University Press, 2007), 57.
142. Jacques Derrida, *The Truth in Painting*, trans. Geoffrey Bennington and Ian McLeod (University of Chicago Press, 1987), 45.
143. Herodotus writes: "when a man desires a woman, he hangs his quiver before her wagon, and has intercourse with her, none hindering." Herodotus, *Histories. Books I and II* (Harvard University Press, 1975), 271.
144. Inga Stasevich, *Sotsial'nyi status zhenshchiny u kazakhov: traditsii i sovremennost'* (Nauka, 2011), 40.
145. Stasevich, *Sotsial'nyi status*, 42.
146. Stasevich, *Sotsial'nyi status*, 131.
147. There is a Kazakh equivalent of the tree of life: Bayterek. According to a Kazakh legend, its roots are in the underworld, the trunk is located in the worldly domain, and its crown reaches up toward the celestial realm inhabited by Samruk, a magic bird of happiness.
148. Vladimir Toporov, *Mirovoe derevo: Universal'nye znakovye kompleksy. Tom 2* (Rukopisnye pamiatniki Drevnei Rusi, 2010), 316.
149. Sergei Eisenstein, "The Incarnation of Myth" in *Writings, 1934–47*, 160.
150. J. H. Philpot, *The Sacred Tree: Or, the Tree in Religion and Myth* (Macmillan, 1897), 75.
151. Eisenstein was commissioned to stage *Die Walküre* at the Bolshoi Theater. While working on the stage production, Eisenstein's experience of staging Richard Wagner's opera made him once again explore the cinematic potential of mythological narratives. His article "The Incarnation of Myth" explains his approach to the production that was marked by the universal appeal of the seemingly nation-specific material. Eisenstein, "The Incarnation of Myth," 143.
152. Eisenstein, "The Incarnation of Myth," 156.
153. Eisenstein, "The Incarnation of Myth," 159.
154. In the 1920s, Petr Kozlov's expedition excavated the royal Xiongnu tombs at the Noin-Ula burial site in northern Mongolia. The Xiongnu was a tribal confederation of nomadic peoples who inhabited the eastern Eurasian Steppe from the third century BC to the late first century AD. One of the artifacts found was a silver plaque of a yak, the lower section of which is almost identical to Eisenstein's drawing "In Memory of Mountain Goat Hunters."
155. Gertrude Jobes, *Dictionary of Mythology, Folklore and Symbols* (Scarecrow Press, 1962), 665.
156. The Central Asian onager, also known as the Asiatic wild ass, is not horned.
157. Sergei Eisenstein, "How I Learned to Draw (A Chapter about My Dancing Lessons)," in *Beyond the Stars*, 579.

158. Eisenstein, "How I Learned to Draw," 580.
159. Sergei Eizenshtein, "[O sobstvennom risovanii]," in *Metod. Tom 2. Tainy masterov*, 497.
160. Luka Arsenjuk, *Movement, Action, Image, Montage: Sergei Eisenstein and the Cinema in Crisis* (University of Minnesota Press, 2018), 34.
161. RGALI, f. 1923, op. 2, d. 1173, l. 1.
162. Sergei Eisenstein, *Disney* (Potemkin Press, 2013), 15.
163. Jay Leyda, ed., *Eisenstein on Disney* (Seagull Books, 1985), 5.
164. Eizenshtein, "[O sobstvennom risovanii]," 497.
165. Sergei Eizenshtein, "Disnei," in *Metod. Tom 2. Tainy masterov*, 267.
166. The *Disney* manuscript contains the following note: "Examples in Veselovsky: *Historical Poetics*, p. 522–24. Copy when I have some free time." Eizenshtein, "Disnei," 613.
167. The date of purchase was written inside the cover of the book held at the Museum of Cinema in Moscow.
168. Aleksandr Veselovskii, *Istoricheskaia poetika* (Khudozhestvennaia literatura, 1940), 130.
169. Veselovskii, *Istoricheskaia poetika*, 132.
170. Veselovskii, *Istoricheskaia poetika*, 317.
171. Veselovskii, *Istoricheskaia poetika*, 53.
172. Veselovskii, *Istoricheskaia poetika*, 62.
173. Veselovskii, *Istoricheskaia poetika*, 376.
174. Sergei Eizenshtein, "Siuzhet v obshchei sisteme formy. Siuzhet kak forma voploshcheniia idei," in *Metod. Tom 2. Tainy masterov*, 362.
175. Shklovsky, *Theory of Prose*, 20.
176. Viktor Zhirmunsky, "On the Study of Comparative Literature," *Oxford Slavonic Papers* 13 (1967): 4.
177. Fadeev, while criticizing Nusinov's Pushkin book, identifies Veselovsky as a precursor of the formalist and cosmopolitan approach. The work of his brother, Aleksei Veselovsky, was also under critical attack but *Historical Poetics* remained a primary target. Aleksandr Fadeev, "Doklad general'nogo sekretaria SSP SSSR," *Literaturnaia gazeta* (June 29, 1947): 1–2.
178. I. Dmitrakov and M. Kuznetsov, "Aleksandr Veselovskii i ego posledovateli," *Oktiabr'*, no. 12 (1947): 168.
179. A historical poetics perceives literary phenomena as "having a history (participating in the history of forms), responsive to history (produced by a particular historical conjuncture), and formative of history (defining present and future historical experience and practice)." Ilya Kliger and Boris Maslov, "Introducing Historical Poetics: History, Experience, Form," in *Persistent Forms: Explorations in Historical Poetics*, ed. Ilya Kliger and Boris Maslov (Fordham University Press, 2016), 15.
180. Veselovsky, *Istoricheskaia poetika*, 511.
181. Viktor Zhirmunskii, "Istoricheskaia poetika A. N. Veselovskogo," in Veselovskii, *Istoricheskaia poetika*, 34.
182. Zhirmunskii, "Istoricheskaia poetika A. N. Veselovskogo," 21.
183. Vladimir Shishmarev, "Aleksandr Veselovskii i ego kritiki," *Oktiabr'*, no. 12 (1947): 162–63.
184. Shklovskii, "Aleksandr Veselovskii—istorik i teoretik," 181.
185. Shklovskii, "Aleksandr Veselovskii—istorik i teoretik," 177.
186. Eisenstein, "The Incarnation of Myth," 142.
187. Eizenshtein, "Oshibki 'Bezhina luga,'" 54.
188. Veselovskii, *Istoricheskaia poetika*, 51.
189. Sergei Eizenshtein, "Oderzhimost' (Idée fixe)," in *Metod. Tom 1. Grundproblem*, 215.
190. RGALI, f. 1923, op. 2, d. 1162, l. 24. Eisenstein incorrectly writes "shchir" instead of Kruchenykh's "shchyl."
191. Lukács, *The Meaning of Contemporary Realism*, trans. John and Necke Mander (Merlin Press, 1963), 104.

EPILOGUE: "END" POINTS

1. RGALI, f. 1923, op. 2, d. 1157, l.88.
2. Fredric Jameson, "Modernism and Imperialism" in *Nationalism, Colonialism, and Literature*, ed. Terry Eagleton et al. (University of Minnesota Press, 1990), 50.
3. See, among others, Gleb Albert, "International Solidarity With(out) World Revolution: The Transformation of 'Internationalism' in Early Soviet Society," *Monde(s)* 2, no. 10 (2016): 33–50, and James van Geldern, "The Centre and the Periphery: Cultural and Social Geography in the Mass Culture of the 1930s" in Stephen White (ed.), *New Directions in Soviet History* (Cambridge University Press, 1991), 62–80.
4. Viacheslav Ivanov, "O veselom remesle i umnom veselii," in *Sobranie sochinenii*, (Foyer Oriental Chrétien, 1979), 3:77.
5. Michael Kunichika, *"Our Native Antiquity": Archaeology and Aesthetics in the Culture of Russian Modernism* (Academic Studies Press, 2015), 13.
6. Evgeny Dobrenko, *Late Stalinism: The Aesthetics of Politics*, trans. Jesse M. Savage (Yale University Press, 2020), 18.
7. Dobrenko, *Late Stalinism*, 12.
8. Stalin's Russocentrism was, as David Brandenberger puts it, "designed to mobilize rather than enfranchise." See David Brandenberger, "Stalin's Populism and the Accidental Creation of Russian National Identity," *Nationalities Papers* 38, no. 5 (2010): 728.
9. The Soviet anti-cosmopolitanism campaign has loose temporal boundaries, but it is generally assumed to have evolved within the context of the political-ideological development of the Stalinist regime in the postwar period, and to have been initiated by the aggressive cultural politics of Andrei Zhdanov. The latter's policies, known collectively as *Zhdanovshchina*, flowed seamlessly into a larger campaign of anti-cosmopolitanism. The infamous resolution of August 14, 1946, on the journals *Zvezda* and *Leningrad*, was a precursor of the latter. Aleksandr Fadeev characterized Zoshchenko's and Akhmatova's literary work as a provincial adoption of the decadent values of the "corrupted" West, which is represented by the "subjective idealist views of Nietzsche, Bergson and Freud." See Aleksandr Fadeev, "Zadachi sovetskoi literatury," in *Sobranie sochinenii v semi tomakh*, (Khudozhestvennaia literatura, 1971), 5:491.
10. In 1948 the United States ratified the Marshall Plan and Israel was declared an independent state. In March 1948, talks for a wider military alliance between Western countries began and they consequently culminated in the formation of the North Atlantic Treaty Organization in 1949.
11. Aleksandr Maksimov, "Protiv reaktsionnogo einshteinianstva v fizike," *Krasnyi flot* (June 13, 1952): 3–4. Leading physicists such as Petr Kapitsa and Vladimir Fok courageously argued against politicizing science. See Dzhahangir Nadzhafov, ed., *Stalin i kosmopolitizm. Dokumenty Agitpropa TsK KPSS. 1945–1953* (Materik, 2005), 130.
12. Nadzhafov, *Stalin*, 451.
13. Nadzhafov, *Stalin*, 23.
14. Nikolai Tikhonov, "V zashchitu Pushkina," *Kul'tura i zhizn'* (May 9, 1947): 4. The 1937 Pushkin Jubilee was a powerful endorsement of the Russian "national form" that was immediately endowed with a universal appeal. But during the Pushkin Jubilee of 1949, Stalin sought to reestablish Pushkin as a messianic figure whose cultural contribution to the Soviet "salvation" of Europe was undeniable. See Olga Voronina, "'The Sun of World Poetry': Pushkin as a Cold War Writer," *Pushkin Review* 14 (2011): 73.
15. In a 1947 memorandum addressed to Molotov, the Jewish Anti-Fascist Committee was characterized as a political entity that had played an instrumental role during World War II but had subsequently acquired a pronouncedly "nationalistic, Zionist character." The committee's connection with Jewish organizations in the West was deeply problematic for the repressive state apparatus. See Nadzhafov, *Stalin*, 99.

16. Frank Grüner, "'Russia's Battle Against the Foreign': The Anticosmopolitanism Paradigm in Russian and Soviet Ideology," *European Review of History / Revue européenne d'histoire* 17, no. 3 (2010): 446. The public antisemitic campaign, endorsed by the state, took place between late January and late March of 1949. Nadzhafov, *Stalin*, 10. According to Ilya Erenburg, in late March of 1949, Stalin instructed newspaper editors to stop revealing the real surnames of Jewish writers and scholars who were writing under assumed names, stating that it "smacks of antisemitism." This marked the end of the openly antisemitic aspects of the anti-cosmopolitan campaign. Il'ia Erenburg, *Sobranie sochinenii v deviati tomakh. Tom 9* (GIKhL, 1967), 574.
17. This was evident in discussions of Soviet Yiddish literature during the anti-cosmopolitan campaign. Some Yiddish writers at a meeting of Moscow Soviet Jewish writers were blamed for "hypertrophying the sense of national identity" and "cultivating religious mystical moods"; see Nadzhafov, *Stalin*, 136.
18. "Ob odnoi antipatrioticheskoi gruppe teatral'nykh kritikov," *Pravda* (January 28, 1949): 3.
19. "Ob odnoi antipatrioticheskoi gruppe," 3, my emphasis.
20. Editorial, "Do kontsa razoblachit' antipatrioticheskuiu gruppu teatral'nykh kritikov," *Literaturnaia gazeta* (January 29, 1949): 1.
21. In Nadzhafov, *Stalin*, 23.
22. Aleksandr Poskrebyshev, "Velikoe mnogonatsional'noe sovetskoe gosudarstvo," *Pravda* (December 30, 1952): 1.
23. See Viktor Vinogradov, *Velikii russkii iazyk* (OGIZ, 1945), 157. However, Stalin had argued the opposite in 1930: "Is it not evident that in advocating a single, common language within the borders of a *single* state, within the borders of the USSR, they [proponents of social chauvinism] are, in essence, striving to restore the *privileges* of the formerly predominant language, namely, the *Great-Russian* language?" Stalin, "Political Report of the Central Committee to the Sixteenth Congress of the CPSU(B), June 27, 1930," 376.
24. Vinogradov, *Velikii russkii iazyk*, 170.
25. See Nadzhafov, *Stalin*, 159.
26. Nadzhafov, *Stalin*, 159–60.
27. Walter Benjamin, *The Arcades Project*, trans. Howard Eiland and Kevin McLaughlin (Belknap Press, 1999), 17.
28. Vera Mukhina, "Monumental'no-dekorativnye skul'pturnye resheniia v ansamble gorodov," in Fedor Fedorovskii, ed., *Monumental'no-dekorativnoe i dekorativno-prikladnoe iskusstvo* (Akademiia Khudozhestv SSSR, 1951), 46. In contrast, the facade-averse avant-gardists were deeply convinced that architectural form should be unadorned, deriving simply from an analysis of function (utility) and an expression of new structural methods (construction) with no reference to outdated historical styles. Rational, analytic, and socially engaged Soviet avant-garde architects aspired to find design solutions to society's collective needs. They rejected ornamentation by forcibly professing its supplementary character in relation to the structure of the building. Construction for the constructivists, like form for the formalists, comprises a self-sufficient core and rejects anything superfluous.
29. The Uzbek and Tajik pavilions featured restaurants that offered national cuisine dishes in addition to the generic Vostochnyi (Eastern) restaurant. This created unexpected and even undesired affinities with colonial fairs that employed the rhetoric of imperialism. The VSKhV's staging of peoples evoked the 1900 Paris Exposition wherein French colonial subjects from Africa, Asia, and Oceania lived on the grounds and were presented purely as objects of display.
30. Tat'iana Astrakhantseva, "Stil' 'Pobeda' v dekorativno-ornamental'nom iskusstve 1940–1950-kh godov," in Iuliia Kosenkova, ed., *Arkhitektura stalinskoi epokhi: Opyt istoricheskogo osmysleniia* (Kom-Kniga, 2010), 142–49.
31. Irina Belintseva, "Iz istorii sozdaniia VSKhV (K voprosu ob otnoshenii k narodnym traditsiiam)," in *Traditsii i sovremennost': aktual'nye problemy izobrazitel'nogo iskusstva i arkhitektury*, ed. Grigorii Sternin (VNII, 1989), 146.

32. Clement Greenberg, "Avant-Garde and Kitsch," in *Clement Greenberg: The Collected Essays and Criticism*, vol. 1, *Perceptions and Judgments, 1939–1944*, ed. John O'Brian (University of Chicago Press, 1986), 19.
33. Vladimir Kliavin, a civil engineer, was responsible for the structural design. Unexpectedly, Topuridze edited a translation of Le Corbusier's *L'Unité d'habitation de Marseille* (1950) in the Soviet Union in 1970.
34. The exhibition site underwent multiple designs and redesigns in 1937 and 1939, as well as substantial reconstruction from 1948 to 1954.
35. VDNKh, f. 1 (indeks 94), op. 7, d. 5–1/12, l. 2.
36. See, for example, Iosif Stalin, "Politicheskii otchet Tsentral'nogo komiteta XVI S"ezdu VKP(b)," in *Sochineniia. Tom 12* (GIPL, 1949), 369, 370.
37. The exhibition itself was an immense display of flora: forty thousand trees, four hundred fifty thousand bushes, and about five million flowers adorned the site. The parterre that connects the two fountains initially took the form of a Russian flower ornament. See I. Petrov, "Dekorativnoe ozelenenie Vsesoiuznoi sel'skokhoziaistvennoi vystavki," *Arkhitektura i stroitel'stvo Moskvy*, no. 9 (1954): 24, 27.
38. It was referred to simply as "Sheaf" (Snop) in archival documentation. According to the initial designs, the golden sheaf of wheat of the fountain was supposed to release water jets that would form a "water sheaf" illuminated with golden light. VDNKh, f. 1 (indeks 94), op. 7, d. 5–1/4, ll. 2, 4. It appears to mirror the wheat sheaf in the form of a crown at the Ukrainian pavilion, which is positioned along the same main axis.
39. The sixteenth was the Karelo-Finnish Soviet republic that existed from 1940 until its integration into the Russian Soviet Federative Socialist Republic (RSFSR) in 1956.
40. Chaikov was responsible for six fountain figures—those representing Estonia, Georgia, Moldova, Tajikistan, the Karelo-Finnish Republic, and Russia. His early period was marked by an engagement with avant-garde trends and by the bold presence of oriental motifs, which he employed to elaborate an emerging Yiddish socialist identity. He was an active member of Kulturlige, a secular socialist Jewish organization established in Kyiv in 1918, whose goal was "to assist in creating a new Yiddish secular culture in the Yiddish language, in Jewish national forms . . . in the spirit of the working man"; see Victor Margolin, *The Struggle for Utopia: Rodchenko, Lissitzky, Moholy-Nagy, 1917–1946* (University of Chicago Press, 1997), 27.
41. Teneta was responsible for the sculptures representing Armenia, Belarus, Kyrgyzstan, Lithuania, and Ukraine. However, there is a plaster prototype for the Russian figure in Teneta's collection in London.
42. Bazhenova sculpted five figures—those representing Azerbaijan, Latvia, Kazakhstan, Turkmenistan, and Uzbekistan.
43. The monograph also establishes that "formalist infatuations did not affect Bazhenova at all; they did not influence her simple, clear, fundamentally realistic perception of life." See Galina Rostovtseva, *Zinaida Vasil'evna Bazhenova* (Sovetskii khudozhnik, 1961), 5, 9.
44. Contemporaneous critics condemned the monotony of the composition and deemed the movement of the women's hands, which was supposed to establish the dynamism of the circular composition, deficient. Sara Valerius, "Vsesoiuznaia sel'skokhoziaistvennaia vystavka. Skul'ptura," *Iskusstvo*, no. 6 (1954): 14.
45. The pumping station of the fountain is housed in the basement of the RSFSR pavilion and connected with the fountain through an underground passage; see Konstantin Topuridze, "Fontany Vsesoiuznoi sel'skokhoziaistvennoi vystavki," *Arkhitektura i stroitel'stvo Moskvy*, no. 7 (1954): 15. Significantly, the initial plan did not include a pavilion for the RSFSR. It was built in a hurry, a few months before the opening, after an inspection by the minister of culture and Kliment Voroshilov, the chairman of the Presidium of the Supreme Soviet. The two were astounded to find out that the Russian nation had not been given its own exhibition hall. See RGALI, f. 2943, op. 1, d. 764, l. 54.
46. VDNKh, f. 1 (indeks 94), op. 7, d. 5–1/2, l. 21.

47. Pavel Bazhov, "Kamennyi tsvetok," *Literaturnaia gazeta* (May 10, 1938): 3.
48. Viktor Pertsov, "Skazki starogo Urala," *Literaturnaia gazeta* (May 10, 1938): 3. See also Mark Lipovetsky, "Zloveshchee v skazakh Bazhova," *Quaestio Rossica*, no. 2 (2014): 213.
49. The Russocentric tendency was further amplified in Sergei Prokofiev's last ballet, *The Tale of the Stone Flower*, based on the same story. Prokofiev's rendering of the tale was written between 1948 and 1949 and first staged in 1953—at the height of the anti-cosmopolitan campaign. The composer defined its central themes as "the joy of creative labor for the benefit of the people" and "the spiritual beauty of the Russian man." See Semen Shlifshtein, ed., *S.S. Prokof'ev: materialy, dokumenty, vospominaniia* (GMI, 1956), 131.
50. Walter Benjamin, *The Origin of German Tragic Drama* (Verso, 1998), 177–78.
51. RGALI, f. 2943, op. 1, d. 764, l. 6.
52. RGALI, f. 2943, op. 1, d. 764, l. 6.
53. RGALI, f. 2943, op. 1, d. 764, l. 46.
54. Gradov, upon his graduation from MARKhI in 1937, joined the state architectural bureau in Kyrgyzstan and quickly became the head of the Kyrgyz division of the Union of Soviet Architects. He served as a military engineer during World War II and chaired a research group on public buildings at the Academy of Architecture of the USSR after the war.
55. Resolution Number 1871, "On the Elimination of Excesses in Design and Construction," Central Committee of the Communist Party of the Soviet Union and of the Council of Ministers of the Soviet Union, November 4, 1955.
56. Nikita Khrushchev, "Rech' tov. Khrushcheva N.S.," *Vsesoiuznoe soveshchanie stroitelei, arkhitektorov i rabotnikov promyshlennosti stroitel'nykh materialov, stroitel'nogo i dorozhnogo mashinostroeniia, proektnykh i nauchno-issledovatel'skikh organizatsii. 30 noiabria—7 dekabria 1954 g. Sokrashchennyi stenograficheskii otchet* (Gosudarstvennoe izdatel'stvo literatury po stroitel'stvu i arkhitekture, 1955), 393.
57. Yuri Tynianov, "Interlude," in *Permanent Evolution: Selected Essays on Literature, Theory and Film* (Academic Studies Press, 2019), 175.

BIBLIOGRAPHY

Abashin, Sergey. "Sovetskaia vlast' i uzbekskaia makhallia." *Neprikosnovennyi zapas* 78, no. 4 (2011): 95–110.
Abashin, Sergey, and Andrew Jenks, eds. "Soviet Central Asia on the Periphery." *Kritika: Explorations in Russian and Eurasian History* 16, no. 2 (2015): 359–74.
Abdel-Malek, Anouar. "Orientalism in Crisis." *Diogenes* 44 (1963): 103–40.
Abikeyeva, Gul'nara. "Central Asian Documentary Films of the Soviet Era as a Factor in the Formation of National Identity." http://www.kinokultura.com/2009/24-abikeeva.shtml, accessed 27 January 2018.
A Commission of the Central Committee of the C.P.S.U.(B.). *The History of the Communist Party of the Soviet Union (Bolsheviks) [Short Course]*. International Publishers, 1939.
Adalis, "Osedaiut kochevniki." *Nashi dostizheniia*, no. 9 (1931): 49–55.
Adorno, Theodor. *The Culture Industry: Selected Essays on Mass Culture*. Routledge, 1991.
Adorno, Theodor, Walter Benjamin, Ernst Bloch, Bertolt Brecht, and Georg Lukács. *Aesthetics and Politics*. Verso, 2010.
Akhmet'ev, V., and G. Volchek. "Fotografiia v glavnom pavil'one," *Sovetskoe foto*, no. 7 (1939): 9.
Akinsha, Konstantin, Katia Denysova, and Olena Kashuba-Volvach. eds. *In the Eye of the Storm: Modernism in Ukraine, 1900–1930s*. Thames & Hudson, 2022.
Al'pert, Maks. "Sotsializm pereplavliaet cheloveka." *Proletarskoe foto*, no. 7/8 (1932): 8
Albéra, François. *Eisenstein et le constructivisme russe: dramaturgie de la forme*. L'Age d'homme, 1990.
Albert, Gleb. "International Solidarity With(out) World Revolution: The Transformation of 'Internationalism' in Early Soviet Society." *Monde(s)* 2, no. 10 (2016): 33–50.
Alekseev, M.P., S.D. Balukhatyi, N.P. Berkov, and A.P. Riftin, eds. *Trudy iubileinoi nauchnoi sessii LGU. Sektsiia filologicheskikh nauk*. LGU, 1946.
Amaglobeli, Sergo, *Iskusstvo narodov SSSR*. Uchpedgiz, 1932.
Anderson, K.M., and L.V. Maksimenkov, eds. *Kremlevskii kinoteatr. 1928–1953. Dokumenty*. ROSSPEN, 2005.
Andreev, Nikolai. "Russkii fol'klor." *Literaturnyi kritik*, no. 10/11 (1939): 267–71.
Andronikashvili, Zaal. "National Form: The Evolution of Georgian Socialist Realism." *Slavic Review* 81, no. 4, (2022): 914–35.
Arsenjuk, Luka. *Movement, Action, Image, Montage: Sergei Eisenstein and the Cinema in Crisis*. University of Minnesota Press, 2018.
Arsharuni, Arshaluis. "Khudozhestvennaia literatura Srednei Azii." *Krasnaia niva* 16 (1929): 10–11.
Arvatov, Boris. *Iskusstvo i proizvodstvo*. Proletkul't, 1926.
Aseev, Nikolai. *Rabota nad stikhom*. Priboi, 1929.

Astakhov, A. "Diskussiia o sushchnosti i zadachakh fol'klora v Leningradskom Institute rechevoi kul'tury (IRK), 11 iiunia 1931 g." *Sovetskaia etnografiia*, no. 3/4 (1931): 239–42.

Auerbach, Jonathan, and Russ Castronovo, eds. *The Oxford Handbook of Propaganda Studies*. Oxford University Press, 2013.

Auezov, Mukhtar. *Mysli raznykh let. Po literaturnym tropam*. KGIKhL, 1961.

___. *Neizvestnoe v nasledii Mukhtara Auezova: arkhivnye dokumenty*. Biblioteka Olzhasa, 2013.

Auezov, Mukhtar, and Leonid Sobolev. "Epos i fol'klor kazakhskogo Naroda." *Literaturnyi kritik* 10/11 (1939): 210–33 and *Literaturnyi kritik* 1 (1940): 169–80.

Bakhtin, Mikhail. *Art and Answerability: Early Philosophical Essays by M.M. Bakhtin*, ed. Michael Holquist and Vadim Liapunov; trans. Vadim Liapunov. University of Texas Press, 1990.

Balakrishnan, Gopal, ed. *Mapping the Nation*. Verso, 2012.

Balibar, Etienne. "The Nation Form: History and Ideology." *Review (Fernand Braudel Center)* 13, no. 3 (1990): 329–61.

Barr, Alfred H. *Cubism and Abstract Art*. MoMA, 1936.

___. "Russian Diary 1927–28." *October* 7 (1978): 10–51.

Barthes, Roland. *Camera Lucida: Reflections of Photography*, trans. Richard Howard. Hill & Wang, 1982.

___. *The Rustle of Language*. Trans. Richard Howard. Hill & Wang, 1986.

Bassin, Mark, Sergey Glebov, and Marlene Laruelle, eds. *Between Europe and Asia: The Origins, Theories, and Legacies of Russian Eurasianism*. University of Pittsburgh Press, 2015.

Bataille, Georges. *The Accursed Share: An Essay on General Economy*. Vol. 1, *Consumption*. Zone, 1998.

Bazhov, Pavel. "Kamennyi tsvetok." *Literaturnaia gazeta* (May 10, 1938): 3.

Beckman, Karen, and Jean Ma, eds. *Still Moving: Between Cinema and Photography*. Duke University Press, 2008.

Behrends, Jan, and Martin Kohlrausch, eds. *Races to Modernity: Metropolitan Aspirations in Eastern Europe, 1890–1940*. Central European University Press, 2014.

Belyi, Andrei. "Chekhov." *Vesy* 8 (1904): 1–9.

Belyi, Andrei, et al. *Kak my pishem*. Kniga, 1930.

Benjamin, Walter. *The Arcades Project*. Trans. Howard Eiland and Kevin McLaughlin. Belknap Press, 1999.

___. *The Origin of German Tragic Drama*. London: Verso, 1998.

___. *Selected Writings*. Vol. 2, Part 1: *1927–1930*. Ed. Michael W. Jennings, Howard Eiland, and Gary Smith; trans. Rodney Livingstone. Belknap Press, 2005.

___. *Selected Writings*. Vol. 2, Part 2: *1931–1934*. Ed. Michael W. Jennings, Howard Eiland, and Gary Smith; trans. Rodney Livingstone. Belknap Press, 2005.

Benson, Timothy, ed. *Central European Avant-Gardes: Exchange and Transformation, 1910–1930*. MIT Press, 2002.

Berman, Jessica. *Modernist Fiction, Cosmopolitanism, and the Politics of Community*. Cambridge University Press, 2001.

Berman, Marshall. *All That Is Solid Melts Into Air: The Experience of Modernity*. Penguin, 1988.

Bhabha, Homi. *The Location of Culture*. Routledge, 1994.

Blitstein, Peter. "Cultural Diversity and the Interwar Conjuncture: Soviet Nationality Policy in Its Comparative Context." *Slavic Review* 65, no. 2 (2006): 273–93.

Bloch, Ernst. *Heritage of Our Times*. Trans. Neville and Stephen Plaice. Polity, 1991.

Boltianskii, Grigorii. *Lenin i kino*. Gosudarstvennoe izdatel'stvo, 1925.

Bor'ba za klassovye proletarskie pozitsii na fronte prostranstvennykh iskusstv. IZOGIZ, 1931.

Bordwell, David. *The Cinema of Eisenstein*. Harvard University Press, 1993.

___. "Eisenstein's Epistemological Shift." *Screen* 15, no. 4 (1974–75): 29–46.

Bowlt, John, ed. *Russian Art of the Avant-Garde Theory and Criticism, 1902–1934*. Viking Press, 1976.

Bowlt, John, and Matthew Drutt, eds. *Amazons of the Avant-Garde: Alexandra Exter, Natalia Goncharova, Liubov Popova, Olga Rozanova, Varvara Stepanova, and Nadezhda Udaltsova*. Deutsche Guggenheim, 1999.

Boym, Svetlana. *Common Places: Mythologies of Everyday Life in Russia.* Harvard University Press, 1994.

Bradbury, Malcolm, and James McFarlane, eds. *Modernism, 1890–1930.* Penguin, 1976.

Brandenberger, David. "Global and Transnational in Form, Soviet in Content: The Changing Semantics of Internationalism in Official Soviet Discourse, 1917–1991." *The Russian Review* 80 (2021): 562–80.

———. *National Bolshevism: Stalinist Mass Culture and the Formation of Modern Russian National Identity, 1931–1956.* Harvard University Press, 2002.

———. "Stalin's Populism and the Accidental Creation of Russian National Identity." *Nationalities Papers* 38, no. 5 (2010): 723–39.

Brandist, Craig, and Katya Chown, eds. *Politics and the Theory of Language in the USSR, 1917–1938: The Birth of Sociological Linguistics.* Anthem Press, 2010.

Brik, Osip. "Ot kartiny k foto." *Novyi Lef*, no. 3 (1928): 29–33.

Brilliant, Richard. *Portraiture.* Reaktion Books, 1991.

Brooker, Peter, and Andrew Thacker, eds. *Geographies of Modernism: Literatures, Cultures, Spaces.* Routledge, 2005.

Brooker, Peter, Andrzej Gąsiorek, Deborah Longworth, and Andrew Thacker, eds. *The Oxford Handbook of Modernisms.* Oxford University Press, 2010.

Brubaker, Rogers. *Nationalism Reframed: Nationhood and the National Question in the New Europe.* Cambridge University Press, 1996.

Buchloh, Benjamin. "From Faktura to Factography." *October* 30 (1984): 82–119.

Bulgakowa, Oksana. *Sergei Eisenstein. A Biography.* Potemkin Press, 2001.

———. *Sovetskii slukhoglaz: Kino i ego organy chuvstv.* NLO, 2010.

Bürger, Peter. *Theory of the Avant-Garde.* University of Minnesota Press, 1984.

Burghardt, Anja. "Picturing Non-Russian Ethnicities in the Journals *Sovetskoe foto* and *SSSR na stroike* (1920s–1930s)." *Russian Literature* 103–105 (2019): 209–33.

Bustanov, Alfrid. *Soviet Orientalism and the Creation of Central Asian Nations.* Routledge, 2016.

Cavarero, Adriana. *For More Than One Voice: Toward a Philosophy of Vocal Expression.* Stanford University Press, 2005.

Cheng, Anne Anlin. *Ornamentalism.* Oxford University Press, 2019.

Cheremukhin, Mikhail. "O narodnykh pesniakh sovetskikh fil'mov." *Iskusstvo kino*, no. 2 (1939): 54–56.

Chicherov, Vladimir. *Voprosy teorii i istorii narodnogo tvorchestva.* Sovetskii pisatel', 1959.

Chion, Michel. *The Voice in Cinema.* Columbia University Press, 1999.

Chuzhak, Nikolai, ed. *Literatura fakta: Pervyi sbornik materialov rabotnikov LEFa.* Federatsiia, 1929.

Clark, Katerina. *Eurasia Without Borders: The Dream of a Leftist Literary Commons, 1919–1943.* Harvard University Press, 2021.

———. *Moscow, the Fourth Rome: Stalinism, Cosmopolitanism, and the Evolution of Soviet Culture, 1931–1941.* Harvard University Press, 2011.

———. *The Soviet Novel: History as Ritual.* University of Chicago Press, 1981.

Clark, T. J. *Farewell to an Idea: Episodes from a History of Modernism.* Yale University Press, 1999.

Coggeshall, Samuel. "Stalin, 'National Content,' and National Destiny." Unpublished paper.

Conrads, Ulrich, ed. *Programs and Manifestoes on 20th Century Architecture.* MIT Press, 1975.

Dabrowski, Magdalena, Leah Dickerman, and Peter Galassi, eds. *Aleksandr Rodchenko.* MoMA, 1998.

Degot', Ekaterina. *Russkoe iskusstvo XX veka.* Trilistnik, 2002.

"Deklaratsiia ob"edineniia 'Oktiabr'.'" *Pravda* (June 3, 1928): 7.

Deleuze, Gilles. *Cinema 1: The Movement-Image.* Trans. Hugh Tomlinson and Barbara Habberjam. University of Minnesota Press, 1986.

———. *Cinema 2: The Time-Image.* Trans. Hugh Tomlinson and Barbara Habberjam. University of Minnesota Press, 1997.

———. *The Fold. Leibniz and the Baroque.* Trans. Tom Conley. University of Minnesota Press, 1993.

Denber, Rachel, ed. *The Soviet Nationality Reader: The Disintegration in Context.* Westview Press, 1992.

Derrida, Jacques. *The Truth in Painting*. Trans. Geoffrey Bennington and Ian McLeod. University of Chicago Press, 1987.

Dickerman, Leah. "David King, *The Commissar Vanishes: The Falsification of Photographs and Art in Stalin's Russia*." *The Art Bulletin* 80, no. 4 (1998): 755–57.

Dimanshtein, Semyon. "Rekonstruktivnyi period i rabota sredi natsional'nostei SSSR." *Revoliutsiia i natsional'nosti*, no. 1 (1930): 9–19.

Diskussiia ob aziatskom sposobe proizvodstva. Po dokladu M. Godesa. GSEI, 1931.

Dmitrakov, I., and M. Kuznetsov. "Aleksandr Veselovskii i ego posledovateli." *Oktiabr'*, no. 12 (1947): 165–73.

Dobrenko, Evgeny. *Late Stalinism: The Aesthetics of Politics*. Trans. Jesse M. Savage. Yale University Press, 2020.

———. *Political Economy of Socialist Realism*. Trans. Jesse M. Savage. Yale University Press, 2007.

———. "Total'naia lingvistika: Vlast' grammatiki i grammatika vlasti." *Russian Literature* 63, no. 2–4 (2008): 533–621.

"Do kontsa razoblachit' antipatrioticheskuiu gruppu teatral'nykh kritikov." *Literaturnaia gazera* (January 29, 1949): 1.

Dolar, Mladen. *A Voice and Nothing More*. MIT Press, 2006.

Dorson, Richard. *American Folklore*. University of Chicago Press, 1977.

Drieu, Cloé. *Cinema, Nation, and Empire in Uzbekistan, 1919–1937*. Indiana University Press, 2019.

Dubinskaia-Dzhalilova, T., and A. Chernev, eds. "Perepiska M. Gor'kogo i I.V. Stalina." *Novoe Literaturnoe Obozrenie* 40, no. 6 (1999): 223–50.

Dubrovskii, Sergei. *K voprosu o sushchnosti "aziatskogo" sposoba proizvodstva, feodalizma, krepostnichestva i torgovogo kapitala*. Nauchnaia assotsiatsiia vostokovedeniia, 1929.

Dulguerova, Elitza. "Introduction to Iakov Tugendkhol'd, 'In the Iron Dead-end' (1915)." *Modernism/modernity* 17, no. 4 (2010): 899–903.

Dwyer, Anne. "Standstill as Extinction: Viktor Shklovsky's Poetics and Politics of Movement in the 1920s and 1930s." *PMLA* 131, no. 2 (2016): 269–88.

Eagleton, Terry. *Exiles and Émigrés: Studies in Modern Literature*. Schocken, 1970.

Eagleton, Terry, Fredric Jameson and Edward Said, eds. *Nationalism, Colonialism, and Literature*. Minneapolis: University of Minnesota Press, 1990.

Eding, Dmitrii. *Reznaia skul'ptura Urala. Iz istorii zverinogo stilia*. GIM, 1940.

Eisenstein, Sergei. *Disney*. Potemkin Press, 2013.

———. "The Film About the Fergana Canal." *Studies in Russian and Soviet Cinema* 5, no. 1 (2011): 157–60.

———. *Film Form: Essays in Film Theory*. Ed. and trans. Jay Leyda. Harcourt Brace & World, 1949.

———. *Izbrannye proizvedeniia v shesti tomakh. Tom 1*. Iskusstvo, 1964.

———. *Izbrannye proizvedeniia v shesti tomakh. Tom 5*. Iskusstvo, 1968.

———. *Izbrannye proizvedeniia v shesti tomakh. Tom 6*. Iskusstvo, 1971.

———. "The Land Has Become Unrecognizable." *Studies in Russian and Soviet Cinema* 5, no. 1 (2011): 160–61.

———. *Metod. Tom 1. Grundproblem*. Muzei kino, 2002.

———. *Metod. Tom 2. Tainy masterov*. Muzei kino, 2002.

———. "[Moia sistema]." *Kinovedcheskie zapiski* 36/37 (1997–1998): 23–27.

———. *Montazh*. Muzei kino, 2000.

———. *Neravnodushnaia priroda. Tom 1. Chuvstvo kino*. Muzei kino, 2004.

———. *Nonindifferent Nature: Film and the Structure of Things*. Intro. Herbert Eagle. Trans. Herbert Marshall. Cambridge University Press, 1987.

———. "Piat' epoch." *Pravda* (July 6, 1926): 6.

Eizenshtein, Sergei, et al. *O fil'me 'Bezhin lug' Eizenshteina*. Iskusstvo, 1937.

Erlich, Victor. *Modernism and Revolution: Russian Literature in Transition*. Harvard University Press, 1994.

———. *Russian Formalism: History and Doctrine*. Yale University Press, 1981.

Erenburg, Il'ia. *Sobranie sochinenii v deviati tomakh. Tom 9*. GIKhL, 1967.

BIBLIOGRAPHY

Erofeev, V., and Z. Zalkind. "Tekhnika zvukovoi kinoekspeditsii." *Proletarskoe kino*, no. 6 (1932): 43–48.
Etkind, Alexander. *Internal Colonization: Russia's Imperial Experience*. Polity, 2011.
Eysteinsson, Astradur. *The Concept of Modernism*. Cornell University Press, 1992.
Fadeev, Aleksandr. "Doklad general'nogo sekretaria SSP SSSR." *Literaturnaia gazeta* (June 29, 1947): 1–2.
___. *Sobranie sochinenii v semi tomakh. Tom 5*. Khudozhestvennaia literatura, 1971.
Fauchereau, Serge. *Art of the Baltic States: Modernism, Freedom and Identity 1900–1950*. Thames & Hudson, 2022.
Favorskii, Vladimir. *Literaturno-teoreticheskoe nasledie*. Sovetskii khudozhnik, 1988.
Fedorovskii, Fedor, ed. *Monumental'no-dekorativnoe i dekorativno-prikladnoe iskusstvo*. Akademiia Khudozhestv SSSR, 1951.
Feldman, Leah. *On the Threshold of Eurasia: Revolutionary Poetics in the Caucasus*. Cornell University Press, 2018.
___. "Orientalism on the Threshold: Reorienting Heroism in Late Imperial Russia." *boundary 2* 39, no. 2 (2012): 161–80.
Fitzpatrick, Sheila, ed. *The Russian Revolution*. Oxford University Press, 2017.
___. *Stalinism: New Directions*. Routledge, 2000.
Fore, Devin. *Realism after Modernism: The Rehumanization of Art and Literature*. MIT Press, 2012.
Fridliand, Semyon. "Zametki o tvorcheskoi praktike: k publikuemym rabotam gruppy ROPF." *Proletarskoe foto*, no. 2 (1931): 13–16.
Friedman, Susan Stanford. *Planetary Modernisms: Provocations on Modernity Across Time*. Columbia University Press, 2015.
Fülöp-Miller, René. *The Mind and Face of Bolshevism: An Examination of Cultural Life in Soviet Russia*. Harper & Row, 1962.
Galushkin, Aleksandr. "'Nastupaet nepreryvnoe iskusstvo . . .' V.B. Shklovskii o sud'be russkogo avangarda nachala 1930-kh." *De Visu*, no. 11 (1993): 25–38.
___. "[Razgovory s Viktorom Shklovskim]." *Novoe Literaturnoe Obozrenie* 131, no. 1 (2015): 220–39.
Gan, Aleksei. *Constructivism*. Tenov Books, 2014.
Gel'fand, Mark. "Deklaratsiia tsaria Midasa, ili chto sluchilos's Viktorom Shklovskim." *Literaturnaia gazeta* (March 13, 1930): 2.
Ginzburg, S. "Kino-Pravda." *Iskusstvo kino*, no. 1/2 (1940): 87–88.
Glaser, Amelia, and Steven Lee, eds. *Comintern Aesthetics*. University of Toronto Press, 2020.
Glebova, Aglaya. *Aleksandr Rodchenko: Photography in the Time of Stalin*. Yale University Press, 2022.
Glisic, Iva. "Terror and Dream: The Photobooks of Aleksandr Rodchenko and Varvara Stepanova, 1936–39." *Modernism/modernity* 28, no. 4 (2021): 707–34.
Gor'kii, Maksim. "O formalizme." *Literaturnaia gazeta* (March 27, 1936): 2.
___. "O iazyke." *Pravda* (March 18, 1934): 2.
___. *Sobranie sochinenii v 30 tomakh. Tom 27*. GIKhL, 1953.
___. "Za druzhnuiu tvorcheskuiu sredu." *Literaturnaia Gazeta* (August 23, 1934): 3.
Gorbachev, Georgii. "My eshche ne nachinali drat'sia." *Zvezda*, no. 5 (1930): 124–25.
Gor'kii, Maksim, Lev Mekhlis, and Aleksei Stetskii, eds. *Tvorchestvo narodov SSSR*. Pravda, 1937.
Gough, Maria. *The Artist as Producer: Russian Constructivism in Revolution*. University of California Press, 2005.
___. "Faktura: The Making of the Russian Avant-Garde." *RES* 36 (1999): 32–59.
Gouldner, Alvin. "Stalinism: A Study of Internal Colonialism." *Telos*, no. 34 (1978): 5–48.
Gourmont, Remy de. *La culture des idées*. Mercure de France, 1916.
Grant, Barry Keith, and Jeanette Sloniowski, eds. *Documenting the Documentary: Close Readings of Documentary Film and Video*. Wayne State University Press, 1998.
Greenberg, Clement. *The Collected Essays and Criticism. Vol. 1, Perceptions and Judgments, 1939–1944*. University of Chicago Press, 1986.

___. *The Collected Essays and Criticism.* Vol. 4, *Modernism with a Vengeance, 1957–1969.* University of Chicago Press, 1986.

Groys, Boris. *The Total Art of Stalinism: Avant-garde, Aesthetic Dictatorship, and Beyond.* Princeton University Press, 1992.

Grüner, Frank. "'Russia's Battle Against the Foreign': The Anticosmopolitanism Paradigm in Russian and Soviet Ideology." *European Review of History / Revue européenne d'histoire* 17, no. 3 (2010): 445–72.

Günther, Hans, and Evgenii Dobrenko, eds. *Sotsrealisticheskii kanon.* Akademicheskii proekt, 2000.

Günther, Hans, and Sabine Hänsgen, eds. *Sovetskaia vlast' i media.* Akademicheskii proekt, 2006.

Hansen-Löve, Aage. *Russkii Formalizm: Metodologicheskaia rekonstruktsiia razvitiia na osnove printsipa ostraneniia.* Iazyki russkoi kul'tury, 2001.

Herodotus. *Histories. Books I and II.* Ed. Carolyn Dewald and Rosaria Vignolo Munson. Cambridge: Harvard University Press, 1975.

Hicks, Jeremy. *Dziga Vertov: Defining Documentary Film.* IB Tauris, 2007.

Hirsch, Francine. "Getting to Know 'The Peoples of the USSR': Ethnographic Exhibits as Soviet Virtual Tourism, 1923–1934." *Slavic Review* 62, no. 4 (2000): 683–709.

Hobsbawm, Eric, and Terence Ranger, eds. *The Invention of Tradition.* Cambridge University Press, 1983.

Hoffmann, David. "Was There a 'Great Retreat' from Soviet Socialism? Stalinist Culture Reconsidered." *Kritika: Explorations in Russian and Eurasian History* 5, no. 4, (2004): 651–74.

Holzberger, Helena. "National in Front of the Camera, Soviet Behind It: Central Asia in Press Photography, 1925–1937." *Journal of Modern European History* 16, no. 4 (2018): 487–508.

Iakobson, Roman. *Roman Iakobson: Teksty, Dokumenty, Issledovaniia,* ed. Henryk Baran and S. I. Gindin. RGGI, 1999.

Iampol'skii, Mikhail. *Uskol'zaiushchii kontekst: Russkaia filosofiia v postsovetskikh usloviiakh.* Ad Marginem, 2002.

Ignatovich, Boris. "Po tvorcheskim gruppirovkam." *Proletarskoe foto,* no. 3 (1932): 27.

Ignatovich, Boris, et al. "Otkrytoe pis'mo gruppy 'Oktiabr'' v redaktsiiu 'Proletarskoe foto.'" *Proletarskoe foto,* no. 2 (1932): 3.

Ioffe, Dennis, and Frederick White, eds. *The Russian Avant-Garde and Radical Modernism: An Introductory Reader.* Academic Studies Press, 2012.

Ismailov, Esmagambet. *Akyny: Monografiia o tvorchestve Dzhambula i drugikh narodnykh akynov.* Kazakhskoe gosudarstvennoe izdatel'stvo khudozhestvennoi literatury, 1957.

Ivanov, Viacheslav. *Sobranie sochinenii. Tom 3.* Foyer Oriental Chrétien, 1979.

Jameson, Fredric. "Modernism and Imperialism." In *Nationalism, Colonialism, and Literature,* ed. Terry Eagleton et al. (University of Minnesota Press, 1990).

___. *The Political Unconscious: Narrative as a Socially Symbolic Act.* Routledge, 2002.

___. *Postmodernism, or, the Cultural Logic of Late Capitalism.* University of North Carolina Press, 1991.

___. *The Prison-House of Language: A Critical Account of Structuralism and Russian Formalism.* Princeton University Press, 1975.

Jencks, Charles. *Late-Modern Architecture and Other Essays.* Rizzoli, 1980.

Jobes, Gertrude. *Dictionary of Mythology, Folklore and Symbols.* Scarecrow Press, 1962.

Jones, Malcolm, and Robin Feuer Miller, eds. *The Cambridge Companion to the Classic Russian Novel.* Cambridge University Press, 1998.

Harrison, Charles, and Paul Wood, eds. *Art in Theory: 1900–1990. An Anthology of Changing Ideas.* Blackwell, 1992.

Hirsch, Francine. *Empire of Nations: Ethnographic Knowledge and the Making of the Soviet Union.* Cornell University Press, 2005.

"K partii. Ko vsem trudiashchimsia." *Pravda,* no. 19 (January 24, 1924): 1.

"K svedeniiu svobodnykh khudozhnikov." *Proletarskoe foto,* no. 1 (1932): 13.

Kaganovsky, Lilya. *The Voice of Technology: Soviet Cinema's Transition to Sound, 1928–1935.* Indiana University Press, 2018.

Kaganovsky, Lilya, and Masha Salazkina, eds. *Sound, Speech, Music in Soviet and Post-Soviet Cinema*. Indiana University Press, 2014.

Kahn, Douglas. *Noise, Water, Meat: A History of Sound in the Arts*. MIT Press, 1999.

Kalinin, Ilya. "USSR: The Union of National Form and Socialist Content." *Russian Studies in Philosophy* 60, no. 5 (2022): 382–94.

———. "Viktor Shklovskii, ili prevrashchenie literaturnogo priema v literaturnyi fakt." *Zvezda*, no. 7 (2014): 198–221.

Kant, Immanuel. *The Critique of Judgement*. Oxford University Press, 2007.

Kaplan, Isabelle. "Comrades in Arts: The Soviet Dekada of National Art and the Friendship of Peoples." *RUDN Journal of Russian History* 19, no. 1 (2020): 78–94.

Karasik, Mikhail, and Manfred Heiting, eds. *The Soviet Photobook, 1920–1941*. Steidl, 2015.

Katsman, R. "Kinokhronika vchera i segodnia." *Sovetskoe kino*, no. 1 (1935): 68–76.

Kaufman, Mikhail. "Poslednee interv'iu Mikhaila Kaufmana." *Kinovedcheskie zapiski*, no. 18 (1993): 143–50.

Kazakhskii narodnyi ornament. Iskusstvo, 1939.

Khalid, Adeeb. *Making Uzbekistan: Nation, Empire, and Revolution in the Early USSR*. Cornell University Press, 2015.

———. "Russian History and the Debate over Orientalism." *Kritika: Explorations in Russian and Eurasian History* 1, no. 4 (2000): 691–99.

Khan-Magomedov, Selim. *Il'ia Golosov*. Stroiizdat, 1988.

———. *Konstruktivizm: kontseptsiia formoobrazovaniia*. Stroiizdat, 2003.

———. *Rodchenko: The Complete Work*. Ed. Vieri Quilici. MIT Press, 1987.

Kiaer, Christina. *Imagine No Possessions: The Socialist Objects of Russian Constructivism*. MIT Press, 2005.

King, David. *The Commissar Vanishes: The Falsification of Photographs and Art in Stalin's Russia*. Henry Holt, 1997.

Kleiman, Naum. "Fergana Canal and Tamburlaine's Tower." *Studies in Russian and Soviet Cinema* 5, no. 1 (2011): 103–22.

———. *Formula finala: Stat'i, vystupleniia, besedy*. Eizenshtein-Tsentr, 2004.

Kleiman, Naum, and Antonio Somaini, eds. *Sergei M. Eisenstein: Notes for a General History of Cinema*. Amsterdam University Press, 2016.

Kliger, Ilya, and Boris Maslov, eds. *Persistent Forms: Explorations in Historical Poetics*. Fordham University Press, 2016.

Kliuchevskii, Vasilii. *Sochineniia v deviati tomakh. Tom IX*. Mysl', 1990.

Kol'tsov, Mikhail. "Poslednii reis." *Pravda*, no. 19 (24 January, 1924): 2.

Kosenkova, Iuliia, ed. *Arkhitektura stalinskoi epokhi: Opyt istoricheskogo osmysleniia*. KomKniga, 2010.

Kotkin, Stephen. *Magnetic Mountain: Stalinism as a Civilization*. University of California Press, 1997.

Kovalev, Andrei. "Russkaia zhivopis' i Vostok: desiatye gody XX veka." In *Nauchnye soobshcheniia. Gosudarstvennyi muzei iskusstva narodov vostoka. Vypusk XIII*, 22–47. Moscow: GMINV, 1980.

Kozlov, Leonid. *Izobrazhenie i obraz: Ocherki po istoricheskoi poetike sovetskogo kino*. Iskusstvo, 1980.

Kracauer, Siegfried. *The Mass Ornament: Weimar Essays*. Harvard University Press, 1995.

Krasnov, P. "A.M. Rodchenko (profili masterov)." *Sovetskoe foto*, no. 7 (1935): 16–26.

Krasovskii, Iu. "Pis'ma S.M. Eizenshteinu." *Iskusstvo kino*, no. 1 (1958): 99–105.

Kristi, L. "Zametki o SSR na stroike." *Sovetskoe foto*, no. 2 (1940): 8–12.

Kunichika, Michael. *"Our Native Antiquity": Archaeology and Aesthetics in the Culture of Russian Modernism*. Academic Studies Press, 2015.

Kushner, Boris. "Otkrytoe pis'mo." *Novyi Lef*, no. 8 (1928): 38–40.

Lahusen, Thomas, and Evgeny Dobrenko, eds. *Socialist Realism Without Shores*. Duke University Press, 1997.

Langman, Eleazar. "Moi universitet." *Sovetskoe foto*, no. 1 (1936): 26.

———. "Tvorcheskie poiski." *Sovetskoe foto*, no. 5/6 (1936): 27–29.

Latour, Bruno. *Science in Action: How to Follow Scientists and Engineers through Society*. Harvard University Press, 1987.

Laruelle, Marlène. *Central Peripheries: Nationhood in Central Asia*. UCL Press, 2021.
Lavrentiev, Aleksandr. *Varvara Stepanova*. Russkii avangard, 2009.
Lavrentiev, Alexander, ed. *Alexander Rodchenko. Experiments for the Future: Diaries, Essays, Letters and Other Writings*. MoMA, 2005.
Lee, Steven. *The Ethnic Avant-Garde: Minority Cultures and World Revolution*. Columbia University Press, 2015.
"Lenin i fotografiia." *Sovetskoe foto*, no. 2 (1929): 33–35.
Lenin, Vladimir. *Collected Works*. Vol. 6, *January 1902–August 1903*. Progress, 1961.
___. *Collected Works*. Vol. 19, *March–December 1913*. Progress, 1977.
___. *Collected Works*. Vol. 20, *December 1913–August 1914*. Progress, 1964.
___. *Collected Works*. Vol. 22, *December 1915–July 1916*. Progress, 1964.
___. *Collected Works*. Vol. 33, *August 1921–March 1923*. Progress, 1973.
___. *What Is to Be Done? Burning Questions of Our Movement*. International Publishers, 1969.
Lenoe, Matthew. "In Defense of Timasheff's Great Retreat." *Kritika: Explorations in Russian and Eurasian History* 5, no. 4 (2004): 721–30.
Lesnik-Oberstein, Karin. *Children's Literature: Criticism and the Fictional Child*. Clarendon Press, 1994.
Levenson, Michael, ed. *The Cambridge Companion to Modernism*. Cambridge University Press, 2011.
Levchenko, Jan. "Poslevkusie formalizma. Proliferatsiia teorii v tekstakh Viktora Shklovskogo 1930-kh godov." *Novoe Literaturnoe Obozrenie* 128, no. 4 (2014): 125–43.
Levine, Caroline. *Forms: Whole, Rhythm, Hierarchy, Network*. Princeton University Press, 2015.
Lévy-Bruhl, Lucien. *Primitive Mentality*. Macmillan, 1975.
Leyda, Jay, ed. *Eisenstein on Disney*. Seagull Books, 1985.
Lindsay, Kenneth, and Peter Vergo, eds. *Kandinsky: Complete Writings on Art*. Vol. 1, *1901–1921*. G. K. Hall & Co, 1982.
Lipovetsky, Mark. "Zloveshchee v skazakh Bazhova." *Quaestio Rossica*, no. 2 (2014): 212–30.
Listov, Viktor. *Istoriia smotrit v ob'ektiv*. Iskusstvo, 1973.
___. "Mikhail Kol'tsov i 'Desiataia muza.'" *Kinovedcheskie zapiski*, no. 5 (1990): 41–52.
___. "Vertov: odnazhdy i vsegda." *Kinovedcheskie zapiski*, no. 18 (1993): 121–43.
Livak, Leonid. *In Search of Russian Modernism*. Johns Hopkins University Press, 2018.
Livshits, Benedikt. "My i Zapad." In *Terent'evskii sbornik. Vypusk 1*, 256–57. Gileia, 1996.
Lodder, Christina. *Russian Constructivism*. Yale University Press, 1983.
Loos, Adolf. "Ornament and Crime." In *Programs and Manifestoes on 20th-Century Architecture*, ed. Ulrich Conrads. The MIT Press, 1975, 19–24.
Lovell, Stephen. "Tynianov as Sociologist of Literature." *The Slavonic and East European Review* 79, no. 3 (2001): 415–33.
Lukács, Georg. *The Meaning of Contemporary Realism*. Trans. John and Necke Mander. London: Merlin Press, 1963.
Lunacharskii, Anatolii. "Khudozhestvennoe tvorchestvo natsional'nostei SSSR." In *Iskusstvo narodov SSSR. Vypusk 1*, 9–24. GAKhN, 1927.
MacKay, John. "Allegory and Accommodation: Vertov's *Three Songs of Lenin* (1934) as a Stalinist Film." *Film History: An International Journal* 18, no. 4 (2006): 376–91.
___. *Dziga Vertov: Life and Work*. Vol. 1, *1896–1921*. Academic Studies Press, 2018.
Mad'iar, Liudvig. *Ekonomika sel'skogo khoziaistva v Kitae*. Gosudarstvennoe izdatel'stvo, 1928.
Maksimov, Aleksandr. "Protiv reaktsionnogo einshteinianstva v fizike." *Krasnyi flot* (June 13, 1952): 3–4.
Malkin, Boris, ed. *15 let Kazakhskoi ASSR*. Ogiz-Izogiz, 1936.
Mandel'shtam, Osip. *Sobranie sochinenii v chetyrekh tomakh. Tom 3. Stikhi i proza, 1930–1937*. Art-Bizness Tsentr, 1994.
Mao, Douglas, and Rebecca Walkowitz. "The New Modernist Studies." *PMLA* 123, no. 3 (2008): 737–48.
Margolin, Victor. *The Struggle for Utopia: Rodchenko, Lissitzky, Moholy-Nagy, 1917–1946*. University of Chicago Press, 1997.

Martin, Terry. *The Affirmative Action Empire: Nations and Nationalism in the Soviet Union, 1923–1929.* Cornell University Press, 2001.

Marx, Karl. *Capital: A Critique of Political Economy.* Vol. 1. Ed. Ernest Mandel, trans. Ben Fowkes and David Fernbach. Penguin Books, 1990.

———. *Capital: A Critique of Political Economy.* Vol. 3. Ed. Ernest Mandel, trans. Ben Fowkes and David Fernbach. Penguin Books, 1991.

———. *A Contribution to the Critique of Political Economy.* Trans. N. I. Stoke. New International Publishers, 1970.

———. *Grundrisse: Foundations of the Critique of Political Economy.* Penguin Books, 1993.

Marx, Karl, and Frederick Engels. *Collected Works.* Vol. 5, *Marx and Engels, 1845–47.* Lawrence & Wishart, 2010.

———. *Collected Works.* Vol. 6, *Marx and Engels, 1845–48.* Lawrence & Wishart, 2010.

———. *Collected Works.* Vol. 12, *Marx and Engels, 1853–54.* Lawrence & Wishart, 2010.

Medvedev, Pavel, and Mikhail Bakhtin. *The Formal Method in Literary Scholarship: A Critical Introduction to Sociological Poetics.* Johns Hopkins University Press, 1978.

Meierkhol'd, Vsevolod. "Iz pisem o teatre." *Vesy* 6 (1907): 93–98.

Men'shikov, Mikhail. *Vyshe svobody.* Sovremennyi pisatel', 1998.

Merrill, Jessica. "Fol'kloristicheskie osnovaniia knigi Viktora Shklovskogo 'O teorii prozy.'" *Novoe Literaturnoe Obozrenie* 133, no. 3 (2015): 197–213.

Mezhericher, Leonid. "Segodniashnii den' sovetskogo fotoreportazha." *Proletarskoe foto*, no. 1 (1931): 9–12.

———. "Tvorcheskie profili: Mnogogrannyi khudozhnik [Abram Shterenberg]." *Sovetskoe foto*, no. 1 (1934): 16–23.

———. "Veshch' gromadnoi vospitatel'noi sily." *Proletarskoe foto*, no. 7/8 (1932): 9–10.

Michaels, Paula. *Curative Powers: Medicine and Empire in Stalin's Central Asia.* Pittsburgh: University of Pittsburgh Press, 2003.

Michelson, Annette. "The Kinetic Icon in the Work of Mourning: Prolegomena to the Analysis of a Textual System." *October* 52 (1990): 16–39.

Michelson, Annette, ed. *Kino-Eye: The Writings of Dziga Vertov.* University of California Press, 1984.

Miller, Aleksandr. *Istoriia iskusstv vsekh vvremen i narodov. Kniga 1-a. Pervobytnoe iskusstvo.* P. P. Soikin, 1929.

Miller, Tyrus. *Late Modernism: Politics, Fictions, and the Arts Between the World Wars.* University of California Press, 1999.

Moholy-Nagy, László. *The New Vision and Abstract of an Artist.* Wittenborn, Schultz, Inc., 1947.

Morozov, Sergei. *Fotoillustratsiia v gazete.* Goskinoizdat, 1939.

———. "Lineinoe postroenie kadra." *Sovetskoe foto*, no. 9 (1937): 6–10.

———. "Na putiakh k realizmu, k narodnosti." *Sovetskoe foto*, no. 5/6 (1936): 3–16.

———. "Preodolenie ekzotiki." *Sovetskoe foto*, no. 6 (1933): 14–15.

———. *Sovetskaia khudozhestvennaia fotografiia.* Iskusstvo, 1958.

Morozov, Viatcheslav. *Russia's Postcolonial Identity: A Subaltern Empire in a Eurocentric World.* Palgrave Macmillan, 2015.

Morrison, Alexander. "*Internal Colonization. Russia's Imperial Experience* by Alexander Etkind (review)." *Ab Imperio*, 3 (2013): 445–57.

Musrepov, Gabit. *Kozy Korpesh and Baian Slu.* Iskusstvo, 1945.

N-k, A. [Nurok, Alfred]. "Vystavki 'setsessionistov' v Berline i Vene." *Mir Iskusstva*, 15 (1899): 14–16.

Nadzhafov, Dzhahangir, ed. *Stalin i kosmopolitizm. Dokumenty Agitpropa TsK KPSS. 1945–1953.* Materik, 2005.

"Na pervom etape tvorcheskoi diskussii." *Proletarskoe foto*, no. 1 (1932): 10–12.

Nesbet, Anne. *Savage Junctures: Sergei Eisenstein and the Shape of Thinking.* I. B. Tauris, 2003.

North, Michael. *The Dialect of Modernism: Race, Language, and Twentieth-Century Literature.* Oxford University Press, 1994.

Northrop, Douglas. *Veiled Empire: Gender and Power in Stalinist Central Asia.* Cornell University Press, 2004.

Novitskii, Pavel, ed. *Izofront: Klassovaia bor'ba na fronte prostranstvennykh iskusstv. Sbornik statei ob'edineniia "Oktiabr'".* OGIZ–IZOGIZ, 1931.
Nunan, Timothy. "Soviet Nationalities Policy, *USSR in Construction*, and Soviet Documentary Photography in Comparative Context, 1931–1937." *Ab Imperio* 2 (2010): 47–92.
Nusinov, Isaak. "Natsional'naia literature." In *Literaturnaia entsiklopediia.* Vol. 7, 627–41. OGIZ, 1934.
Obertreis, Julia. *Imperial Desert Dreams: Cotton Growing and Irrigation in Central Asia, 1860–1991.* V&R unipress, 2017.
"Ob odnoi antipatrioticheskoi gruppe teatral'nykh kritikov." *Pravda* (January 28, 1949): 3.
Ogden C. K., and I. A. Richards, eds. *The Meaning of Meaning: A Study of the Influence of Language Upon Thought and of the Science of Symbolism.* Harcourt, Brace & World, 1923.
Oinas, Felix. *Essays on Russian Folklore and Mythology.* Slavica Publishers, 1985.
Ol'denburg, Sergei, "Sovetskoe vostokovedenie." *Front nauki i tekhniki*, no. 7/8 (1931), 64–66.
Ol'khovyi, Boris. "O prostote i poniatnosti." *Literaturnaia gazeta* (March 31, 1930): 2.
Olcott, Martha Brill. *The Kazakhs.* Stanford University Press, 1994.
Olofsson, Kerstin, ed. *From Orientalism to Postcoloniality.* Södertörns högskola, 2008.
Ong, Walter. *Orality and Literacy: The Technologizing of the Word.* Routledge, 2002.
Osipov, D. "Kinopoema o Lenine." *Pravda*, no. 201 (July 23, 1934): 4.
P., V. "Zvukovaia produktsiia sovetskoi' kinopromyshlennosti." *Proletarskoe kino*, no. 5 (1931): 11–13.
Papazian, Elizabeth Astrid. *Manufacturing Truth: The Documentary Moment in Early Soviet Culture.* Northern Illinois University Press, 2009.
Paperny, Vladimir. *Architecture in the Age of Stalin: Culture Two.* Cambridge University Press, 2002.
Pavlenko, Petr, and Sergei Eisenstein, "The Great Fergana Canal." *Studies in Russian and Soviet Cinema* 5, no. 1 (2011): 123–55.
Pavlov, Iu. "Kosmopolitizm—ideologicheskoe oruzhie amerikanskoi reaktsii." *Pravda* (April 7, 1949): 3.
Payne, Matthew. *Stalin's Railroad: Turksib and the Building of Socialism.* University of Pittsburgh Press, 2001.
———. "Viktor Turin's *Turksib* (1929) and Soviet Orientalism." *Historical Journal of Film, Radio and Television History* 21, no. 1 (2001): 37–62.
Pertsov, Petr. "Zheltye ili belye?" *Novyi put'*, no 2 (1904): 269–78.
Pertsov, Viktor. "Skazki starogo Urala." *Literaturnaia gazeta* (May 10, 1938): 3.
"Pervye itogi obsuzhdeniia statei 'Pravdy'." *Iskusstvo kino*, no. 4 (1936): 16–18.
Pervyi vsesoiuznyi s'ezd sovetskikh pisatelei 1934: Stenograficheskii otchet. Khudozhestvennaia literatura, 1990.
Petric, Vlada. "Vertov, Lenin, and Perestroika: The Cinematic Transposition of Reality." *Historical Journal of Film, Radio, and Television* 15, no. 1 (1995): 3–17.
Petrov, I. "Dekorativnoe ozelenenie Vsesoiuznoi sel'skokhoziaistvennoi vystavki." *Arkhitektura i stroitel'stvo Moskvy*, no. 9 (1954): 24–29.
Philips, Christopher, ed. *Photography in the Modern Era: European Documents and Critical Writings, 1913–1940.* MoMA, 1989.
Phillips, William. "Our Country and Our Culture: A Symposium (III)." *Partisan Review* 19, no. 5 (1952): 562–98.
Philpot, J. H. *The Sacred Tree, or the Tree in Religion and Myth.* Macmillan, 1897.
Platonov, Andrei. *Sobranie. Usomnivshiisia Makar: Rasskazy 1920-kh godov. Stikhotvoreniia.* Vremia, 2011.
Poggioli, Renato. *The Theory of the Avant-Garde.* Harvard University Press, 1968.
Poskrebyshev, Aleksandr. "Velikoe mnogonatsional'noe sovetskoe gosudarstvo." *Pravda* (December 30, 1952): 1.
Pratt, Mary Louise. "Arts of the Contact Zone." *Profession* (1991): 33–40.
Prunes, Mariano. "Dziga Vertov's *Three Songs of Lenin* (1934): A Visual Tour through the History of the Soviet Avant-Grade in the Interwar Years." *Criticism* 45, no. 2 (2003): 251–78.
R., L. "Zamechatel'naia rabota!" *Pravda* (December 21, 1934): 4.

BIBLIOGRAPHY

Ram, Harsha. "Decadent Nationalism, 'Peripheral' Modernism: The Georgian Literary Manifesto between Symbolism and the Avant-Garde." *Modernism/modernity* 21, no. 1, (2014): 343–59.

———. "National Mythopoesis: Georgian Symbolism, the National Question, and Socialist Realism." Unpublished paper.

Ramazani, Jahan. *A Transnational Poetics*. University of Chicago Press, 2009.

Rempel', Lazar'. "O natsional'nom iskusstve." *Brigada khudozhnikov*, no. 7 (1931): 1–3.

———. *Zhivopis' sovetskogo Zakavkaz'ia*. OGIZ-IZOGIZ, 1932.

Riegl, Alois. *Problems of Style: Foundations for a History of Ornament*. Princeton University Press, 1992.

Robin, Régine. *Socialist Realism: An Impossible Aesthetic*. Stanford University Press, 1992.

Rodchenko, Aleksandr. "Master i kritika. Nechitannoe vystuplenie." *Sovetskoe foto*, no. 9 (1935): 4–5.

———. *Stat'i. Vospominaniia. Avtobiograficheskie zapiski. Pis'ma*. Sovetskii khudozhnik, 1982.

Rodchenko, Aleksandr, and Varvara Stepanova. *Al'bom*. Kniga, 1989.

Rolf, Malte. *Soviet Mass Festivals, 1917–1991*. University of Pittsburgh Press, 2013.

Romberg, Kristin. *Gan's Constructivism: Aesthetic Theory for an Embedded Modernism*. University of California Press, 2019.

Rosenberg, Harold. *The Tradition of the New*. Horizon Press, 1959.

Roshal', Lev. "Stikhi kinopoeta." *Kinovedcheskie zapiski*, no. 21 (1994): 80–96.

Roshal', Lev, et. al., " 'Pryzhok' Vertova." *Iskusstvo kino*, no. 11 (1992): 96–108.

Rostovtseva, Galina. *Zinaida Vasil'evna Bazhenova*. Sovetskii khudozhnik, 1961.

"RSFSR." *Pravda* (February 1, 1936): 1.

Rubin, William, ed. *"Primitivism" in 20th-Century Art: Affinity of the Tribal and the Modern*. Vol. 1. MoMA, 1984.

Ruskin, John. *The Seven Lamps of Architecture*. Wiley & Halsted, 1857.

Rzhevsky, Nicholas, ed. *The Cambridge Companion to Modern Russian Culture*. Cambridge University Press, 2012.

Said, Edward. *Culture and Imperialism*. Knopf, 1993.

———. *Orientalism*. London: Penguin Books, 2003.

Saint-Amour, Paul. "Weak Theory, Weak Modernism." *Modernism/modernity* 25, no. 3 (2018): 437–59.

Salazkina, Masha. *In Excess: Sergei Eisenstein's Mexico*. University of Chicago Press, 2009.

Sarkisova, Oksana. "Edges of Empire: Representations of Borderland Identities in Early Soviet Cinema." *Ab Imperio*, no. 1 (2000): 225–52.

———. *Screening Soviet Nationalities: Kulturfilms from the Far North to Central Asia*. IB Tauris, 2017.

Savina, A., ed. *Vrubel': Perepiska. Vospominaniia o khudozhnike*. Iskusstvo, 1963.

Schild, Kathryn Douglas. *Between Moscow and Baku: National Literatures at the 1934 Congress of Soviet Writers*. PhD diss., University of California, Berkeley, 2010.

Schivelbusch, Wolfgang. *The Railway Journey: The Industrialization of Time and Space in the 19th Century*. University of California Press, 1986.

Semper, Gottfried. *Style in the Technical and Tectonic Arts; or, Practical Aesthetics*. Getty Research Institute, 2004.

Shaikhet, Arkadii, and Maks Al'pert, "Kak my snimali Filippovykh." *Proletarskoe foto*, no. 1 (1931): 46–47.

Sharp, Jane. *Russian Modernism Between East and West: Natal'ia Goncharova and the Moscow Avant-Garde, 1905–1914*. Cambridge University Press, 2006.

Shevelenko, Irina. *Modernizm kak arkhaizm: natsionalizm i poiski modernistskoi estetiki v Rossii*. NLO, 2017.

Shishmarev, Vladimir. "Aleksandr Veselovskii i ego kritiki." *Oktiabr'*, no. 12 (1947): 158–64.

Shklovsky, Viktor. "Aleksandr Veselovskii—istorik i teoretik." *Oktiabr'*, no. 12 (1947): 174–82.

———. *Bowstring: On the Dissimilarity of the Similar*. Trans. Shushan Avagyan. Dalkey Archive Press, 2011.

———. *Eizenshtein*. Iskusstvo, 1976.

———. *Gamburgskii schet: Stat'i, vospominaniia, esse*. Sovetskii pisatel', 1990.

___. *Gornaia Gruziia: Pshaviia. Khevsuretiia. Mukheviia.* Molodaia gvardiia, 1930.
___. *A Hunt for Optimism.* Trans. Shushan Avagyan. Dalkey Archive Press, 2012.
___. *Ikh nastoiaschee.* Knigopechat', 1927.
___. *Knight's Move.* Trans. Richard Sheldon. Dalkey Archive Press, 2011.
___. *Marko Polo.* Zhurnal'no-gazetnoe ob"edinenie, 1936.
___. *Marko Polo, razvedchik.* OGIZ, 1931.
___. "O liudiakh, kotorye idut po odnoi i toi zhe doroge i ob etom ne znaiut. Konets barokko." *Literaturnaia gazeta* (July 17, 1932): 4.
___. "O formalizme." *Literaturnyi Leningrad*, no. 20 (1936): 3.
___. *O teorii prozy.* Sovetskii pisatel', 1983.
___. "Pamiatnik nauchnoi oshibke." *Literaturnaia gazeta* (January 27, 1930): 1.
___. "Pamiatnik nauchnoi oshibke [vtoraia redaktsiia]." *Novoe Literaturnoe Obozrenie* 44, no. 4 (2000): 154–58.
___. *Podenshchina.* Izdatel'stvo pisatelei v Leningrade, 1930.
___. "Prostota—zakonomernost'." *Literaturnaia gazeta* (June 5, 1933): 2.
___. *A Sentimental Journey: Memoirs, 1917–1922.* Trans. Richard Sheldon. Cornell University Press, 1970.
___. *Theory of Prose.* Trans. Shushan Avagyan. Dalkey Archive Press, 2009.
___. *Third Factory.* Trans. Richard Sheldon. Dalkey Archive Press, 2002.
___. *Turksib.* Gosudarstvennoe izdatel'stvo, 1930.
___. *Viktor Shklovsky: A Reader.* Ed. and trans. Alexandra Berlina. Bloomsbury Academic, 2017.
___. *Za 60 let: Raboty o kino.* Iskusstvo, 1985.
___. *Zemli razvedchik: Istoricheskaia povest'.* Molodaiia gvardiia, 1969.
___. *Zhili-byli: Vospominaniia. Memuarnye zapisi.* Sovetskii pisatel', 1966.
___. *Zoo, or Letters Not About Love.* Trans. Richard Sheldon. Dalkey Archive Press, 2001.
Shlifshtein, Semen, ed. *S.S. Prokof'ev: materialy, dokumenty, vospominaniia.* GMI, 1956.
Shorin, Aleksandr. *Kak ekran stal govoriashchim.* Goskinoizdat, 1949.
Shumiatskii, Boris. *Kinematografiia millionov. Opyt analiza.* Kinofotoizdat, 1935.
Slezkine, Yuri. "Imperialism as the Highest Stage of Socialism." *Russian Review* 59, no. 2 (2000): 217–34.
___. "Primitive Communism and the Other Way Around." In *Socialist Realism Without Shores*, ed. Thomas Lahusen and Evgeny Dobrenko (Duke University Press, 1997).
___. "The USSR as a Communal Apartment, or How a Socialist State Promoted Ethnic Particularism." *Slavic Review* 53, no. 2 (1994): 414–52.
Sokolov, Yurii. *Russian Folklore.* Trans. Catherine Ruth Smith. Folklore Associates, 1966.
Sosfenov, Il'ia. "Dva fronta. Zametki ob osnovakh tvorcheskikh ustanovok." *Proletarskoe foto*, no. 5 (1932): 14–8.
"Sovetskaia kinematografiia v period rekonstruktsii. Zadachi assotsiatsii rabotnikov revoliutsionnoi kinema-fotografii." *Kino* 331, no. 2 (January 11, 1930): 4–5.
Spivak, Gayatri Chakravorty. *A Critique of Postcolonial Reason: Toward a History of the Vanishing Present.* Harvard University Press, 1999.
Stalin, Joseph. *Sochineniia. Tom 12.* GIPL, 1949.
___. *Works.* 13 vols. OGIZ, 1946–1954.
___. *Works.* Vol. 14. Red Star Press, 1978.
Stasevich, Inga. *Sotsial'nyi status zhenshchiny u kazakhov: traditsii i sovremennost'.* Nauka, 2011.
Stasov, Vladimir. *Russkii narodnyi ornament.* Obshchestvennaia pol'za, 1872.
Steiner, Peter. *Russian Formalism: A Metapoetics.* Cornell University Press, 1984.
Stepanova, Varvara. *Chelovek ne mozhet zhit' bez chuda.* Grant, 1994.
___. *Varvara Stepanova: The Complete Work.* Ed. and trans. John E. Bowlt. MIT Press, 1988.
Sternin, Grigorii, ed. *Traditsii i sovremennost': aktual'nye problemy izobrazitel'nogo iskusstva i arkhitektury.* VNIII, 1989.

Struve, Vasilii. "Problema zarozhdeniia, razvitiia i upadka rabovladel'cheskikh obshchestv drevnego Vostoka." In *Izvestiia Gosudarstvennoi akademii istorii material'noi kul'tury*. Vypusk 77, 32–111. OGIZ, 1934.

"Sumbur vmesto muzyki." *Pravda* (January 28, 1936): 3.

Suny, Ronald Grigor, and Terry Martin, eds. *A State of Nations: Empire and Nation-Making in the Age of Lenin and Stalin*. Oxford University Press, 2001.

Taylor, Richard. *Film Propaganda: Soviet Russia and Nazi Germany*. IB Tauris, 1998.

———. "On Stalin's Watch: The Late-night Kremlin Screenings: May to October 1934." *Studies in Russian and Soviet Cinema* 7, no. 2 (2014): 243–58.

Taylor, Richard, ed. *S.M. Eisenstein: Selected Works*. Vol. 1, *Writings, 1922–34*. BFI, 1998.

———. *S.M. Eisenstein: Selected Works*. Vol. 3, *Writings, 1934–47*. BFI, 1996.

———. *S.M. Eisenstein: Selected Works*. Vol. 4, *Beyond the Stars: The Memoirs of Sergei Eisenstein*. BFI, 1995.

Teichmann, Christian. "Canals, Cotton, and the Limits of De-Colonization in Soviet Uzbekistan, 1924–1941." *Central Asian Survey* 26, no. 4 (2007): 499–519.

Tihanov, Galin. "Viktor Shklovskii and Georg Lukács in the 1930s." *The Slavonic and East European Review* 78, no. 1 (2000): 44–65.

Tikhonov, Nikolai. "V zashchitu Pushkina." *Kul'tura i zhizn'* (May 9, 1947): 4

Timasheff, Nicholas. *The Great Retreat: The Growth and Decline of Communism in Russia*. E. P. Dutton, 1946.

Tippner, Anja. "Viktor Shklovskii's *Marko Polo—Razvedchik*: Medieval History vs. Geopoetic Representation of Imperial Space." *Detskie chteniia* 6, no. 2 (2014): 102–11.

Tisse, Eduard. "Bol'shoi khudozhestvennyi fil'm o kanale." *Ferganskaia Pravda* (August 16, 1939): 1.

Toddes, Evgenii. "B.M. Eikhenbaum v 30–50-e gody." In *Tynianovskii sbornik: Deviatye Tynianovskie chteniia*, 563–691. OGI, 2002.

Tolz, Vera. *Russia's Own Orient: The Politics of Identity and Oriental Studies in the Late Imperial and Early Soviet Periods*. Oxford University Press, 2011.

Toporov, Vladimir. *Mirovoe derevo: Universal'nye znakovye kompleksy*. Tom 2. Rukopisnye pamiatniki Drevnei Rusi, 2010.

Topuridze, Konstantin. "Fontany Vsesoiuznoi sel'skokhoziaistvennoi vystavki." *Arkhitektura i stroitel'stvo Moskvy*, no. 7 (1954): 13–19.

Tret'iakov, Sergei. "B'em trevogu." *Novy Lef*, no. 2 (1927): 1–5.

———. "Kak desiatiletit'." *Novyi Lef*, no. 4 (1927): 35–37.

———. "Ot fotoserii k dlitel'nomu fotonabliudeniiu." *Proletarskoe foto*, no. 4 (1931): 20–45.

Trotsky, Leon. *The History of the Russian Revolution*. Trans. Max Eastman. Haymarket Books, 2008.

———. *Literature and Revolution*. Ed. William Keach, trans. Rose Strunsky. Haymarket Books, 2005.

Tsivian, Yuri, ed. *Lines of Resistance: Dziga Vertov and the Twenties*. Le Giornate del cinema muto, 2004.

Tucker, Robert. *Stalin in Power: The Revolution from Above, 1928–1941*. Norton, 1990.

Tugendkhol'd, Iakov. *Iskusstvo oktiabr'skoi epokhi*. Akademiia, 1930.

———. "Iskusstvo SSSR i natsional'nyi element." *Novyi mir*, no. 8 (1925): 119–24.

———. "K izucheniiu izobrazitel'nogo iskusstva SSSR." In *Iskusstvo narodov SSSR*. Vypusk 1, 43–56. GAKhN, 1927.

———. "K voprosu o natsional'nosti v iskusstve." *Natsional'nye problemy*, no. 2 (1915): 23–25.

———. "Sovremennoe iskussstvo i narodnost'." *Severnye zapiski*, no. 11 (1913): 153–56.

Turkestano-Sibirskaia Magistral'. SNK RSFSR, 1929.

Turner, Bryan. *Marx and the End of Orientalism*. Routledge, 1978.

Tursunkhodzhaev, M., ed. *10 let Uzbekistana*. Ogiz-Izogiz, 1934, 1935.

Turvey, Malcolm. *Doubting Vision: Film and the Revelationist Tradition*. Oxford University Press, 2008.

Tynianov, Iurii. *Permanent Evolution: Selected Essays on Literature, Theory and Film*. Academic Studies Press, 2019.

———. *Poetika. Istoriia literatury. Kino*. Nauka, 1977.

Tynianov, Iurii, and Roman Jakobson. "Problemy izucheniia literatury i iazyka." *Novyi LEF*, no. 12 (1928): 35–37.
Ushakov, Dmitrii. *Tolkovyi slovar' russkogo iazyka*. OGIZ, 1935.
V., L. "Na prosmotre fil'my 'Tri pesni o Lenine'." *Kino*, no. 49 (October 28, 1934): 1.
Vaingurt, Julia. *Wonderlands of the Avant-Garde: Technology and the Arts in Russia of the 1920s*. Northwestern University Press, 2013.
Vaisfel'd, I. V. *Voprosy kinodramaturgii. Vypusk III. Sbornik statei*. Moscow: Iskusstvo, 1959.
Valerius, Sara. "Vsesoiuznaia sel'skokhoziaistvennaia vystavka. Skul'ptura." *Iskusstvo*, no. 6 (1954): 11–16.
Van Ree, Erik. *The Political Thought of Joseph Stalin: A Study in Twentieth-Century Revolutionary Patriotism*. Routledge, 2002.
___. "Socialism in One Country: A Reassessment." *Studies in East European Thought* 50, no. 2 (1998): 77–117.
Vertov, Dziga. *Iz Naslediia. Tom 1: Dramaturgicheskie opyty*. Eizenshtein-Tsentr, 2004.
___. *Iz Naslediia. Tom 2: Stat'i i Vystupleniia*. Eizenshtein-Tsentr, 2008.
___. "O liubvi k zhivomu cheloveku." *Iskusstvo kino*, no. 6 (1958): 95–99.
___. *Stat'i. Dnevniki. Zamysly*. Iskusstvo, 1966.
___. *Tri pesni o Lenine: Zvukovoi fil'm*. Mezhrabpomfil'm, 1934.
Vertova-Svilova, Elizaveta. *Tri Pesni o Lenine*. Iskusstvo, 1972.
Veselovskii, Aleksandr. *Istoricheskaia poetika*. Khudozhestvennaia literatura, 1940.
Vinogradov, Viktor. *Velikii russkii iazyk*. OGIZ, 1945.
Vishnevskii, Vsevolod. *Eizenshtein*. Goskinoizdat, 1939.
Vol'gemut, A. "Fotomontazh i fotopanno." *Sovetskoe foto*, no. 7 (1939): 4–5.
Volkov-Lannit, L. *Aleksandr Rodchenko risuet, fotografiruet, sporit*. Iskusstvo, 1968.
___. "Problema skhodstva v fotoportrete." *Sovetskoe foto*, no. 9 (1940): 6–10.
Voronina, Olga. "'The Sun of World Poetry': Pushkin as a Cold War Writer." *Pushkin Review* 14 (2011): 63–95.
"Vostokovedenie (inache orientalistika)." In *Bol'shaia sovetskaia entsiklopediia*. Vol. 9, 193–202. Sovetskaia Entsiklopediia, 1951.
Vsesoiuznoe soveshchanie stroitelei, arkhitektorov i rabotnikov promyshlennosti stroitel'nykh materialov, stroitel'nogo i dorozhnogo mashinostroeniia, proektnykh i nauchno-issledovatel'skikh organizatsii. 30 noiabria—7 dekabria 1954 g. Sokrashchennyi stenograficheskii otchet. Gosudarstvennoe izdatel'stvo literatury po stroitel'stvu i arkhitekture, 1955.
Wallerstein, Immanuel. *The Essential Wallerstein*. The New Press, 2000.
Weis, Elisabeth, and John Belton, eds. *Film Sound: Theory and Practice*. Columbia University Press, 1985.
Wells, H. G. *Anticipations: Of the Reaction of Mechanical and Scientific Progress Upon Human Life and Thought*. Chapman and Hall, 1901.
White, Stephen, ed. *New Directions in Soviet History*. Cambridge University Press, 1991.
Widdis, Emma. *Socialist Senses: Film, Feeling, and the Soviet Subject, 1917–1940*. Indiana University Press, 2017.
Williams, Raymond. *The Politics of Modernism*. Verso, 1989.
Wittfogel, Karl. "Geopolitika, geograficheskii materializm i marksizm." *Pod znamenem marksizma*, no. 2/3 (1929): 16–42 and no. 6 (1929): 1–29.
___. *Oriental Despotism: A Comparative Study of Total Power*. Yale University Press, 1957.
Wölfflin, Heinrich. *Renaissance and Baroque*. Cornell University Press, 1966.
Worringer, Wilhelm. *Form Problems of the Gothic*. G. E. Stechert, 1920.
Za bol'shevistskii plakat. OGIZ–IZOGIZ, 1932.
"Za konsolidatsiiu sil. Za sozdanie proletarskoi fotografii. Deklaratsiia initsiativnoi gruppy ROPF." *Proletarskoe foto*, no. 2 (1931): 14–15.
Zherebtsov, B. "Montazh fotograficheskoi serii: O serii "Sem'ia Filippovykh." *Proletarskoe foto*, no. 9 (1932): 6–11.
___. *Tekstovka k foto-snimku*. Biblioteka gazety Fotokor, 1932.
Zhirmunskii, Viktor. *Fol'klor zapada i vostoka: Sravnitel'no-istoricheskie ocherki*. OGI, 2004.
___. "On the Study of Comparative Literature." *Oxford Slavonic Papers* 13 (1967): 1–13.
Zorkaia, Neia. "Veshchie sny Alma-Aty." *Iskusstvo kino*, no. 7 (1999): 125–39.

INDEX

Page numbers in *italics* indicate illustrations.

Abdel-Malek, Anouar, 15
abstraction, xvii, 193, 224, 246; Eisenstein and, 197, 235–37; generalization as, 222, 230
Adorno, Theodor, 7–8
Academy of Architecture of the USSR, 263
acmeism, 6
acousmatic voice, 176
aerial shots, 123, 125, 166, 182
aesthetics, aesthetic form and, 4–6, 41, 78, 92, 98–99, 232, 269n52, 272n104; avant-garde, 52, 155; continuity and, 197–98, 201, 208, 210, 221, 241, 245; evolution of, xxiii, 3, 13, 201; excess and, 52–53, 230, 256–63, *261*; kino-eye, 139–40; modernist, 14, 16–18, 41, 147, 250; of Rodchenko and Stepanova, 86, 93, 102–3, 123–24; socialist realism, 253, 267n38; Soviet, 3, 86, 88, 96, 272n108; of Stalinism, 46, 263, 267n38; of Vertov, 152, 155, 190–92; VSKhV, 255–60
agit-train, "Red East," 137–38
Akhmatova, Anna, 275n159, 301n9
akrostikh, 252
akyn (Kazakh folk singer), 250–51, 292n133, 293n143, 293n154; in *The Front, to You!*, 171–72, 174–75, 178–79, 182, 184–85
Al'pert, Max, 102, 104–5
Aleksandr Nevsky (film), 197
Aleksandrov, Grigorii, 202
Aleksei Gan, 89

alienation, 44, 184
allegorical imagery, *233*, 234, 258–59
All-Union Agricultural Exhibition (VSKhV), 129, 255–63, *261*, 302n29, 303nn37–38. *See also* Exhibition of Achievements of the National Economy (VDNKh)
All-Union Creative Conference of Soviet Filmworkers, 206–7
Alma-Ata, Kazakhstan USSR, 170, 197–98, 231–32
alterity, xxi, 28, 50–51, 53, 86, 250–51, 260; ethnic, xix, xxiii, 44, 46–47, 78, 260
Amaglobeli, Sergo, 34
AMP. *See* Asiatic Mode of Production
Anderson, Benedict, 28–29
Andreev, Nikolai, 157, 179
anti-cosmopolitanism, Soviet, 1, 252–55, 275n159, 301n9, 302nn16–17, 304n49; Shklovsky and, 51, 245; Veselovsky and, 243
anti-Semitism, 253, 301n15, 302n16
appropriation, 97, 208
Arbeiter Illustrierte Zeitung (Workers' Illustrated Newspaper), 105
architecture, xx, 9–10, 256–57, 262–63, 304n54
Aristotle, 44
Armenia, 37–38, 266n9, 271n84
"Art as Device" ("Iskusstvo kak priem") (Shklovsky), 44
Art Deco, 256

artistic construction (*khudozhestvennoe konstruirovanie*), 90, 116, 281n24
artistic continuity, 197–98, 201, 208, 210, 221, 241, 245
art nouveau, 166n13
Arvatov, Boris, 130–31
Aseev, Nikolai, 158
Asiatic Mode of Production (AMP), 25, 271n95, 271n97
assimilation, 4, 28, 72–73, 243–44, 249
astrakhan fur, 120, 285n129
Atasheva, Pera, 194, 223
audiovisual, 176–77
Auezov, Mukhtar, 174, 223, 292n135, 292n137, 294n177, 298nn116–17
authority, 19, 152, 175–76, 179, 256
authorship, 81, 92, 179
automatization, 82–83
avant-garde, xvii, 6–20, 132, 144, 288n37
avant-garde, Soviet, xix, 135, 189, 246–47, 257, 268n40, 274n158, 285n126; aesthetics and, 52, 155; collectivity, 11; foreshortening, *113*, 114; formal experimentation and, 4, 248–50; institutional support and, 248–49; montage, 149, 151; montage and, 149, 151; October Group as, 96–97; ornament and, 134, 228, 230; photomontage by, 99; Rodchenko and, 3, 11, 84, 103, 105–6, 116; Shklovsky and, 3, 43, 82; sound and, 148; Stalinist state and, 20; Vertov and, 3, 155, 191–93; Working Group of Constructivists and, 87
"Avant-Garde and Kitsch" (Greenberg), 257
Azerbaijan, 266n5, 271n84
aziatchina, xxii

backwardness, 107, 205, 211, 215–16, 228; Barr on, xix; Dimanshtein on, 63; feudalism and, xxi; nomadic, 73; October group and, 96–98; Orientalism and, 36; of Russia, 22
Baduev, Said, 36
Baiganin, Nurpeis, 171–72, 175, 184, 187, 213, 292n136, 294n174, 294n179, 298n118
Bakhtin, Mikhail, 20, 35
Balzac, Honoré de, 57
Barbusse, Henri, 162
baroque, 47, 52–56
Barr, Alfred, xvii–xxi, *xviii*, 17, 194, 263, 265n2
Barthes, Roland, 130, 138
Bartold, Vasily, 24–25
Basmachi resistance movement, 79

Bataille, Georges, 25
Battleship Potemkin (*Bronenosets Potemkin*) (film), 195
Bauer, Otto, 28–29
Bauhaus, xix, 265n3
Bayterek, 299n147
Bazhenova, Zinaida, 259–60, 303n42
Bazhov, Pavel, 261–62
Belik, Maria, 152
Belomor Canal, Russia, 102–8, *106*, *109*, 110–12, 114, 283n77
Bely, Andrei, 11, 266n13
Benjamin, Walter, 132, 192, 256, 262
Bezhin Meadow (*Bezhin lug*) (film), 194–97
Bhabha, Homi, 15
Bloch, Ernst, 16
Blok, Aleksandr, 201
Bolsheviks, 3, 11, 24, 29, 196; imperialism and, 19; Russian Civil War and, 21; Shklovsky fighting against, 43
book design, 86, 90–91, 103, 115–17, 281n24
borderlessness, 20–21, 28, 137–38, 144, 166, 250
borders, Soviet Union, 21–24, 192, 253, 302n23
bottom-up perspectives, 125, 282n34
Bowstring (*Tetiva*) (Shklovsky), 44
Boym, Svetlana, 195
Brenner, Anita, 208
Brigade of Artists (journal), 98
Brik, Osip, 95
Bukharin, Nikolai, 161–62
Bürger, Peter, 7
Burliuk, David, 84
Byronic echoes in Pushkin, 252

cameras: film, 137–42 147, 188; photography, 92, 104
capitalism, 21–23, 28, 38, 73, 156, 243–44, 285n129
cartoons, animated, 238–40
Catholicism, 201, 203, 208, 210, 221, 241
Caucasus, xx, 21, 66, 72
censorship, Stalinist, 12, 37, 127, 274n158
Central Asia, 2–4, 85, 210–11, 231, 266n9, 289n57; Eisenstein and, 197, 202, 223; Mácza on, 98; Shklovsky on, 67; Soviet Union controlling, 21–27; in *Ten Years of Soviet Uzbekistan*, 86, 101, 111, 115–27, *119*, *124*, *126*, 130, 135, 210, 250–51; Turkestan-Siberian (Turksib) railway and, 61–63, *64*, 65–70, *71*, 72–73; Vertov and, 148, 162, 166–68 172. *See also* Soviet Orient; *USSR in Construction*; *specific countries, republics*

INDEX

Central Asian Bureau, 162
Central Committee of the Communist Party of the Soviet Union, 159–60, 263
Central Committee of the Communist Party of Uzbekistan, 212
Chaikov, Iosif, 259–60m 303n40
chauvinism, Russian, xxii, 32, 34
Cheremukhin, Mikhail, 148
Chicherov, Vladimir, 179
children, children's literature and, 62–63, 66, 68, 70, 73–74
China, xxi, 1–2, 48, 74–75, 271n97
Chion, Michel, 176
Christianity, 201, 208, 237, 241
Chulkov and Levshin (*Chulkov i Levshin*) (Shklovsky), 80
Cine-Eye (*Kinoglaz*) (film), 184
cinema, films and, 287n9, 287n11, 289n57, 291n101, 291n111, 292n116; Eisenstein on, 206–7, 211; formalism and, 142–44; historicization and, 290n86; Lenin on, 138; sound technologies in, 138–39, 143–44, 192, 202; Stalin on, 138, 162, 189; Vertov on, 137–38, 189–91. *See also specific films*
"Circus Mystery Play" (Eisenstein), 200
Civil War, Mexican, 202–3
Civil War, Russian, 21
clarity, 4–5, 30, 47, 52–56, 156, 179
Clark, Katerina, 157, 269n70
Clark, T. J., 6–7
class consciousness, 30, 32, 38, 141, 156
collectivity, 11, 184, 186–87, 191–93, 196, 203, 214; abstraction and, 134; authorship and, 179; individualism and, 87–88; Stalinism and, 168
collectivization campaign, Soviet, 73, 79, 108
colonialism, 16, 32, 174, 207, 211–14, 230, 244; Russian/Soviet, 34, 46, 61–62, 67, 72, 79–80, 182, 248–49, 255, 268n41, 270n77
Comintern (Communist International), 269n70, 271n97, 292n116
commodities, 38–39, 65, 184, 256
communism, 21–22, 24, 73; primitive, 26, 72, 101–5
Communist Manifesto, The (Marx), 205–6
consciousness, 56, 152, 204–7, 215; class, 30, 32, 38, 141, 156; individual, 51, 168, 216; *narodnost'*, 80, 114, 155–56, 243, 255; national, 29, 38, 98, 218–19, 226, 228; self, 219, 240; socialist, 23, 168, 196–97, 219

construction, socialist, 35, 39, 41, 56, 92, 97–98, 158, 168; Eisenstein and, 132; Kazakh people and, 132; Shklovsky on, 58–60, 81; in Uzbekistan, 127; Vertov on, 144, 148, 170, 192
constructivism, 6, 249, 280n15, 283n78, 296n41; *faktura* in, 41, 89–90, 92, 132, 135 280n15; of Rodchenko and Stepanova, 84, 86–95, 103, 116, 128, 135–36, 172, 280n10, 281n22, 281n24
"Content of Form, The" (Eisenstein), 205–6
continuity: artistic, 197–98, 201, 208, 210, 221, 241, 245; historical, 105, 187, 201, 212, 245; Soviet succession-continuity, 162, 165
cosmology, 165, 234–35
cosmopolitanism, 38, 244, 251–55
Cossacks, The (Tolstoy), 46
"Critical Remarks on the National Question" (Lenin), 33
Critique of Judgment (Kant), 232
Cubism and Abstract Art (exhibition), xvii–xviii, *xviii*
cubo-futurism, 6
cultural difference, 23, 107, 249–51, 255, 266n8, 283n93
Cultural Revolution, Soviet, xxii, 2–3
Cyrillization, 172

Dada, 7, 274–75n158
Dagestan, 36, 157
"Death of Lenin, The" ("Smert' Lenina") (poem), 158–59
decadence, 11, 52, 88
defamiliarization, 2, 56, 89, 222, 246–47, 249–50; photography and, 94, 123; Shklovsky and, 51, 58, 81–82; socialist realism and, 43–44. *See also ostranenie*
Deineka, Aleksandr, 96, 127
Deleuze, Gilles, 52, 188, 203
delimitation, national, 23–25, 48, 271n89
depiction (*izobrazitel'nost*), 86, 89–91, 94, 128, 135–36
Derrida, Jacques, 232
de-Stalinization, 263
Dialectical and Historical Materialism (Stalin), 26
dialectic-materialism, 99, 101
dialectics, 44, 152, 168–69, 177, 191–92, 203–6, 217–18; form-content, 5, 56, 99, 132, 155–56, 198–201, 207–8, 210, 219–21, 245, 251; progress-regress, 195, 197, 203–7, 211–16, 228, 240, 245–47

Diaz, Porfirio, 203
diegetic sound, 144, 151, 176
difference, cultural, 23, 107, 249–51, 255, 266n8, 283n93
difference, ethnic, 19, 30, 33–34, 38, 53, 283n93, 289n62; collectivity and, 191; in "Friendship of the Peoples" fountain, 259–60; homogenization and, 255
difference, national, 30, 33–34, 38, 53
Dimanshtein, Semyon, 63
Disney, Walt, 238–40
diversity, ethnic, 170, 187, 259–62, 266n5, 274n146, 302n29, 303nn41; communism and, 251; Russian national form and, 255; subjectivity and, 191
Dneprostroi, 152, 155
documentary fact, 91, 104–5, 126, 137, 139, 143–44, 156, 174
documentary genre, 148, 182; Vertov and, 137–38, 142, 144, 156, 161–62, 165, 170, 175–76, 180, 187–93
documentary truth, 103, 193
drawings, 91–92, *261*; by Eisenstein, 221–24, *225*, *226*, *227*, *229*, 231–38, *233*, *236*, *239*, 298n101, 299n154
dynamism, 97, 190, 207, 218, 226, 231, 237–40, 259, 303n44; photography and, 87, 105–6; Shklovsky and, 46, 77
Dzhabayev, Dzhambul, 171, 293n154, 294n179

Eagleton, Terry, 17, 269n60
École nationale supérieure des arts décoratifs, 259
Eding, Dmitrii, 232
"'Eh!' On the Purity of Film Language" (Eisenstein), 200
Eikhenbaum, Boris, 51, 242
Einführung (Eisenstein), 220
Einstein, Albert, 252
Eisenstein, Sergei, 3, 248, 250–51, 295n2, 297n68, 297nn74–75; constructivism and, 296n41; drawings by, 221–24, *225*, *226*, *227*, *229*, 231–38, *233*, *236*, *239*, 298n101, 299n154; formalism and, 194–96, 200–201, 214–15, 242–43, 246; on form and content, 199; Great Fergana Canal and, 29n65, 210–16, 297n68, 297n76; late modernism and, 195, 203–4, 212–13, 247; in Mexico, 197–98, 202–8, *209*, 210, 236–37, 248; on multiculturalism, 295n18; national form and, 197–202, 212, 216–22, 226, 228, 245; ornament and, 28, 198, 223–24, *225*, 226, *227*, 228, *229*, 230–32, *233*, 234–47, *236*, *239*; on Shklovsky, 52, 203, 216; stage productions by, 299n151; temporality and, 195–97, 202–8, 210–11, 241; on Veselovsky, 241–42. *See also specific works*
embellishment (*ukrashatel'stvo*), 256, 262
Engels, Friedrich, xxii, 72
Enthusiasm (*Entuziazm*) (film), 138–39, 146–48, 188, 192–93
epic genre, 156, 177, 196, 213–14, 216–17, 223–24, 246, 298n116
"Epos and Folklore of the Kazakh People" ("Epos i fol'klor kazakhskogo naroda") (Auezov, Sobolev), 223
Erenburg, Ilya, 302n16
Esperanto, 179–80
essentialism, 28, 253–55
ethnic alterity, xix, xxiii, 44, 46–47, 78, 260
ethnic difference, 19, 255, 259–60, 283n93, 289n62
ethnic diversity, Soviet, 170, 187, 255, 259–62, 266n5, 274n146, 302n29, 303nn41–42; communism and, 251; Russian national form and, 255; subjectivity and, 191
ethnic heterogeneity, 4, 250
ethnic minorities, 83, 153–54, 161, 256
ethnic other, 4, 6, 198, 266n8
ethnic particularism, Soviet, 18, 35, 107, 182, 266n8, 294n191
Eurasia, 18–19, 232
Eurocentrism, 26, 85
excess, aesthetic, 52–53, 230, 256–63, *261*
Exhibition of Achievements of the National Economy (VDNKh), 255; *See also* All-Union Agricultural Exhibition (VSKhV)
exoticism, xxii, 60, 68–69, 74, 155, 249–50, 256–57; Amaglobeli on, 34; colonialism and, 200; Orientalist, 5, 37, 213; *ostranenie* and, 62–63; Shklovsky and, 79
eyesight, human, 139–41, 149

fact, documentary, 104–5, 139, 143–44, 156, 174; cinematic, 137; photography and, 91; photomontage and, 126
factography, 59–60, 92, 104, 121, 156
Fadeev, Aleksandr, 300n177, 301n9
fakelore, Soviet, 158, 193, 291n94
faktura (texture), 41, 89–90, 92, 132, 135, 280n15
famine, 73, 108

Favorsky, Vladimir, 115, 132
February 1905 Revolution, 10–11
Fergana, 211–20
fetishism, fetishization and, 65, 107–8, 142, 250, 272n108
feudalism, xxii, 73, 153, 271n97
fictional representation, 89, 91–92, 128, 131
Fifteen Years of Kazakhstan, USSR in Construction, 107–8, *109*, 110–12, 122
film cameras, 137–42 147, 188
film industry, Soviet, 142, 162. *See also* cinema, films and
"Final Journey, The" ("Poslednii reis") (Kol'tsov), 154
fin de siècle, 11
First Soviet Writers' Congress, 35–36, 60, 79, 82, 157, 227n56, 277n56
"Five Epochs, The" (Eisenstein), 204–5
Five-Year Plan, Soviet, 18, 25, 48, 61, 73, 115, 158, 182
folkloric narratives, folklore and, 196, 213–14, 223–24, 235, 241, 245–46; Central Asian, 148; Shklovsky on, 78–81; Tugendkhol'd on, 32; Vertov and, 28, 139, 153–61, 166–72, 174, 177–79, 186, 192–93
foreignness, 3, 79, 249
foreshortening, 93–94, 100–101, 103–4, 122–23, 130, 283n69; by Langman, 111–12, *113*, 114; Persian miniatures and, 221
form, 28–30, 37, 41; form-content dichotomy, 5, 56, 99, 132, 155–56, 198–201, 207–8, 209, 219–21, 245, 251; literary, 17, 50. *See also* aesthetics, aesthetic form and; national forms
formal experimentation, 19, 41, 56, 269n52, 281n22; of the avant-garde, 4, 248–50
formalism, 28, 86, 104, 114, 156–57, 167, 253, 255, 272n108, 276n22; cinema and, 142–44; Eisenstein and, 194–96, 200–201, 214–15, 242–43, 246; Shklovsky and, 2, 43, 45–48, 50–61, 65, 78, 80–82, 242–43, 246
form-content dichotomy, 5, 99, 198–201, 207–8, 209, 219–21, 245, 251; Eisenstein and, 245; ornament and, 132; Shklovsky and, 56; Vertov and, 155–56
forms: pagan, 201, 208, 237, 241; vernacular, 197, 201, 208
French Polynesia, 32; Polynesian masks, 200
Fridliand, Semyon, 99–100, 102
friendship of the peoples (Stalinist concept), 37–39, 184, 186–87, 214, 217, 251, 253–61

"Friendship of the Peoples" fountain, 255–61, *261*, 303n38, 303nn44–45
"From Dombra to Opera, From the Legend to the Novel" (Auezov), 292n135
"From the Photo-Series to the Prolonged Photo-Observation" (Tretiakov), 105
Front, to You!, The (*Tebe, front!*) (film), *178*, 190, 192–93, 293n150; orality and, 139, 170–72, *173*, 174–80, *178*, *181*, 182–84, *185*, 186–87
Fülöp-Miller, René, 147
functionalism, 89, 91, 128, 135–36, 280n15
future, socialist, 23, 62, 72, 155, 192, 196, 206
futurism, 45–46, 84, 90, 146

GAKhN. *See* State Academy of Artistic Sciences
Galushkin, Aleksandr, 51, 276n23, 276n28
Gan, Aleksei, 132, 274n158
Gauguin, Paul, 32
Gel'fand, Mark, 51, 53
gender, 153–54, 199n143, 260, 286n143; in "Kozy-Korpesh and Baian-Sulu" drawings, 223–24, *225*, *226*, *227*, *229*; labor and, 170–71, *185*; masculinity and, *239*, 239–40; orality and, 184; ornament and, 230; power and, *233*, 234; representation, 126, *126*
General Governorate of Turkestan, 21
General History of Cinema, A (Eisenstein), 206
generalization, 95, 196–97, 217, 222, 230, 246
Georgia, 266n9, 271n84
Georgian modernism, 266n5
Germany, xvii, 21; Nazi, 170, 174–75, 183, 186–87
Gesamtkunstwerk (Groys), 13–14
Ginzburg, Semen, xix–xx, 191
göl, 119–20
Golden Horde civilization, 278n110
Goloshchekin, Filip, 73
Goncharova, Natal'ia, 18, 31, 287n171
Gorbachev, Mikhail, 43
Gorky, Maxim, 110, 157, 177, 196, 200, 277n56; on language, 53–54; on orality, 36–37
Gourmont, Remy de, 201
Gradov, Georgii, 263, 304n54
graphic design, 90–92, 103, 115
Great Break of 1929, Soviet Union, xix, xxii, 10–12, 248–49
Great Fergana Canal, 29n65, 210–17, 220, 297n68, 297n76
Great Fergana Canal, The (film), 197, 211–17, 220

Great Friendship, The (*Velikaia druzhba*) (opera), 254–55
Great Patriotic War (1941), 3
great-power chauvinism, 39
Great Retreat, The (Timasheff), 267n38
Great Russian Language, The (*Velikii russkii iazyk*) (Vinogradov), 254
Greenberg, Clement, 7–8, 257
Gropius, Walter, xix
Groys, Boris, 12–13, 268n40
GULAG (Main Directorate of Correctional Labor Camps), 103
Gurvich, Abram, 253

Habsburg Empire, 15, 268n41
hammer and sickle symbolism, 259–60, *261*
Hegel, Georg Wilhelm Friedrich, 56, 203, 241
heritagization, 24
Herodotus, 234, 299n143
heterogeneity, 4, 31–32, 40, 47, 53, 155, 251
hierarchies, 56, 90, 201, 251, 253, 291n101
historical continuity, 105, 187, 201, 212, 245
historical development, 26, 56–58, 219, 243
Historical Novel, The (*Istoricheskii roman*) (Lukács), 78
Historical Poetics (Veselovsky), 240, 243–46, 300n179
historicism, 58, 78, 245
historicity, 182, 240, 249
historicization, 17–18, 57–58, 290n86
historiography, xviii–xix, 22, 252
Hitler, Adolf, 174–75
Hobsbawm, Eric, 158
homogeneity, homogenization and, 192, 205 164–65, 251, 255
horizontality, xx–xxi, 93–94, 130, 226, 251, 258
"How I Learned to Draw (A Chapter about My Dancing Lessons)"(Eisenstein), 235–36
"How One Writes and How One Ought to Write about Technical Equipment" ("Kak pishut i kak pisat' o tekhnike") (Shklovsky), 61
Hunt for Optimism, A (*Poiski optimizma*) (Shklovsky), 47
hydraulic culture, Soviet, 25–26, 160–61, 258

iconicity, 98, 130, 156
identity, 24, 27, 31, 180, 251, 303n40; national, 21–22, 41, 147, 255, 258–59, 302n17; Russian Soviet, 19, 21–22, 72, 149, 176, 253–54, 259

ideology, 6, 91, 127–28, 138; friendship of the peoples, 37–39, 184, 186–87, 214, 217, 251, 253–61; Soviet, 3–4, 38, 138, 196–97, 251–55, 258, 272n108
Idols Behind Altars (Brenner), 208
Ignatovich, Boris, 102, 111
Ikramov, Akmal, 210, 286n147
imaginism, 6
immateriality, 29, 88, 249
imperialism, 2, 177–78, 208, 243–44, 255, 268n41; Bolsheviks and, 19; Jameson on, 17, 67; Russian, 60; Said on, 14–15; Stalinism and, 251
Imperialism, the Highest Stage of Capitalism (Lenin), 22
"In a Black Prison Was My Face" (song), 153
"Incarnation of Myth, The" (Eisenstein), 299n151
indexicality, 87, 91–92, 98–99, 130
individual consciousness, 51, 168, 216
individualism, individuality and, 8, 87–88, 179, 196
industrialization, 61, 87–88, 107–8, 184, 260; formalism and, 65; hydraulic culture and, 160–61; primitivsm and, 32
instantaneity, 95, 136
Institut Khudozhestvennoy Kultury [Institute of Artistic Culture] (INKhUK), 248
interdependence, 157, 184, 226, 228, 231
inter-ethnic relations, 1, 38–39, 214, 253–55, 262
interiority, 189–90, 230
International Exhibition of Modern Decorative and Industrial Arts (1925), 31, 84–85
internationalism, 21, 38, 210, 244–46; Soviet, xxii, 20, 35, 55–56, 143–44, 162, 166–67, 192, 251–56
intertitles, film, 172, *173*, 175, 179–80
"In the Great City of Stone" (V bol'shom kamennom gorode) (song), 154–55
"In the Interests of Form" (Eisenstein), 199–200
Ion (Plato), 168
Iskusstvo kino (magazine), 190–91, 294n194
Islam, Muslim people and, 25, 153
Ismailov, Esmagambet, 178, 293n154
Iusupov, Usman, 212
Ivanov, Viacheslav, 250, 301n4
Ivan the Terrible (film), 197, 242–43
Izogiz (State Fine Arts Press), 96, 283n70
Izvestiia (newspaper), 87

Jakobson, Roman, 48
Jameson, Fredric, 9, 17, 58, 67, 249
Jazz Singer, The (film), 145

INDEX

Jencks, Charles, 9
Jewish Anti-Fascist Committee, 301n15
Jones, Owen, 132
Journey to Armenia (*Puteshestvie v Armeniiu*) (Mandelstam), 37–38
Joyce, James, 7, 8
Justus, Ursula, 157

Kadochnikov, Valentin, 223
Kaganovich, Lazar, 52, 158
Kaiumov, Malik, 297n68
Kamensky, Vasilii, 84
Kandinsky, Wassily, 132–33
Kant, Immanuel, 232
Kara-Kyrgyz, 60
Karelo-Finnish Soviet republic, 303n39
Kaufman, Denis Arkad'evich. *See* Vertov, Dziga
Kaufman, Mikhail, 237
Kazakh people, culture and, 60, 250–51, 292n128, 292n135, 293n154, 299n147; Eisenstein drawings of, 223–24, *225*, *227*, *229*, 231–33, *233*, *236*, *239*, 298n101, 299n154; in *Fifteen Years of Kazakhstan*, 107–8, *109*, 110–12; in *The Front, to You!*, 139, 170–72, *173*, 174–80, *178*, *181*, 182–84, *185*, 186–87, 293n150; in *Kazakhstan*, 86, 128–35, *133*; Langman photographs of, *113*, 114; Turkestan-Siberian (Turksib) railway impacting, 61–62
Kazakhstan, Soviet Republic of, 86, 107–8, 170, 197–98; Eisenstein in, 223–24; Shklovsky and, 2, 59–62, 66–69
Kazakhstan (photobook), 86, 128–35, *133*
Kazan, Russia, 84
Khalip, Yakov, 99
Khan, Kublai, 74
Khan-Magomedov, Selim, 9–10, 283n78
Khlebnikov, Velimir, 18
Khodzhaev, Faizulla, 210
khorovod (Slavic pagan circle dance), 260
Khrushchev, Nikita, 304n56
Kino (newspaper), 142
kino-eye (*kino-glaz*), 138–49, 153, 188, 190–93
"Kino-Eyes" (Vertov), 145
Kino-Pravda (*Leninskaia kino-pravda*) (films), 165
kitsch, 257
Kliuchevsky, Vasilii, 20
Klodt, Evgenii, 131–32, 135
Klutsis, Gustav, 96
Kol'tsov, Mikhail, 154

Konstantinovsky, Grigorii, 257–58, 260–61
Kopalin, Ilya, 162, 164
korenizatsiia (Soviet policy), 37
Kozlov, Leonid, 203
Kozlov, Petr, 299n154
Kracauer, Siegfried, 134
Krasnaia Zvezda (newspaper), 187
Kretschmer, Ernst, 231, 238
Kruchenykh, Aleksei, 247
Krupskaia, Nadezhda, 164
Kushner, Boris, 94
Kuzembaev, Tusup, 111, 114, 284n104, 284n107
"Kuzimbayev," *Sovetskoe foto*, *113*, 114
Kyrgyz people, culture and, 250–51

"Laboratory of Hearing (Vertov)," 145–46, 153
Lady Macbeth of the Mtsensk District (opera), 55
Lahouti, Abolqasem, 36
Langman, Eleazar, 111–12, *113*, 122–23, 284n105
language, 88, 117, 144–46, 155, 168–69; common, 161, 302n23; Gorky on, 53–54; Jameson on, 58; Russian, 174–75, 178, 184, 186, 254; Shklovsky on, 54–55; translation and, 151–52, 157–60, 176, 178, 192, 250–51, 287n1, 288n15; written traditions and, 90, 161, 172, *173*, 177–80, *178*, 274, 293n150, 293n161. *See also* writing, written traditions and
Larionov, Mikhail, 18
late modernism, Soviet, 9–14, 45–47, 50, 245, 248, 250–52; avant-garde and, 103; of Eisenstein, 195, 203–4, 212–13, 247; of Shklovsky, 82; of Vertov, 151, 191, 193
Latour, Bruno, 141, 288n21
Le Corbusier, xix, 303n33
Left Front of the Arts (*Levyi front iskusstv*) (LEF), 58, 82, 84, 99, 101, 137–38
leftist art (*levoe iskusstvo*), 6, 10
Lenin, Vladimir, 22–23, 110, 117–18, 138–39, 142, 292n116; death of, 149, 151, 153–55, 159–62, 164–69; Rodchenko and, 95, 100; Shklovsky on, 54–55; two nations concept of, 33–34. *See also specific works*
Leningrad Institute of Oral Culture, 157
Leninism, 110, 144; Vertov and, 142, 161–62, *163*, 164–69
Lermontov, Mikhail, xx
Lévy-Bruhl, Lucien, 203, 206
Lezgin, 36
life caught off-guard (*zhizn' vrasplokh*), 140

"Light from the East" (Stalin), 85
linearity, 129, 143, 237, 283n69
Linnaeus, Carl, 228
Lissitzky, El, 274n158
Literary Encyclopedia (Nusinov), 252
"Literary Fact" (Literaturnyi fakt) (Tynianov), 77
literary forms, 17, 50
Literary Gazette (*Literaturnaia gazeta*) (newspaper), 48–49, 51, 53–54, 66, 253
Literature and Revolution (Trotsky), 167
Livshits, Benedikt, 18
Lodder, Christina, 88, 92, 281n24
long shot, in photography, 112
Loos, Adolf, 134, 230
Lubok, 80, 98
Lugovskoi, Vladimir, 186
Lukács, György (Georg), 8, 56, 78, 247
Lullaby (*Kolybel'naia*) (film), 194n191
Lunacharsky, Anatolii, 164

Macheret, Aleksandr, 63
Mácza, János (Ivan Matsa), 98
Magnitostroi, 104, 155
Magyar, Lajos (Liudvig Mad'iar), 271n97
Maiakovsky, Vladimir, 84, 274n158
Malevich, Kazimir, 81, 121, 128, 274n158
Malinowski, Bronisław, 167
Mandelstam, Osip, 37–38
Man with a Movie Camera (*Chelovek s kinoapparatom*) (film), 144–45, 161–62
"March of the Radio-Eye" (Vertov), 144, 146
Marco Polo (Shklovsky), 75–76
Marco Polo, Explorer (*Marko Polo*) (Shklovsky), 47–48, 62–63, 73–75
Marinetti, Filippo Tommaso, 18
Marshak, Samuil, 63
Marx, Karl, 26, 33, 65, 67, 259
Marxism, 18–19, 22–23, 79, 87, 141, 196, 271n95, 281n22; AMP and, 25; Shklovsky and, 48–49
Marxism and the National Question (Stalin), 29
mass production, 82, 88, 135
Masters of Soviet Photography exhibition, 101, 106, 125
materiality, materialism and, 55, 67, 81, 120, 142, 204, 223, 285n129; constructivism and, 88–91, 98–99
material production, 87–88, 281n22, 285n129
matter, 42, 58, 65, 183–84, 226, 237–38
Matvei Komarov, Resident of the City of Moscow (*Matvei Komarov, zhitel' goroda*) (Shklovsky), 80

Mayakovsky, Vladimir, xix
Medizinische Psychologie (*Medical Psychology*) (Kretschmer), 231
Medvedev, Pavel, 78
Mel'nikov, Konstantin, 31
Men'shikov, Mikhail, xx–xxii
mentalité primitive, La (Lévy-Bruhl), 203
Method (Eisenstein), 198, 204, 206, 218–19, 226, 245–46
Mexico, Eisenstein in, 197–98, 202–8, *209*, 210, 236–37, 248
Meyerhold, Vsevolod, 266n13
Mezhericher, Leonid, 99, 104, 106–7
Mighty Flow, The (*Moguchii potok*) (film), 297n68
miniatures, Persian, 98–99, 198, 220–22
Mir Iskusstva (journal), xx, 265n6
mnogoukladnost' (coexistence of socio-economical forms), 205, 296n50
modernism, Russian/Soviet modernity and, 3–4, 11, 168, 170, 248–50, 266n5, 267n24; internationalism and, 255–56; Men'shikov on, xx–xxii; Shklovsky and, 61–63, *64*, 65–70, *71*, 72–73; socialist future and, 205; socialist realism and, 8–9, 40–41; Stalinist, 60, 62, 168, 243–44, 252. *See also* late modernism, Soviet
modernity, modernism and, xvii–xx, *xviii*, 6–13, 116, 156–57, 183, 206, 269n52; abstraction and, 134; Constructivism and, 87, 93–95; individualistic, 240, 242; Orientalism and, 14–20; socialist, 258–59, 263, 271n89 85
modernization, 18, 65, 251, 283n93; Soviet, 47, 70, 107, 143, 153, 155, 165, 210–11
Moholy-Nagy, László, 133–34
Mongolia, 299n154
montage, 195, 200, 203–4, 216, 285n133; avant-garde, 149, 151; internal, 93, 114; Vertov and, 137, 145–46, 154
Montage (Eisenstein), 217
"Monument to a Scholarly Error" ("Pamiatnik nauchnoi oshibke") (Shklovsky), 47–51, 75, 197, 245
Morozov, Pavlik, 194, 197
Morozov, Sergei, 93, 114, 125, 283n69
Moscow 800 (film), 296n49
Mountainous Georgia (*Gornaia Gruziia*) (Shklovsky), 46
Mukanov, Sabit, 174

INDEX

Mukhina, Vera, 256
multiculturalism, 30–31, 253–54, 256–57, 259–60, 295n18
multilingualism, 198
Muradeli, Vano, 254–55
Museum of Cinema, Moscow, 194
Museum of Modern Art, New York, xvii–xviii, *xviii*
musical notation, 146
Musrepov, Gabit, 174, 292n136, 294n174, 298n117
mythology, 157, 186–87, 192–93, 195–97, 234–35, 246. *See also* folkloric narratives

narodnost' (popular spirit), 80, 114, 155–56, 243, 255
narrative line (*siuzhetnost'*), 99–100
narrators, narration and, 47, 61–63, 66–67, 175–76, 179, 182
national consciousness, 29, 38, 98, 218–19, 226, 228
national delimitation, 24, 48, 271n89
national difference, 30, 33–34, 38, 53
national form, xxii, 86, 114, 170, 272n108, 272nn105–6; Eisenstein and, 13, 197–202, 212, 216–22, 226, 228, 245; October Group on, 97–99; ornament as, 134, 198, 223–24, *225*, 226, *227*, 228, *229*, 230–32, *233*, 234–47, *236*, *239*; Rempel on, 34–35; Russian, 39, 197–98, 251–53, 255, 301n14; socialist, 4–5, 27–40, 216–22; Soviet, xxiii, 248–53, 255, 274n139, 301n14; Stalinism and, 27, 46, 199, 201, 250; Uzbek, 119–20
national identity, 21–22, 41, 147, 255, 258–59, 302n17
nationalism, xxi, 15, 38, 258, 272n108, 301n15; Soviet, 24, 251–52, 266n5
Nationalities Council of the Supreme Soviet of the Soviet Union, 187
nationality, Soviet, 22–23, 25, 31, 184, 186, 198, 253, 262
nation-building, Soviet, 24, 79, 115, 156
"Nation Form, The" (Balibar), 27
nation-states, 15–16, 21
Nazi Germany, 170, 174–75, 183, 186–87
Neoclassicism, 256
Neo-Primitivism, 250
New Economic Policy, Soviet Union, 11, 20
New LEF (*Novyi LEF*) (journal), 48, 95, 276n22
nomadic peoples, nomadism and, 69, 73–81, 223, 278n110, 299n154
non-diegetic sound, 175, 293n143
nonlinearity, 203, 248

non-objectivity, 84, 91, 101, 120, 128
nonsynchronization, visual-auditory, 143–44
normalization, colonial, 67
North Atlantic Treaty Organization (NATO), 301n10
Notes for a General History of Cinema (Eisenstein), 206
"Notes on Line and Ornament" (Eisenstein), 230
noviny (contemporary Soviet folklore), 158, 171
Nusinov, Isaak, 35, 252–53, 300n177

OBERIU (Union of Real Art), 274–75n158
Obidova, Jahon, 126–27
objective representation, 8, 11, 135, 137, 288n21
objectivity, 8, 143, 188, 190
oblique angle, in photography, 112
October (film), 52, 231–32
October Group (All-Russian Association of Workers of New Types of Artistic Labor "October"), 86, 96–102, 111, 122
October Revolution, Soviet Union, 10, 19–20, 31, 39–40, 182, 201
OGPU. *See* Soviet secret police
Olesha, Iurii, 36
Ol'denburg, Sergei, 15
Ol'khovyi, Boris, 53
"On Cultivated Speech" ("O kul'ture rechi") (Shklovsky), 54
"On Formalism" (Gorky), 55
"On Formalism" (O formalizme) (Shklovsky), 57
Ong, Walter, 167–68, 177
"On Language" (Gorky), 53
"On Literary Evolution" (Tynianov), 77–78
"On National Art" (Rempel'), 98
"On One Antipatriotic Group of Theatre Critics" (*Pravda* article), 253
"On Simplicity" ("O prostote") (Shklovsky), 54
"On Simplicity and Intelligibility" ("O prostote i poniatnosti") (Ol'khovyi), 53
On Soviet Prose (O *sovetskoi proze*) (Shklovsky), 54
"On the Elimination of Excesses in Design and Construction" (Central Committee of the Communist Party of the Soviet Union), 263
On the Film 'Bezhin Meadow' by Eisenstein (*O fil'me 'Bezhin lug' Eizenshteina*) (booklet), 194–96
"On the National Pride of the Great Russians" (Lenin), 54–55
"On the Question of: 'National in Form, Socialist in Content'" (Eisenstein), 197–98, 200–201, 210

"On the Square Stands a Tent" ("Na ploshchadi stoit kibitka") (song), 159
"On the Struggle against Formalism" (Vertov), 156
operas, 234–35, 254–55, 299n151
OPOIAZ (Society for the Study of Poetic Language), 48
optics of perception, Soviet, 42, 87
oral tradition, orality and, 81, 167–69, 216, 292n135, 293n150, 293n161; Gorky on, 36–37; Vertov and, 139, 148–49, *150*, 151–61, 170–72, *173*, 174–80, *178*, *181*, 182–84, *185*, 186–87, 192
Ordzhonikidze, Sergo, 254
Oriental Despotism (Wittfogel), 25
Orientalism, xx–xxi, 36, 61–62, 86, 98, 182, 221–22, 271n95; exoticism and, 5, 37, 213; modernism and, 14–20; socialism and, 20–27; Soviet, 26, 249–50, 266n9, 271n89; Stalinist, 23–24, 28, 30
Origin of German Tragic Drama, The (Benjamin), 262
ornament, ornamentation and, 256–58, 262, 286n165, 287n171, 302n28; in *Kazakhstan*, 131–35, *133*; as national form, 134, 223–24, *225*, *226*, *227*, *228*, *229*, 230–32, *233*, 234–47, *236*, *239*
ostranenie (defamiliarization), 41, 94, 215, 246–47, 249; Shklovsky and, 42, 44–48, 50, 58–59, 61, 66, 83
otherness, Other and, xxi, 13, 16–17, 206, 251, 255, 266n9; Bakhtin on, 20; Eisenstein and, 213; ethnic, 4, 6, 198, 266n8; Shklovsky and, 46–48, 60, 80–81; Soviet Orient and, 107
Ottoman Empire, 15, 21

Paris Exposition (1900), 302n29
Panfilov Division, 177, 186–87
pagan forms, paganism and, 201, 208, 237, 241
painterliness (*zhivopisnost'*), 86, 89, 128
painting, xx–xxi, 88, 92, 94, 101, 120–21, 127–28
Paris, France, 31, 84–85, 259
particularity, 14, 197, 246 166; ethnic, 18, 35, 107, 182, 266n8; national, 249, 255, 266n8
Pasternak, Boris, 26, 266n9
"Paths of Contemporary Photography, The" (Rodchenko), 93
patriarchy, 184, 251
Pavlenko, Petr, 211
Penson, Maks, 122, 125
People's Commissariat of Enlightenment, 45
periodization, 6, 275n7
Persian people, culture and, 250–51

perspective: foreshortening, 93–94, 100–101, 103–4, 111–12, *113*, 114, 122–23, 130, 221, 283n69; top-down, 123–25, 282n34; vertical, 106–7, 130, 221–22, 236
"Perspectives" (Eisenstein), 199
Petersburg (Bely), 11
Philpot, J. H., 234
photo-epic, 135–36
photography, 86, 90–92, 95–96, 98, 103, 136; aerial shots in, 123, 125, 166, 182; captions and, 110–11; dynamism and, 87, 105–6; in *Kazakhstan*, 86, 128–35, *133*; *rakurs* in, 93–94, 101, 117, 123–25, 165, 282n35, 283n69; retouching and, 130–31; socialist realism and, 102; in *Soviet Photo*, 94, 99, 111, *112*, 114, 125–26, 283n69; staging and, 104–7, 130; Stalinism and, 87, 123–24; synthetic, 99–101; in *USSR in Construction*, 104–6, *106*, 107–8, *109*, 110–12
Photo-Illustration in the Newspaper (brochure), 125
photojournalism, 99, 101, 122
photomontage, 90–92, 101, 115, 118, 120, 122, 129, 136; avant-garde, 99; as documentary fact, 126; in *Kazakhstan*, *133*, 134–35; of Stalin, 103, 117
"Photomontage" (Stepanova), 91
photo-painting, 131, 135–36
Picasso, Pablo, 7, 17
Pil'niak, Boris, 36
Pioneer Truth (*Pionerskaia Pravda*) (newspaper), 100
plasmaticity, 238
plasticity, 89, 238–40
Plato, 168, 249
Platonov, Andrei, 76
Poem Without a Hero (*Poema bez geroia*) (Akhmatova), 275n159
poetics, poetry and, 146, 240–42; orality and, 178–79
Poggioli, Renato, 7
Poland, 21
Pollock, Jackson, 263
Popov, Gavriil, 186
populism, 78
Poskrebyshev, Aleksandr, 253–54
post-avant-garde (*postavangard*), 10
postcolonialism, 14–15, 17
post-constructivism, 9–10
postmodernism, 9
Potboiler Work (*Podenshchina*) (Shklovsky), 47, 58, 62, 65, 68

Pound, Ezra, 6–7
power, 22, 42, 139, 166, 241, 251, 270n79, 285n143; gender and, *233*, 234
Pravda (newspaper), 31, 87, 154, 156, 158, 204–5, 253–54; Eisenstein in, 211, 213; Gorky in, 53; October Group in, 96; Shklovsky in, 55; on *Ten Years of Soviet Uzbekistan*, 115
pre-Columbian culture, 208
Prekhner, Mikhail, 102
present, socialist, 79–80, 128, 153, 156, 198, 213, 215, 217, 245
primitive communism, 26, 72, 204–6
primitivism, 18, 61, 210, 245, 249, 273n128, 299n139; Eisenstein and, 197, 203–7, 210–16, 228, 237; Five-Year Plan and, 73; industrialization and, 32; Turin and, 63
private property, 14, 215
privilege, 14, 214, 251, 255, 270n80, 302n23
"Problem of the Genesis, Development, and Disintegration of the Slave Societies of the Ancient Orient, The" (Struve), 26
"Problem of the Materialist Approach to Form, The" (Eisenstein), 198
productivism, 91, 97, 249
progress-regress dichotomy, 195, 197, 203–7, 211–16, 228, 240, 245–47
Prokofiev, Sergei, 297n71, 304n49
proletarianism, 20, 21, 38–39, 51, 83, 125, 128, 249; assimilation and, 72–73; folklore and, 80; Lenin on, 33; October Group on, 96–98; racial discrimination and, 61; realism and, 97, 99; Stalinism and, 85; Stalin on, 29–30; statelessness and, 27
Proletarian Photo (periodical), 100, 105
propaganda, 87, 105, 127–28, 136, 170
Propp, Vladimir, 80, 177
protoplasm, 237–38
psychoanalysis, 204
psychology, 188–90
"Psychology of Paganism, The" ("Psychologie du paganisme") (Gourmont), 201
Pudovkin, Vsevolod, 143, 288n32
Pumpianskaia, Semiramida, 162, 164
Pushkin, Alexander, 252, 300n177, 301n14
Pushkin and World Literature (*Pushkin i mirovaia literatura*) (Nusinov), 252
pyshnost', 262

¡Queviva México! (film), *109*, 197–98, 202, 207–8

racialization, 17, 230
racism, 61, 145, 207
Radek, Karl, 161–62
radio, 144, 147–48
radio-eye, 28, 138–48
railway, Turkestan-Siberian (Turksib), 61–63, *64*, 65–70, *71*, 72–73
rakurs (diagonal camera angle, foreshortening), 41, 93–94, 101, 117, 123–25, 165, 282n35, 283n69
raw materials, 65–66, 81, 107, 183–84, 284n95
realism, 8, 11, 92, 97, 98, 99, 197. *See also* socialist realism
"Realism in the Balance" (Lukács), 8
"Reconstruction of an Artist" (Rodchenko), 101–2
Red Army, Soviet, 21, 154, 183–84, 186–87
"Red East" agit-train, 137–38
religion, religious symbolism and, 99, 195, 208
"Religion of Art, A" ("Une religion d'art") (Gourmont), 201
Rempel', Lazar, 34–35, 98, 274n139
reorientation, 5, 40, 86, 112, 121, 123, 138, 219; Shklovsky and, 47, 65–66, 80, 244; Vertov and, 143, 151, 190
representation, 5, 86, 98, 129, 217, 221–22, 260, 291n108; allegorical, 262; constructionism and, 91–92, 95; containment and, 249; documentary genre and, 128; *faktura* and, 90; fictional, 89, 91–92, 128, 131; gender and, 126, *126*; kino-eye and, 142; objective, 8, 11, 135, 137, 288n21; Orientalist, 182; ornament and, 230; *ostranenie* and, 94; realism and, 197; socialist mode of, 104–5, 108, 112, 123–26, *124*, 134–35; sound and, 146–48
repression, Stalinist, 12, 37, 127, 274n158
Republic, The (Plato), 87
retouching, photographic images, 130–31
revolutionary, 142, 198–99
Riegl, Alois, 132
Rivera, Diego, 221
Rodchenko, Aleksandr, 84, 86, 130–31, 283n79, 285n126, 285n130, 285n137; Belomor Canal and, 102–8, *106*, *109*, 110–12, 114, 283n77; constructivism and, 87–95, 172, 280n10, 281n24; on depiction and painterliness, 281n18; Kazakhstan folio by, 127–236, *133*; October Group and, 96–102; photographs retouched by, 130–31; Uzbek Soviet Socialist Republic commemorated by, 115–27, *119*, *124*, *126*. *See also specific works*

romanticism, 34, 204
ROPF. *See* Russian Association of Proletarian Photographers
Rosenberg, Harold, 7
"Rough Outline of the Mexican Picture" (Eisenstein), 208
RSFSR. *See* Russian Soviet Federative Socialist Republic
Ruskin, John, 132
Russia, Russian Empire and, 20–22, 39, 68, 85, 252–255, 268n41, 270n79; chauvinism, Russian, xxii, 32, 34. *See also* Soviet Union
Russian Association of Proletarian Photographers (ROPF), 99–101
Russian Folklore (Sokolov), 179
Russian language, 174–75, 178, 184, 186, 254
Russian national form, 39, 197–98, 251–53, 255, 301n14
Russian Silver Age, xx, 250
Russian Soviet Federative Socialist Republic (RSFSR), 36, 107, 271n84, 303n39
Russian-Soviet identity, 19, 21–22, 72, 149, 176, 253–54, 259
Russification, 21–22, 72, 176, 214, 270n70
Russocentrism, 78, 198, 214, 252, 262, 301n8, 304n49
Russo-Polish War, 21
Ryleeva, Zoia, 258

Said, Edward, 14–16, 19, 271n95
sarape (Latin American blanket worn as a cloak), 208
Satpaev, Kanysh, 183
Scriabin, Aleksandr, 146
Scythianism, Scythian cultures and, 231–32, 299n139
secularism, 126, 201
sedentarization, mass, 73
Seifullin, Saken, 60
self-consciousness, 219, 240
Self-Orientalization, xxi–xxii
self-transformation, 216, 249
Semper, Gottfried, 132
Sentimental Journey (*Sentimental'-noe puteshestvie*) (Shklovsky), 43
Shadr, Ivan, 165, 259
Shaikhet, Arkadii, 102, 105
Shishmarev, Vladimir, 243–44
Shklovsky, Viktor, 82–83, 250–51, 275n8, 276n22, 279n135, 280n148, 283n77, 298n118; the

baroque and, 52–56; on Eisenstein, 52, 203, 216; foreshortening and, 94; formalism and, 2, 43, 45–48, 50–61, 65, 78, 80–82, 242–43, 246; "Monument to a Scholarly Error," 48–51; on *ostranenie*, 42, 44–48, 50, 58–59, 61, 66, 83; otherness and, 46–48, 60, 80–81; reorientation of, 47, 65–66, 244; on sound film, 143; Soviet modernity and, 61–63, *64*, 65–70, *71*, 72–73; on strangeness, 62–63, 65–66, 73–81; Vertov and, 174–75; on Veselovsky, 1, 182, 244. *See also specific works*
Shorin, Aleksandr, 146–48
Shostakovich, Dmitri, 55, 254
Shterenberg, Abram, 102, 122
Shterenberg, David, xix, 11, 31
Shtro, Petr 3, 15
Shub, Esfir', 96
Shul'kin, David, 111
Shumiatsky, Boris, 162, 195
silhouette portraiture, profile and, 118–19, *119*
Silk Road, 1, 245
Silver Age, Russian, xx, 250
Sinclair, Upton, 202
Sixth Part of the World, A (*Shestaia chast' mira*) (film), 184, 192
Smolian, Aleksandr, 104
Sobolev, Leonid, 223
socialism, 153, 162, 187, 204–5, 248–54; alterity and, 28, 251; consciousness and, 23, 196–97, 219; labor and, 63, 193, 215; national forms and, 27–40, 216–22; Orientalism and, 20–27; representation and, 104–5, 108, 112, 123–26, *124*, 134–35; subjectivity and, 19, 195; universality and, 19, 31, 258. *See also* construction, socialist
socialist future, 23, 62, 72, 155, 192, 196, 205
"Socialist Metabolism," *USSR in Construction*, 107–8
socialist present, 79–80, 128, 153, 156, 198, 213, 215, 217, 245
socialist realism, 4, 116, 135, 196, 201, 253, 263, 285n142, 289n65; baroque intricacy and, 52–56; foreshortening and, 112; Groys on, 13–14, 268n40; in high and late Stalinism, 267n38; imitation and, 97; Marxism and, 57; Rodchenko and, 102; Shklovsky and, 43–44; Soviet modernism and, 8–9, 40–41; Vertov and, 143, 155–57
Society for the Study of Poetic Language (OPOIAZ), 48, 51, 77

Society of Russian Sculptors, 259
Sokolov, Iurii, 179
Sosfenov, Ilya, 100, 282n66
Songs of Lenin, The (film), 149, 290n65
sound, sound films and, 42, 138–39, 143–49, 151–62, 164, 192–93, 202
Soviet Art (newspaper), 136
Soviet Artists' Union, 131–32
Soviet East, 36, 78, 139, 149, 153, 193, 289n62, 293n150
Soviet internationalism, 143, 250, 255
Soviet Jews, 253, 302n17
Soviet national forms, xxiii, 248–53, 255, 274n139, 301n14
Soviet Orient, 2–4, *112*, 128–29, 192, 198, 203, 250–51, 271n89; Cyrillization and, 172; Eisenstein and, 211–16; generic, 149; primitiveness of, 18; "Red East" agit-train in, 137–38; temporality and, 72; in *Ten Years of Soviet Uzbekistan*, 86, 101, 111, 115–27, *119*, *124*, *126*, 130, 135, 210, 250–51; in *USSR in Construction* and, 107–8, *109*, 110–11; vanguardism and, 40. *See also specific republics*
Soviet Photo (*Sovetskoe foto*) (journal), 94, 99, 111, *112*, 114, 122, 125–26, 283n69
Soviet secret police (Unified State Political Directorate) (OGPU), 103
Soviet Union (Union of Soviet Socialist Republics) (USSR). *See specific republics*; *specific topics*
Spain, 208
Spivak, Chakravorty, 26
spontaneity, 196–97
stadialism, 207, 210, 219–20, 226, 228, 249
staging, photography and, 104–7, 130
Stakhanovite movement, 259
Stal'sky, Suleiman, 36–37, 157
Stalin, Joseph, 108, 164, 166, 196, 198, 253, 274n156, 302n23; on Bauer, 29; on capitalism, 21; on cinema, 138, 162, 189; death of, 258, 262; mass production and, 32; Orientalism of, 23–24, 28, 30; photomontages of, 103, 117; on proletarianism, 29–30; Rodchenko on, 136; silhouette portraiture of, 118–19, *119*. *See also specific works*
Stalinism, 138–39, 162, 167, 190, 192, 249, 270n79; aesthetics and, 46, 263, 267n38; Cultural Revolution, 2–3; Eisenstein and, 194–95, 214, 231; formalism and, 255; friendship of the peoples in, 37–39, 184, 186–87, 214, 217, 251, 253–61; Great Terror, 54, 127, 248, 262; high, 5, 19, 156; late, 12, 243–45, 251–52, 262, 267n38; national forms and, 27, 46, 199, 201, 250; nomadic sedentarization under, 73; Orientalism and, 23–24, 28, 30; photography and, 87, 123–24; on proletarian resistance, 85; repression under, 12, 274n158; Russian/Soviet modernism and, 60, 62, 168, 243–44, 252; Shklovsky and, 47; Wittfogel on, 26; written culture and, 177
Stalin White Sea-Baltic Canal, The (Shklovsky), 283n77
Stasov, Vladimir, 286n165
State Academy of Artistic Sciences (GAKhN), 31
Stein, Gertrude, 17
Stepanova, Varvara, 84–86, 250–51, 281n18, 281n24, 285n126, 285n130, 285n133; constructivism and, 87–95, 281n22; *Kazakhstan* folio by, 127–236, *133*; Uzbek Soviet Socialist Republic commemorated by, 115–27, *119*, *124*, *126*. *See also specific works*
Steppe Warrior, The (*Stepnoi batyr*) (film), 223
stil' modern (modern style), xx, 266n13
"Stone Flower, The" ("Kamennyi tsvetok") (Bazhov), 261–62, 304n49
"Stone Flower" fountain, 260–62
strangeness, 4–5, 36, 62–63, 65–66, 73–81
Struggle for Proletarian Class Positions on the Front of Spatial Arts (*Bor'ba za klassovye proletarskie pozitsii na fronte prostranstvennykh iskusstv*) (brochure), 96
Struve, Vasily, 26
subjectivity, 8, 79–80, 88, 154, 180, 188, 190–93; socialist, 19, 195; Soviet, 4, 14, 27, 41, 123, 250
succession-continuity, Soviet, 162, 165
suprematism, 121
surrealism, xix
Svilova, Elizaveta, 162, 164
symbolism, 6
synchronism, 140, 145
syncretism, 240
synthetic photography, 99–101

Tansykbayev, Ural, 126
Tajikistan, Soviet Republic of, 2, 78–80
Tale of the Stone Flower, The (ballet), 304n49
Tansykbayev, Ural, 126, 285n142
Tatar, 36
Tatlin, Vladimir (Volodymyr), 11

"Teacher of the Sands, The" (*Peschanaia uchitel'nitsa*) (Platonov), 76
Technique of the Writing Craft (*Tekhnika pisatel'skogo remesla*) (Shklovsky), 58–59
technology, 46, 69–70, 88, 90–91, 136, 203; film camera, 137–42; sound, 192, 202
Telingater, Solomon, 96
Teneta, Aleksei, 259–60, 303n41
Ten Years of Soviet Uzbekistan (Rodchenko, Stepanova), 86, 101, 111, 115–27, *119*, *124*, *126*, 130, 135; Ikramov and Khodzhaev defamed in, 210; Soviet subjectivity and, 250–51
texture (*faktura*), 41, 89–90, 92, 132, 135, 280n15
theatricality, 137, 256
Theory of Prose (Shklovsky), 1, 49–50, 80, 215, 244
Theory of the Avant-Garde (Bürger), 7
Theses on Feuerbach (Marx), 142
Third Factory, The (*Tret'ia fabrika*) (Shklovsky), 49, 76
Three Heroines, The (*Tri geroini*) (film), 194n191
Three Songs of Lenin (*Tri pesni o Lenine*) (film), 148–49, *150*, 151–62, *163*, 164–70, 175–76, 192–93, 292n118; booklet accompanying, 291n108; folklore and, 186; orality and, 139
Tikhonov, Nikolai, 76
Timasheff, Nicholas, 267n38
time, temporality and, 7, 58, 67, 72, 139, 151, 243, 246; Eisenstein and, 195–97, 202–8, 210–11, 241
Tisse, Eduard, 202
Tolstoy, Leo, 46, 215
Tolstoy, Vladimir, 262
top-down perspectives, 123–25, 282n34
Topuridze, Konstantin, 257–58, 260–61, *261*
Total Art of Stalinism, The (Groys), 12
totalitarianism, 4–5, 12–13, 25, 42, 249
"Towards Realism and Narodnost'" (Morozov), 114
To You, the Front! (film), 216, 250–51, 298n117
Transcaucasia, 266n9, 271n84
translation, 151–52, 157–60, 176, 178, 192, 250–51, 287n1, 288n15
Treaty of Brest-Litovsk (1918), 21
Treaty of Riga (1921), 21
tree of life, 234–35, 299n147
Tretiakov, Sergei, 105, 133, 147–48, 274n158
Troshin, Nikolai, 111
Trotsky, Leon, 270n80m 167
truth, documentary, 103, 193
truthful image (*istinnyi obraz*), 216–18

tuberculosis, 158, 274
Tugendkhol'd, Iakov, 31–32, 258
Turin, Viktor, 63, *64*, 65, 70, *71*, 142
Turkestan-Siberian (Turksib) railway, 61–63, *64*, 65–70, *71*, 72–73
Turkmen people, culture and, 250–51
Turksib (documentary), 63, *64*, 65, 69–70, *71*, 72–73
Turksib (Shklovsky), 47–48, 62–63, 65–70, 72–74, 76, 250–51, 278n104
two nations (concept), 33–34
Tynianov, Yuri, 20, 51, 77–78, 263

Ukraine, 21, 25, 35–36
Ukrainian modernism, 266n5
ukrashatel'stvo
underdevelopment, 205, 266n9, 270n77, 271n84
Union of Soviet Architects, 304n54
Union of Soviet Artists, 262
United States, xvii, 238–40, 252, 301n10
universality, universalism and, 35, 249, 251–52, 255, 260, 271n97; Eisenstein and, 198, 245–46; socialist, 19, 31, 258
Urgench, Uzbekistan, 211–12, 295n18
Ushakov, Dmitrii, 87
USSR. *See* Soviet Union
USSR in Construction (publication), 86, 101–8, *106*, 135, 283n70, 283n77; *Fifteen Years of Kazakhstan*, 107–8, *109*, 110–12
Uzbek people, culture and, 256–57, 285n142, 292n128, 297n68, 297n75; in *Ten Years of Soviet Uzbekistan*, 86, 101, 111, 115–27, *119*, *124*, *126*, 130, 135, 210, 250–51; Uzbek national form, 119–20
Uzbek Soviet Socialist Republic, Uzbekistan and, 2, 222, 259, 274n145, 275n159, 286n147; Great Fergana Canal, 29n65, 210–17, 220, 297n68, 297n76; Rodchenko, Stepanova commemorating, 115–27, *119*, *124*, *126*; Vertov in, 149

Vaingurt, Julia, 280n10
Vaisfel'd, Ilya, 195
vanguard (*avangard*), 6, 10, 23, 40, 251, 255, 266n9
vanishing point, 117, 221–22
Varlamov, Leonid, 297n68
Vasil'ev, Petr, 131
VDNKh. *See* Exhibition of Achievements of the National Economy

Velikanov, Vasilii, 186
Venice Biennale, 252
vernacular forms and, 197, 201, 208
verticality, 106–7, 130, 165, 182–83, 221–22, 236
Vertov, Dziga (Denis Arkad'evich Kaufman), 13, 250–51, 287n1, 289n47, 289n62, 289n65, 292n116, 297n117; documentary genre and, 187–93; Eisenstein compared to, 213, 216; on human vision, 287n11; Kino-eye technique and, 138–48; Leninism and, 144, 161–62, *163*, 164–69; MacKay on, 287n9; orality and, 139, 148–49, *150*, 151–61. *See also specific works*
Veselovsky, Aleksandr, 1, 240–46
Veselovsky, Aleksei, 300n177
Vesnin, Viktor, 96
Victory style (*stil' Pobeda*), 257
Vienna Secession, xx–xxi
Vinogradov, Viktor, 254
Vishnevskii, Vsevolod, 296n50
vision, 42, 87–88, 95; human, 94, 188, 283n69, 287n11
VKhUTEMAS (Higher Art and Technical Studios), 96, 116, 132, 259, 280n10
vostokofil'stvo, 18, 31
Vrubel, Mikhail, xx–xxi
VSKhV. *See* All-Union Agricultural Exhibition

Wagner, Richard, 299n151
Walküre, Die (stage production), 234–35, 299n151
Wallerstein, Immanuel, 23
Wanderers, the Russian, 89
"Way I Write, The" ("Kak ia pishu") (Shklovsky), 59–60
Wells, H. G., 69–70, 152
"We Loved Him . . ." (My liubili ego . . .) (song), 153–54
Weltanschauung, 56
Westernization, 85

"We Will Not Forget the Name of Lenin" ("Ne zabudem my imeni Lenina") (Tajik folk song), 166
"Where Is Dziga Vertov Striding?" (Shklovsky), 182
White Sea–Baltic Canal, 57, 101–2
Wilhelmine empire, 15
"Without Words" ("Bez slov") Vertov, 152
Wittfogel, Karl, 25–26, 271n92
Wölfflin, Heinrich, 52
"Word, The" (Slovo) (film), 293
Working Group of Constructivists, 87
"Work with a Band on the Canal" ("Rabota s orkestrom na kanale"), 106–7
World of Art (*Mir Iskusstva*) (journal), xx
world tree, 234–35
World War I, 15, 21
World War II, 170–71, 198, 251–52, 257, 259, 267n24, 301n15, 304n54; deaths, 186–87; late modernism and, 9; Soviet expansionism after, 1
Worringer, Wilhelm, 132
writing, written traditions and, 90, 161, 172, *173*, 177–80, *178*, 274, 293n150, 293n161

xenikon (aliénation), 44
xenophobia, 61
Xiongnu tribal confederation, 299n154

Yggdrasil mythology, 234–35
Yiddish literature, 35, 302n17, 303n40
Yusupov, Usman, 210

Zhanak, 223
Zhdanov, Andrei, 301n9
Zhirmunsky, Viktor, 80, 157, 168, 242
zhizn' vrasplokh (life caught off-guard), 140, 288n15
Zionism, 301n15
Zoo (Shklovsky), 77
Zoshchenko, Mikhail, 275n159, 301n9

GPSR Authorized Representative: Easy Access System Europe, Mustamäe tee
50, 10621 Tallinn, Estonia, gpsr.requests@easproject.com